A330.01

D0314472

NEW DIRECTIONS IN ECONOMIC METHODOLOGY

Recent years have witnessed a dramatic growth in interest in economic methodology. However, this work has moved in a number of significantly different directions, and it is not easy to see how several of these might be reconciled. The dominance of 'falsificationism' and the ideas associated with Kuhn, Lakatos and Popper that had emerged by the late 1970s has gone, and has been replaced by a range of more or less exclusive approaches.

In *New Directions in Economic Methodology* some of the figures most closely associated with the most important of these new approaches provide new and definitive statements of their positions. The result reflects the diversity of work currently being undertaken in economic methodology. Much, but by no means all, of this work reflects a dissatisfaction with the current practice of economics and in the course of the book various attempts to reform or replace existing practices are proposed.

The book begins with chapters which examine some of the big questions which underlie economics. What are – and what should be – the aims of economics? How might these be pursued? It proceeds with a section which considers what is left of 'falsificationism'. This includes chapters which advocate, criticize and reformulate what is still the dominant position within economic methodology.

The third and fourth sections of the book reflect the extent to which recent developments are influenced by areas outside economics, especially philosophy (both analytical and continental), discourse analysis and various forms of analytical theory. The perspectives addressed here include different incarnations of realism, pragmaticism, those of the 'rhetoric' school and other approaches which see the economy as a 'text'.

Roger Backhouse is Reader in the History of Economic Thought at the University of Birmingham.

ECONOMICS AS SOCIAL THEORY

Series Edited by Tony Lawson
University of Cambridge

Social theory is experiencing something of a revival within economics. Critical analyses of the particular nature of the subject matter of social studies and of the types of methods, categories and modes of explanation that can legitimately be endorsed for the scientific study of social objects, are re-emerging. Economists are again addressing such issues as the relationship between agency and structure, between economy and the rest of society, and between inquirer and the object of inquiry. There is renewed interest in elaborating basic categories such as causation, competition, culture, discrimination, evolution, money, need, order, organization, power, probability, process, rationality, technology, time, truth, uncertainty and value etc.

The objective for this series is to facilitate this revival further. In contemporary economics the label 'theory' has been appropriated by a group that confines itself to largely a-social, a-historical, mathematical 'modelling'. *Economics as Social Theory* thus reclaims the 'theory' label, offering a platform for alternative, rigorous, but broader and more critical conceptions of theorizing.

ECONOMICS AND LANGUAGE
Edited by Willie Henderson, Tony Dudley-Evans and Roger Backhouse

RATIONALITY, INSTITUTIONS AND ECONOMIC METHODOLOGY
Edited by Uskali Mäki, Bo Gustafsson and Christian Knudsen

WHO PAYS FOR THE KIDS?
Gender and the structures of constraint
Nancy Folbre

NEW DIRECTIONS
IN ECONOMIC
METHODOLOGY

Edited by Roger E. Backhouse

London and New York

First published 1994
by Routledge
11 New Fetter Lane, London EC4P 4EE

Simultaneously published in the USA and Canada
by Routledge
29 West 35th Street, New York, NY 10001

Selection and editorial matter © 1994 Roger E. Backhouse
Individual chapters © of the respective authors

Typeset in Garamond by Intype, London

Printed and bound in Great Britain by
Mackays of Chatham PLC, Chatham, Kent

British Library Cataloguing in Publication Data
A catalogue record for this book is available from the British Library.

Library of Congress Cataloging in Publication Data
New directions in economic methodology/edited by Roger E. Backhouse.
p. cm.
Includes bibliographical references and index.
ISBN 0-415-09636-7
1. Economics–Methodology. I. Backhouse, Roger.
HB131.N48 1994
330'.01–dc20 93-37623
CIP

ISBN 0-415-09636-7   0-415-09637-5 (pbk)

CONTENTS

CONTRIBUTORS

Roger E. Backhouse is Reader in the History of Economic Thought at the University of Birmingham. He has published on macroeconomics, the history of economic thought and economic methodology, and is author of *A History of Modern Economic Analysis, Economists and the Economy* and is co-editor of *Economics and Language*. He is Review Editor of the *Economic Journal*.

Mark Blaug is Professor Emeritus, University of London, and Visiting Professor of Economics at the University of Exeter. He is author of *Economic Theory in Retrospect, Economic Theories: True or False* and *The Methodology of Economics*.

Lawrence A. Boland is Professor of Economics at Simon Fraser University. He is author of numerous articles and books on economic methodology, including *The Foundations of Economic Method, Methodology for a New Microeconomics, Methodology of Economic Model Building* and *The Principles of Economics: Some Lies My Teacher Told Me*.

Vivienne Brown is Lecturer in Economics at the Open University, UK. Her research interests include the history of economic thought and language/discourse. She is author of *Adam Smith's Discourse: Canonicity, Commerce and Conscience*.

Bruce J. Caldwell is Professor of Economics at the University of North Carolina at Greensboro. He is author of *Beyond Positivism: Economic Methodology in the Twentieth Century* (recently reissued by Routledge) and is editor and co-editor of *Carl Menger and His Legacy in Economics, The Philosophy and Methodology of Economics* and *Austrian Economics: Tensions and New Directions*.

David Colander is Christian A. Johnson Distinguished Professor of Economics at Middlebury College. He is co-author of *The Making of an*

Economist and *A History of Economic Theory* and co-editor of *The Spread of Economic Ideas.*

D. Wade Hands is Professor of Economics at the University of Puget Sound. He has published many articles on general equilibrium theory, the history of economic thought and methodology. He is author of *Testing, Rationality and Progress: Essays on the Popperian Tradition in Economic Methodology* (1993).

Daniel M. Hausman is Professor of Philosophy at the University of Wisconsin-Madison. He is co-editor of *Economics and Philosophy*. His writings on the philosophy of economics include *Capital, Profits and Prices: An Essay in the Philosophy of Economics*, *The Inexact and Separate Science of Economics*, and *Essays on Philosophy and Economic Methodology*. He is editor of *The Philosophy of Economics: An Anthology*, and is currently writing a book on ethics and economics.

Willie Henderson is Senior Lecturer in the School of Continuing Studies at the University of Birmingham. He has a long-standing interest in methodological, language and educational issues in economics. He is co-editor of *The Language of Economics: The Analysis of Economics Discourse* (1990) and *Economics and Language* (1993).

Kevin D. Hoover is Professor of Economics at the University of California, Davis. He is author of *The New Classical Macroeconomics: A Sceptical Inquiry*, as well as articles on macroeconomics, the methodology of economics, and philosophy. He is currently writing a book entitled *Causality in Macroeconomics*.

Terence W. Hutchison is Emeritus Professor of Economics at the University of Birmingham. He has published extensively on the history of economic thought and economic methodology. His publications on methodology include *The Significance and Basic Postulates of Economic Theory* (1938), *Positive Economics and Policy Objectives* (1964), *Knowledge and Ignorance in Economics* (1977) and *Changing Aims in Economics* (1992). He is currently compiling a selection of essays under the title *The Uses and Abuses of Academic Economics*.

Tony Lawson is Lecturer in Economics at the University of Cambridge. He has published on economic methodology and on general economics, including industrial relations and UK industrial decline. He is a member of several editorial boards, and is joint coordinator of the European Association for Evolutionary Political Economy's Research Group on Methodology.

Donald N. McCloskey is Professor of Economics at the University of Iowa. He has published numerous articles and books on British economic history and the rhetoric of economics, including *The Rhetoric of Economics* and *If You're So Smart: The Narrative of Economic Expertise.*

Uskali Mäki is currently Senior Research Fellow at the Academy of Finland. He has published papers on the metatheory of economics, including Friedman's, Austrian and institutionalist views, the rhetoric, sociology and metaphysics of economics, and various facets of the issue of realism. He is co-editor of *Rationality, Institutions and Economic Methodology* (1993) and is preparing a monograph on *Economics and Realism.*

Philip Mirowski is Carl E. Koch Professor of Economics at the University of Notre Dame. He is author of *Against Mechanism* and *More Heat Than Light*, and editor of *Natural Images in Economics: Markets Read in Tooth and Claw.*

Alexander Rosenberg is Professor of Philosophy at the University of California, Riverside. He is author of seven works on the philosophy of social science and biology, including *Philosophy of Social Science* and *Economics – Mathematical Politics or Science of Diminishing Returns?*

PREFACE

The idea for this book arose out of conversations with Alan Jarvis, at Routledge. We were discussing the possibility of producing an anthology of articles on economic methodology that would be more up-to-date than what was then available. After considering the various alternatives we decided that this was not an attractive option. Instead, we decided that the best way to provide a broad perspective on recent work was to invite a wide range of people working in the area to write something new. The invitation was very general, potential contributors being invited to write about a topic that they thought was important. The brief was to write something that was clear and accessible to students, whilst at the same time saying something that would be of interest to specialists in the field. In my view the contributors have succeeded in both tasks. Some view their previous work from a new perspective. Others take old arguments a stage further. Others explore new avenues.

I am grateful to Alan Jarvis for his assistance and encouragement, and to the contributors who provided valuable criticisms of others' contributions. Without either of these inputs the quality of the book would have been much poorer.

1

INTRODUCTION: NEW DIRECTIONS IN ECONOMIC METHODOLOGY

Roger E. Backhouse

INTRODUCTION

Since the 1970s, interest in economic methodology has grown dramatically, to the extent that it is now possible to view economic methodology as a clearly identifiable subdiscipline within economics. The result of this growth has been a proliferation of ideas and perspectives, projects and themes that are not yet reflected in textbooks or collections of readings. The aim of this volume is to bring together papers which represent some of the main themes in this recent literature. Some papers provide clear introductions to ideas already in the literature, whilst others go on from these to introduce new ideas.

ECONOMIC METHODOLOGY BEFORE 1980

Before the 1970s the literature on economic methodology was very limited. There were the classic discussions by Senior (1836), Mill (1844), Cairnes (1875), Menger (1883/1963), Keynes (1891), Robbins (1932), Hutchison (1938) and Machlup (1963). There were briefer methodological statements by a small number of very prominent post-war economics, such as Samuelson (1963), Koopmans (1957) and, standing above all the others, Friedman (1953). There were also methodological statements by economists who were very critical of mainstream economics, such as Myrdal (1953), Dobb (1937) and Robinson (1962). Methodological issues were also raised very clearly in Lipsey's introductory textbook (1964). In addition, scattered amongst general journals it was possible to find a small number of articles on methodology, mostly commenting directly on issues raised by these works.

In the 1970s, the situation began to change, with an increase in the number of articles on methodology, many of which appeared in *History of Political Economy*, started in 1968. The dramatic growth in work on economic methodology, however, did not take place until around 1980.

There began to appear books by specialists in economic methodology (of the authors listed above only Hutchison and Machlup could be so labelled), such as Rosenberg (1976), Stewart (1979), Klant (1979/1984), Hausman (1981), Hollis and Nell (1975), Boland (1982) and Caldwell (1982).

This rise in interest in economic methodology was associated with a change in the nature of the issues discussed, a change which paralleled developments in the philosophy of science. Early work on economic methodology was concerned largely with the status of the propositions of economic theory – with verification, testing and the logical structure of theories. The 1970s, however, saw the impact of Kuhn's *The Structure of Scientific Revolutions* (1962/1970) with its emphasis on the historical dynamics of scientific knowledge. Economists explored the relevance to economics first of Kuhn's ideas – Gordon (1965), Coats (1969), Bronfenbrenner (1971), Kunin and Weaver (1971) – and later those of Lakatos, a particularly important contribution being the symposium published as Latsis (1976). In part these developments can be seen as a response to changes in the philosophy of science. It is also arguable, however, that changes in both disciplines reflected wider intellectual developments, and that developments in economic methodology were, to some extent, a response to the breakdown, around 1970, of the Keynesian–neoclassical synthesis that had dominated economics since the 1950s.

Alongside these developments there was also an increase in methodological discussions by heterodox economists – Austrians, post-Keynesians and institutionalists. For many economists associated with these schools methodology provided a way to criticize orthodox economics. Some of this heterodox work addressed issues related to those discussed above, raising questions concerning, for example, the nature of explanations in economics. Thus Wilber and Harrison (1978) argued for the importance of storytelling. Much heterodox methodological writing, however, was concerned with different issues, such as the treatment of time and uncertainty (post-Keynesians), the nature and role of knowledge (Austrians) and conceiving of the economy as a system of power rather than a series of interrelated markets (institutionalists). Such writing, though clearly methodological, is very closely linked with the heterodox traditions out of which it arises and to a certain extent stands apart from the developments discussed elsewhere in this chapter.

BLAUG'S *METHODOLOGY OF ECONOMICS*

The book which, arguably, defined the subject as it existed around 1980 was Mark Blaug's *The Methodology of Economics* (1980/1992).[1] It opened with a survey of the philosophy of science, discussing not only traditional issues such as the hypothetico-deductive model, but also the more recent ideas associated with Kuhn, Lakatos and Feyerabend. This was followed,

2

after a survey of the history of economic methodology, by a series of case studies of different branches of economics. The book was important for several reasons. The first is that it provided a textbook, thereby defining a subject. That subject was defined as covering not only traditional concerns (tendency laws, the irrelevance-of-assumptions thesis, positive and normative economics), but also the new issues, raised by Popper, Kuhn and Lakatos, of how the subject developed. The series of case studies made the point that the way to understand economic methodology was through examining its history in the light of ideas taken from philosophy.

The main reason why Blaug's book was so important, however, was that it set the agenda for much of the 1980s. The dominant theme running through the book was falsificationism. More specifically, it can be argued that it was Blaug who was responsible for placing Popper at the centre of methodological discussion in economics. Prior to Blaug's book Popperian ideas were, with the exceptions of Hutchison and Boland, not discussed much outside the London School of Economics (LSE) (the notable example there being perhaps Klappholz and Aggassi (1959);[2] after it, they were, at least for the rest of the decade, central.

Blaug's account of the philosophy of science is in two chapters. The first starts with the so-called 'received view' of the philosophy of science, ending with Popper. The second chapter presents Kuhn, Lakatos and Feyerabend as providing alternatives to Popperian falsificationism. Popperian falsificationism, with its emphasis on the importance of methodological rules for scientific progress, is thereby presented as the orthodoxy against which the ideas of Kuhn and Feyerabend, who challenged traditional notions of science, should be seen.[3] Lakatos's methodology of scientific research programmes emerged as embodying the best of both worlds, combining the hardness of Popperian falsificationism with the historical sensitivity of Kuhn's approach.[4] Falsificationism, whether Popperian or Lakatosian, is the methodology against which the branches of economics analysed later in the book were evaluated. Blaug ends with a bold conclusion concerning the role of methodology in economics.

> What methodology can do is to provide criteria for the acceptance and rejection of research programs, setting standards that will help us to discriminate between wheat and chaff. These standards, we have seen, are hierarchical, relative, dynamic, and by no means unambiguous in terms of the practical advice they offer to working economists. Nevertheless, the ultimate question we can and indeed must pose about any research program is the one made familiar by Popper: what events, if they materialized, would lead us to reject that program? A program that cannot meet that question has fallen short of the highest standards that scientific knowledge can attain.
>
> (Blaug 1980: 264)

This conclusion, arguably, underlay much methodological work during the 1980s. Even though the trend was away from such a point of view, it was Blaug's position with which people took issue.

ECONOMIC METHODOLOGY SINCE 1980

During the 1980s the literature on economic methodology mushroomed. In the second edition of his book, Blaug cites thirty books published in the twelve years since the first edition. In addition to new monographs, there appeared textbooks (e.g. Pheby 1988; Glass and Johnson 1989) and books of readings aimed at students (Caldwell 1984; Hausman 1985; Marr and Raj 1983). The journals *Research in the History of Economic Thought and Methodology* (1983), *Economics and Philosophy* (1985) and *Methodus* (1989)[5] were established, specializing in whole or in part in economic methodology. The number of articles and books on economic methodology increased dramatically during the 1980s. Hausman (1994) lists fifty books published between 1984 and 1993, compared with nineteen for the period 1975–83. By the end of the 1980s, economic methodology had become a recognizable subdiscipline within economics.

Though many new themes emerged during the 1980s, most economic methodologists seeking alternatives to falsificationism, Blaug's work was frequently in the background. Even where people were opening up new areas, his work was frequently taken as the orthodoxy against which it was necessary to fight. Though it is hard to summarize this literature without oversimplifying it, it is possible to pick out two main strands within the criticism of Blaug's methodology. One comprises philosophical criticisms of falsificationism, arguing that it is not cogent. The other is a desire to 'recover practice' – the notion that before methodologists can offer criticism, they must understand what it is that economists are actually doing. These strands are, of course, tangled up together – arguing that one needs to recover practice is a criticism of the cogency of falsificationism – but between them they provide a route through much of the literature.

DEBATING FALSIFICATIONISM

Pluralism

Caldwell's *Beyond Positivism* (1982) argued the case for what was termed 'critical pluralism'. The positivist approach to science, dominant till the 1960s, involved looking for rules to govern theory appraisal or theory choice: rules which, if followed, would lead scientists towards correct theories. Popperian falsificationism provides an alternative to this – it is not claimed that falsificationism leads to the establishment of true theories,

4

merely that it leads to the elimination of error. Caldwell (1982: 236), however, claimed that falsificationism was not viable, for three reasons: (1) Falsificationism is not viable as a methodology for *any* scientific discipline. When interpreted narrowly, falsificationism is far too restrictive; when interpreted broadly it loses its prescriptive force. (2) There is little reason to expect falsificationism to work in a social science like economics. Reasons include the large number and uncheckability of initial conditions in most economic theories; the absence of general laws; that tests of models are not tests of theories; and that economic data rarely correspond exactly to the concepts that arise in economic theories. (3) Falsificationism had never been practised to a significant extent in economics (as even some of its proponents freely admit).

Caldwell's response was that to abandon the search for a unique set of rules for choosing between theories did not involve anarchism. Rather, he advocated methodological pluralism, this being defined as involving methodologists in three tasks.

> 1. The starting point of methodological analysis is the rational recon-struction of the methodological content both of the writings of economic methodologists and of the various research programs within the discipline ... 2. The next step is the critical assessment of the methodological content revealed in the rational reconstructions. 3. The role of the methodologist is first to show that there is no single 'given' method, and then to demonstrate that reasonable and fruitful criticism and debate is still possible .... This latter task is achieved by the critical discussion of the strengths (if any) and limitations of the rationally reconstructed methodological positions under examination.
>
> (Caldwell 1982: 245–7)

Critical pluralism, therefore, defines an agenda for *methodologists*, not for economists. It thus differs from the pluralism advocated by, for example, Dow (1985) or Harcourt and Hamouda (1988) who advocate plurality of methods within economics. It is based on specific philosophical objections to both positivism and falsificationism.

Constructivism

A more radical critique of falsificationism, and much else besides, is pro-vided by what is perhaps most accurately labelled constructivism, though terms such as post-modernist and post-positivist are sometimes used. A suitable definition is the following.

> *Constructivism* The only independent reality is beyond the reach of our knowledge and language. A known world is partly constructed by the imposition of concepts. These concepts differ from (linguistic,

social, scientific, etc.) group to group, and hence the worlds of groups differ. Each world exists only relative to an imposition of concepts.

(Devitt 1991: 235)

From this perspective knowledge is something that can be defined only with reference to the linguistic practices of a particular community. It follows that theories can be appraised only from within specific communities: the notion that there are standards which transcend specific communities is, it is argued, indefensible.

Such arguments are well known in philosophy (e.g. Rorty 1979), the sociology of scientific knowledge (e.g. Latour and Woolgar 1986) and literary criticism (e.g. Fish 1981). In the 1980s they were introduced into economics by McCloskey (1983, 1986) in his attack on modernism, which he defined in terms of the desire to predict and to control. Modernist methodology was narrow, limiting and, because prediction is impossible in economics, impossible to implement. Falsificationism, like any modernist methodology, was, for McCloskey, incoherent. After quoting Blaug's claim that methodology can provide criteria for the acceptance and rejection of research programmes (see page 3 above) he concluded,

It sounds grand, but Einstein's gods are rolling in the aisles. Why, the voice of pragmatism asks, should a dubious epistemological principle be a test of anything at all, much less of practice, much less the 'ultimate' test? Doesn't science take place most of the time well short of the ultimate?

(McCloskey 1986: 21, quoting Blaug 1980)

It is in similar vein that Weintraub (1989) has argued that 'Methodology doesn't matter'. He defines methodology as the attempt to govern the appraisal of particular economic theories by an account of theorizing in general. This is impossible, for economic theories must be appraised using economic arguments, not using arguments from outside economics. He applies to methodology the arguments Fish applies to 'theory' in literary criticism:

Theory cannot guide practice because its rules and procedures are no more than generalizations from practice's history (and are only a small piece of that history), and theory cannot reform practice because, rather than neutralizing interest, it begins and ends in interest and raises the imperatives of interest – of some local, particular, partisan project – to the status of universals.

(Fish 1985: 438–9, quoted in Weintraub 1989: 272)

When exploring the history of general equilibrium theory, therefore, Weintraub (1991) aims to avoid altogether the issue of appraising the research programme, his objective being to understand the way the literature evolved.

Appraising the Popperian tradition

During the 1980s there were many attempts to take further the debate over the Popperian tradition in economic methodology (defined as including methodology inspired by both Popper and Lakatos), notably a series of volumes edited by de Marchi: *The Popperian Legacy in Economics* (1988); *Appraising Economic Theories: Studies in the Methodology of Research Programmes* (jointly edited with Blaug 1991) and *Post-Popperian Methodology of Economics* (1993). Five categories of contribution can be picked out:

1 'post-modernist' arguments against the project of methodology in general;
2 philosophically-based criticisms of Popperian methodology;
3 attempts to apply falsificationist methodology to the analysis of economics;
4 attempts to 'salvage' something from the Popperian tradition;
5 defences of falsificationism.

(1) The first category contains the work of McCloskey, Klamer and Mirowski (in de Marchi 1988, 1993). McCloskey's critique of falsificationism has been sketched above, and the views of all three are discussed further in the next section.

(2) A clear example of the philosophical objections that have been levelled against falsificationism is provided by Hausman. He has summarized his attitude to Popper by claiming that 'the notion of falsificationism as a purely logical relation between theories and basic statements or observation reports ... is irrelevant to any important questions concerning science [, and that] Popper's relevant views concerning falsificationism as a methodology or a policy are unfounded and unacceptable' (in de Marchi 1988: 65). On the first point, once one accepts, as does Popper, that it is predictions derived from systems of scientific theories that have to be falsifiable, logical falsifiability ceases to play any very important role in appraising individual theories. In addition, Hausman argues, Popperian methodology goes too far in denying that we ever have evidence in support of our views. Even though knowledge is not certain, we do, Hausman claims, have positive grounds for beliefs we hold. On the second point he argues, as will be explained in the next section, that there are good reasons why economists attach greater weight to some of their theories than to disconfirming empirical evidence. It would damage the discipline if economists were to adopt Popperian methodological rules which required one always to reject theories that failed empirical tests.

Rosenberg, another philosopher who has turned his attention to economics, pays little attention to Popperian falsificationism, arguing simply that it is undermined by the argument that testing always requires auxiliary assumptions concerning initial or boundary conditions, with the result that when a test fails one can never be sure whether it is the main hypothesis or one of the auxiliary assumptions that is at fault (Rosenberg 1992: 26). Where Rosenberg differs from Hausman is that, despite their shared objections to falsificationism, he attaches much greater importance to prediction. He argues that natural sciences, including biology, do involve predictions; that 'the best and most prized of scientific theories are in fact those with the greatest predictive power' (1992: 49); and that, whether or not science requires predictions, we need them as a guide to making decisions. He then provides a critique of economics, focusing on the theory of individual behaviour, based on the assumption that economics exhibits a dismal record of predictive success, and the judgement that this record needs to be improved.

(3) Of the many attempts to apply falsificationist methodology (interpreting this to include not only Popperian falsificationism but its Lakatosian offshoot) to economics, one of which has attracted much attention is that of Weintraub (de Marchi 1988; Weintraub 1985).[6] Weintraub interpreted the literature on the existence of general, competitive equilibrium from a Lakatosian perspective. Though general equilibrium analysis dealt with a body of theory that was not falsifiable (since it related to no conceivable economy), it could be defended as forming part of a research programme which did successfully predict novel facts: it was, in Lakatos's terms (see Chapter 9) empirically progressive. In contrast, heterodox programmes such as post-Keynesian economics were not (Weintraub 1982).

The most wide-ranging series of attempts to appraise the relevance of Lakatos's methodology for economics is the series of essays in de Marchi and Blaug (1991). These exhibit much greater scepticism about Lakatosian ideas than was evident in Latsis (1976). Of the contributors who sought to apply Lakatosian methodology to various branches of economics, most concluded that it did not fit, and that to condemn economics for not exhibiting empirical progress was to pay insufficient attention to the nature of economics. The main reason for playing down the importance of empirical progress was placing a high weight on theoretical progress. This emerges particularly clearly in Steedman's attempt to view Sraffian economics through Lakatosian spectacles. The main contributions of Sraffian economics, Steedman claimed, were negative theoretical ones: Sraffian economics had contributed towards eliminating theoretical error in economics. Such contributions, he argued, were more important than Lakatosian, or any other falsificationist, methodology admitted. Hoover argued a similar case with respect to the new classical macroeconomics.

(4) Other methodologists have sought to face up to the criticisms of falsificationism, and yet retain, at least to some extent, something of the

Popperian perspective. Caldwell (1991) thinks that economists could learn more from Popper's situational logic than from his falsificationism. He also agrees with Boland's (1982, 1992) focusing on Popper's emphasis on criticism and on the importance of starting from problems. A somewhat different approach is taken by Hands, a contributor to all three of de Marchi's volumes (his contributions being reprinted in Hands 1993). In an essay reflecting on these and other essays he starts by claiming that it would be undesirable to save the Popperian tradition as a normative methodology:

> If the Popperian tradition is viewed solely as *a particular normative philosophy of science* – that is, as a particular set of rather narrow *methodological rules* and the associated epistemological claims that underwrite those rules with respect to the *foundations of knowledge* – then no, the Popperian tradition cannot be saved. . . . There simply are *not* convincing arguments that by strictly following a falsificationist methodology or by restricting our attention to research programs that consistently and correctly predict novel facts we will necessarily be assured that our theories will produce economic Knowledge.
>
> (Hands 1993: 149–50; original emphases)

He proposes instead to save the Popperian tradition as 'a general philosophical backdrop' that is better than the alternatives.

Popper, Hands points out, recognizes that theories or beliefs cannot be justified in the sense of grounding them on secure foundations. This does not, however, mean that choice between theories cannot be rational. The Popperian position is that rationality is based on *criticism* rather than justification. Conjecture and the testing of theories are recommended not as infallible methodological rules, but only in so far as they serve the goal of furthering critical discussion. Popper is a realist, but also a fallibilist: 'Although we strive for theories that correspond to the world, they are forever conjectural, forever capable of (and likely to be) overthrown' (Hands 1993: 162–3). Such a response, Hands argues, provides a reasoned response to post-modernist and constructivist trends, placing Popper 'outside the range of Rorty's sweeping critique' (ibid.; see also Backhouse 1992: 76–7).

(5) The main representatives of the final category are Hutchison and Blaug. Both defend Popperian methodology on normative grounds, arguing that falsificationism is something to which economists ought to adhere if the subject is to progress. Hutchison (in de Marchi 1988; Hutchison 1992) points out that because economics is a policy-science, offering advice to policy-makers, prediction is vital. Blaug (in de Marchi 1988, 1993; and in de Marchi and Blaug 1991) also emphasizes the importance of appraising economics in terms of its predictive power, but he chooses to approach this from a Lakatosian perspective. First, he interprets Popper's notion of

a theory having empirical content in terms of the ability of a research programme to predict novel facts. Second, he is prepared to argue that economists *are* concerned with predicting novel facts: that economists are falsificationists.

'RECOVERING PRACTICE'

Rhetoric and discourse analysis

In *The Rhetoric of Economics* (1986) McCloskey urged economists to pay attention to their own rhetoric. When economists do economics they are concerned to persuade, which means we can understand what it is they are doing by finding out what it is that economists find persuasive. He produced a series of brilliant case studies from which he drew the conclusion that what persuaded economists was not empirical testing or successful prediction, but things that no explicit methodology took into account: mathematical virtuosity, arguments by analogy, symmetry and so on.

The importance of analysing economists' rhetoric was also stressed by Klamer, though from a different starting point. Whereas McCloskey started from an analysis of economists' publications, Klamer started with a series of interviews, finding out how economists saw their work when talking about it in a more informal way. His conclusion, however, was similar. Theoretical disagreements were not settled by accumulating empirical evidence.

> Economists do not only construct models and conduct empirical tests, they also argue what a good model should look like. Moreover, they philosophize, appeal to common sense, and talk about other economists and their work. Economics involves the art of persuasion. In the absence of uniform standards and clearcut empirical tests, economists have to rely on judgements, and they argue to render their judgements persuasive. This process leaves room for nonrational elements, such as personal commitment and style, and social discipline.
>
> (Klamer 1984: 234)

He contrasts this perspective with that of Popper and Lakatos, with its emphasis on the rational elements in science.

McCloskey and Klamer have both emphasized the importance of analysing the way economists argue – of analysing economics discourse. This approach follows naturally from their post-modernist approach to methodological issues, for analysing economics discourse provides a way to think about what economists are doing without passing judgement on it. These concerns have led McCloskey into literary criticism as a perspective from which to view economics (McCloskey 1990) and Klamer into placing economics into a much wider cultural setting, involving art as well as literature (Klamer 1987). Economics discourse has, however, also been approached via applied linguistics (see Henderson *et al.* 1993). Applied linguists have looked at language use in relation to authors' purposes and the reading practices of the communities they are addressing. Much of this literature, though not all of it, is oriented towards education rather than methodology. It can, however, lead into a discussion of the values held by economists, and of the way economic knowledge is created and conceived. A good example is the demonstration, on the basis of a purely linguistic analysis of the way economists modify propositions, that empirical statements about the economy (about the real world) appear not to be regarded by economists as central to their field – in dramatic contrast to the situation in natural sciences (Bloor and Bloor 1993).

Sociology of scientific knowledge

Scientific knowledge is produced by communities of scientists. It is, therefore, possible to analyse the processes whereby scientific knowledge is created from a sociological point of view: exploring the ways in which networks of scientists operate and how they interact; how scientific ideas are communicated and negotiated; how reputations are created and sustained; how entry into science is regulated; how funding decisions are made, and so on. This is sociology of science. Many sociologists, however, take the argument a stage further, developing the notion that the social processes involved have implications for the content of scientific knowledge itself – that what counts as scientific knowledge is the product of the social system that produces it. This is often termed the sociology of scientific knowledge. This perspective leads to a view of scientific knowledge that is very different from that underlying most philosophy of science. The emphasis is not on the epistemic or cognitive status of scientific ideas, but on the social processes whereby meanings are negotiated.

The perspective provided by the sociology of scientific knowledge can lead in a variety of directions. One is to very detailed examination of how specific claims to knowledge are established: of what goes on within science laboratories and of how controversies in science are conducted (see, for example, Collins 1985). Another direction is into an analysis of scientific discourse. Here the emphasis is on the need for knowledge claims to be expressed in language and on the nature and implications of the languages that are used in scientific papers, grant applications, textbooks and other types of scientific writing (see, for example, Bazerman 1988, or Myers 1989).

The contrast between the philosophical and sociological perspectives is

11

well illustrated by two papers on the issue of replication in econometrics by Collins (1991) and Cartwright (1991). Both are concerned with the role of replication in the establishment of knowledge claims, but beyond that their perspectives differ. Cartwright, the philosopher, sees the replication as establishing that there is a phenomenon to be explained. In contrast, Collins, the sociologist, sees replication as being achieved when consensus is reached within the scientific community, making no claims beyond this.

Philosophical analysis of practice

Rhetorical and sociological analysis of economists' practices tends to set aside traditional philosophical concerns with issues such as the epistemic or cognitive status of economic theories, and the rationale for the way economists do things. These issues have, however, not been neglected. Hausman (1991) has argued that much of what economists do can be rationalized by seeing economics as an inexact and separate science. Inexactness is understood in the sense defined by John Stuart Mill: economic laws can never hope to be complete – they describe only some of the laws which will be operating in any situation which means that it is always necessary to ask what disturbing causes are also operating. His perspective on empirical testing is that the quality of empirical data, and the nature of the tests employed, mean that economists often have very good reasons to place more confidence in their theories than in empirical evidence. What Blaug dubs 'innocuous falsificationism' is, Hausman claims, a rational response to the situation in which economists find themselves.

Hausman's other theme is that economists are concerned for the separateness, or autonomy, of their science – that it should not depend on sociology or psychology as would be the case if economists were to turn to these disciplines for their behavioural assumptions. This desire that economics be separate accounts for economists' attachment to the notion of rational behaviour. This attachment can also be explained by the notion that the theory of rational behaviour describes how individuals *ought* to behave. If people do not learn, they can be systematically exploited, providing them with an incentive to learn.

The centrality of rationality as a normative theory of individual behaviour is also emphasized by Rosenberg (1992) who makes a case for treating economic theory as a part of political philosophy. General equilibrium theory, he argues, is central to economics, but if economists were concerned with providing explanatory theories or with predictive success, this would be hard to explain. General equilibrium theory explains very little, it is not a necessary precondition for undertaking partial equilibrium analysis, and it generates no useful predictions. As part of a normative enterprise, however, the rationale for general equilibrium theory is clear. In the words of two leading general equilibrium theorists, it shows how

12

A decentralized economy motivated by self-interest and guided by price signals would be compatible with a coherent disposition of economic resources that could be regarded, in a well-defined sense, as superior to a large class of possible alternative dispositions.... It is important to understand how surprising this claim must be to anyone not exposed to this tradition.

(Arrow and Hahn 1971: vii; quoted in Rosenberg 1992: 218)

General equilibrium theory is, as Rosenberg puts it, 'the formalized approach to the systematic study of this claim about how the unintended consequences of uncoordinated selfishness result in the most efficient exploitation of scarce resources in the satisfaction of wants' (1992: 219).

This view of economics as a branch of contractarian political philosophy is consistent with the view, also explored by Rosenberg, that much of economics (at least as it now is) should be viewed not as science but as applied mathematics. This is a point that has been voiced somewhat more vigorously by several economists who, unlike Rosenberg, see it as an indictment of modern economics. McCloskey (1991) has argued that much economic theory should be seen as a search through what he calls the 'hyperspace of assumptions'. Hutchison has repeatedly criticized economic theory for having become no more than an intellectual game (1992, 1938; and in de Marchi 1988; see also Mayer 1993).

Economics has also been analysed from the perspective provided by realism. Realism is, loosely, the notion that the world exists independently of our knowledge of it. Different varieties of realism arise from different specifications of what it is that is claimed to exist: commonsense realism involves asserting that commonsense objects exist; scientific realism asserts the existence of the objects of scientific research. It is also possible to distinguish between realism about scientific theories and realism simply about the entities postulated in such theories.

One way to approach economic methodology from a realist perspective is that of Mäki (1989). Much of his work is critical, in the sense that he is concerned not with constructing some grand methodology, but with seeking to achieve clarity and precision in analysing economists' methodological positions. To this end he has analysed a range of issues, including Austrian economics (1990), Friedman's essay (1992), and McCloskey's work on rhetoric (1988, 1993). The constructive side of his work involves providing precise conceptual tools which can be used to clarify the nature of economic arguments. The concepts of idealization and isolation, for example, can be used to explain what it is that economists are doing when they construct abstract, theoretical models.

Also rooted in realist philosophy, but very different, is the approach of Lawson (1989).[7] His claim is that reality, whether natural or social, comprises not only the phenomena we experience directly (events, actions,

13

states of affairs) but also structures, mechanisms, powers and tendencies that underlie and govern such phenomena. Science, therefore, should be concerned not with elaborating event regularities (regularities of the form 'whenever event x occurs then event y occurs'), but with uncovering the structures and tendencies that produce the phenomena of experience. This perspective leads to an acknowledgement of the concept-dependent nature of social life (social structure is seen as dependent upon human concepts and actions) whilst at the same time a limited naturalism is preserved.

A very different philosophical basis for economic methodology is provided by pragmatism. This has been used by Hirsch and de Marchi (1990) to make sense of Friedman's 'The methodology of positive economics' (1953) in the light of his work on economics. This essay, they argue, should be understood against the background, not of Popperian falsificationism, but of Dewey's pragmatism. A Popperian reading of Friedman's essay fails to make sense of the way in which Friedman undertook his research into economics. Friedman is, for example, very concerned about where hypotheses come from – it is important that they arise out of a close familiarity with empirical data and are not the result simply of the theorist's imagination. Similarly, Friedman does not see his work in simple falsificationist terms: theories are never knocked out by a single piece of empirical evidence. Instead, Friedman stresses the importance of a range of different tests, approaching a problem from as many angles as possible. Like McCloskey in *The Rhetoric of Economics*, Hirsch and de Marchi read economics in the light of Dewey, but they reach different conclusions.

In Hirsch and de Marchi's work on Friedman we find an increased emphasis on where economic ideas come from. The argument that the context of discovery has epistemic significance has been explored in the philosophy of science literature (e.g. Pera 1987). De Marchi has taken up this notion, which provides one of the motives for his collection of essays subtitled 'Recovering practice' (1993; see also the introduction to de Marchi and Blaug 1991). Backhouse (1993a) has suggested that such a perspective provides a way to justify Lakatos's emphasis on the prediction of novel facts as an appraisal criterion.

Reforming practice

The work discussed above has all had what might, somewhat loosely, be termed a philosophical orientation. There have, however, also been attempts by economists to reflect on their discipline directly. By now the critiques of economic theory offered by Hahn, Leontief and others in the early 1970s are well known (see Backhouse 1993b; Mayer 1993). McCloskey's arguments about formalization fall into the same category. One of the main themes in this literature has been the existence of distortions in the incentives facing economists, inducing them to devote disproportionate effort to refining abstract theory at the expense of developing the subject's empirical foundations. In the past few years, however, a few economists have sought to go beyond this to analyse the specific problems facing the subject in more detail.

One area to be examined in this way is industrial organization, a field that has, during the 1980s, been transformed by the application of game theory. Fisher (1989), however, has argued that this explosion of theoretical work has enabled us to say almost nothing about the working of oligopolistic markets that could not be said on the basis of earlier theory: both the new theory and the old tell us that many outcomes are possible. Fisher locates the reason for this failure in economists' having turned away from theorizing about what must happen towards theorizing about what might happen – from 'generalizing' to 'exemplifying' theory. The move towards exemplifying theory was widespread during the 1980s, and arises, at least in part, from economists' having come to realize that there are few extremely general theoretical results to be obtained. Its cost, however, is that we do not know which theories, if any, are relevant to the real world, with the result that we can obtain few testable predictions.

A second example is provided by Summers's critique of what he terms 'The scientific illusion in empirical macroeconomics' (1991). As the cost of computing has plummeted, and the availability of suitable software has increased, econometric research into macroeconomics has been undertaken on a larger and larger scale, with more and more sophisticated econometric techniques being employed. Yet this effort, Summers claims, has had little impact on the evolution of macroeconomic theory. The type of empirical work that has had the greatest impact is more informal, such as Friedman's demonstration that money matters. Such work does not attempt to provide a single, formal, decisive test of a highly developed theory, but relies on the accumulation of a variety of evidence at a lower level.[8] Related arguments have been developed by Mayer (1993) who has argued that economists have devoted excessive attention to the strongest links in their chains of reasoning, neglecting the all-important weakest links, and that they have claimed an unwarranted degree of precision for their results.

What sets apart the arguments of economists such as Fisher and Summers from the other arguments discussed here is that they are reflections by practising economists concerned directly to improve work in the areas in which they are working. Though not necessarily philosophically unsophisticated, such arguments are driven by practical, not philosophical, concerns. The goal of reforming practice is dominant.

ROGER E. BACKHOUSE

THE CHAPTERS WHICH FOLLOW

General perspectives

The following chapters explore and develop many of the themes which have arisen in economic methodology since 1980, starting with three papers exploring general issues concerning economic methodology. Hutchison (Chapter 2) argues that before discussing the nature of the methods appropriate for economics, it is vital to be clear about the aims of the subject. This is important to us in a way that it was not important for previous generations. Fifty years ago, he claims, most economists took it for granted that the provision of advice to policy-makers, and hence prediction, was the overriding aim. With the expansion of academic economics, and the demands made on academic economists, however, he sees the profession as having turned inwards, away from real-world relevance and policy as the aim of the subject.

The relationship between economics and policy-making is also stressed by Colander (Chapter 3). He approaches this through returning to the terminology of J. N. Keynes (1891) in which the 'art' of economics is used to refer to the 'engineering branch' of economic science – to applied policy analysis. This has, of necessity, to draw on both positive and normative economics. Colander's motivation for resurrecting this terminology is the argument that the goals of positive economics and applied policy analysis are different. Though his work falls squarely in the tradition of work by practising economists such as Kamarck (1983) and Mayer (1993), he differs from them in attaching greater importance to abstract theory. The practical rules he suggests, therefore, apply only to applied policy analysis, and should not be used to criticize pure theory.

Mirowski (Chapter 4) is also critical of the contemporary economics, but from a different perspective. His main thesis is that methodologists should be asking awkward questions, very different from those discussed so far. Is it justifiable to assume that the natural and the social can be clearly separated? Is economic thought a simple reaction to changes in the 'economy', or is the latter constituted by our inquiries? What are the implications of economists' involvement in society for any claims to objectivity? How do the mathematical tools used by economists influence the content of their theories? Why have economists paid so little attention to experimentation and the problems involved in current econometric practices?

The sociology of scientific (and economic) knowledge is taken up by Hands (Chapter 5). This chapter provides an account of the rise and origins of the sociology of scientific knowledge literature, distinguishing on the one hand between this literature and the, older, sociology of science literature, and on the other hand between the major schools of thought within it. Hands goes on to point out the importance of interests in the sociology of scientific knowledge literature. For contributors to this literature, scientific knowledge is created by scientists motivated by their own interests. When undertaking scientific work scientists are concerned with reputation and other rewards. This has led several sociologists to use economic concepts in their analysis of science: to talk of a market for information, with supply, demand and value. This leads Hands to argue that the *economics* of scientific knowledge may be as important as the sociology of scientific knowledge. Economists could bring to the study of scientific knowledge tools that are very different from those used by sociologists. He explores some of the possibilities that may exist and uses the experience of the sociology of scientific knowledge to identify some of the problems that might arise. Of particular importance is the problem of reflexivity: the economist exploring the economics of scientific knowledge is a part of the system that is being analysed.

Falsificationism: for and against

Blaug's *Methodology of Economics* placed falsificationism at the centre of discussions of economic methodology. Since then it has been subjected to an immense amount of criticism. The first chapter in this section (Chapter 6) contains Blaug's response to his many critics. He reiterates his commitment to certain key features of Popperian methodology, notably the priority of prescriptive methodology (deriving methodological norms which should govern science) and opposition to the inductive fallacy (the notion that we can find out about the world simply by observing it).

Attaching primacy to prescriptive methodology, however, does not mean that the methodologist ignores what economists actually do – Blaug recognizes a tension between seeking to appraise science and learning from what scientists actually do, arguing that confronting this question explicitly is one of the most attractive features of Lakatos's methodology. His commitment to prescriptive methodology does mean, however, that Blaug views interpretations of Popper that stress 'critical rationalism' as having too little content, and 'recovering practice' as a way of defending economics just as it is. Constructivism is even worse, for it goes even further in undercutting the empirical aspirations of economists. It provides a defence of formalism, where this is understood as involving not simply the use of formal methods but the ranking of rigour and precision higher than relevance.

In the following chapter (Chapter 7) Caldwell, one of Blaug's critics, outlines his objections to falsificationism and direction in which he believes economic methodology should be moving. Falsification, he argues, is both unhelpful to economists and inconsistent with Popper's methodology of the social sciences, situational analysis. He argues that in embracing Lakatosian ideas, Blaug has himself moved significantly away from falsificationism, thus undermining his earlier arguments based on falsificationism. Instead, Caldwell argues (his first proposal) that situational analysis provides one way (though not the only one) to understand what economists are doing. His aim is not to distinguish between good and bad practice, but to analyse what economists are doing. His second proposal is to explore the limits to what economists can achieve – what he calls 'epistemic pessimism'. He contrasts this with the 'epistemic optimism' of Blaug and Hausman, both of whom believe (for different reasons) that appropriate investment in empirical work would lead to empirical progress. The two proposals are linked, for exploring the limits of economics means exploring the constraints under which economists are acting.

Criticism is also the main emphasis in Boland's interpretation of Popper (Chapter 8). Boland distinguishes between what he calls 'the popular Popper' (the falsificationist, as found in Blaug's work) and 'the Socratic Popper', for whom the problem situation is critical, providing the setting in which criticism can be undertaken. Socratic dialogue, Boland argues, is the appropriate model for science. One of the reasons this has not been recognized, he contends, is that Lakatos recast Popper's views in a way that brought them much closer to Kuhn's. This may have made them more popular, but at the expense of their all-important Socratic dialectical elements.

Backhouse (Chapter 9) explores Lakatos's methodology of scientific research programmes. His conclusion is that whilst it cannot be regarded as providing a simple recipe for evaluating economic theories – there are too many difficulties for that – it does provide a valuable starting point for many issues in economic methodology. Though Lakatos's characterization of a research programme may not tell us much about the structure of economics, the notion of a research programme defined in terms of heuristics is one that can be developed. In addition, prediction of novel facts, an appraisal criterion that appeals to many economists, can be defended. Perhaps most important, Lakatos's methodology preserves the important tension between positive and normative methodology – between understanding practice and appraising it – that is absent from much recent work on methodology.

Philosophical perspectives on economics

Though he, like the authors of the previous four chapters, discusses Lakatos's methodology of scientific research programmes, Hausman (Chapter 10) is concerned with rather different issues. He explicitly sets aside the issue of theory appraisal in order to ask about the structure of economic theories. It was Kuhn who opened up this idea with his theory of paradigms and scientific revolutions. He showed the importance to science of disciplinary matrices – the sets of assumptions and rules that govern scient-

ific work. Hausman then analyses Lakatos's notion of a research programme, arguing that, when we confine ourselves to what it says about
the structure of science (i.e. setting aside questions to do with appraisal),
it takes us hardly any distance beyond Kuhn. Furthermore, he claims,
neither perspective provides any useful recipe for grasping the overall
structure and strategy of contemporary economics. A much better recipe
is provided by a modified version of Mill's inexact deductive method,
which Hausman describes in detail. Kuhn and Lakatos do no more than
get one started in trying to understand the structure of economic theories.

Rosenberg (Chapter 11) tackles the puzzling question of the cognitive
status of economic theory. Are economic theories laws about the causes of
behaviour, analogous to laws in physics or biology, or are they something
else? The problem with regarding economic theories as laws in this sense
is that not only have they been very unsuccessful, but economists show
no interest in modifications to their theories which might make them more
successful. They refuse, for example, to learn from psychology in order to
improve the predictive success of economic theories. Instead, Rosenberg
offers the suggestion that we should think of economic theory either as a
normative discipline, or as a branch of applied mathematics.

Mäki (Chapter 12) returns to the question which once dominated discussions of economic methodology – the realism of assumptions, arguing
that there is a need to reorient the discussion. The question of whether or
not assumptions are realistic is, he points out, not an interesting one. All
assumptions are, in various ways, unrealistic. The important issue is the
role assumptions play in a theory.

Lawson's purpose (Chapter 13) is to introduce, describe and argue for
a specific perspective on the nature of social reality and science, which he
labels 'critical realism'. His starting point is that it is not enough to assert
a priori that the methods employed in social science should, or should not,
be the same as those that have been found to be successful in natural
sciences. The aim must be to find methods, techniques and modes of
reasoning that are appropriate to what we know about the nature of the
social phenomena we are studying. This requires paying specific attention
to questions of ontology. From this realist perspective Lawson argues that
the methods and techniques that prevail in economics are usually inadequate, and that they are preserved because they are believed to have been
successful in certain spheres of natural science.

Recent discussions of pragmatism in the context of economics have
focused primarily on Dewey and Rorty. Kevin Hoover (Chapter 14) argues
that economists would do better to turn to the pragmatism (which he
termed pragmaticism) of Peirce, the source of many of Dewey's ideas. In
many respects Peirce's theory of truth and scientific knowledge resembles
that of Dewey and Rorty: truth involves beliefs being coherent, with
knowledge being relative to the presuppositions of a given community.

Peirce, however, does not rest here. Central to his work is a theory of inquiry in which criticism is central. Truth is also a regulatory ideal governing inquiry, involving correspondence between propositions and facts of the world. Peirce is thus prepared, unlike Rorty, to speak of Truth (with a capital T). Such Truth is parasitic on beliefs but cannot be private and subjective because knowledge is social, its growth being ensured by the method of science. Peirce thus combines pragmatism and realism, providing a much sharper version of pragmatism, or of more use to economists, than the Deweyian or Rortian versions.

Economics as discourse

Donald McCloskey (Chapter 15) takes as his starting point the fact that economists are, like most other people, concerned to persuade: they, like any scientists, are writing with intent. Rhetoric is the study of such writing with intent and involves reading with understanding. To aid such understanding McCloskey lists and explains a number of terms that need to be used in rhetorical analysis. These include: ethos (the character of the implied author of a text); point of view (personal, or impartial narrator?); style (inextricably linked with content); appeals to authority; metaphor (tied up with the structure of arguments); irony (saying one thing but meaning the opposite); story; and deconstruction. His thesis is that science uses far more of the resources of language than conventional philosophical accounts imply, and that to understand science one must understand the way in which language is used.

Willie Henderson (Chapter 16) takes up one particular aspect of language – metaphor. An important aspect of metaphor, he argues, is that it involves a transfer of ideas without implying a comparison that can be spelled out. It is thus very different from analogy where the aspects of a comparison are spelled out, for the power of metaphor derives from its involving more than mere comparison. Useful metaphors extend meanings and are important in creating new ways of thinking. Thus what counts as metaphor changes over time. A term (e.g. human capital) may start out as a metaphor (education is like investment, not consumption) but with constant repetition its metaphorical aspects may become lost, resulting in its becoming dead as a metaphor. It is also important to distinguish between different types of metaphor (single-sentence metaphors; extended metaphors; root metaphors) which need to be considered separately.

Vivienne Brown (Chapter 17) considers the implications of a specific metaphor – seeing the economy as text, and economic discourse as involving reading a text. This perspective implies that where McCloskey sees the economist as a persuader, she sees the economist as a reader and interpreter of the signs of the economy. It follows that in the same way that the nature of language means that texts are open to different interpretations, so too is the economy. Seeing the economy as text raises the issue of its nature. Brown argues that the economy is, unlike literary texts, not clearly defined: it is fragmentary, needing to be constructed from incomplete, approximate and inconsistent series of data. The economy is also fragmentary in the sense that its boundaries are not clearly defined. A further important characteristic of the economy is that it is not a static text, but one that is constantly changing over time. For this reason, Brown argues, the economy should not be read in terms of an invarying plot structure: there is no single narrator in full control of the story. The economy should, therefore, be read as a multi-voiced discourse.

ACKNOWLEDGEMENTS

I am grateful to participants in the first NPPE Workshop in Economic Methodology, and to Lawrence Boland, Bruce Caldwell, Wade Hands, Daniel Hausman and Tony Lawson for helpful discussion of an earlier draft of this paper.

NOTES

1 The main exceptions to this statement are heterodox methodological writings.
2 For a discussion of how Popperian ideas were received by economists at the LSE in the 1960s, see de Marchi (1988).
3 Though this is true of Lakatos, who was explicitly seeking to develop Popperian ideas, it was not true for Kuhn. The 'received view' was not Popperian. Neither was the prevailing view of economic methodology, influenced primarily by Friedman. It is arguable that, with the exceptions cited above, economists interested in methodology turned to Kuhn and Lakatos from the 1970s, and to Popper only after 1980: that in economics Popper effectively came *after* Kuhn and Lakatos.
4 These ideas are discussed more fully in several chapters in Parts II and III, notably Hausman (Chapter 10) and Backhouse (Chapter 9).
5 To become the *Journal of Economic Methodology* from 1994.
6 For a list of other attempts, see de Marchi's introduction to de Marchi and Blaug (1991).
7 See also the references to Chapter 13 below.
8 This point is also made by Friedman and Schwartz (1991). See also the discussion on page 14 above.

BIBLIOGRAPHY

Arrow, K. J. and Hahn, F. H. (1971) *General Competitive Analysis*, Edinburgh: Oliver & Boyd.
Backhouse, R. E. (1992) 'The constructivist critique of economic methodology', *Methodus* 4(1): 65–82.
Backhouse, R. E. (1993a) 'Realism and the prediction of novel facts in economics', Discussion Paper 93–01, Department of Economics, University of Birmingham.

Backhouse, R. E. (1993b) *Economists and the Economy*, 2nd edn, New Brunswick, NJ: Transaction Publishers.

Bazerman, C. (1988) *Shaping Written Knowledge: The Genre and Activity of the Experimental Article in Science*, Madison, WI: University of Wisconsin Press.

Blaug, M. (1980/1992) *The Methodology of Economics: How Economists Explain*, 2nd edn 1992, Cambridge: Cambridge University Press.

Bloor, M. and Bloor, T. (1993) 'How economists modify propositions', in Henderson *et al.* (1993).

Boland, L. (1982) *The Foundations of Economic Method*, London: Allen & Unwin.

Boland, L. (1992) *The Principles of Economics: Some Lies My Teachers Told Me*, London: Routledge.

Bronfenbrenner, M. (1971) 'The "structure of scientific revolutions" in economic thought', *History of Political Economy* 3: 136–51.

Cairnes, J. E. (1875) *The Character and Logical Method of Political Economy*, London.

Caldwell, B. (1982) *Beyond Positivism*, London: Allen & Unwin.

Caldwell, B. (ed.) (1984) *Appraisal and Criticism in Economics*, London: Allen & Unwin.

Caldwell, B. (1991) 'Clarifying Popper', *Journal of Economic Literature* 29(1): 1–33.

Cartwright, N. (1991) 'Replicability, reproducibility and robustness: comments on Harry Collins', *History of Political Economy* 23(1): 143–55.

Coats, A. W. (1969) 'Is there a "structure of scientific revolutions" in economics?' *Kyklos* 22: 289–96.

Collins, H. (1985) *Changing Order: Replication and Induction in Scientific Practice*, London and Beverly Hills: Sage.

Collins, H. (1991) 'The meaning of replication and the science of economics', *History of Political Economy* 23(1): 123–42.

de Marchi, N. (ed.) (1988) *The Popperian Legacy in Economics*, Cambridge: Cambridge University Press.

de Marchi, N. (ed.) (1993) *Post-Popperian Methodology of Economics: Recovering Practice*, Boston, Dordrecht and London: Kluwer.

de Marchi, N. and Blaug, M. (eds) (1991) *Appraising Economic Theories: Studies in the Methodology of Research Programmes*, Aldershot: Edward Elgar.

Devitt, M. (1991) *Realism and Truth*, 2nd edn, Oxford: Basil Blackwell.

Dobb, M. (1937) *Political Economy and Capitalism*, London: Routledge.

Dow, S. C. (1985) *Macroeconomic Thought*, Oxford: Basil Blackwell.

Fish, S. (1981) *Is There a Text in this Class?* Cambridge, MA: Harvard University Press.

Fish, S. (1985) 'Consequences', *Critical Inquiry* II: 433–58.

Fisher, F. (1989) 'Games economists play: a noncooperative view', *Rand Journal of Economics* 20(1): 113–24.

Friedman, M. (1953) 'The methodology of positive economics', in Milton Friedman (ed.), *Essays on Positive Economics*, Chicago: Chicago University Press.

Friedman, M. and Schwartz, A. J. (1991) 'Alternative approaches to analysing economic data', *American Economic Review* 81(1): 39–49.

Glass, J. C. and Johnson, W. (1989) *Economics: Progression, Stagnation or Degeneration?* Brighton: Harvester Wheatsheaf.

Gordon, D. F (1965) 'The role of history of thought in the understanding of modern economic theory', *American Economic Review* 55 (Papers and Proceedings): 119–27.

Hands, D. W. (1993) *Rationality, Testing and Progress*, Lanham, MD: Rowman & Littlefield.

Harcourt, G. C. and Hamouda, O. (1988) 'Post Keynesianism: from criticism to coherence?' *Bulletin of Economic Research* 40(1): 1–34.

Hausman, D. M. (1981) *Capital, Profits and Prices: An Essay in the Philosophy of Economics*, New York: Columbia University Press.

Hausman, D. M. (ed.) (1985/1994) *The Philosophy of Economics: An Anthology*, Cambridge: Cambridge University Press.

Hausman, D. M. (1991) *The Inexact and Separate Science of Economics*, Cambridge: Cambridge University Press.

Henderson, W., Dudley-Evans, T. and Backhouse, R. (eds) (1993) *Economics and Language*, London: Routledge.

Hirsch, A. and de Marchi, N. (1990) *Milton Friedman: Economics in Theory and Practice*, Brighton: Harvester Wheatsheaf.

Hollis, M. and Nell, E. J. (1975) *Rational Economic Man: A Philosophical Critique of Neoclassical Economics*, Cambridge: Cambridge University Press.

Hutchison, T. W. (1938) *The Significance and Basic Postulates of Economic Theory*, London: Macmillan.

Hutchison, T. W. (1992) *Changing Aims in Economics*, Oxford: Basil Blackwell.

Kamarck, A. (1983) *Economics and the Real World*, Oxford: Basil Blackwell.

Keynes, J. N. (1891) *The Scope and Method of Political Economy*, London: Macmillan.

Klamer, A. (1984) *The New Classical Macroeconomics: Conversations with New Classical Macroeconomists and Their Opponents*, Brighton: Harvester Wheatsheaf.

Klamer, A. (1987) 'The advent of modernism', mimeo, University of Iowa.

Klant, J. J. (1979/1984) *The Rules of the Game: The Logical Structure of Economic Theory*, translated by Ina Smart, Cambridge: Cambridge University Press.

Klappholz, K. and Aggassi, J. (1959) 'Methodological prescriptions in economics', *Economica* 26(101): 60–74.

Koopmans, T. C. (1957) *Three Essays on the State of Economic Science*, New York: McGraw-Hill.

Kuhn, T. S. (1962/1970) *The Structure of Scientific Revolutions*, 2nd edn 1970, Chicago: University of Chicago Press.

Kunin, L. and Weaver, F. S. (1971) 'On the structure of scientific revolutions in economics', *History of Political Economy* 3: 391–7.

Latour, B. and Woolgar, S. (1986) *Laboratory Life: The Construction of Scientific Facts*, 2nd edn, Princeton: Princeton University Press.

Latsis, S. J. (1976) *Method and Appraisal in Economics*, Cambridge: Cambridge University Press.

Lawson, T. (1989) 'Abstraction, tendencies and stylized facts: a realist approach to economic analysis', *Cambridge Journal of Economics* 13: 59–78.

Lipsey, R. G. (1964) *An Introduction to Positive Economics*, London: Weidenfeld.

Machlup, F. (1963) *Essays on Economic Semantics*, Englewood Cliffs: Prentice-Hall.

McCloskey, D. N. (1983) 'The rhetoric of economics', *Journal of Economic Literature* 21(2): 481–517.

McCloskey, D. N. (1986) *The Rhetoric of Economics*, Brighton: Harvester Wheatsheaf.

McCloskey, D. N. (1990) *If You're So Smart: The Narrative of Economic Expertise*, Chicago and London: University of Chicago Press.

McCloskey, D. N. (1991) 'Economic science: a search through the hyperspace of assumptions?', *Methodus* 3(1): 6–16.

Mäki, U. (1988) 'How to combine rhetoric and realism in the methodology of economics', *Economics and Philosophy* 4(1): 89–109.

Mäki, U. (1989) 'On the problem of realism in economics', *Ricerche Economiche* 43: 176–98.

Mäki, U. (1990) 'Mengerian economics in realist perspective', in B. Caldwell (ed.), *Carl Menger and his Legacy in Economics*, annual supplement to *History of Political Economy* 22: 289–310.

Mäki, U. (1992) 'Friedman and realism', *Research in the History of Economic Thought and Methodology*, 10: 171–95.

Mäki, U. (1993) 'Two philosophies of the rhetoric of language', in Henderson *et al.* (1993).

Marr, W. L. and Raj, B. (eds) (1993) *How Economists Explain: A Reader in Methodology*, Lanham, MD: University Press of America.

Mayer, T. (1993) *Truth versus Precision in Economics*, Aldershot: Edward Elgar.

Menger, K. (1883/1963) *Problems of Economics and Sociology*, translated by F. J. Nock. Urbana, IL.

Mill, J. S. (1844) *Essays on Some Unsettled Questions of Political Economy*, London: Parker. Reprinted Bristol: Thoemmes Press, 1992.

Myers, G. (1989) *Writing Biology: Texts in the Social Construction of Scientific Knowledge*, Madison, WI: University of Wisconsin Press.

Myrdal, G. (1953) *The Political Element in the Development of Economic Theory*, translated by Paul Streeten, London: Routledge & Kegan Paul.

Pera, M. (1987) 'The rationality of discovery: Galvani's animal electricity', in J. Pitt and M. Pera (eds), *Rational Changes in Science*, Dordrecht: Reidel.

Pheby, J. (1988) *Methodology and Economics: A Critical Introduction*, London: Macmillan.

Robbins, L. (1932) *An Essay on the Nature and Significance of Economic Science*, London: Macmillan.

Robinson, J. (1962) *Economic Philosophy*, Harmondsworth: Penguin Books.

Rorty, R. (1979) *Philosophy and the Mirror of Nature*, Oxford: Basil Blackwell.

Rosenberg, A. (1976) *Microeconomic Laws: A Philosophical Analysis*, Pittsburgh: University of Pittsburgh Press.

Rosenberg, A. (1992) *Economics – Mathematical Politics or Science of Diminishing Returns?* Chicago: University of Chicago Press.

Samuelson, P. A. (1963) 'Problems of methodology – discussion', *American Economic Review* 53 (Papers and Proceedings): 231–6.

Senior, N. (1836) *An Outline of the Science of Political Economy*, Reprinted London: LSE.

Stewart, I. M. T. (1979) *Reasoning and Method in Economics*, London: McGraw-Hill.

Summers, L. (1991) 'The scientific illusion in empirical macroeconomics', *Scandinavian Journal of Economics* 93(2): 129–48.

Weintraub, E. R. (1982) 'Substantive mountains and methodological molehills', *Journal of Post Keynesian Economics* 5(2): 295–303.

Weintraub, E. R. (1985) *General Equilibrium Analysis: Studies in Appraisal*, Cambridge: Cambridge University Press.

Weintraub, E. R. (1989) 'Methodology doesn't matter, but the history of thought might', *Scandinavian Journal of Economics*; reprinted in S. Honkapohja (ed.), *The State of Macroeconomics*, Oxford: Basil Blackwell, pp. 263–79.

Weintraub, E. R. (1991) *Stabilizing Dynamics: Constructing Economic Knowledge*, Cambridge: Cambridge University Press.

Wilber, C. K. and Harrison, R. S. (1978) 'The methodological basis of institutionalist economics: pattern modelling, storytelling and holism', *Journal of Economic Issues* 12: 61–89.

Part I
GENERAL PERSPECTIVES

2

ENDS AND MEANS IN THE METHODOLOGY OF ECONOMICS

Terence W. Hutchison

I

The shift in the aims of economists which has taken place since the Second World War is unprecedented, or virtually so, in the modern history of political economy and economics, or even, perhaps, since Aristotle. The major transformation in the subject which marked the transition from the Scholastics to the 'mercantilists' was certainly, in some respects, fundamental and it took well over a century. However, with regard to their aims, or ends, scholastics and mercantilists both focused on the actions or policies of individuals and governments in a manner which could be said, in both cases, to a significant extent, to have involved or implied prediction.[1] The shift in recent decades has, of course, affected only academics, not businessmen or government economists – and only a part of academia. In the absence of satisfactory surveys, however, it is impossible to gauge at all precisely how widely, and by what particular groups, the traditional aim of the subject, in terms of policy guidance, has been replaced by other aims. It seems clear, however, that an important sector (involving 'the best minds'), claiming (and to some extent regarded as possessing) high 'status' and prestige, is quite seriously affected, or infected. My hypothesis is that interest in policy problems has declined significantly, in roughly the last half-century, in the key graduate-school sector among both teachers and students; while the aim of prediction has been explicitly rejected, or inexplicitly demoted, by a growing number of academics; though, of course, for all, or virtually all, *non*-academic economists, improved prediction remains a prime aim or preoccupation.

II

The sociological–institutional approach to the explanation of the development of economic thought and theory never seemed to me more than moderately interesting or useful regarding the great first generation of neoclassicals, or in helping to explain the association between the rise of neoclassicism and increasing academicism and 'professionalism'. Admittedly, higher standards of precision were attained in the formulation of economic analysis, with mathematics being very effectively employed in presenting the new marginal concepts. Certainly, however, by the end of the nineteenth century, or even down to the inter-war period, there were few signs of the abandonment by neoclassical economists, as compared with their classical predecessors, of the overriding aim of real-world policy guidance and relevance. Alfred Marshall had, in fact, proclaimed in his *Principles* (1961: 42) that 'the dominant aim of economics in the present generation is to contribute to a solution of social problems'; and Marshall and his pupils, notably Pigou and Keynes, exercised a dominant influence on the subject in Britain and a leading influence in the world, down to the Second World War.

All this time, however, though there was some increase in the 1930s, numbers remained extremely small compared with today. It was an era of great intellectual leaders, with extremely small departments and very few students. Institutions and professional organizations were still embryonic. From 1870 until 1929 or 1939, the development of the subject can probably be studied more fruitfully in terms of biography rather than sociology. It is rather in the second half of the twentieth century that large-scale academicism and academic institutions, together with a kind of 'professionalism', has come significantly to influence, and indeed to introduce considerable confusion and distortion into the aims of economists. It is surely on this most recent and current phase that experts in sociological–institutional analysis, and pathology, should focus their efforts.[2]

III

This shift in economists' views as to the aims or ends of their subject is mainly responsible for, and has much complicated, the explosion of methodological controversy in the last decade or so. Such controversy has taken on a largely new dimension with the breakdown of the long-traditional, though largely tacit, consensus as to the overriding aim of the subject. Profound ambiguities and disagreements, explicit or implicit, have increasingly emerged regarding the main aim, or aims, which economists can, and should, try to pursue. It does not seem to have been sufficiently clearly realized, or acknowledged, that a more normative dimension regarding ends has recently supervened on arguments which were previously mainly about means, so long, that is, as something of a consensus, albeit largely tacit, had prevailed regarding the main overriding end.

Not, of course, that ends and means can be completely separated in this case, any more than they usually can be, more generally, in the analysis of economic policies. Obviously, normative issues as to what the main aim, or end, of the subject should be, are interconnected with positive issues regarding the possibility of their achievement. Indeed the increase in the explicit rejection of prediction by economists, and by philosophical and methodological writers on economics, may be connected with an apparently quite widespread decline of interest in policy among academic economists. If, quite literally, 'PREDICTION IS IMPOSSIBLE IN ECONOMICS' (*sic*, McCloskey 1985: 15) then economics inevitably becomes a largely, or even entirely, policy *ir*relevant subject.[3]

The traditional prime aim, or end, of the subject – the 'job' it was assumed to be trying to 'get done' – has apparently been increasingly replaced, in recent decades, by games-playing (as Sir John Hicks described 'much of economic theory'); by displays of brilliantly wise 'new conversation'; or by technical virtuosity in the form of empirically vacuous mathematical 'rigour' or aesthetics. Such activities are then dignified as promoting some unspecified, non-predictive 'understanding', 'wisdom' or even 'beauty'.

IV

One or two points and questions may be added regarding the vital issue of prediction and forecasting in economics, which for decades there seems to have been a widespread reluctance to confront:

(1) The rejection of prediction as an intellectually respectable, or even 'possible' aim has usually been proclaimed by academic spokespersons in hopelessly ambiguous terms – as, for example, by McCloskey in his upper-case announcement quoted above.

To extricate meaning from such statements one must ask what standards of precision and what sort of margins of error are being envisaged. Obviously, prediction in economics is generally impossible with anything approximating to the precision and near-certainty attainable in physics. Prediction in economics is also obviously impossible with the standards of accuracy and margins of error achievable in meteorology and medicine (which, of course, are well below those of physics and, therefore, much less irrelevant in respect of standards of prediction in economics). In fact, the degree of accuracy with which it may be 'possible' for economists to predict may, on the average, be significantly higher than that which would be attained without their efforts; and would certainly be very much less unsuccessful without the various series of economic statistics, built up mostly in the last half to three-quarters of a century.

Many academic economists, bemused by so long envisaging policy-making in the context of abstract, Utopian models of optimization and maximization (based on the assumption of far-reaching omniscience) may fail to realize that the contributions of economists to real-world policy-making inevitably often have to take the form, in a real world of profound

29

ignorance and uncertainty, of damage limitation and attempts to avoid the more fundamentally serious forms of politico-economic catastrophe (such as occurred, for example, in 1929–33). At least it seems to be the 'rational expectation' of the employers of non-academic economists in business and government that whatever techniques, or forms of knowledge, economists may command, are worth investing in for the sake of less inaccurate and less unreliable predictions.

(2) Predictions are described as 'scientific' if they are based on laws and reasonably precisely-stated initial conditions. Since the pretensions of the English 'Classicals' regarding 'the Laws of Political Economy', it has been increasingly recognized by economists, especially since about the middle of this century, that there are very few, and arguably no statements in economics and the social sciences which should be dignified with the title 'law' – and certainly not in the sense in which the term is used in physics.

Predictions in economics have, therefore, to be based on trends, tendencies, patterns and precedents which it may seem pointless and pedantic to reject as too unreliable as a basis for predictions, if one accepts the seriousness of the needs of business and government for less inaccurate predictions.

(3) It seems to be very difficult for economists to maintain balanced and moderate views on the subject of economic predictions. Over the last two centuries there have been, at one extreme, the excessively pretentious claims for English Classical Political Economy in the middle decades of the nineteenth century, which were echoed roughly a century later by the pretentious over-optimism of some 'Keynesian' academics in the 1950s and early 1960s. At the other extreme we have today a form of outright intellectual nihilism, which not only describes prediction in economics as 'impossible' but denounces attempts as ridiculous and even dishonest.

It is also difficult for *critics* to preserve a balance. The world being the place it is, the most conscientious, disciplined and expert predictors, or forecasters, may put forward seriously erroneous predictions which nevertheless it may be quite unfair to criticize too severely. Unfortunately, however, there are also quite a number of economic predictions, advanced by those whose conscientiousness, discipline and expertise may, and should, be questioned. For there are few, if any, subjects where constant, robust and forthright criticism is socially more desirable than is the case with regard to political economy.

(4) Alex Rosenberg has recently condemned, in severe but justifiable terms, the lack of predictive improvement achieved by both microeconomic and macroeconomic 'theory' in this century, or even, in the case of consumer behaviour, since Adam Smith. Rosenberg even puts forward the extremely drastic proposal that the pretence be abandoned that 'economics any longer has the aims or makes the claims of an empirical science of human behavior' (1992: 247). (Such abandonment might be happily

accepted by some leading academics but not, for one moment, by any 'real-world' governmental or business economist.)

Though finding it impossible not to agree with a considerable part of Rosenberg's criticisms, I would like to advance one or two countervailing points, first regarding his charge that 'macroeconomic theory has had a relatively poor record of predictive success' (1992: 249). Relative to what, it must be asked? Comparisons with other sciences (which are on many occasions very expertly undertaken throughout his book) may be of little or no relevance if the material these sciences deal with is very different in kind from that faced by economists. Anyhow, it might reasonably be maintained that macroeconomic theory was first created as recently as the 1930s partly as a result of the most catastrophic economic policy failure of this or any other century, which was responsible for the great depression, and its obvious consequences, the rise to power of Hitler and the Second World War.

The vital omission by Rosenberg, however, has been that of the relatively very considerable quantity of empirical–statistical material, including a number of quite fundamental, vital and previously non-existent statistical series, which the creation of macroeconomic theory, in its various forms, has generated in the course of the last fifty to sixty years. National income accounting was largely the offspring of Keynesian macroeconomic theory, while monetarist macroeconomics has generated a large expansion of new monetary and banking statistical series. The creation of such series has made possible the discovery of trends, tendencies, patterns and precedents, on which often unreliable, but certainly not worse than useless (but vitally necessary) tentative predictions can be based.[4]

How far the macroeconomic predictions, regularly indulged in over the last half-century by government and business, have been derived from formal 'theory', going beyond more-or-less sophisticated extrapolation, may be difficult to determine. However that may be, though it could be argued that it is pure historical luck which has prevented the various quite serious depressions since the Second World War from developing into the kind of catastrophic collapse and politico-economic nightmare such as occurred in 1929–33, it can reasonably be maintained that the creation of a considerable databank of fundamental statistical series – inaccurate and belated though they often may be – has played a crucial part in damage limitation.

It should also be borne in mind that even if the predictive record has been poor, or perhaps, in a sense, actually has deteriorated, it seems quite possible, or probable, that economic prediction, in particular macro-economic prediction, may, in the last half-century, have become significantly more difficult, and more liable to error, because of mounting politico-economic instabilities, in the form of a markedly more rapid rate of technical innovation, and much more extensive worldwide economic interdependence. It is quite possible (or probable) that improvements in techniques, and in the statistical material, may be failing to show up in improved predictive performance, because greater instability in the social–political–economic world is making prediction more difficult, and not because of any inadequacies or errors on the part of predicting economists. This kind of deterioration does not, however, affect any margin of advantage economists may or may not have over non-economists in providing less inaccurate predictions, assuming that prediction, explicit or implicit, remains an inevitable activity in real-world economic life, and that reduction in the inaccuracy of prediction becomes more, rather than less, important, the greater and more dangerous the instabilities of the real world.

In conclusion, however, it seems highly desirable to reiterate, once more, that before positive methodological analysis can be fruitfully discussed, much clearer statements must be available as to what are held, or assumed, to be the ends and aims of the subject.

NOTES

1 Questions of the possibility and nature of economic predictions, their essential role in policy-making and the predictive record of economists, have long seemed to me among the most important of those confronting anyone interested in the methodology of the subject – while, in fact, these issues have seldom, if ever, received the attention they deserve (see Hutchison 1964: 88–102; 1977: 8–33; 1992: 66–88 and 156–67).

2 An examination would seem interesting of how 'the medium' (of large-scale academic institutions) may, in recent decades, have shaped some important aspects of 'the message' (the output of economic literature and the motives in turn shaping this output). The sheer size of 'the profession' and the vast numbers of 'peers' may have turned inward an increasing number of economists, so that they look for their aims and criteria more esoterically, and away from real-world relevance and policy. To see how a somewhat similar process has engulfed the academic subject of literary criticism, see Lehmann (1991).

However, I would now alter somewhat the emphasis in seeking to explain the abstractionist–formalist 'revolution' of recent decades from that adumbrated in Hutchison (1992: 30–8). I would not now put quite such a preponderant weight on an 'internal' explanation in terms of the academic propensity to abstraction, but emphasize rather more the possible 'external' sociological–institutional factors.

3 See Hutchison (1992: 166), especially the quotations from Rosenberg. Prediction has also been rejected as an aim for economists by the late George Shackle and some of his 'Austrian' followers, notably Ludwig Lachmann. Shackle, however (incidentally in a typically generous review of a book of mine) also, very ambiguously, claimed that there are theories 'which claim only to set bounds to the diversity of things which *can* happen' (1983: 224). The question here is whether these theories are empirically falsifiable, or what kind of 'can' or 'cannot' is involved here? Is any possibility excluded by these 'predictions' apart from logical or mathematical impossibilities?

4 I would like, with some relevance, I think, at this point to correct a view,

indirectly attributed to me by Alexander Rosenberg, when he states that some writers, 'following T. W. Hutchison' (1938) 'have derided it [economics] as a body of tautologies, as a pure system of implicit definitions without any grip on the real world' (1992: 244–5). I must concede that if I have been misinterpreted it may be, to a considerable extent, my own fault, since quite a number of critics seem to have misunderstood that part of my juvenile book.

On re-reading, however, I find that although I did indeed describe what I called – in the terminology of the period – 'pure theory' as consisting of tautologies and implicit definitions, I made it clear that 'pure' theory was not the whole of theory, and that 'applied theory' did, indeed, possess empirical content. I certainly did not describe the whole of economics as consisting of tautologies, nor did I say that *all* 'pure theory', though without empirical content, was 'without any grip on the real world'. On the contrary, I pointed out that the 'propositions of pure theory', by providing precisely defined concepts, could and sometimes did facilitate the formulation of precise empirical questions. In Chapter II, section 3 (pp. 33–6), entitled 'The use and significance of propositions or pure theory', I observed that: 'A sharply and clearly defined system of concepts enables sharp and clear answers to be obtained from empirical investigation', adding the Baconian apophthegm *prudens interrogatio dimidium scientiae*.

This attempt to defend a very ancient text is not irrelevant to the argument at this point; because it was just such a precise set of concepts, generated by Keynesian, macroeconomic analysis (or 'pure theory') which facilitated the development of national income accounting and national income statistics. Whatever, or how far, in addition, the analysis, or 'pure theory', of consumer behaviour has generated a system of precise concepts useful to statistical market researchers, trying to construct firms' *ex-ante* demand curves, I am not able to answer with any authority. But it seems possible that precise concepts, such as the income and substitution effects of price changes, may have helped market researchers to get a 'grip on the real world' at some points.

Rosenberg apparently maintains that the contemporary 'theory of consumer behavior does not actually improve(s) on our ability to predict consumer behavior any better than Adam Smith' (1992: 235). This seems to me unduly pessimistic. My own hypothesis would be that although market researchers today are very far from attaining the standards of precision and reliability which their customers hope for, with the aid of trends, tendencies, patterns and precedents, derived from statistical series – in turn possibly aided by the precise concepts provided by modern 'theory' or analysis – they can, and do today, on the average, predict considerably less inaccurately than Adam Smith would have done, in the almost complete absence of statistical market research, though in the far less complex conditions of 1776. If any such predictive improvement has indeed occurred, I would award more credit to those who created the statistical series than to the 'pure' theorists, even though the latter may have assisted with the provision of more precise concepts.

On the dust cover of his book, the blurb states (though Rosenberg himself may not be responsible for this) that: 'Economics' (*tout simple*) 'is no better at predicting the likely outcome of specific events today than it was in the time of Adam Smith'. I would disagree strongly with this statement with regard to quite a wide range of important and interesting economic events. In assessing the improvement, or non-improvement, of the ability of economists, from Adam Smith to the present day, to predict less inaccurately, it is a highly misleading academic error to draw a pessimistic conclusion simply from the development of 'theory' or analysis, without taking into account the vast growth (which has been the most valuable achievement of economists in the twentieth century) in many forms of empirical material, including a number of vitally useful statistical series, whatever their failings in up-to-dateness and reliability.

BIBLIOGRAPHY

Hutchison, T. W. (1938) *The Significance and Basic Postulates of Economic Theory*, London: Macmillan.

Hutchison, T. W. (1964) *'Positive' Economics and Policy Objectives*, London: Allen & Unwin.

Hutchison, T. W. (1977) *Knowledge and Ignorance in Economics*, Chicago: University of Chicago Press.

Hutchison, T. W. (1992) *Changing Aims in Economics*, Oxford: Basil Blackwell.

Lehman, D. (1991) *Signs of the Times: Deconstruction and the Fall of Paul de Man*, New York: Poseidon Press.

McCloskey, D. N. (1985) *The Rhetoric of Economics*, Madison, WI: University of Wisconsin Press.

Marshall, A. (1961) *Principles of Economics*, 2 vols, edited by C. W. Guillebaud, London: Macmillan.

Rosenberg, A. (1992) *Economics – Mathematical Politics or Science of Diminishing Returns?* Chicago: University of Chicago Press.

Shackle, G. L. S. (1983) 'Review of *The Politics and Philosophy of Economics* by T. W. Hutchison', *Economic Journal* 93: 223–4.

3

THE ART OF ECONOMICS BY THE NUMBERS

David Colander

Most textbooks divide economics into two categories: positive and normative economics. They then go on to discuss the methodology of positive
economics, focusing on broad rules that can be reduced to variants of the
following: develop a formal model; derive an hypothesis and empirically
test that hypothesis with technical econometrics. These broad rules may
or may not be appropriate for the building and testing of general theories,
laws or insights that are meant to become the structural basis for economic
thinking; they are not appropriate for what most economists do, which is
applied policy economics. Applied policy economics is a third branch of
economics, a branch that builds down – that relates the abstract insights
of economic models to real-world problems.

Exactly where applied policy economics fits into the positive/normative
criteria is subject to some confusion. Many economists today, following
Friedman, see it as part of the positive branch of economics. Others see it
as belonging in welfare economics and hence as part of the normative
branch of economics. This confusion about where to place it is understand-
able, since it belongs in neither positive nor normative economics. It
belongs in a third category that J. N. Keynes, to whom Friedman credits
the positive/normative distinction, called the art of economics.[1] According
to Keynes, the art of economics was that branch of economics that relates
the insights learned in positive economics to the goals determined in
normative economics.

In making this positive/art distinction it is not necessary to place art in
juxtaposition to science. Both positive economics and the art of economics
can fall under the broad rubric of economic science. Regardless of whether
it is necessary, Keynes's use of the term 'art' to describe one of the three
branches of economics has bothered many economists who are sympathetic
to the need to do applied policy work. They see calling applied policy work
'art' and the development of theories 'positive' economics as demeaning to
applied policy work. I do not see the term 'art' as demeaning, nor do I
see 'science' as a higher level of activity than art. I would be delighted
were people to think of me as an economic artist. However, given the

35

normal economist's reaction to the term 'art', it may have been better to have called this branch the 'engineering branch' of economic science.

WHY DISTINGUISH THREE BRANCHES OF ECONOMICS?

There are a number of reasons for distinguishing among three branches of economics rather than between two. The most important reason is that different methodological rules apply to each. In building up a theory, or general law, about how the economy works, the task is to generalize from specifics – to abstract from the specifics of one's knowledge and develop models that elegantly capture relationships that transcend any specific instance. In the pursuit of general rules, Friedman's F-twist is relevant. The more elegant the theory, the more removed from real-world assumptions the theory is.

An example of a successful generalization is the general constrained maximization model of choice. Once learned, that model captures many of the specific insights of production and choice theory. Another would be the rules of optimal taxation, such as the Ramsey rule, which elegantly captures specific insights about efficiency and taxation. An even more elegant model is general equilibrium theory, which captures insights into the aggregate economy.

There is an empirical aspect to this search for general theories; somehow one must determine when a generalization, law or theory is to be accepted as tentatively true and when a generalization is to be rejected. Most discussion in the philosophy of science and in the methodology of economics has focused on rules relevant to generalization, formalizing and accepting or rejecting these generalizations or theories.

In this methodological discussion of positive economics it is generally accepted that economists are trying to understand the economy for the sake of understanding; they are designing abstract models and formal tests of those models to determine whether they are 'true', or at least not yet falsified.

The reason the methodological rules in the art of economics are different is that in applied policy economics one's objective is fundamentally different. In the art of economics one accepts the general laws and models that have been determined by the profession and one tries to apply the insights of economic models to real-world problems. Applied policy economics has nothing to do with testing a theory; it has to do with applying the insights of that theory to a specific case.

In applied policy economics Friedman's F-test is quite inappropriate because one is trying to translate down from abstract theories to the real world. This means that one must take account of real-world institutions and frictions that were abstracted from in the development of the theory. There is an empirical element of applied policy economics, just as there is in the developing of the theory, but it involves a fundamentally different type of empirical work; it follows that the distinction between art – applied policy economics – and positive economics – developmental theory economics – *is not* based on an empirical/deductive theory distinction as some, especially Thomas Mayer (1992), have suggested. The distinction is based on whether one is working towards developing theories, or towards *applying* theories that have already been developed.

A second reason for differentiating the art of economics from positive economics is to separate out the normative goals from the positive theory. This was the reason Keynes gave for separating them. Otherwise, one will have a tendency to give too much 'scientific' weight to precepts which do not follow from theory but are, instead, based upon a combination of theory and institutional and political scientific judgements. Keynes writes that 'unless the distinction between theorems and precepts is carefully borne in mind, the relativity of the former is likely to be overstated' (Keynes 1891: 65). Terence Hutchison (1964) extending Keynes's reasoning, similarly argued for the importance of separating positive economic theory from normative economic thinking as much as possible.[2]

Let us consider an example: tariffs. Economic theory does not say whether or not tariffs are desirable for individual countries. There are numerous theoretical exceptions to their use, and qualifications to the proposition that tariffs reduce welfare. Tariffs can help individual countries at the expense of others. But, based on judgements about historical study of real-world cases, most economists are willing to ignore these qualifications and support free trade. But that support is based on historical and institutional judgement. It is not a theoretical law of positive economics; it is an applied policy precept. Often this distinction is not made because economists do not make the positive/art distinction.

An argument can be made that much of the formalist development of positive theory was done to offset the tendency of some economists to claim too much for the market. Examples of claiming too much for the market include J. B. Clark's well-known argument that the market distribution of income was fair, the well-known utilitarian arguments that the market maximized societal welfare, and the Chicago view that *laissez-faire* was the appropriate policy that followed from economic theory. Formal theorists have shown that the logical reasoning for each of these arguments does not follow directly from economic theory without large numbers of provisos. For such conclusions to be drawn from theory, additional elements must be added to the analysis. These additional elements involve judgements on which reasonable people may differ and hence precepts – rules to guide policy – based on them belong in the art of economics and not in the positive branch of economics.

THE GROWING IMPORTANCE OF SEPARATING POSITIVE ECONOMICS FROM THE ART OF ECONOMICS

The need to distinguish applied policy work from positive work is an important one. Its importance has grown over time because of the increasing technical sophistication of positive economic research which increases the importance of division of labour. Adam Smith's insight applies to economics as well as to pins.

In the early stages of a discipline, as theory and initial insights in a field are developing, a formal separation of an applied policy branch from a positive developmental theory branch is far less important, and probably impossible: general theories develop from specific applications as one tries to separate out the generalities from the specifics. But, over time, as more areas are looked into, agreement on more generalities becomes widespread, and these general insights are codified into elegant formal models. This happened to neoclassical microeconomics in the 1930s, 1940s and 1950s, as economists such as Abba Lerner, John Hicks and Paul Samuelson codified the static individual maximization model into what has become the core of economic theory.

Once this codification occurs, combining applied policy and positive theoretical work no longer makes sense, since doing so does not take full advantage of the codification. One of the primary reasons for codifying insights is to be able to convey them more efficiently to others, including those doing applied policy work. Once one knows the generalized maximization principle, one knows the way it will work out in a variety of general settings. To take advantage of the codification, individuals doing applied policy work should not technically work out the implications of the maximization principle in each individual case. It is wasteful and inefficient to redevelop the wheel in each specific case to which the theory is being applied. One only need adapt the generally known result to the specifics of the case being considered.

It follows that the development of a codified theory requires a significant change in how applied policy economics is conducted. *After codification, the further development of theory and applied policy work must be separated and that separation increases as theory is more developed.* One group of researchers – those in the positive branch – need to become more abstract and technical, further developing, extending and testing the theoretical dimensions of the model. A second group of researchers – the applied policy branch – needs to become less technical and more institutionally oriented, as they determine how the insights of the codified theory can be applied in specific instances where the particulars of the case do not fit the assumptions of the theory.

Each of these branches involves both a theoretical component and an empirical component, but the structure and rules used in these components will differ between the two branches. For example, formally modifying the generalized model to particular cases may be a useful exercise for students to teach them the generalized model, but it is not a good way to conduct applied policy economics. Similarly, once a generalized model is developed, it makes little sense to test specific implications of that generalized model, other than as an educational exercise. If one believes the generalized model, one believes it applies; applied policy economics has nothing to do with empirically testing theories; it has to do with applying theories – theories that one is willing to tentatively accept as true – to the real world. To do that, one must add back into the model all the assumptions that were made as it was being generalized. The question in applied policy economics concerns whether the theory fits the application, not whether the theory is true. The applied policy issue is: how can the insights of positive economic theory be translated into real-world policies which achieve society's goals, taking account of real-world institutions, as well as the sociological and political dimensions of the policy?

PREVIOUS WORK ON THE METHODOLOGY FOR THE ART OF ECONOMICS

Keynes, who developed the three-part division of economics, provided little guidance to researchers as to how to do applied policy economics. His discussion of methodology of the art of economics was almost Feyera-bendish – almost everything goes. He simply said that it would be loose and would include many non-economic factors. He did not try to provide any methodological benchmarks by which to judge applied policy work.

This lack of discussion about the methodology appropriate for the art of economics is unfortunate. The mere fact that methodological prescriptions for the art of economics must deal with integrating abstract theory with real-world observations, and hence must include many non-economic factors, does not mean that anything goes. If anything, when work is loose and includes non-economic factors, there is more need for methodological prescriptions.

Later economists also have had little to say about methodological prescriptions for applied policy work, at least in the literature with which I am familiar. One exception is Andrew Kamarck, whose excellent book, *Economics and the Real World* (1983) makes a number of the same points that I make in this paper.

A second exception is Thomas Mayer's *Truth and Precision in Economics* (1992), whose methodological discussion parallels mine in many ways. The difference is that Mayer specifically *does not* distinguish the methodology appropriate for applied policy economics from the methodology appropriate for positive economics. Instead, he discusses the methodology for what he calls 'empirical science economics'.[3]

My approach differs from Mayer's in advocating a distinct split between the methodology and teaching of positive economics – how to develop and test theories, and the methodology and teaching the art of economics – applying theories to the real world to policy issues.[4] I am making no claims about how positive economics should be undertaken. Whereas Mayer laments positive theory becoming more abstract and technical, I see such abstract work as necessary to refine theoretical insights. Somehow Mayer, like Friedman, of whose work Mayer's is a continuation, sees the insights of economic theory as simply existing, rather than being developed by a separate branch of economics – the branch that I call positive economics.

The difference between Mayer's and my approaches can be seen in our evaluation of what he calls 'fingertip economics', which he defines as 'a less formal, more intuitive theory that can be applied to every nook and cranny of economic life' (1992: 16). His book calls for a return to fingertip economics – which most people will remember as the old Chicago approach. I do not. In my view much of fingertip economics was the equivalent to the playing of *Chopsticks* on the piano. It is wonderful as an exercise for teaching students economic theory, but it is not a good way to conduct applied policy analysis. Because it fails to distinguish art from positive economics, the Chicago approach tends to confuse economic precepts and economic laws, and to make it seem as if the economic theory leads to policy conclusions without the addition of the researcher's judgement. A second reason I oppose fingertip economics is that much of it is too formal for applied policy work and not formal enough for good positive economic work.

Much of fingertip economics is simply modifying the general model to particular cases. Because it is generally done in a semi-formal maximizing model, it requires the researcher to abstract from real-world institutions and explain everything within a pure economic framework, rather than to integrate non-quantifiable, non-economic factors into the analysis. The type of semi-formal theory and semi-formal empirical work fingertip economics involved led to enormous confusion, and to a tendency to use methodology appropriate for building up theory when doing applied policy work. Thus whereas my approach calls for two increasingly polar branches of economics: a positive branch – a highly abstract, deductive branch in which work is subject to rigorous empirical tests before it allows an insight to become a law, and an art branch: a loose, non-formal application of the theoretical insights to the real world, Mayer's approach calls for a single semi-formal methodology and no separation of art/positive branches.

Despite this difference, one will notice a distinct similarity between the methodological rules I will list for the art of economics and those that could be gleaned from Mayer's book. Given the overwhelming dominance of formalism in the modern economics profession, we are far more in agreement than we are in disagreement.

METHODOLOGICAL RULES FOR THE ART OF ECONOMICS

I will now proceed to list and discuss some methodological rules for the art of economics that I believe would be useful ones for applied policy economists to follow. The methodological rules are not meant to be binding constraints, but are instead meant as rough guides to approaching issues of applied policy. I fully recognize that every case is different and believe that if a good reason (consistent with the sense, if not the letter, of these rules) exists for breaking a rule, then it should be broken. But a methodological rule should be broken by explicit intent, not out of lack of consideration.

Rule 1: Do not violate the law of significant digits

I list this rule first because it is the one I believe is most often violated. Failure to follow this law of significant digits does not make the research wrong, it simply makes the research far less relevant than it otherwise would be. Let me give an example of violating the law of significant digits. Say you are multiplying these numbers:

$$2.04271 \times 4.0446 \times y$$

where $3 < y < 4$. What is the appropriate way to carry out the multiplication? One could fully multiply out the first two numbers and then multiply the result by 3 and 4 and use some averaging procedure. The answer arrived at by that process is not logically wrong; the process is, however, inefficient, and in violation of the law of significant digits. It involves much wasted work with no gain in accuracy. Thus, it would be an inappropriate method according to the law of significant digits. Instead, one would more reasonably round off to, say, the nearest 10th and get an approximate answer between 24 and 32. Any more precise result presents false accuracy and would likely be misleading. A result can be no more accurate than the least significant digit.[5]

Much of what goes under the name of applied economic policy work violates this law all the time. Inevitably one needs to create a proxy which is only a loose representation of the variable one is interested in. Alternatively, there are qualitative variables that cannot be precisely measured but which must be integrated into the analysis to come to a policy conclusion. That is the nature of applied policy economics.

The current standard practice of most academic applied economists is to create a precise model, to calculate precise results, and then to add vague qualifiers. Doing so is just as wrong as carrying on the above multiplication to ten decimal points.

The law of significant digits also applies to empirical work. If adding back the real-world assumptions is an imprecise process, then there is no advantage to precise empirical work. Applied policy statistical work should be far less precise than developmental theory statistical work which is not applying accepted theory, but is determining whether accepted theory should be changed.[6]

Rule 2: Be objective; use the Reasonable Person Criterion to judge policy

The normative goals of society are many, and policies are ultimately made to achieve society's normative goals. Good applied policy work explains how the real-world goals of society are advanced by a policy.

Positive economic methodology that focuses on a formal model is not especially helpful in meeting this criterion. The problem is that the generalized maximization model sheds little light on the multidimensional, and possibly lexicographic, goals of society. That formal model leads researchers to focus on efficiency in the formal model, treating distributional, moral and institutional issues as addenda. Doing so is inappropriate for applied policy work. All considerations which could lead the model to differ from a researcher's sense of the appropriate concerns of society should be given equal marginal consideration.

Unlike the situation in positive economics where, potentially (although in practice they seldom do) the formal empirical tests determine whether one accepts or rejects a theory, in the art of economics there is no escaping judgement. Society's goals are inevitably poorly specified, and they are often contradictory. Yet, to come to a conclusion about a real-world policy proposal, one must come to grips with these contradictory goals and either help clarify them (which falls under the category of normative economics), or show how one's policy proposal will best meet the real-world contradictory goals. Focusing on Pareto-optimality as a goal, or on some abstractly specified social welfare function, as is generally done in much of what goes under the name, 'welfare economics', is unacceptable for applied policy work since Pareto-optimality or abstractly specified social welfare functions are not descriptions of real-world goals. Instead, one should use a reasonable person criterion: would a representative reasonable person in society favour a policy proposal once he or she understood the implications and effects as well as the researcher does? Thus, questions like the following must be explicitly dealt with. What are the distributional consequences of the policy? What groups will be helped and what groups will be hurt, in both the short run and the long run? What senses of morality will the policy upset? Why should those senses be overruled? What effect will the policy have on existing institutions?

Applied policy work requires the researcher to make value judgements, but that does not mean the researcher should not maintain objectivity. The goals in relation to which a researcher discusses policies should be well specified. (They very likely will have been determined by others specializing in normative economics.) Those goals might be quite different from the economists' own goals. Since the art of applied policy is so messy, and since one cannot rely on formalization to help keep one's values out of the analysis, the researcher must be even more careful than in positive economics to be open about his or her judgements about society's goals, the value of existing institutions, and the way in which government works to achieve those goals.

Rule 3: Use the best economic theory available

Work in applied policy economics – in the art of economics – has a symbiotic relationship with work in positive theory. Work in positive economics should be constantly challenging assumptions of the currently accepted model, testing the models as best one can, and providing alternative formulations of existing theories and models. The work will often be highly technical and obscure. Most of it will have little relevance to applied policy economics, but some will, and the applied policy theorist will have to make judgements about the relevance of new theoretical developments.

An applied policy economist would stay familiar with advances in positive theory, but would be unlikely to take part in it. Where there are competing theories, he or she would know the competing theories, considering their policy proposals and analysis in relation to all competing theories.

One example of what I mean is the following: the standard theory of the labour markets suggests that wages and salaries follow certain laws; modern efficiency wage theories have called standard theories into question and an applied policy economist should be aware of the different implications of the new theory and, where needed, change his or her policy prescriptions to fit the 'new common sense' that follows from the new theory.

A second example concerns recent developments in game theoretic foundations of general equilibrium which suggest that multiple aggregate equilibria will exist and that sunspot and bubble equilibria cannot be ruled out. These developments have profound implications for applied policy macroeconomics that the applied policy economist would have to deal with.

Rule 4: Take in all dimensions of the problem

Formal work in positive economics is necessarily limited by the formal tools available. Thus, the model will not necessarily fit the problem; the problem will be constructed to fit the available techniques. In a sense it will be focused on parts of the chain of analysis that are the strongest, and develop those. In applied policy economics a formal model exists only as an aid to one's understanding. It is not being tested.

Work in applied policy economics cannot take that approach. The problem being considered, not the techniques, must guide the analysis. If administrative costs are important to the policy and they are not included in the formal model, they must be built into the analysis; effects of the policy on institutions are important but are not considered in the theoretical model, then those must be taken into account. If some of those effects are only roughly quantifiable, then, following the law of significant digits, there is little sense in precisely quantifying other aspects of the analysis. Similarly, there is little gain in carrying out statistical tests of significance on a well-defined model.

Rule 5: Use whatever empirical work sheds light on the issue at hand

The role of empirical work in the art of economics is quite different from the role of empirical work in positive economics. In positive economics one is trying to test the validity of theories; in the art of economics one is trying to apply theories. Empirical work is giving one a feel for the data; data mining is quite acceptable, even encouraged, as a way of getting a handle on the intricate dynamic interrelationships that are beyond the formal theory. Vector auto-regression and other measurement without theory techniques are acceptable.

This freedom to use data to get a feel for the problem comes at a cost, however. That cost is that the standard classical statistical tests which were designed to formally test theories are no longer valid. A researcher cannot rely on them to tell him or her whether his or her statistical work is meaningful; the researcher must rely on his or her judgement.

In the art of economics, often, a scatterplot of one variable against another is more useful than a formal econometric analysis. The need for informality in empirical work is reinforced by the fact that much of the relevant empirical facts will be non-quantifiable. When this is the case, the law of significant digits makes most precise empirical work a waste of time.

Rule 6: Do not be falsely scientific; present only empirical tests that are convincing to you

Rule 6 does not mean that statistical tests should not be done; it does, however, mean that they are to be used as a guide to the researcher, not as a scientific test of the model of the effects of a policy. To present them as something other than they are is to be falsely scientific and that is a fundamental methodological error in the art of economics.

Currently, as Mayer nicely discusses (1992: 132–51), economists violate this rule all the time. In fact, they violate it so much that all economists reading another economist's work can discount the scientific claim and reasonably correctly interpret the results. But as Mayer also discusses, there is a tendency not to do robustness tests, which would be required to make empirical work convincing and in the art of economics one would do, and report whatever empirical work that is helpful to guide you to a policy conclusion.

THE INTERACTION OF WRITTEN AND UNWRITTEN METHODOLOGICAL RULES

For the majority of economists who are working in applied policy jobs directly subject to market forces, the above-stated methodological rules are the ones they already follow. Their advancement depends on the relevance of their work; since the above rules are designed to see that applied policy work is relevant, they relate closely to the institutional incentives they face. Thus, these rules are not directed at them. They are, instead, directed at academic economists. Even though the majority of these academic economists consider themselves applied policy economists and they are training students in applied policy economics. They find themselves subject to the methodological rules of developmental theory science in their unwritten rules even as they are teaching and doing research in applied policy economics. They face implicit directives to develop formal models and rigorously test these models and, since they are doing applied policy economics, to make those formal models relevant to policy. These are *impossible* directives, but if one's job depends on meeting directives, they are directives that will be superficially met with tests that look rigorous, but often are not, and models that look impressive and formal but that are vacuous, or simply reformulations of models that already exist. It is those academic economists that I am interested in affecting.

I do not expect to affect these academic economists directly. Almost the only people who read methodological discussions are other methodologists. Put simply, most economists do not care about formal methodology; they are concerned with institutional requirements for advancement. So I am under no illusion that the above methodological rules will be considered by anybody other than methodologists.

But that does not mean that formal methodological discussions are irrelevant; far from it. Methodologists have much greater influence than they realize. But that influence is indirect, through the brief general discussion of methodology that filters into textbooks, and the influence that discussion has on tenure rules and editorial decisions. In that filtering process, the prescriptions and insights of methodological specialists are likely to be perverted, but something will remain. That something has been Friedman's positive/normative distinction and the implicit acceptance that economists' work should be judged by the rules of formal positive science. Almost all methodological writings in economics have accepted that premise and have carried out the methodological discussion of positive economics to high levels, taking up the problems in defining science, in carrying out good science, and in choosing among competing theories. Much of that writing has been critical of what economists do, but because it has accepted the proposition that economists are supposed to do positive theoretical science, that writing has reaffirmed the positive/normative distinction and thereby reinforced, rather than challenged, the existing methodological practices.

If methodologists no longer reaffirm the positive/normative distinction, the textbooks will have to deal with the issue. If methodologists agree that applied policy economics should have a different set of methodological rules than does the positive science of economics, the textbooks will have to deal with the issue since there is a strong demand by students and society to have economists teach applied policy economics. As that happens, those rules will begin filtering down through textbooks to incoming students, and thereby make a difference in what they see as good economics. As it does so, it will have other impacts and eventually it will influence what really matters to academic economists – tenure criteria and editorial policy of journals.

The current positive methodological prescriptions have created unwritten rules for academic economists which go something like the following: publish often in those journals that are highly ranked; do not worry about real-world applicability of the analysis; adopt a new technique; do not waste time discussing institutions; make sure you do some empirical test, the more formal the better, and see that you get reasonably good results; briefly mention policy implications at the end, but state that more work is needed. Variants of these rules are also conveyed to graduate and undergraduate students as they choose their research or dissertation topics: choose a topic that is feasible; choose a topic for which you can develop a formal model; choose a topic for which there is some data with which you can empirically test the model, ideally using a new econometric technique that has just been developed; choose a topic that you can divide up into publishable papers relatively quickly.

In short, the combination of this push for publication and the background positive methodological rules leads academic researchers to do precisely what I argued makes little sense for applied policy work – to modify one assumption of an existing model at a time and to examine the result, while leaving out many assumptions that intuitively would fundamentally change the model's results when applied to reality.[7] If a journal can be found to publish it, the incentives are for a professor to publish such an article. If one cannot be found, the incentives are for a group of professors to get together and start one.

One could argue that the existence and growth of applied journals of the type I am describing implies that there is a demand by society for their output. I find that argument unpersuasive. The demand for most applied economics journals is generated by university libraries which generally respond to requests of professors themselves. Publishers see academic journals as potential cash cows for which they can charge up to hundreds of dollars per subscription.[8] Even if only a few professors succeed in getting their libraries to buy that journal, it will generate enough income to be sustainable. Moreover, librarians have an inherent compulsion to acquire complete sets and, once started, they dislike breaking off a subscription. The result is that many, if not most, applied policy journals exist in large part to provide publication outlets for academic economists, not to influence policy. Since the process of supplying journal articles has value to the writer independent of the value of those articles to society, it pays faculty either to subsidize the demand for these journals themselves or to get their schools to subsidize demand, by having their library subscribe.

There are many journals of applied economics out there – and there are more every day. But many of the articles in these journals are pedagogical exercises. They take the general maximizing model; modify it slightly, sometimes by simply redefining some terms; and show how the modified general maximizing model looks in this particular case. Such articles give little or no guidance to real-world policy because they do not address the policy-relevant questions. Are the assumptions reasonable? Do the goals the model achieves match the normative goals one has decided upon? Is the suggested policy administratively feasible? The economist often has ideas about these issues, but the current methodological rules do not allow the author to discuss them; it would not be good science. It would, however, be good applied policy work. The reality is that issues relevant for policy seldom have a general answer. The reality is that most of these applied policy issues cannot usefully be considered in relation to technical models. The reality is that applied policy issues inevitably must be done by someone with an intricate knowledge of real-world institutions.

Many academic economists I have talked with agree that much of what is currently called applied policy work is actually simply a ticket to tenure. Researchers who believe that, but do currently acceptable applied policy work anyhow, justify what they are doing with the argument that everyone is doing it; if they did not, they would not get tenure and they would be out of a job. And they are right. The unwritten methodological rules state that if a journal will accept an article modifying the wheel for the nth time, it is an article worth writing.

CONCLUSION

I believe the above description of what happens when positive economic methodology is used in applied economics is understood by most economists. Nonetheless, most economists would prefer to ignore it, either because they are caught up in the tenure/publication process or find that their training has not prepared them to do good applied policy work. Given individual incentives, I can understand that position. But methodological prescriptions are not designed to make people's lives easy, or to get them tenure; they are designed to make compatible the goals of what the discipline is trying to achieve with what individuals are trying to achieve, given existing institutional incentives.

Where the institutional framework creates perverse incentives, strong methodological rules must exist to counter them. These rules, however, are not for young economists; they are for the economists who determine the institutional rules; they are for reviewers of journals; they are for tenure committees; they are for dissertation advisers; they are for outside reviewers of academic programmes. These are the groups who determine institutional incentives. If these groups judge young economists by the methodological guidelines of the art of economics rather than by the guidelines of positive economics, then applied policy work will become more relevant.

ACKNOWLEDGEMENTS

I would like to thank Kevin Hoover, Abe Hirsch, Thomas Mayer and Roger Backhouse for helpful comments on earlier drafts of this paper.

NOTES

1 The term 'art of economics' was not new to Keynes. It was much discussed in the literature in juxtaposition to science. Keynes's contribution was in focusing on a tripartite division, establishing art as a buffer between positive economics and normative judgements.
2 Hutchison uses the term positive in a different way. In Hutchison's usage it includes much of what I classify as art, whereas his art includes much of what I include in normative economics. In my view, however, the differences between

Hutchison and myself are primarily terminological; our substantive approaches to economic methodology are similar.

3 In a separate paper (Mayer 1993), he makes clear that he sees his methodological approach as a continuation of Friedman's methodological approach.

4 The issue is not whether different people do the work. I have no objection to the same people sometimes doing applied policy and sometimes doing developmental theory, but I argue that, if they do, they should use fundamentally different methodologies in each; Mayer seems to be arguing that only one methodology should be used in economics.

5 The theory of significant digits can itself become complicated, and precisely where one should round off can be a matter of debate. But the law is subject to itself, and in applied policy work, precisely where one rounds off is less important than that one does not grossly violate the law.

6 Mayer discusses a similar rule, which he calls the 'strongest link' rule, citing Kamarck's and my discussion of the law of significant digits. It is reasonable to apply this law to all aspects of economics, but I argue that in applied policy work one must add back dimensions of the problem that are highly imprecise and hence in applied policy work it is a much stronger argument against the use of precise, formal models. In developmental theory, one can separate out parts of the chain that consist solely of stronger links, and hence one can achieve more rigour and precision.

7 Salim Rashid told me a wonderful story in which one economist tells another that an idea can be demonstrated forty-two different ways, and the other responds, 'Great, that's forty-two articles we can get out of it.'

8 One well-known applied economic policy journal currently costs libraries $775 per year.

BIBLIOGRAPHY

Colander, D. (1991) *Why Aren't Economists as Important as Garbagemen?* Armonk, NY: Sharpe.

Colander, D. (1992) 'The lost art of economics', *Journal of Economic Perspectives*, Summer, 6(3): 191–8.

Hutchison, T. W. (1964) *Positive Economics and Policy Objectives*, London: Allen & Unwin.

Hutchison, T. W. (1992) *Changing Aims in Economics*, Oxford: Basil Blackwell.

Kamarck, A. (1983) *Economics and the Real World*, Philadelphia: University of Pennsylvania Press.

Keynes, J. N. (1891) *The Scope and Method of Political Economy*, London: Macmillan.

Mayer, T. (1992) *Truth and Precision in Economics*, Aldershot: Edward Elgar.

Mayer, T. (1993) 'Friedman's methodology', *Economic Inquiry*, April, XXXI(2): 213–23.

4

WHAT ARE THE QUESTIONS?

Philip Mirowski

There was a time when a reference to 'economic methodology' or 'philosophy of economics' meant that the author was claiming a licence to discuss the larger issues often neglected in the day-to-day practice of economics. One text in that erstwhile tradition bore the same title as the present essay: Joan Robinson's 1977 'What are the questions?'[1] That characteristically uncompromising essay broached such signal topics as: to what extent is orthodox economics driven by ideological error, and why does it persist? Does the subject matter of economics change too frequently to underwrite its putative 'laws'? Why cannot neoclassicals adequately encompass the passage of historical time in social life? What is economic growth for, or what can we hope to achieve as an affluent society? Why does so much of economics take the organizing principle of the nation-state for granted? And finally, to what extent can the evolution of economic explanation be comprehended as the 'choice' of (in)appropriate methods, for instance, opting for mathematics instead of participant ethology?

But now, Robinson is dead, deprived of the Nobel Prize that was rightfully hers; and I glance at various recent books with 'Philosophy' or 'Methodology' yoked to Economics in their titles, or at the journals *Economics and Philosophy* or *Methodus*, or attend various conclaves of economists and philosophers, and, by and large, those questions are no longer on the agenda. Perhaps some of my colleagues think that is just as well, bidding good riddance to what they perceive as naive rubbish. But some, myself included, feel that what we have left is diminished, desiccated, and not a little sad. I shall not recapitulate Robinson's questions here – the student can best do that themselves by consulting the original – but propose instead to toddle along inadequately in her footsteps by suggesting a few more large questions for the consideration of the student of economics who may feel that the title of 'Worldly Philosophy' was the one prize worth the candle. If the student then comes to feel that the quasi-speciality of 'Methodology' was a space where her own nascent whys and wherefores could take root and flourish, and not be dismissed in the interest of getting on with 'real economics', then all the nagging questions will not have been in vain.

QUESTION 1: WHAT ARE THE STANDARDS?

In the bad old days, the answer to this question was not so much discussed and dissected as simply taken for granted. It was just assumed that the standards were identical with the 'scientific method' properly applied; and since there existed a hierarchy of successful sciences – King Physics and Queen Maths on top, guess who on the bottom – then the obvious next move was to get some philosopher of physics to tell us what their practices were and how it was all done so tidily. The history of economics is rife with this sort of reasoning, further back than one might initially imagine, and I have expended a fair amount of effort uncovering these presumptions in my earlier books *Against Mechanism* and *More Heat than Light*. For reasons that will become clearer as we proceed, I do not believe that this mode of entry into the discussion of standards is any longer interesting or fruitful. That is not to say that there is absolutely nothing to be learned from the history of physics, or of mathematics, or of cosmology, for that matter: quite the contrary. Yet what I would suggest is that we must instead relinquish the idea that the fore-ordained role of the methodologist is to sit at the feet of the latest greatest guru in the philosophy of science community, and then return home from the pilgrimage to proselytize watered-down versions of this fresh minted wisdom for the average economist operating in the trenches. That vocation has proven a dismal failure; and the failure cannot simply be laid at the door of the dismal science.

Almost no one wishes to deny that there are standards of legitimate and indeed superior work in economics; just as there exist such standards in any community at any given juncture organized into an academic discipline. The problem becomes: what happens when we no longer take those conventional hierarchies of legitimation for granted? This is the problem which confronts any potential critic, from Blaug and McCloskey to Lawson and Hodgson. Abstract philosophical ukases are generally perceived as a waste of time and effort. In other words: how do practitioners recognize good work on a quotidian basis and act accordingly? The ultimate arbiter in such matters is history, and not philosophy, in the sense that only fine-grained narratives of the evolution of the particular language-communities could ever provide anything more than a fleetingly satisfying version of real standards in action (Latour 1987). Nevertheless, there are a few broadly philosophical statements some might find it helpful to introject any time the Standards Question rears its ungainly head. One move brandishes the formidable name of Ludwig Wittgenstein, whilst the other proposes a reconsideration of the self-image of the persona of the economic methodologist.

Like many others in the Social Studies of Knowledge (SSK) community (Pickering 1992; Bloor 1983; Hacking 1984), I have been extremely impressed with Wittgenstein's later discussions of the various problems of 'following a rule'.[2] Through numerous examples of deceptive simplicity, the mature Wittgenstein explored various conundrums associated with hastily presuming that someone has been transparently following a rule. Briefly, the process of clarifying such activities always flounders on the mistaken presumption that a rule can somehow dictate how to employ itself; the upshot is that any explicit rule can be undermined by further reference to context. 'However many rules you give me – I give a rule which justifies *my* employment of your rules. . . . The employment of the word "rule" is interwoven with employment of the word "same" ' (Wittgenstein 1978: I, 113; VII, 59). The problem is not that (as some would have it) all rules are at bottom unjustifiable, but rather that there are distinctly thorny problems with asserting that observed conduct is rule-following, or that the observer has correctly grasped the rule at issue.

> Grammatical conventions cannot be justified by describing what is represented. Any such description already presupposes the grammatical rules. That is to say, if anything is to count as nonsense in the grammar which is to be justified, then it cannot at the same time pass for sense in the grammar of the propositions that justify it. You cannot use language to go beyond the possibility of evidence.
>
> (Wittgenstein 1975: 55)

One way to put these insights to work is to empathize with the hostility often expressed towards the economic methodologist: namely, an outsider to economic practice is no better situated to explicate whether or not an economist is following a rule than an insider; and the insider, if truly such, will see no point in the project of an external generic codification of her grammar.[3] (This, of course, ignores certain pedagogical considerations of inculcating respect in rebellious youth.) But an even better use of Wittgensteinian aphorisms, such as those quoted above, is to destabilize all the various unspoken oppositions which are implied in the Standards Question: why are any particular representations of the activities of the economist better or worse than the engaged practices in themselves? How are various representations of the other (economist/actor, scientist/subject, academic/businessman, theorist/empiricist, philosopher/economist) made to appear as though they have found purchase on an Archimedian point – outside language, outside society, outside history? These are the sorts of themes broached in our subsequent questions.

But that should not be taken to imply that there is no place for anyone to construct large-scale narratives of 'Whither goest we' and 'The meaning of it all'; methinks the Lyotards (1984) of the world protesteth too mightily that all meta-narratives are henceforth obsolete and an anathema to the post-modern mind. The one legitimate inference that can be drawn from recent post-modern discontents is that the rise and fall of meta-narratives are part and parcel of the projects which they promote and legitimate; and that the best meta-narratives are those which simultaneously transform narrative practice. I should like to suggest that this (Nietzschean?) position taken with respect to Standards in effect would divide the world into Weak Methodologists and Strong Methodologists.

The Weak Methodologist, as an inheritor of Comtist Positivism, dearly wants to dole out praise and blame according to his unspoken presumed hierarchy of knowledge. In this view, it is necessary for the hierarchy to remain unspoken, for otherwise, the problems of reflexivity would immediately intrude (Woolgar 1988; Pickering 1992). Here is one weak methodological syllogism: Karl Popper says physics is falsificationism; economists do not practise falsificationism; ergo (and note the slipperiness of the syllogism) economics is not (yet?) a science. Or here is another example, from the opposite corner of the Two Cultures: Richard Rorty (1991) tells us that 'Natural science is not a natural kind', and some historians tell us that neoclassical economics is a debased imitation of natural science, so we should all become practitioners of literary criticism instead. This sort of 'methodology', by itself, leads nowhere, in the sense that all subsequent conversation gets deflected onto whether the esteemed philosopher's ukases 'apply' in our benighted case.

The Strong Methodologist, by contrast, realizes that every discipline has its own foundation myth and its own version of its historical conditions of success; to construct such meta-narratives is a major component of foundational work in science. Here, then, is a different role for philosophy. It is no accident that most of the major characters in the economist's hall of fame – from Adam Smith to Karl Marx, from Francis Edgeworth to Thorstein Veblen, from John Maynard Keynes to Nicholas Georgescu-Roegen – had their initial socialization in the precincts of philosophy, and not in economics. It takes a certain modicum of disciplinary distance to believe true originality springs from reconfiguring the boundaries of thought, provoking the shock of the new, rather than reconfirming standardized prejudices about the Humdrum Order of Things. Whenever the Strong Methodologist realigns the vectors of influence to foster a different vision of what economics could entail, then it is also likely that the concepts and histories of other disciplines will undergo revision. For instance, to assert that neoclassicism is bowdlerized nineteenth-century energetics not only changes our perspective upon present practices in economics; it could also change our impressions of and attitudes toward the main lines of the history of physics. Instead of shrinking from such a prospect, Strong Methodologists doggedly fashion contentious meta-narratives of the world according to their disciplines; it is not their job to reconcile them all into one standardized method. The contested terrains are resolved by the ongoing operations of the rival disciplines; and in the case of two well-ensconced *Denkollectivs*, guerilla warfare can extend over many generations (Hacking 1992). And to police faithful conformity to the posited rules of the specific meta-narrative – well, that is not the job of the Strong Methodologist, either. This is not to deny the role of socialization in graduate school, or in the referee's report, or the faculty coffee lounge; intellectuals and cows love herds. Nevertheless, any person moderately literate in history and philosophy will realize that you cannot control what others do with your text.

Hence the purpose of this essay is to imagine some of what the project of Strong Methodology might look like in the present historical nexus of economics, philosophy and history of science. By no means is it the only possibility, or even the most logical of alternatives, given the present situation in departments of economics, and, let it be said, science studies, gender studies, anthropology, comparative literature and history. Yet something must be done about the fact that no one seems to care about Popper any more, except a few economists.

QUESTION 2: WHAT IS SO 'SOCIAL' ABOUT SOCIAL SCIENCE?

> Is it unfair . . . to suppose that the glee the computer scientist commonly feels when speculating about the duplicability of human behavior springs from an underlying sense of himself as less than human? Isn't he in effect saying to the rest of us, *See? Even you, who have so often called me clumsy and empty and soulless, are nothing better than a machine?* It is only a fool, surely, who would underestimate the degree to which feelings of inadequacy and spite motivate the scientist. . . . Or the philosopher, for that matter.
>
> (Leithauser 1989: 108)

Rather than just jumping straight into the vast mass of literature about how economists want to be scientists, it might give us a different perspective on our problems if we instead asked why so much of our discourse revolves around what is Natural and what is Social. There was a time when economic methodologists would have asserted that the matter had been settled long ago in the *Methodenstreit* between Gustav Schmoller and Carl Menger; but I doubt that anyone now knows what the hubbub was all about.[4] The reason is simple: the hegemony of American social science in the post-Second World War period has wiped the slate clean of any trace of an operant distinction between the *Naturwissenschaften* and the *Geisteswissenschaften*. It has been suggested (Proctor 1991; Ross 1991) that the importation of an unreflective scientism characterized most of the American social sciences from the 1920s onward; and that the rallying cry of the unity of the sciences, while very effective, was remarkably vague about the exact character of what was shared. The academic erasure of continental philosophy, in conjunction with the confusion of the technologies of statistics with the practices of the natural sciences in the post-Second World War period (Gigerenzer and Murray 1987), fostered the impression that 'science' was itself a species of generic procedure which any social inquiry could readily appropriate, due to the intrinsic unity of Nature and Society, be it economics or literary criticism or personnel management.

Those days are now past, although many economists seem still not to have got the message. The problem of demarcating the Natural and the Social is one of the most active research areas in the Sociology of Scientific Knowledge; the best introduction to these controversies is to consult some of that literature (Collins and Pinch 1993; Pickering 1992; McMullin 1992; Bloor 1976). Yet in the interests of pedagogy, we might at minimum provide a scorecard for the present state of play. To that end, I reproduce as Table 1 a taxonomy which I have discussed in greater detail elsewhere.[5]

Table 1 The Natural and the Social

---

(1) Are identical in:
    (a) every respect (extreme physical reductionism);
    (b) laws;
    (c) epistemic methods;
    (d) metaphorical structures.
(2) Are disjunct but individually lawlike due to:
    (a) epistemic status of knowledge;
    (b) ontological status of subject matter;
    (c) purposes of research.
(3) The Natural is objective and stable, whereas the Social is patterned upon it but is unstable, due to:
    (a) the sociology of collective knowledge;
    (b) sociology as naturalized epistemology.
(4) Are both unstable and hence jointly constructed:
    (a) out of interests;
    (b) out of practices;
    (c) out of will.

I would maintain that most orthodox economists (and not just neoclassicals!) seem to travel in the extremely narrow orbit of positions (1b) and (1c), although attention in detail to their history would reveal that the best that has ever been actually achieved by their efforts is a *metaphorical* resemblance between the procedures of physics and economics (Mirowski 1989). For instance, the mathematics of constrained optimization gains much of its cachet from its close resemblance to the same mathematics' appearance in rational mechanics, rather than from any explicit justification on either epistemological or ontological grounds found within economics. Nature and Society are implicitly united through the inscription of a few partial differential equations.

While clarification of the nature of the asserted identity of the natural and social by partisans of position (1) is one task still awaiting its methodologist, I should like to assert that the above taxonomy is the necessary point of departure in every further question raised in this paper. Whether it be the contemporary deference to the role of the scientist, or the place of mathematics in economics, or the meaning of probability, or the nature of empirical practice, or the presumed relationship of the actors *vis-à-vis* the economist, or even the impact of forms of expression upon the content of the message, in each and every case the presumed orientation with regard to the Natural and the Social will largely govern the positions taken.

For instance, take position (2). If one agrees with Heinrich Rickert and Max Weber that the natural sciences purposely abstract from concrete particulars in order to uncover laws, whereas the social sciences, dealing as they must in self-interpreting beings, relish the historical particulars and must work in terms of meanings and values, then the pervasive envy of the physical sciences in economics will be deemed the root of all error, as it is by their followers Friedrich Hayek and Ludwig von Mises.[6] Or perhaps, with Jurgen Habermas and Herbert Dreyfus, if one insists that the purposes of the social sciences are inherently distinct from those of physics or biology – essentially evaluative rather than manipulative – therefore all talk of 'prediction' and 'control' is fundamentally misguided and perhaps even pernicious. Or perhaps, so as not to inadvertently portray this option as implacably opposed to mathematical formalism, we might with Michael Bacharach (1989) attempt to reconceptualize the modern project of game theory as an attempt at modelling the way *Verstehen* works in psychological or intentional mental states.

Consider, alternatively, position (3). Suppose we presume with Emile Durkheim and Karl Mannheim that the subject matter of the natural sciences provides them with a benchmark against which they may readily judge their successes; but that the social sphere affords no commensurate talisman. These folks tend to want to ask the question, 'Why is economics not *yet* a science?' Then relevant questions revolve around such issues as what configuration of interests are served by various specific constructions of social life, such as the disembodied authority of mathematics, the moral and political authority of the scientist (Ezrahi 1990), and the 'invisible hand' portrayal of the marketplace. Here the methodologist might seek to challenge the claims of disinterested analysis with regard to themes of gender (Moore 1993), or the marketplace of ideas,[7] or the morality of the speech community (McCloskey 1990).

Finally, consider position (4), the closest to the present author's heart, but also the one most under-represented orientation in the economic methodology literature. If neither the natural nor the social sciences possess the kind of stability in method or subject matter which would permit simple one-way evaluations of success or failure of inquiry, as now maintained by such philosophers as Bruno Latour, Joseph Rouse and others, then the project of economic methodology must undergo drastic revision. Absent the usual smug cynicism, economics would now be defined as whatever economists do. One would jettison such categories as falsification or realism or rationality in favour of detailed studies of actual practices, following the lead of authors such as Andrew Pickering, Harry Collins and Simon Schaffer in physics, George Stocking in anthropology and Roy Weintraub in economics. Mathematics would be treated as neither pure logic nor as convenient language, but rather as yet another form of trial-and-error practice on all fours with congressional testimony, tenure evaluations, literature searches and arbitrage operations. Fascination with abstract 'science' would presumably wither away, to be replaced by a serious curiosity about how other disciplines construct the objects of their inquiry. Under this regime, methodologists might simply drift free of their moorings in economics departments and become more like generalist historians of science. Where their paychecks would come from is another matter.

QUESTION 3: ARE WE CONSTITUTED BY OUR SUBJECT MATTER?

There is another question to ask: why should we believe that there exists an 'economy' with its own integrity and self-sufficient laws? For most of human history this has not been treated as some species of categorical *a priori*, even though many neoclassicals claim that they can discern their notion of scarcity all the way back to Adam. Indeed, the constitution of the economy as an entity amenable to a narrow construction of analysis is a nineteenth-century phenomenon, precipitated out of a debate over the potential for a unified science of society. While references to an 'Oeconomy' of domestic or rural cast, patterned upon the analogy of management of the household, date from antiquity, and a 'political economy' in the eighteenth century, 'the' economy is clearly a stepchild of French enthusiasm for a 'science sociale' and the British response to Comtist hubris.[8] By the end of the nineteenth century we can begin to have books with titles like *Economy and Society*, which certainly tells us something new has happened: there are now two things, whereas before there was simply one. This parthenogenesis would appear to be of an eminently ontological character, but I think it fair to point out that no extant school of economics ventures to sanction the bifurcation as a metaphysical postulate.

There are at least two ways to approach this question, the one epistemological, the other historicist. The epistemological approach takes the bull by the horns and attempts to incorporate a theory of the quarantine of the economy within the ambit of the specification of the social environment. Marxism provides an example of this option, with the theory of alienation explaining why various classes themselves view their provisioning activities as intrinsically out of their control, and therefore alien to their conceptions of daily life. The historicist move, on the other hand, stresses the contested status of the carving up of the social sphere, and then posits various reasons why the political economists in particular seemed to have been the first off the mark to successfully exit the broad church of generic 'moral philosophy' or 'sociology' or 'social science' (Hirschman 1977). This latter tradition would stress the intrinsically imprecise character of notions of barter, exchange and money in actual historical practice and discourse, as well as the exile of convictions that they are (or were) intrinsically embedded in social structures such as kinship, ceremonial gift behaviour, religious and political structures; thenceforth only to be found in the nether antipodes of modern anthropology and sociology.[9]

Notably, both approaches start out with an essential denial of any discrete existence of an 'economy', as do neoclassical approaches, which bypass altogether any specification of the phenomenal economy in favour of a generic rational choice by an actor completely stripped of all context. It may indeed be that all modern schools of thought depend implicitly upon untutored impressions of the economy as having something to do with money and labour and commodities as their external justification for their discipline, although none actually wishes to delimit the bounds of their discourse in any fixed sense. The methodologist would then ask: how are the boundaries of the economy set in practice, even if only in a temporary and conditional way? One thing is certain, however: the conjectural anthropology that traces the 'economic problem' back to year one has got to go. And then another bit of common wisdom is at risk: namely, that economic thought is a simple reaction to changes in the 'economy'.

QUESTION 4: HOW ARE WE SO PURE?

Economics is a political activity, and this has been a persistent source of embarrassment in the history of its institution as an academic discipline, a fact ably illustrated by Mary Furner (1975). Indeed, we tend to forget just how much of our revealed preferred heritage of the philosophy of science was itself a reaction to political events in our turbulent century.[10] But fascination with the philosophy of physics has obscured one of the major preoccupations of methodological discourse, namely, the quest for 'objectivity'. It is a precept hallowed by all and questioned by few, but fewer still can say exactly what it would involve; thus it is honoured mostly in the breach. It should seemingly create special problems for the economist, since in the activity of portraying a world riven by interest and greed, where everything can be indifferently bought and sold, it would seem there was no room left for objectivity, other than empty pious incantations. (Indeed, that is precisely how it is treated in the so-called 'cheap talk' literature in game theory.) Notions of objectivity are all bound up with prohibitions of anthropomorphism and anthropocentrism in the history of the West. They date back to the Judaeo-Christian critique of attributing human attributes to God, and continue into the modern period as an eschewal of vitalism, teleology and natural theology. The goal has been to attain a 'view from nowhere', untainted by human presence (Nagel 1986). Lately, historians of science have been unpacking this notion, so very rich in ambiguity.

> Aperspectival objectivity is both conceptually ... and historically distinct from the ontological aspect of objectivity that pursues the ultimate structure of reality, and from the mechanical aspect of objectivity that forbids judgement and interpretation in reporting and picturing scientific results. Whereas ontological objectivity is about the world, and mechanical objectivity is about suppressing the universal human propensity to judge and aestheticize, aperspectival objectivity is about eliminating individual (or occasionally group, as in the case of national styles of anthropomorphism) idiosyncracies.
>
> (Daston 1992: 599)

Inverting our common equation of 'science' with objectivity, Daston claims the aperspectival version grew up, not in natural philosophy, but rather in moral philosophy in the later eighteenth century, using as her prime examples Adam Smith and David Hume. This offers a completely different approach to objectivity, especially for economic methodologists, who should rejoice in yet another vindication of the importance of their progenitors. It is a reorientation that brings the focus of objectivity back to the social context and to the *ethos* projected by the researcher. The multivalent shifting meanings of objectivity in history lend credence to the rhetoric programme in economics, although it also reveals a hostility to its aestheticizing moves; it could also be employed in lending structure to numerous apparently technical discussions of the crisis in econometrics (Hendry *et al.* 1990), including the problem of replication.

The problems of advocacy and objectivity can also be posed on a less abstract (if perhaps not less elevated) plane. It has been noted by various perceptive writers such as Ezrahi (1990) that the role of the scientist in the modern polity is a bit self-contradictory. Every noble ethos associated with science is, it seems, compromised by scientists' practice and location in late twentieth-century discourse. For instance, they often claim to strive to serve only mankind in general, but they also jealously assert their prerogative to be held accountable to no one except a very circumscribed group of self-defined peers. Scientists testify to holding truth as a vocation above all personal ambition, but take it for granted that they deserve to be accorded elite status in their society. They extol their role as detached disinterested intellects, but show unseemly haste in stumbling over them-selves to be politically useful to just about any movement that attains power. Scientists love to portray their history as a sequence of godlike individual unfettered geniuses, but in their quotidian activities construct social structures unparalleled in their rigidity, hierarchy and pedestrian inhabitants. And, of course, scientists pay elaborate homage to their vocation, the dissemination of knowledge, but spend most of their waking hours in attributing ownership of ideas and contesting the boundaries of their closed corporate control of intellectual traditions.[11]

Perhaps all of this would not matter much, except for the fact that other political structures themselves often depend upon an image of an asocial aperspectival science in order to secure their own stability. A very instruc-tive example is inadvertently provided by Huber (1991). Huber complains that the American judicial system has taken the ideal image of impartial science too literally: it allows each side to hire its own experts to buttress its case, usually in personal injury or negligence suits, finally allowing twelve impartial citizen-jurors to decide what are exceedingly complex technical issues. Because huge sums of money are involved, the purchase and sale of expertise unmasks the scientists for what they really are, namely, a shifty bunch of self-seeking sharks no better than the amoral lawyers who argue the cases. Huber's remedy is to have the court peremptorily define the relevant expert community *a priori*, with truth defined as majority rule of the court-defined peer-review literature, and to hold the expert witnesses under penalty of perjury to expression of the consensus of the above-defined orthodoxy, rather than their own personal opinions. Of course, this remedy is naive in the extreme. It essentially transfers the right of definition of the disciplinary orthodoxy to the courts. It subjects the scientists to a political regimen they will not accept, and seeks to remove them forcibly from the realms of economic activity and human individuality. It reveals in a stark manner the basic hostility of the social structures of science to democratic practices.

It is time to give up the idea that 'science' has solved the problem of objectivity, mainly because there is no such single problem to be solved. The injunction to withhold judgement is not at all identical to the prohibi-tion of biases of analysis; and both have very little to say about the problems of projecting our own wishes and desires into the very structures of our sciences. Appeals to objective criteria are as much a function of the internal contradictions of the social structures of modern science as they are a species of categorical imperative. Methodologists of economics might find themselves shaking 'policy economists' out of their dreamlike complacency (or is it venal cynicism?) if they could manage to get them to take this lesson to heart. Or to put it more in the local jargon: it wasn't just Keynes who took a Polyanna approach to the relationship between the government and the economy.

QUESTION 5: WHY DOES SO MUCH ECONOMICS LOOK LIKE BAD APPLIED MATHEMATICS?

It is a failing of the methodology literature that, if there is one question many students of economics would actually like to discuss, it is that of the role of mathematics in the discipline; but that is precisely the question which has been neglected in the literature since about 1955. The reasons for it are fairly straightforward. Complaints about mathematics which surfaced in the 1940s and 1950s were suppressed primarily by *ad hominem* attacks; while those who expressed reservations were tarred as analytical incompetents. As the issue became a generational one, where older economists were displaced by younger colleagues whose major claim to excellence was a greater facility with various new and unfamiliar mathematical formalisms, it has become such second nature that the standard of technique rachets upward with each new crop of graduates, that a certain curmudgeonly grumpiness on the part of older economists nearing retirement is taken in stride. The only intellectual deficiency which can flunk a student out of an American-style graduate programme in economics these days is the suspicion of a lack of mathematical facility (Klamer and Colander 1990).

Methodologists, who already take enough abuse in the course of their endeavours, have been in no mood to participate in this not-so-subtle form of masochism as well. But that has been unfortunate, since this is one of the areas where the philosophers and historians of science have had some very interesting things to say to their brethren labouring in adjoining fields. Long gone are the days when all one could manage to do was to marvel at the 'unreasonable effectiveness of mathematics' in science, or repeat the old chestnut about mathematics being pure unadulterated logic (Wigner 1967). The philosophy of mathematics has been in a persistent state of upheaval since the 1930s, so long that many good popularizations of the basic issues are now available (Kline 1980; Kitcher 1983; Gilleis 1992). I can only strongly suggest that the methodologist sample this cornucopia of ideas, since I cannot possibly survey the wealth of implications this literature has for economics in this venue.[12]

What can be attempted here is an indication of the different images of the role of mathematics in economics, and to intimate how efforts by methodologists could change them. To put it in an extremely crude fashion, there are two broad defences of the use of mathematics in economics: the *procedural defence* and *the book of nature* defence. The procedural defence hinges upon an ideal of rigour which is independent of the uses and purposes in which the mathematics is embedded. My favourite advocate of this position is Tjalling Koopmans, if only because, for him, mathematical rigour was the only thing standing between us and the chaos of shoddy argumentation, duplicity and the 'noise' in communication due to human frailty.[13] Sometimes this defence is repackaged as the catch-phrase that 'mathematics is language', but a funny species of language that banishes all error by rendering meanings interpersonally transparent. However phrased, this is patently a restatement of the Hilbert formalist programme from turn-of-the-century mathematics, perhaps filtered through the Bourbakist lens of the axiomatization of all mathematics, and, ultimately, all knowledge. The major development in twentieth-century mathematics has been the spreading of utter disillusionment with all the formalist goals. Historians now regularly deride 'the mythical character of the "Euclidean method" . . . the widespread belief that the mathematician begins by setting out a cluster of definitions, axioms and postulates, and then deduces from them one theorem after another in a more or less mechanical manner' (Crowe, in Gilleis 1992: 315; Horgan 1993). One of the lessons of the modern history of mathematics is that the actual practice of mathematics cannot be reduced to a simple logic-chopping machine; and indeed, it was the example of the machine-assisted Appel-Haken proof of the four-colour theorem which drove this point home (Tymoczko 1986; Shankar 1987). Mathematicians have repeatedly encountered situations that were not resolvable by logic alone; and while they have triumphed more often than not, it is sheer misplaced nostalgia to envy mathematicians their calm unilinear progress towards truth.

The other common defence of mathematics in economics echoes Galileo's marvelling that the Book of Nature was written in those very mathematical tropes. This defence dates back to Jevons, and has been recently seconded by Debreu (1986):

> Economics was in a privileged position to respond to this invitation, for two of its central concepts, commodity and price, are quantified in a unique manner. . . . The differential calculus and linear algebra were applied to that [commodity–price] space as a matter of course.

This position is flawed on at least two counts: first, the employment of mathematical expression in economics was halting, slow and riven with doubts and disillusion; and second, it is not at all clear, either historically or now, that the subject matter of economics is 'naturally' quantitative. I have argued elsewhere that there are many good reasons to think that the metric structure of 'commodity space' is not at all isomorphic to that assumed for physical space, and that the presumed algebraic structure of prices may not hold in actual practice.[14] The thrust of these arguments is not that a mathematical economics is an impossible project, but rather that the logical justification of its use has been egregiously suppressed and neglected by mathematical economists, thus potentially leaving the field wide open for students of philosophy, as well as for those seeking a somewhat less cynical set of foundational principles than those rooted in accidents of disciplinary pecking-order.

A different approach to understanding mathematical discourse could start with the premise that applied mathematics (and even much of pure mathematical research) consists of deployment of analogical reasoning (Steiner 1989). This would have the advantage of rendering loose comparisons of mathematics to the vernacular much more pointed and precise, as well as stressing the critical role of the specifications of symmetries and equivalence classes as a primary move in the mathematicization of any discourse. Another particular advantage for economic methodologists would be to jettison vague images of 'rigour' based upon rumours of the experiences of other sciences, and replace them with explicit attention to the question of the existence of invariants in the realm of economic discourse: for instance, when is value conserved in the economy? In exchange, or production, in accounting, or nowhere at all (Mirowski 1989)?

These topics do not even begin to exhaust the questions which revolve around the uses of mathematics and language in economics. For instance, there is a well-developed literature in philosophy of mathematics which discusses the various alternative foundations of probability theory, best represented by Fine (1973). When one partakes of such sophisticated discussions of the at least *five* different developed approaches therein (classical, frequentist, logicist, personalist and complexity theory), and discovers that the standard Kolmogorov axioms may not hold indifferently across them all, then one can only blanch at the naive bickering of Bayesians versus frequentists in orthodox econometrics, or at the halting discussions of uncertainty in the post-Keynesian literature. Indeed, one might be tempted to make the case that, however much it initially appears to the contrary, the discipline of economics has not fully reconciled itself to the implications of a stochastic world view. There is a clear role here for methodological inquiry.

One could continue to list various technical issues begging for enthusiasm and elucidation, from the recent frisson of interest in chaos theory to the insistence of game theorists on the conceptual primacy of the Nash programme, philosophical reflections not forthcoming from mathematical economists due to their training and inclinations. But rather than lay out a programme, it may repay the effort to ask what it is about the mathematicization of a discourse that seems to render it so inhospitable to such larger questions. I find it astounding that no methodologist has deemed it worth his or her while to wonder if there might be some salient sociological aspects to the mathematicization of economics, or at least to the structure of a discipline which has been recast to conform largely to its imperatives. Nicholas Georgescu-Roegen (1971) has initiated an inquiry into what he calls the 'arithmomorphic' bias; and the exclusionary aspects of a regime of pure formalism in graduate school should be grist for the same mill. But I wonder if methodologists are brave enough to entertain the idea that mathematical discourse itself influences the very content of the social theories it supports and maintains. This could range from the motivating 'physics envy' encouraging the importation of an excessively deterministic conception of order, all the way to the very selection effect of choosing those economist candidates who find mathematical pedagogy salubrious. After all, mathematics in the West has come to represent the epitome of the possibility of self-enforcing rule structures: the pedagogy is arranged so that the student can come to believe that *the mathematics* on its own can dictate the right or wrong answer. If those of a mathematical bent are then encouraged to come to economics, is it not unsurprising that they will prefer to view economic structures in the same manner? Instead of shrouding the Invisible Hand in lurid dark shadows, this inquiry could promise to bring its elusive character out into the light of day.

QUESTION 6: IS EXPERIMENTATION REALLY IMPOSSIBLE IN ECONOMICS?

For all the ink that has been spilled over the empirical status of economics, it is astounding how little clarification has been achieved in showing where empirical practice has led in the history of the discipline. It is my contention in this section that the fascination with Popper, Duhem and Lakatos on the part of economic methodologists has misled them into believing that there was a single yardstick of 'empiricism' shared by all sciences to which economists had to live up; and further, this has therefore blinded them to the historical fact that rival schools in economics have been constructing their own versions of empirical practices over the course of the last century. Methodologists might earn their keep if they could address the concerns of those in the throes of construction of practice, rather than coming fifty years too late to programmes already repudiated.

For instance, take the first two generations of neoclassical economics. There, the premise of a truly scientific economics was primarily identified with its mathematical expression, and only secondarily with some version of a subordinate empirical research programme. Some progenitors like Jevons did actually innovate some empirical practices, while others like Walras evinced no interest at all, and some others still like Edgeworth wrote in detail about the theory of statistical empiricism. Nevertheless, I have yet to discover one methodologist who has seen the significance of the fact that, no matter who the specific neoclassical was, they all: (a) despaired of any possibility of controlled experiment; and (b) never ultimately engaged in any empirical practice which linked up directly to the core of their new programme, i.e., neoclassical price theory. Utility was deemed inherently inaccessible, demand curves were treated as irretrievable by both Marshall and Edgeworth, and the one empirical exercise which Pareto claimed had led to the discovery of a factual regularity, namely, his Law of Distribution, had no foundation in his mathematical theory. This lacuna compromised claims to scientific status, and this was held against the neoclassical programme by such figures as Henry Ludwell Moore, Wilhelm Lexis and Frederick C. Mills. And yet our 'histories' of economic thought bequeath us no glimpse of any of this; instead they relegate the vanquished to the footnotes, if not to the margins, of discourse, and cast the history as solely one of a sequence of theories.

Of course, one explanation of this great gaping void is a common impression that it was merely a temporary setback for the neoclassicals, rectified by the rise of econometrics in the 1930s and 1940s. The recent history by Morgan (1990) exemplifies this position, asserting that early inchoate empirical practice in both price and macro theory could achieve legitimacy only once its foundations in probability theory were made explicit: the writings of Haavelmo and the efforts of the Cowles Commission put the practice of economic empiricism on a solid basis, which it still enjoys today. Briefly, Haavelmo accomplished this by claiming that actual economic data could be treated as if it were a drawing from an infinite hypothetical population; say, actual 1993 GNP as one outcome of an 'experiment' run by Nature which might have produced any of an infinite range of values of GNP. Again, I find it disappointing that no economic methodologist has come forward to challenge this version of events, especially since evidence of the empirical disarray of modern ortho- dox econometrics is thick on the ground.

One need only peruse contemporary econometrics journals to note that the Cowles Commission version of standard econometrics is a sham- bles. Neyman–Pearson hypothesis testing was brought over from agricul- tural experimentation in the 1930s, but without its accompanying techniques of randomization, sampling design and controls it rapidly became an empty rationalization for a supposedly scientific procedure which could produce almost any result the investigator desired. This experience was not unique with economics, but also happened roughly contemporaneously in psychology (Gigerenzer and Murray 1987). Anyone with sufficient ingenuity could produce t-statistics above two and R-squareds approaching one; and with infinite freedom to alter variables and estimation procedures, the so-called 'Law of Demand' was merely an injunction to keep trying alternative specifications until you got a negative coefficient on the price variable. All that massive effort sunk into identi- fication and simultaneous-equation estimation techniques came to naught because it seemed to make little difference in actual practice when com- pared to single-equation techniques. The lack of robustness of results conditional upon alternative specifications was only exacerbated in the simultaneous-systems context. Few seem to realize that the Cowles Commission itself lost interest in econometrics as the panacea for scientific progress around 1950, and instead turned to arcane mathematical theory far removed from empirical questions, such as the Arrow–Debreu existence proofs.

Recent econometricians have regarded this debacle as largely a problem of econometric *theory*, and have taken to disputing the relative merits of a Neyman–Pearson frequentist versus a Bayesian subjectivist approach to estimation (Hendry *et al.* 1990). It should be the role of the methodologist to point out that in general the larger and graver issues get obscured by assuming (as an econometric theorist would) that the crux of the problem lies in technique. The reason the frequentist/Bayesian bickering seems interminable is that Neyman–Pearson is a deeply flawed theory of inductive inference on the frontiers of research, as opposed to a theory of something like industrial quality control, whereas even Bayesians will admit that efforts to get researchers to behave in a consistently subjectivist fashion have been roundly ignored (Leamer, in Granger 1990). I might instead suggest that what is needed is an entirely different approach to the study of inductive inference, one which looks at the social implications of stabilizing notions of error in physics, psychology and economics (Mirowski 1994b).

The ramifications of such a reorientation would be profound. For example, we should stop asking if any theory had ever been falsified in the history of economics, and start asking whether any controversy with something really substantial at stake had ever been settled for any appreciable length of time by means of econometrics.[15] I fear that the answer would be no, but we methodologists should be encouraged to nurture our own empirical traditions. Other implications would involve paying attention to other disciplines in the social sciences and discovering what they came to regard as legitimate empirical practices. This would disabuse us of the notion that there exists a single generic statistical inference procedure, or indeed the oft-repeated refrain that some generic kind of experimentation is impossible in the social sciences.[16] Methodologists should take note that there never has been a sole claimant to the mantle of inductive inference in economics – although it is the case that econometrics became tightly bound to the neoclassical programme in the period around 1940–80 – and that the failure of econometrics is causing various rivals to come out of the woodwork even as I write. At the very least there are the historian's narrative model, ill-formed notions of 'calibration' of mathematical models, and of course the growing amorphous field of 'experimental economics'.

The questions being raised by experimental economics cry out for philosophical evaluation, while methodologists are still busy rehashing simpler versions of probabilistic causality and other instances of correlation exercises run amok. As Vernon Smith, the champion of the experimental literature, writes,

> Why is it that human subjects in the laboratory frequently violate the canons of rational choice when tested as isolated individuals, but in the social context of exchange institutions serve up decisions that are consistent (as though by magic) with predictive models based on individual rationality?
>
> (1991: 893)

One need not accept either purported 'finding' to realize that this betokens a major clash between empirical practices in psychology (Hogarth and Reder 1987) and nascent practices in neoclassical economics, with profound implications for the espousal of methodological individualism. Are both camps being driven by outdated images of 'scientific' practice of an earlier vintage, or is there something rather more novel and interesting going on here? What relationship do the new practices have to observations on the difficulties of replication in the physical sciences (Collins 1985)? How have images of 'experimentation' changed over the course of economics?

To take just one example, as neoclassical images of science have come under persistent attack from various quarters, there has been of late a casting about for a replacement consensus view on the foundations of their practices. They can no longer appeal to the hallowed positions of their early forebears, such as Jevons or Edgeworth, who were convinced that the theory was based upon impersonal psychological precepts derived from energy physics. A logical empiricist image of science devoid of metaphysics also has proved a disappointment in the interim, as documented by other authors in this collection. One novel attempt to recast the foundations of neoclassical practice by locating the objective character of the analysis in animal Nature can be found in the series of papers by a research group at Texas A&M and elsewhere, attributing 'Demand Curves [to] Animal Consumers.'[17] It is a shame that methodologists have chosen only to ridicule this literature (Boulier and Goldfarb 1991), since it reveals with some poignancy how an imaginative group of researchers can make use of the resurgent trends of anthropomorphism in the larger culture in order to bolster the *status quo*. In this instance, animals are purported to display both 'preferences' and behaviours consistent with neoclassical price theory, a finding which is then asserted to support orthodox theory in its application to human affairs. For late twentieth-century man, animals have come to represent a pristine innocent Nature untainted by human corruption (if they have so far managed to escape extinction), a beguiling platform from which to gain an objective perspective upon human nature: hence the endless fascination with sociobiology, animal rights, environmentalism, and so on. The Texas A&M group has parlayed this insight into an impressive network of laboratories, articles in prestigious journals, and government grants. One contribution of the methodologist would be to point out that such a tactic would never have worked in the eighteenth century: Adam Smith went out of his way to insist that dogs do not trade, as a prelude to situating his discourse in a non-anthropomorphic civilized society.

QUESTION 7: WHAT IS NEOCLASSICAL ECONOMICS, ANYWAY?

This question may seem naive, but it is important to ask it anyway, since it bears directly upon explanations of the success of the present orthodoxy over the last century. Although its opponents often treat it as a monolithic doctrine, the historian is forced to concede that, in fact, it is best described as a sequence of distinct orthodoxies, surrounded by a penumbra of quasi-rivals; and that it is this, more than any deductive or inductive 'successes', which accounts for its longevity. The idea that it was all there nascent in Adam Smith (Arrow and Hahn 1971: 1) or Marshall or Walras has been a great obstacle to the construction of an interesting methodological meta-narrative.

The following is a brief characterization of the changing shape of neo-classical theory, based on Mirowski (1989, 1992b, 1993) and Ingrao and Israel (1990) offered in the hope of provoking further research. In the period roughly 1870–90, the main aspects of the programme that allowed the far-flung practitioners to recognize one another as comrades-in-arms were three-fold: (a) the unapologetic use of mathematics; (b) the importa-tion of concepts of potential from physics, and especially energetics; and (c) the attendant variational principle displaying the maximization of a mental entity of uncertain character. The definition was transformed in the Anglophone world with the appearance of Marshall's *Principles*, which instead asserted a profound continuity between Ricardian and Jevonian theory by means of the artifice of demand-and-supply functions, which were not themselves central to the previous tradition. A third minor rival stream grew up in the Austrian context, a tradition which eschewed (a)–(c) but persisted in using a psychologistic language similar to that of the other schools, and maintaining that they were part of the larger language community. The next major rupture occurred in the 1930s, with compara-tively large numbers of scientists and engineers moving over into eco-nomics, and redefining the tradition in a more formal and Walrasian direction. Simultaneously, the Marshallian tradition produced the Keynesian variant, which was itself absorbed as a separate division (macroeconomics) within the orthodoxy. All of these variants were taught, often in the same text, as though they were mutually compatible in the middle of the twentieth century, even though they demonstrably were not. As the Walrasian formalist variant and Keynesian macroeconomics ran into insuperable internal contradictions in the latter half of the twentieth century, and the Marshallian variant was increasingly relegated to introductory contexts, game theory (a formalism not necessarily or intrinsically neoclassical in character) was being groomed to replace the other variants. Crude similarities in the types of preferences posited or the use of some kind of maximum principle were all that buttressed the claim that a deep continuity drove the programme.

I think that many if not most historians will find this narrative uncontroversial, but it does raise an interesting question: does neoclassicism consist of anything more than a bald assertion of continuity in the face of repeated ruptures every two or three generations? Then why do outsiders so regularly have the impression that economics is the most stable and cumulative of the social sciences? And, to the shame of our profession, why has a history of the conflict between the various strains not yet been written?

ACKNOWLEDGEMENTS

A large number of people have made extensive comments upon earlier drafts, even though they considered them fatally wonky. I would like to thank Bruce Caldwell, Dan Hausman, Roger Backhouse, Willie Henderson, Arjo Klamer and Wade Hands for their merciless criticisms. None should be held responsible for what remains. Further, a somewhat more lengthy bibliography than might be standard is appended, so that the student might have some indication of the less conventional sources of this paper.

NOTES

1 The essay is reprinted in volume 5 of her *Collected Papers* (1980).
2 The problem of 'following a rule' is discussed in Wittgenstein's *Philosophical Investigations* and especially his *Remarks on the Foundations of Mathematics*. One of the best discussions of what is an exceedingly thorny topic is by Levison (in Fann 1967). A truly amazing biography of Wittgenstein which manages to get the point across in a narrative manner is Monk (1990).
3 It has struck me (Mirowski 1992b: 125) that this might be a starting point for a serious critique of the modern project of game theory; though that case cannot be made in this context. It has sometimes been used to argue against the possibility of a sociology of science as well.

> The consensual culture of mathematics is expressed and described mathematically; that is, it is available in the actions of doing intelligible mathematics. To say this does not imply that mathematicians' practices are given a complete and determinate representation by mathematical formulae, but that no such representation can be constructed and none is missing.
>
> (Lynch, in Pickering 1992: 230)

> The use of Wittgenstein against the programme of artificial intelligence (which I have elsewhere linked to the programme of game theory) is entertainingly deployed in Collins (1990).

4 Menger's side of the controversy has been translated into English as *Problems of Economics and Sociology* (1963), but Schmoller's mostly has not; and most people get their impressions on what the controversy was about second-hand either from Popper or Schumpeter or Blaug, none of whom is a reliable guide. What is interesting is that the Natural/Social distinction becomes a dominant trope in anthropology in America, from Durkheimian functionalism to Douglas to Sahlins, but entirely drops out of economics once the American version of neoclassicism rises to the fore. Sociology remains an intermediate case.

5 See Mirowski (1994a), where the positions are linked to various philosophers who represent paradigm cases. Much of the dispute between Harry Collins and Bruno Latour in Pickering (1992) is over the more fruitful position to occupy.

6 The signal critique of 'scientism' from the right is Hayek (1979). Left anti-scientism is perhaps exemplified by Michel Foucault. The best overall critique of position (2) is Oakes (1988). Few methodologists realize that (2) is roughly Thomas Kuhn's position as well. See his comments in Hiley *et al.* (1991).

7 See the article by Hands in this volume.

8 This is nicely covered in Tribe (1976). The words 'socialism' and 'individualism' also take on their modern references in this period. On this, see Claeys (1986).

9 The classic statement of the Marxist position is Ollman (1976). The contested history of concepts of barter, exchange and money is surveyed in my 'Tit for tat' (unpublished Notre Dame working paper, March 1993). Parenthetically, the specification of what it is that precisely constitutes the economy is not so abstract or removed from practical concerns as the text may make it seem. Many discussions of the causes of Japan's rise to economic predominance, such as Thurow (1992), are explicitly about where one should draw the boundaries of the economy. Controversies over the legitimacy of Gary Becker's work on marriage, suicide and irrationalty also are exercises in transgression.

10 The experiences of Terence Hutchison and Karl Popper in the era of competing ideologies of Marxism and National Socialism had much to do with their earlier positions, whereas one might see the political drift of the Western market economies after the 1970s reflected in more recent post-modern currents.

11 These contradictions are illustrated by three vignettes from recent economics in Mirowski (1992a).

12 However, for the beginnings of this movement, see Weintraub (1991, forthcoming), Hands (forthcoming), Sent (forthcoming), Leonard (forthcoming) and Mirowski (1991a, 1991b, 1992b, 1993). Tymoczko (1986) is a particularly useful introduction to new currents in the philosophy of mathematics.

13 '. . . the mathematical method when correctly applied forces the investigator to give a complete statement of assuredly noncontradictory assumptions has generally been conceded as far as the relations of assumptions to reasoning is concerned. To this may be added that the absence of any natural meaning of mathematical symbols, other than the meanings given to them by postulate or by definition, prevents the associations clinging to words from intruding upon the reasoning process' (Koopmans 1957: 172–3). For those who know a little meta-mathematics, Gödel's theorem contradicts the first assertion (Shankar 1989), while the history of applied mathematics in most fields belies the second. A version of Koopmans's position with a little reverse English may be found in Rosenberg (1992), where mathematical economics is treated as a formalist exercise, but because it is empirically empty, is saddled with a status commensurate with that of navel-gazing. Again, some concerted history of mathematics would transcend these simplistic dichotomies.

14 A first attempt to make this case, one I now think is too awkward and inept,

can be found in my *Against Mechanism*. Somewhat better versions are Mirowski (1991b, 1991c).

15 One of the few attempts along these lines is Gilbert (1991), but even there the inquiry is too coloured by notions of falsification, and therefore the claim that the Permanent Income Hypothesis in macroeconomics is a candidate is not really compelling. The fact that Morgan (1990) can purport to be a history of econometrics without once identifying some empirical 'facts' which were the product of the programme is a symptom of the absence of any historiography of empirical economics.

16 The best history of experimentation in psychology is the thought-provoking book by Danziger (1990), which should give pause to anyone who thinks laboratory experimentation is easily transported into social theory. Another very fine critical study is by Gigerenzer and Murray (1987).

17 A bibliography of the major animal experiments plus a more elaborate analysis of their significance may be found in Mirowski (1994a).

BIBLIOGRAPHY

Arrow, K. J. and Hahn, F. H. (1971) *General Competitive Analysis*, Edinburgh: Oliver & Boyd.

Ashmore, M. (1989) *The Reflexive Thesis*, Chicago: University of Chicago Press.

Bacharach, M. (1989) 'The role of verstehen in economic theory', *Ricerche Economiche* 43: 129–50.

Backhouse, R. (1992) 'How should we approach the history of economic thought?', *Journal of the History of Economic Thought* 14: 18–35.

Blaug, M. (1980) *The Methodology of Economics*, Cambridge: Cambridge University Press.

Bloor, D. (1976) *Knowledge and Social Imagery*, London: Routledge & Kegan Paul.

Bloor, D. (1983) *Wittgenstein: A Social Theory of Knowledge*, New York: Columbia University Press.

Bonar, J. (1992) [1893] *Philosophy and Political Economy*, New Brunswick, NJ: Transaction Press.

Boulier, B. and Goldfarb, R. (1991) 'Pisces Economicus', *Economics and Philosophy* 7: 83–6.

Christie, J. (1987) 'Adam Smith's metaphysics of language', in A. Benjamin *et al.* (eds), *The Figural and the Literal*, Manchester: Manchester University Press.

Claeys, G. (1986) 'Individualism, socialism and social science', *Journal of the History of Ideas* 47: 81–93.

Collins, H. (1985) *Changing Order*, London: Sage.

Collins, H. (1990) *Artificial Experts*, Cambridge, MA: MIT Press.

Collins, H. and Pinch, T. (1993) *The Golem*, Cambridge: Cambridge University Press.

Crowe, M. (1990) 'Duhem and history and philosophy of mathematics', *Synthèse* 83: 431–47.

Danziger, K. (1990) *Constructing the Subject*, New York: Cambridge University Press.

Daston, L. (1992) 'Objectivity and the escape from perspective', *Social Studies of Science* 22: 597–618.

Debreu, G. (1986) 'Theoretical models: mathematical form and economic content', *Econometrica* 54: 1259–70.

de Marchi, N. and Blaug, M. (eds) (1991) *Appraising Economic Theories*, Aldershot: Edward Elgar.

Ezrahi, Y. (1990) *The Descent of Icarus*, Cambridge, MA: Harvard University Press.

Fann, K. T. (ed.) (1967) *Ludwig Wittgenstein: The Man and His Philosophy*, New York: Humanities Press.

Fine, T. (1973) *Theories of Probability*, New York: Academic Press.

Fraser, L. M. (1937) *Economic Thought and Language*, Edinburgh: Black.

Furner, M. (1975) *Advocacy and Objectivity*, Lexington: University of Kentucky Press.

Galison, P. (1988) 'History, philosophy and the central metaphor', *Science in Context* 2: 197–212.

Georgescu-Roegen, N. (1971) *The Entropy Law and the Economic Process*, Cambridge, MA: Harvard University Press.

Gigerenzer, G. and Murray, D. (1987) *Cognition as Intuitive Statistics*, Hillsdale, NJ: Lawrence Erlbaum.

Gilbert, C. (1991) 'Do economists test theories?', in N. de Marchi and M. Blaug (eds), *Appraising Economic Theories*. Cheltenham: Edward Elgar.

Gilleis, D. (ed.) (1992) *Revolutions in Mathematics*, Oxford: Clarendon Press.

Granger, C. (ed.) (1990) *Modelling Economic Series*, Oxford: Oxford University Press.

Hacking, I. (1984) 'Wittgenstein rules', *Social Studies of Science* 14: 469–76.

Hacking, I. (1992) 'Style for historians and philosophers', *Studies in the History and Philosophy of Science* 23: 1–20.

Hands, D. Wade (1992) *Testing, Rationality and Progress*, Lanham, MD: Rowman & Littlefield.

Hands, Wade H. (forthcoming) *Economics and Philosophy*.

Hayek, F. (1979) *The Counter-Revolution of Science*, Indianapolis: Liberty Press.

Henderson, W. (1993) 'The problem of Edgeworth's style', in W. Henderson, T. Dudley-Evans and R. Backhouse (eds), *Economics and Language*, London: Routledge.

Hendry, D., Leamer, E. and Poirier, D. (1990) 'A conversation on econometric methodology', *Econometric Theory* 6: 171–261.

Hiley, D. *et al.* (1991) *The Interpretative Turn*, Ithaca: Cornell University Press.

Hirschman, A. (1977) *The Passions and the Interests*, Princeton: Princeton University Press.

Hodgson, G. (1993) *Economics and Evolution*, Ann Arbor: University of Michigan Press

Hogarth, R. and Reder, M. (eds) (1987) *Rational Choice*, Chicago: University of Chicago Press.

Horgan, J. (1993) 'The death of proof', *Scientific American*, October, 269: 92–103.

Huber, P. (1991) *Galileo's Revenge*, New York: Basic Books.

Ingrao, B. and Israel, G. (1990) *The Invisible Hand*, Cambridge, MA: MIT Press.

Kitcher, P. (1983) *The Nature of Mathematical Knowledge*, Oxford: Oxford University Press.

Klamer, A. and Colander, D. (1990) *The Making of an Economist*, Boulder: Westview Press.

Kline, M. (1980) *Mathematics: The Loss of Certainty*, New York: Oxford University Press.

Koopmans, T. (1957) *Three Essays on the State of Economic Science*, New York: McGraw-Hill.

Latour, B. (1987) *Science in Action*, Cambridge, MA: Harvard University Press.

Leithauser, B. (1989) *Hence*, New York: Knopf.

Leonard, R. (forthcoming) 'Reading Cournot, reading Nash', *Economic Journal*.

Lyotard, F. (1984) *The Postmodern Condition*, Minneapolis: University of Minnesota Press.

McCloskey, D. (1990) *If You're So Smart*, Chicago: University of Chicago Press.

McMullin, E. (ed.) (1992) *The Social Dimension of Science*, Notre Dame: University of Notre Dame Press.

Mäki, U. (1990) 'Methodology of economics: complaints and guidelines', *Finnish Economic Papers* 3: 77–84.

Menger, C. (1963) *Problems of Economics and Sociology*, Urbana: University of Illinois Press.

Meyerson, E. (1991) [1921] *Explanation in the Sciences*, Boston: Kluwer.

Mirowski, P. (1986) *Against Mechanism*, Totawa: Rowman & Littlefield.

Mirowski, P. (1989) *More Heat than Light*, New York: Cambridge University Press.

Mirowski, P. (1991a) 'When games grow deadly serious', in C. Goodwin (ed.), *The Economics of National Defense*, Durham, NC: Duke University Press.

Mirowski, P. (1991b) 'The how, the when and the why of mathematical expression in the history of economic analysis', *Journal of Economic Perspectives* 5: 145–57.

Mirowski, P. (1991c) 'Postmodernism and the social theory of value', *Journal of Post Keynesian Economics* 13: 565–82.

Mirowski, P. (1992a) 'Three vignettes on the state of economic rhetoric', in N. de Marchi (ed.), *Post-Popperian Methodology of Economics*, Boston: Kluwer.

Mirowski, P. (1992b) 'What were von Neumann and Morgenstern trying to accomplish?', in R. Weintraub (ed.), *Toward a History of Game Theory*, Durham, NC: Duke University Press.

Mirowski, P. (ed.) (1993a) *Natural Images in Economics: Markets Read in Tooth and Claw*, New York: Cambridge University Press.

Mirowski, P. (ed.) (1993) 'What could mathematical rigor mean?', *History of Economics Review* 20: 41–60.

Mirowski, P. (ed.) (1994a) *Natural Images in Economics: Markets Read in Tooth and Claw*, New York: Cambridge University Press.

Mirowski, P. (1994b) 'Three ways of thinking about testing in econometrics', *Journal of Econometrics*, forthcoming.

Mirowski, P. (ed.) (1994c) *Ysidro Ycheued*, Totawa: Rowman & Littlefield.

Mommsen, W. and Osterhammel, J. (eds) (1987) *Max Weber and His Contemporaries*, London: Allen & Unwin.

Monk, R. (1990) *Ludwig Wittgenstein*, New York: Free Press.

Moore, D. C. (1993) 'Feminist accounting theory as a critique of natural economics', in Mirowski (1994a).

Morgan, M. (1990) *A History of Economics*, Cambridge, Cambridge University Press.

Nagel, T. (1986) *The View from Nowhere*, Oxford: Oxford University Press.

Nehamas, A. (1985) *Nietzsche: Life as Literature*, Cambridge, MA: Harvard University Press.

Oakes, G. (1988) *Weber and Rickert*, Cambridge, MA: MIT Press.

Ollman, B. (1976) *Alienation*, New York: Cambridge University Press.

Pickering, A. (ed.) (1992) *Science as Practice and Culture*, Chicago: University of Chicago Press.

Porter, T. (1990) 'Natural science and social theory', in R. Olby et al. (eds), *Companion to the History of Modern Science*, London: Routledge.

Porter, T. (1992) 'Quantification and the accounting ideal in science', *Social Studies of Science* 22: 633–51.

Proctor, R. (1991) *Value-Free Science?* Cambridge, MA: Harvard University Press.

Robinson, J. (1980) *Collected Papers*, vol. 5, Cambridge, MA: MIT Press.

Rorty, R. (1991) *Objectivity, Relativism, and Truth*, New York: Cambridge University Press.

Rosenberg, A. (1992) *Economics – Mathematical Politics or Science of Diminishing Returns?* Chicago: University of Chicago Press.

Ross, D. (1991) *The Origins of American Social Science*, New York: Cambridge University Press.

Rouse, J. (1991) 'Philosophy of science and the persistent metanarratives of modernity', *Studies in the History and Philosophy of Science* 22: 141–62.

Searle, J. (1992) *The Rediscovery of the Mind*, Cambridge, MA: MIT Press.

Sent, E.-M. (forthcoming) 'Resisting Sargent', Ph.D. thesis, Stanford University.

Shankar, S. (1987) *Wittgenstein and the Turning-Point in the Philosophy of Mathematics*, Albany: SUNY Press.

Shankar, S. (ed.) (1989) *Godel's Theorem in Focus*, London: Routledge.

Smith, V. (1986) 'Experimental methods in the political economy of exchange', *Science* 234: 167–73.

Smith, V. (1991) 'Rational choice', *Journal of Political Economy*, 99: 877–97.

Steiner, M. (1989) 'The application of mathematics to the natural sciences', *Journal of Philosophy* 86: 449–80.

Taylor, C. (1964) *The Explanation of Behaviour*, London: Routledge & Kegan Paul.

Thurow, L. (1992) *Head to Head*, New York: Morrow.

Tribe, K. (1976) *Land, Labour and Economic Discourse*, London: Routledge & Kegan Paul.

Tymoczko, T. (1986) *New Directions in the Philosophy of Mathematics*, Boston: Birkhauser.

Weintraub, E. R. (1991) *Stabilizing Dynamics*, New York: Cambridge University Press.

Weintraub, E. R. (forthcoming) *Mathematical Formalism and Economic Theory*.

Wigner, E. (1967) 'The unreasonable effectiveness of mathematics in the natural sciences', in E. Wigner (ed.), *Symmetries and Reflections*, Bloomington: Indiana University Press.

Wittgenstein, L. (1975) *Philosophical Remarks*, Chicago: University of Chicago Press.

Wittgenstein, L. (1978) *Remarks on the Foundations of Mathematics*, revised edn. Cambridge, MA: MIT Press.

Woolgar, S. (ed.) (1988) *Knowledge and Reflexivity*, London: Sage.

5

THE SOCIOLOGY OF SCIENTIFIC KNOWLEDGE

Some thoughts on the possibilities

D. Wade Hands

INTRODUCTION

During the last twenty years the sociology of scientific knowledge (SSK) has emerged as an influential new approach to the study of science. Unlike traditional philosophy of science which often emphasizes issues such as demarcation, appraisal and the logic of scientific theory choice, the sociology of scientific knowledge focuses on the inherently social nature of scientific inquiry. According to the SSK, science is practised in a social context, the products of scientific activity are the results of a social process, and scientific knowledge is socially constructed. Although there are a variety of individual points of view within the general framework of the SSK (and the SSK-inspired work in the history of science) these different perspectives are 'united by a shared refusal of philosophical apriorism coupled with a sensitivity to the social dimensions of science' (Pickering 1992b: 2). In other words: most of what philosophers of science have said about science is irrelevant, and science is fundamentally social.

Although the SSK raises a number of provocative challenges to traditional epistemology and the philosophy of science, such global philosophical issues are not the primary focus of this paper; some of these issues will surface briefly toward the end of the discussion, but they are not the main theme. The main theme of this paper is economics and what this recent literature on the SSK might mean to economics and economic methodology. In particular I want to address such questions as whether an 'economics of science' might not be as important to the study of science as the sociology of science, and whether the SSK in any sense 'leads to' such an economic analysis of science. Such an economics-based investigation into the nature of science would certainly raise a number of questions for economic methodology. While the paper will examine a wide range of issues regarding economics and the SSK, my purpose is only to provide a general discussion of these topics and not to advocate any one particular perspective on the relationship between these two fields.

The paper is arranged in the following way. The first section documents the rise of the SSK and briefly discusses some of its intellectual origins. A few of the differences among the various schools of thought within the SSK will be examined in this section. The second section will consider the issue of whether the SSK might 'lead to' an economics of science. In particular the question of 'social interests' in science will be discussed and how such 'interests' might be economically interpreted. The third section considers some of the existing literature that might be classified as 'the economics of science' or 'the economics of scientific knowledge'. Although this literature is hardly voluminous, it has existed for a long time (one of the early contributions dates from the late nineteenth century), and it is currently expanding. The fourth section considers some of the more general philosophical issues raised by the SSK (and inherited by any economics-based alternative to it): particularly the questions of 'circularity' and 'reflexivity'. In the fifth and final section, I will argue that while the economics of science seems to be a fertile area for additional research, interested economists should recognize that the social study of science (by sociologists or economists) represents a virtual Pandora's box of challenges to the beliefs that most economists hold regarding knowledge, science and even nature. These wider philosophical implications will leave many economists feeling rather uncomfortable about the whole project of an economic version of the SSK even though it would otherwise seem to be a rather obvious next step for the application of the economic method.

THE RISE OF THE SOCIOLOGY OF SCIENTIFIC KNOWLEDGE

While the recent literature on the SSK draws its intellectual inspiration from a broad range of sources, two important influences can be rather easily identified: the earlier 'sociology of science' of the Merton tradition, and the historicist (some would add 'relativist') turn within the philosophy of science initiated by authors such as Thomas Kuhn (1970) and Paul Feyerabend (1975).

The origin of the earlier sociology of science is frequently traced to Robert K. Merton's doctoral dissertation in 1935 (Merton 1970). Merton's thesis, in opposition to both 'internal' (usually inductivist) histories of science as well as Marxist 'external' histories,[1] argued that the development of natural science was promoted by the Puritan ethic of seventeenth-century England. Merton's argument that it was a particular social milieu that brought about the rise of science was quite similar to Max Weber's thesis that it was the Protestant ethic that had spurred on the development of capitalism. It is important to note that Merton's sociology of science was a sociology *of science*, and not necessarily a sociology *of scientific knowledge*. The distinction is very important. Neither Merton nor the other members of the Merton school really questioned the objective validity of our scientific knowledge. Science, for the sociology *of science*, employs a particular scientific method that provides reliable and universal knowledge about the objective world; sociology only enters in an attempt to explain the unique characteristics of the social and institutional context that allows such objective knowledge to be obtained. For this early, Mertonian, sociology of science, 'scientific knowledge' – the content of scientific theories – is not inexorably social. There are, for the Merton school, external social factors that promote or impede the development of scientific knowledge, factors that can be studied by the sociology of science, but the objective content of scientific theories exists independently of these social factors. This objective independence of scientific knowledge is not endorsed by many contemporary contributors to the SSK; this is one of the reasons why the recent literature, unlike that of the Merton school, is termed the sociology of *scientific knowledge*, rather than merely the sociology of *science*. Much of the impetus for this (much stronger) claim regarding the constitutively social nature of knowledge itself came from the work of historical philosophers of science like Kuhn and Feyerabend in the 1960s and 1970s.

Thomas Kuhn's (1962) central thesis regarding paradigms, scientific revolutions and normal science is much too familiar to summarize here, but it is useful to review a few individual parts of Kuhn's argument in order to trace the relationship between his influential ideas on the history of science and the development of the SSK. Kuhn's basic claim is that in mature science the members of a given scientific community are always in the grip of a collectively shared paradigm. In 'holding' a certain paradigm what the scientists 'see', or do not 'see', is determined by the paradigm. Observations are not independent and 'theory free', but rather are a product of the paradigm and are 'theory laden'. During a scientific revolution the scientist's way of seeing, the gestalt, changes; what was once seen 'as' one thing, is now seen 'as' something else. On this view there are no theory neutral empirical observations by which scientific theories can be independently judged. Rather it is the scientific theory itself, or more properly the scientific paradigm itself, that actually determines the observations within its domain. Two different paradigms are thus fundamentally 'incommensurable'; they constitute two incomparable ways of viewing the world.

Notice how this Kuhnian view of science introduces an irrevocably social element into science. It is not simply that different scientists have different subjective perspectives that taint their observations in various ways; rather each individual scientist 'participates in' or 'shares' a collective world view – the scientific paradigm – and this collectively held world view determines what they do and do not 'see'. What is 'observed', what is and is not seen as 'evidence', becomes a social product; the 'world' the scientist participates in, the 'world' of science, is socially constructed.[2] This particular aspect of the Kuhnian story – the social construction of the scientist's world – clearly opens the door for a sociological analysis of these scientific worlds (even though such a sociological analysis was not Thomas Kuhn's main interest). Since each individual paradigm constitutes 'the facts' in its domain, it cannot be the case that theory choices are made on the basis of the 'objective facts'. But if it is not the objective evidence that determines the choice between scientific theories then what does? Enter the social studies of science. The scientific community, like any other human community, forms a culture; it is a society. This society, this culture, can be examined like any other society, and since the traditional mode of inquiry for the study of society is sociology, the result is the SSK.[3]

While there are very many different individual points of view within the SSK – some inspired more by anthropology than sociology, and some much more radical than others – there is one group that seems to be cohesive enough to be labelled a particular 'school' within the SSK. This school is the so-called 'strong programme' associated with Barry Barnes, David Bloor and Steven Shapin.[4]

One of the central theses of the strong programme is that 'social interests' determine which scientific theories are successful and which are failures. As Paul Roth has characterized this view:

> The successes of science, both in the laboratory and in the prevailing textbook account, are to be explained by citing those social factors that cause, in a given historical context, a particular scientific theory to triumph (be judged correct) in place of its competitors. More specifically, the considerations determining which scientific theory will prevail, including the standards by which any such theory is deemed better than its alternatives, are tied to perceptions of which theory best rationalizes the interests of the dominant social group. This view differentiates the strong programmers from those . . . (most prominently Karl Mannheim and Robert Merton) who hold that the process of scientific justification is not a form of ideological rationalization and so not to be explained by sociological inquiry.
>
> (Roth 1987: 155–6)

Although the strong programme generally emphasizes the macro-social interests or ideologies that 'bear on national or dynastic politics' (Bloor 1984: 79), other, more micro-oriented social factors, such as the particular interests of the individual members of a given scientific community, may also be considered.

I mean that the social factors concerned may be ones which derive from the narrowly conceived interests or traditions or routines of the professional community.... Much that goes on in science can be plausibly seen as a result of the desire to maintain or increase the importance, status and scope of the methods and techniques which are the special property of a group.

(Bloor 1984: 80)

Notice how much the strong programme's view of scientific knowledge differs from the traditional philosophical characterization of science. The traditional view emphasizes the world 'out there' – either the real objective 'world' of nature (realism) or the 'world' of empirical phenomena (instrumentalism) – as the determining factor in our scientific knowledge. For the strong programme it is not the world 'out there', but rather it is the particular social context – the social interests present in that context – that determines what beliefs scientists hold, and these beliefs in turn determine what comes to be scientific knowledge. The beliefs that scientists hold are shaped by their social context, the social milieu in which they live and work; since these beliefs determine what comes to be scientific knowledge, the result is a scientific knowledge that is fundamentally social, a product of (and in a certain sense 'about') its social context. To explain scientific knowledge within this framework one focuses on the beliefs that scientists hold as the cause of scientific knowledge, and to explain the beliefs that scientists hold one focuses on social context as the cause of those beliefs. This view of science not only elevates the role of 'the social' far beyond that which it has traditionally played in the philosophy of science, but also well beyond the role it played in the earlier Mertonian sociology of science.

Although the strong programme is, in certain respects, quite radical, it remains philosophically traditional in at least two ways. First, the strong programme employs a relatively traditional notion of 'cause'. According to the strong programme the beliefs of scientists have 'social causes' in the rather straightforward and commonsense way that any event A might 'cause' event B.[5] Second, the strong programme practises a type of sociology that is both empiricist and inductive, thus making it quite traditional in its scientific methodology. According to the strong programme one simply determines the social causes of scientists' beliefs by empirically examining actual science. As Bloor admits, 'I am an inductivist.... My suggestion is simply that we transfer the instincts we have acquired in the laboratory to the study of knowledge itself' (Bloor 1984: 83). Such a stance is not only inductivist it is also methodologically monist – it presupposes that social science, in this case the sociology of science, should employ exactly the same methodology as that which has traditionally been characterized as 'the method' of natural science.[6] Critics have used both of these traditional aspects of the strong programme as points of attack.

While I will not say much more about the issue of causality,[7] the questions of inductivism and methodological monism will surface again when 'reflexivity' is discussed in the penultimate section.

No other group of authors within the SSK forms such a clearly defined 'school of thought' as the strong programme; outside the strong programme the SSK is composed of a number of disparate points of view which disagree on a number of issues. Despite this disagreement, if one is willing to live with rather rough-hewn categories, it is possible to characterize one major alternative to the strong programme. This alternative school – the 'constructivist' or 'ethnographic' approach to the SSK – differs from the strong programme in at least two significant ways.[8] Both of these differences could be considered methodological in a broad sense. First, the constructivist approach differs from the strong programme with respect to the sociological categories and the theoretical entities employed in the investigation of science. The strong programme generally (though not exclusively) focuses more on the broad macro-sociological variables at work in the wider society, while constructivist authors tend to focus more on the micro-sociological factors at work in the individual laboratories and other sites of scientific activity. Second, the strong programme and the constructivist approach differ considerably regarding their basic methodology of social inquiry. The strong programme is (as discussed above) narrowly 'scientific' in its approach to understanding the social causes of scientific belief; this rather narrow meta-method does not generally characterize the work of those writing from a constructivist point of view. The constructivist authors draw their methodological inspiration from a much wider range of inquiring traditions: the participant–observer approach in anthropology, ethno-methodology and the hermeneutic tradition to name a few. The constructivist authors are broadly empirical, but it is not the simple inductivism of the strong programme. Those in the constructivist programme seek to understand the social nature of scientific activity and employ a broad range of inquiring frameworks in order to obtain that understanding; it is not simply a matter of applying the natural science method to the study of science as it often is for the strong programme. Constructivist studies in science are generally local, richly detailed and deeply textured investigations into scientific practice as a life activity; they may focus either on a particular historical episode in science or on contemporary scientific activity, but in either case the result generally involves much more contextual solicitousness than the investigations of the strong programme.[9]

SOCIOLOGY, INTERESTS AND ECONOMIC OPPORTUNITY

The SSK seems to leave the door open for an economic analysis of science. If science is done in social communities by individual scientists and we desire to employ social science to help us understand the behaviour of those scientists in that community, then economics seems to be as likely a candidate for the relevant social science as sociology or anthropology. In the SSK, both versions, there is a lot of talk about the 'interests' of those in the scientific community, and while economists do not normally use the term 'interests', they do in fact explain economic behaviour on the basis of the 'interests' of the agents involved. The economics of science, or the economics of scientific knowledge, seems to be a rather obvious next step in the study of science as the product of a social community of individual agents.[10]

Before taking this obvious next step and considering the economics of science explicitly, I would like to examine a few of the quasi-economic arguments that have been offered from within the SSK. Surprisingly there are a number of cases within the SSK where, even though the author was not consciously attempting to apply economic analysis to science, the arguments offered do in fact sound very much like economic arguments.[11] This quasi-economic argumentation is emphasized by Uskali Mäki in his recent examination of the SSK and economics:

> It is interesting from our point of view that much of recent sociology of science is built upon analogies drawn from economics. In these suggestions science is viewed as analogous to a capitalist market economy in which agents are maximizing producers who competitively and greedily pursue their self-interest. The point of emphasis in these suggestions is on scientists' action and on the ends involved in that action.
>
> (Mäki 1992: 79)

It seems useful to examine a few of these quasi-economic discussions from the existing SSK literature before moving on to the explicit consideration of the economic approach in the next section.

The first case I would like to consider is one that is also discussed by Mäki (1992): Bruno Latour and Steve Woolgar's *Laboratory Life* (1986). This work, a work that is generally (and fittingly) considered one of the more radical positions within the SSK, has a surprisingly large amount of economic argumentation. In chapter 5, where Latour and Woolgar discuss the motivation of scientists, there are many references to the 'quasi-economic terms' (p. 190) that scientists, particularly younger scientists, use to describe their own work and professional involvements. The scientists interviewed by Latour and Woolgar repeatedly used the term 'credit' to describe that which was being sought through scientific activity as well as that which participation in science would distribute to those who were successful. This scientific 'credit' clearly has a component that is direct reward, but the scientists in Latour and Woolgar's study seemed to be motivated by, and interested in, more than simply the direct rewards from credit. Latour and Woolgar expand the notion of credit beyond the simple notion of a reward to a broader issue of professional 'credibility'. They argue that when scientists are viewed as 'engaged in a quest for credibility, we are better able to make sense both of their different interests and of the process by which one kind of credit is transformed into another' (Latour and Woolgar 1986: 200). After elaborating on this expanded notion of credibility (pp. 198–208), Latour and Woolgar embed the concept in a general economic characterization of science.

> Let us suppose that scientists are investors of credibility. The result is the creation of a *market*. Information now has value because, . . . it allows other investigators to produce information which facilitates the return of invested capital. There is a *demand* from investors for information which may increase the power of their own inscription devices, and there is a *supply* of information from other investors. The forces of supply and demand create the *value* of the commodity, which fluctuates constantly depending on supply, demand, the number of investigators, and the equipment of the producers. Taking into account the fluctuation of this market, scientists invest their credibility where it is likely to be most rewarding. Their assessment of these fluctuations both explains scientists' reference to "interesting problems," "rewarding subjects," "good methods," and "reliable colleagues" and explains why scientists constantly move between problem areas, entering into new collaborative projects, grasping and dropping hypotheses as the circumstances demand, shifting between one method and another and submitting everything to the goal of extending the credibility cycle.
>
> (Latour and Woolgar 1986: 206, italics in original)

For Latour and Woolgar it is the market for credibility that determines what scientists work on, what they find interesting, what is considered good work and ultimately what becomes scientific knowledge.[12]

The second example of an economic-like characterization from within the SSK is Karin Knorr-Cetina's 'exchange strategy' representation of the scientific activity in experimental particle physics. In her studies of particle physicists she found two basic strategies; one of these was the very economic-sounding 'exchange strategy', which she characterizes in the following way:

I have defined contingency in terms of a negative relationship of dependence between two desired goals, or research utilities, such that one utility can only be obtained or optimized at the cost of the other. In this situation particle physicists resort to a strategy of commerce and exchange: they balance research benefits against each other, and then "sell off" those which they think that, on balance, they may not be able to afford. Particle physicists refer to this commerce with research benefits as "trade-offs." In the experiment we observed, they traded off tracking particles against electron identification; time needed for calibration against granularity of the detector; performance of the calorimeter against cost; dead time against background reduction; and so on.

(Knorr-Cetina 1991: 112–13)

Here again, as in Latour and Woolgar's *Laboratory Life*, scientific activity is described in terms that are quite familiar to economists. It should be noted that this 'exchange strategy' was not the only strategy that Knorr-Cetina found among particle physicists – and she also found a totally different strategy among molecular biologists – but nonetheless it clearly is an economic story about the practice of science.

One very important point about these two examples (and perhaps other examples that one might find in the SSK[13]) is they *are not attempts to 'apply' economics to science*. Economists often find themselves in the position of trying to model something 'as an X'; we might, for example, try to model sticky wages 'as a rational response to asymmetric information', or we might try to model the demand for children 'as the outcome of a noncooperative game'. This is not what is going on in these economic stories about science. The economic argumentation that appears in the literature on the SSK is not a result of the various authors trying to model science 'as a competitive market process'. The intention of these three authors in particular was certainly not to demonstrate the robustness of the economic method; it was simply to examine the social nature of science through careful ethnographic investigation into the actual practice of science. As we will see in the next section, there are in fact some studies that are motivated by an attempt to 'apply' economics to science, but neither Latour and Woolgar nor Knorr-Cetina are such cases. In fact, although it is purely speculation on my part, a reasonable conjecture would be that all three of these authors consider neoclassical economics to be naively reductionist, narrowly individualist, and in general a quite uninteresting approach to studying (any) social process. The point is, despite the fact that none of these authors intended to apply economics, and perhaps do not even particularly like the discipline, the stories that emerge from their ethnographic investigations of science look very much like the product of economic analysis.[14]

For the third and final example of economic analogies in the SSK I will take a slightly different approach. Rather than simply showing that what was produced in a particular sociological or ethnographic study looks very much like what an economist might say about science, I will discuss a case where a particular study in the SSK has been criticized precisely because the study characterizes the behaviour of scientists in the way that a neoclassical economist would characterize individual behaviour.

Andrew Pickering's *Constructing Quarks* (1984) is an influential sociological history of high-energy physics from 1960 to 1980. The study is self-consciously constructivist and it focuses on the intricate details of the 'dynamics of practice' rather than the more general 'social interests' that motivate many studies in the SSK. Pickering's basic claim is that scientific activity in particle physics is best understood as 'opportunism in context'; he characterizes this opportunism in the following way:[15]

> Perhaps the single most conspicuous departure of CQ from the philosophical tradition is that, in CQ, I paid great attention to the dynamic aspect of scientific practice. I advanced a general schema for thinking about this dynamics under the slogan of "opportunism in context." The idea was simple enough. Doing science is real work; real work requires resources; different scientists have different degrees of access to such resources; and resources to hand are opportunistically assembled as contexts for constructive work are perceived. My claim, exemplified many times over in CQ, was that if one understands scientists as working this way then one can understand, in some detail, why individuals and groups acted as they did in the history of particle physics.
>
> (1990: 692)

Many commentators have been critical of Pickering's 'opportunism in context' precisely because it sounds so much like economic haggling in the marketplace. Peter Galison, for instance, comments that experimentation should not be 'parodied as if it were no more grounded in reason than negotiations over the price of a street fair antique' (1987: 277). Similarly, in Paul Roth and Robert Barrett's lengthy critical examination of Pickering's book they make the following remarks about his economic approach:

> Pickering's model of scientific decision-making is thus fundamentally an economic one – scientists invest their expertise in areas promising them the most useful return for this investment. Justification of decision-making is dictated, in this model, by factors completely outside of the purview of traditional philosophy of science.
>
> (1990: 594)

While commentators like Roth and Barrett, and Galison, are critical of the economic aspect of Pickering's story, this is not their only, or even their major, concern. In both cases, the fact that Pickering has characterized science as an economic process is a relatively minor infraction compared to the fact that he has almost totally excluded objective reality as a constraint on the experimental behaviour of scientists.[16] However, in the same series of papers that contains Roth and Barrett's criticism, Steve Fuller (1990) attacks Pickering specifically on grounds that are relevant to microeconomics: the way he characterizes the agency of the individual scientists. In Pickering's story the scientists behave essentially in the way that neoclassical agents behave – they make intentional choices on the basis of their beliefs and desires. For Fuller, this argument (common to all microeconomic explanations) presupposes a teleological framework from folk psychology that is just as philosophically suspect as any of the standard philosophical charaterizations of the epistemologically moral character of scientists. Fuller says:

> The problem is that, contrary to his own intentions, by attributing agency to the scientists, Pickering has already supposed that they have the sort of *post facto* knowledge that he finds so objectionable in the philosophical accounts. The difference is that his scientists do not foresee hidden entities but hidden opportunities; they are master prognosticators of their own interests, if not the state of the external world.
>
> (1990: 671)

While neither Pickering in his original presentation, nor Fuller in his criticism, even mentions neoclassical economics, this criticism of Pickering by Fuller is very relevant to the general question of the economic analysis of science. The point of Fuller's criticism, the implicit folk psychology of Pickering's story about the behaviour of scientists, is precisely the same criticism that certain philosophers of science, particularly Alexander Rosenberg (1988, 1992), have levelled at microeconomics.[17] Thus, not only is it the case that certain ethnographic and historical studies in the SSK have (without any explicit consideration of economic theory) come to characterize the behaviour of scientists and scientific activity in a very (neoclassical) economic way, the similarities to economics are so great that critics of these 'sociological' studies (again without explicit consideration of economics) attack them on exactly the same grounds that economists have recently been attacked by philosophers of science.

In summary, it seems that the SSK exists in some intellectually parallel universe to the universe inhabited by most economists. It is a world in which economic explanations of individual behaviour as well as the social phenomena that emerges from that behaviour (along with some of the criticism of these explanations) clearly exist – not only *do* such explanations exist, but they are generally considered to be both credible and persuasive – and yet it is a world that seems to be totally without economics.[18]

THE ECONOMICS OF SCIENCE AND/OR THE
ECONOMICS OF SCIENTIFIC KNOWLEDGE

The previous section makes clear that many of the studies in the SSK describe science in a way that is much like the way that it might be described if it were approached from an explicitly economic perspective. In this section I would like to discuss a few of the attempts to do just that: to approach science from an explicitly economic perspective.

The first work to consider is perhaps the first work ever written on the topic of the economic approach to science: a paper by the American pragmatist philosopher Charles Sanders Peirce (1967). In this rather amazing paper, Peirce discusses the 'economy of research' in a way that not only employs marginal economic analysis but does so in a very contemporary manner; this paper, originally published in 1879, would not seem too far out of place in a modern economics journal.[19] Peirce's approach is basically to maximize the utility obtained from various research projects subject to the cost constraint imposed by each project The first-order conditions require that the marginal utility per dollar of research cost be equated for each of the research projects undertaken; such a result, while certainly not surprising from the viewpoint of modern economics, seems rather astounding for 1879. As Wible (1992b) shows, Peirce's paper really amounts to a modern cost–benefit analysis of research project selection.[20]

Since nothing short of an actual (and extended) quotation from Peirce's paper could possible convey its contemporary style, the following contains most of the first three paragraphs of the paper.

> The doctrine of economy, in general, treats of the relations between utility and cost. That branch of it which relates to research considers the relations between the utility and the cost of diminishing the probable error of our knowledge. Its main problem is, how, with a given expenditure of money, time, and energy, to obtain the most valuable addition to our knowledge.
>
> Let r denote the probable error of any result, and write $s=1/r$. Let $Ur \cdot dr$ denote the infinitesimal utility of any infinitesimal diminution, dr, of r. Let $Vs \cdot ds$ denote the infinitesimal cost of any infinitesimal increase, ds, of s . . . . Then, the total cost of any series of researches will be
>
> $$\Sigma_i \int V_i s_i \cdot ds_i;$$
>
> and their total utility will be
>
> $$\Sigma_i \int U_i r_i \cdot dr_i.$$
>
> The problem will be to make the second expression a maximum by varying the inferior limits of its integrations, on the condition that the first expression remains of constant value.
>
> (Peirce 1967: 643)

As I said, this was a rather amazing paper for the time that it was published.

While Peirce's paper was clearly 'way ahead of its time' in many respects, it was, if examined in isolation from the rest of his pragmatist philosophy, only an early contribution to the *economics of science*, rather than an early contribution to the *economics of scientific knowledge*. If we mirror the distinction between the sociology of science and the sociology of scientific knowledge, then the economics *of science* would be the application of economic theory, or ideas found in economic theory, to explaining the behaviour of scientists and/or the intellectual output of the scientific community. That is, given the goals of the individual scientists or those of the scientific community (for example, the 'pursuit of truth') the economics of science might be used to explain the behaviour of those in the scientific community or to make recommendations about how those goals might be achieved in a more efficient manner. In this way the economics of science would relate to science in precisely the way that microeconomics has typically related to the firms in the market economy. Peirce's 1879 paper is a very early example of such an economics of science.[21] On the other hand, the economics *of scientific knowledge* (ESK) would involve economics in a philosophically more fundamental way. The ESK would involve economics, or at least metaphors derived from economics, in the actual characterization of scientific knowledge – that is, economics would be involved fundamentally in the epistemological discourse regarding the nature of scientific knowledge. Like the SSK argues that scientific knowledge comes to be constructed out of a social process, the ESK would argue that scientific knowledge comes to be constructed out of an economic process.

Although in isolation Peirce's 1879 paper is more an application of the economics of science than the ESK, Peirce's more general pragmatist philosophy of science does in fact contain elements of an economic theory of knowledge. For Peirce truth is simply that which the community of inquirers converges to over an infinite period of time. His notion of truth is inherently social – a community of inquirers is involved – but it is not merely a product of existing social conditions; it has an independent existence in that it is the limit (ultimate limit) of a process of inquiry by the inquiring community. As Thomas Haskell has characterized Peirce's position:

> The ultimate consensus to be reached by his community of inquiry is of a very special kind, and his theory of reality, though indubitably social, is not at all relativistic, as twentieth-century analogues have tended to be. Like Thomas Kuhn, he regarded science as the practical accomplishment of a community of researchers. Unlike Kuhn, however, he supposed that the universe was so made that an ultimate convergence of opinion was virtually predestined and that the reality

toward which opinion converged was utterly independent, not of thought in general but of what any finite number of human beings thought about it.

(Haskell 1984: 205–6)

The economic element in Peirce's view of science becomes clear when he discusses the nature of this 'convergence' towards communal truth; his story is basically a competitive story. For Peirce it is the 'economy of inquiry' that drives the inquiring community towards truth. The same economic principles that governed the choice of research projects in his 1879 paper, the maximization of return on our collective cognitive investment, that propels the scientific community towards its goal. Again quoting Haskell:

> Indeed, the entire process that causes what Peirce called "the most antagonistic views" to converge in the ultimate consensus is strangely reminiscent of the price mechanism in economic markets. There, in accordance with the natural laws of supply and demand, the jockeying of rival consumers and producers looking out for their own interests generates for each commodity a convergence towards its "natural price." In the community of inquiry the clash of erring individuals produces eventually a convergence of opinion about reality. No one in Peirce's community need feel love toward the other members, nor even love of truth, strictly speaking (since no individual's present ideas can be said to correspond with that opinion which the community will ultimately settle on).

(1984: 211)[22]

Charles Sanders Peirce thus seems to be an earlier contributor to both the economics of science and the ESK. He discussed the 'economy of research' as a way of optimally selecting scientific research projects, but he also integrated this economic argument into his basic philosophy of science and theory of scientific truth.

The second author I would like to discuss, Gerard Radnitzky, is also a philosopher, although a contemporary one, and his view of science is also one that involves economics in both ways: as a tool for explaining what scientists actually do, and as an integral part of his characterization of scientific knowledge. Radnitzky has presented his 'economic theory of science' in a series of recent papers: Radnitzky (1986, 1987a, 1987b, 1989). His basic purpose is '*to investigate what may be gained from applying the economic approach, in particular cost–benefit thinking, to the methodology of research*' (Radnitzky 1986: 125, italics in original).[23] Radnitzky argues that by taking cost–benefit analysis (CBA) as our general point of departure it is possible to clarify a number of lingering controversies within the philosophy of science. In particular, he argues that CBA can help illuminate such philosophical questions as: why do certain scientists hold on to established paradigms even in the face of negative empirical evidence?[24] How are decisions made regarding what is and what is not to count as part of the empirical basis for a scientific theory? And when is it rational to prefer one scientific theory over another? Radnitzky does not say that the economic approach can conclusively 'solve' any of these philosophical problems, but rather 'that the CBA-frame may provide an organizing scheme that helps the researcher to see what sorts of questions he should take into account when dealing with such problems' (1986: 125).

These particular papers that apply the 'economic method' directly to questions of science and economic methodology are really only the tip of the iceberg regarding the importance of economics to Radnitzky's philosophy of science. Radnitzky subscribes to a particular brand of Popperian philosophy; he supports the 'critical rationalist' interpretation of Popper's philosophy associated with the work of W. W. Bartley III.[25] Since the critical rationalist interpretation of Popper is discussed elsewhere in this volume (in the paper by Lawrence Boland) there is no reason to reproduce the argument here.[26] All I would like to note is that in the Bartley/ Radnitzky characterization, 'knowledge' emerges from the competitive process of scientific criticism in the same way that economic welfare emerges from the competitive market process. Their view essentially amounts to an invisible-hand argument for the growth of scientific knowledge and it depends fundamentally on their notion of 'criticism' and its role in error elimination. The Bartley/Radnitzky view also depends heavily on arguments from evolutionary epistemology to connect up these competitively emergent theoretical structures with the underlying physical world; their theory, unlike Peirce's for example, endeavors to hold on to scientific realism. In any case, Radnitzky's view, and to a lesser extent critical rationalism more generally, represents a direct application of economic reasoning to questions about the nature of scientific knowledge; it thus constitutes a version of ESK.

Finally, I would like to mention a few of the studies, some quite recent, and some not so recent, where economists, rather than philosophers, have undertaken various exercises in the economics of knowledge. These are primarily studies in the economics of science – applying the tools of economic analysis to the behaviour of a particular type of economic agent: a scientist – although some of these economists also consider issues that might be part of the ESK.

One of these works is Gordon Tullock's *The Organization of Inquiry*, published in 1966. This book, inspired by 'six months spent working with Karl Popper' (1966: v) applies an early public choice-type analysis to the study of science. For Tullock one of the identifying characteristics of science is that it is conducted in a scientific community and the book is primarily 'devoted to a discussion of this community, the organization which controls inquiry', the main feature of this community is that it is 'a system of voluntary co-operation' (1966: 63). Tullock discusses the incentives of and constraints on this community, and also reflects on a few traditional philosophical (particularly Popperian) questions.[27]

Boland (1971)[28] takes a different approach. He uses economics (particularly welfare economics) to attack what he calls 'conventionalist' methodologies – methodological approaches that attempt to choose the 'best' theory from a set of competing theories. On Boland's view any methodology is considered conventionalist if it recommends choosing scientific theories on the basis of the fact that they are 'more simple', or 'more general', or 'more verifiable', or any other criterion other than truth. In the paper Boland makes an analogy between these conventionalist theory choices and the choices involved in welfare economics. He then uses well-known problems in welfare economics, such as the Arrow impossibility theorem, to show that the conventionalist economic problem is 'unsolvable on its own terms' (1971: 105).

Finally, I would like to mention three quite recent papers that have directly applied 'the economic method' to the practice of science: Diamond (1988) and Wible (1991), (1992a). All three of these papers employ a Gary Becker-based model of rational choice to the problem of science (or a particular problem in science). Diamond (1988) applies Becker's general 'economic approach' to the problem of a rational scientist. The rational scientist is one who maximizes a utility function with 'scope' and 'elegance' as arguments, and faces constraints imposed by time and production functions. Diamond argues that such a 'maximization-under-constraints model holds promise of being able to account for scientific progress in a way consistent with the history of science' (1988: 150).

The papers by Wible are of a similar genre. Wible (1991) discusses the question of replication in science by means of Becker's model of the allocation of time, and Wible (1992a) discusses the question of fraud in science by means of the Becker/Ehrlich model of the economics of crime. All three of these papers are replete with formal economic analysis: first-order conditions, qualitative comparative statistics, Kuhn–Tucker conditions, and even optimization under uncertainty. The following quotation from Wible captures the general flavour of the analysis in, and the results available from, these three papers.

> Reconsidering the first-order condition describing the individual scientist's optimization under uncertainty, equation 5 has additional behavioral implications. The more negative or the greater the slope becomes in absolute value, the less fraud will be committed by the individual. This will occur if the probability of being discovered, P_f, increases, or if the penalty F_f associated with time spent in illegitimate activities increases. Either of these reduces the incentive to engage in

fraudulent activities in science. If the marginal return to fraudulent activities increases relative to legitimate activities, then the individual would be expected to increase the proportion of time spent on illegitimate activities.

(1992a: 19)

These papers are clearly *the economics of science* and they are presented in the language and discursive format of contemporary economics. These papers *may not actually be* any more of a direct application of microeconomics to science than the earlier work by Tullock, Boland or Radnitzky (or even Peirce for that matter), but they certainly *seem* to be, perhaps because of the mathematics, the most direct application of economic analysis to science available in the literature.[29]

The discussion of these quite recent Becker-based models ends the survey portion of the paper. After discussing many of the quasi-economic arguments available in the sociological literature, and also discussing a number of the direct applications of economic theory to science, it is time to return to more philosophical issues.

CAVEAT ECONOMIST: CIRCULARITY, REFLEXIVITY AND EPISTEMIC ANOMIE

Criticisms of the SSK (particularly the strong programme) are legion.[30] From outside the SSK most of this criticism has come from philosophers, but a few philosophically oriented historians of the various scientific disciplines have also been involved. Within the SSK, disagreement has come primarily from one school criticizing the other, although the constructivist approach is sufficiently diverse that serious disagreements often occur between various individuals who share this general point of view. Out of all of the many criticisms that have been, or could be, raised, I would like to focus on only one: the problem of *reflexivity*. The reason for focusing on this one problem is two-fold. First, this seems to be the *major problem*; it gets the most attention in the literature, and many of the other controversies seem to be derived from it. Second, it is also a problem that will trouble any attempt to apply economics to the study of science.

The problem of 'reflexivity' arises in the following way. The SSK argues that science is the product of its social context, either the social interests of the scientists involved or other social factors that constitute the social context of science. What scientists observe and the theories they propose are not simply given by the external world 'out there', but rather it is constituted by the social context 'in here'. Now if one accepts this basic claim of the SSK, then should it not also be true for the sociologists who are doing the SSK as well? The sociologists doing the SSK are a community of scientists; if what a community of scientists produces is constituted by its social context, then the output of the SSK will also be a product of, and constituted by, its social context. As Alexander Rosenberg expresses it: 'This sort of sociology pulls itself down by its own boot straps' (1985: 380). Focusing particularly on the strong programme, Rosenberg characterizes the problem in the following way:

> Proponents of the "strong program" in the sociology of science [Bloor 1976; Barnes 1977] suggest that science is nothing more than such a social institution, and must be understood as such. But if this argument is correct, it must be self-refuting. If scientific conclusions are always and everywhere determined by social forces, and not by rational considerations, then this conclusion applies to the findings of the sociologist of science as well.
>
> (Rosenberg 1985: 379)

Reflexivity is an extremely important issue for the SSK. Many of the advocates of the SSK claim to undermine the hegemony of the natural sciences by showing that what is purported to be objective and 'natural' is neither one of these things, but rather simply a product of the social context in which it is produced. If this is true for all human inquiry, then it must be true for the SSK as well; this makes everything socially/context dependent and thus *relative*.[31] This leads many of those writing the SSK to a version of 'sociological skepticism' (Kitcher 1992) where individuals are always trapped in the categories of a particular social context (or in Wittgensteinian terms, trapped in a particular language game); individuals are either unable to escape these social categories, or if they can escape, there is no way of rationally deciding among the various frameworks that are available.

Collins and Yearley (1992a,b) – both advocates of a version of constructivism, but critical of sociologists who revel in such relativism – refer to this tendency within the SSK as 'epistemological chicken'; they characterize this relativist tendency in the following way:

> In sum, following the lead of the relativists, each new fashion in SSK has been more epistemologically daring, the reflexivists coming closest to self-destruction. Each group has made the same mistake at first; they have become so enamoured of the power of their negative levers on the existing structures as to believe they rest on bedrock. But this is not the case. Though each level can prick misplaced epistemological pretensions, they stand in the same relationship to each other as parallel cultures; no level has priority and each is a flimsy building on the plain. Accepting this we can freely use whatever epistemological "natural attitude" is appropriate for the purpose at hand; we can alternate between them as we will. That is what methodological relativism is all about – the rejection of any kind of foundationalism

and its replacement, not by permanent revolution but by permanent insecurity. To reverse the vertical scale of the metaphor, while SSK showed that science did not occupy the high ground of culture, the newer developments must be taken to demonstrate not the failure of SSK, but that there simply is no high ground.

(Collins and Yearley 1992a: 308)

The particular solution offered by Collins and Yearley is 'social realism' – let social scientists 'stand on social things' to explain natural things (1992b: 382) – but other authors have other solutions.[32] Bruno Latour for example, one of the SSK authors who seems to delight in the problems (opportunities?) of reflexivity, sees the situation quite differently than do Collins and Yearley:

A few, who call themselves reflexivists, are delighted at being in a blind alley; for fifteen years they had said that social studies of science could not go anywhere if it did not apply its own tool to itself; now that it goes nowhere and is threatened by sterility, they feel vindicated.

(Latour 1992: 272)[33]

There are obviously a number of different responses to the reflexivity issue within the SSK. My purpose is not to attempt to defend one of these positions over the others; the purpose is only to point out that *all* of the authors involved in the recent SSK feel impelled to give *some response* to the question of reflexivity and the relativism (that many suggest) it implies. While these questions are clearly relevant to the SSK, it could be argued that if one were only concerned with the *sociology of science*, rather than the SSK, then the problems of reflexivity and relativism would not be relevant (since the cognitive content of scientific theories remains unexamined in the sociology of science). But even here, in the sociology of science, there is a problem if the tools are turned on the carpenter. Even when the focus is only on the culture of science and not on the content of the theories offered, there is clearly a potential problem of regress and circularity when the sociology of science looks at the science of sociology.

Let us now return to the economics of science literature from the previous section; does the reflexivity question also impact the economics of science? The immediate answer is clearly yes. Suppose that one is engaged in a public choice-type analysis of science; for example, suppose that we view individual scientists as acting in their own rational self-interest given the market for professional credibility. This public choice (scientific choice) analysis could just as easily be applied to practising economists – in fact, it could even be applied to the specific public choice economist that was examining the behaviour of scientists. The circularity or reflexivity problem thus occurs in the economics of science just as it does in the sociology of science.

Much of the previously considered work on the economics of science encounters such reflexivity problems. For example, in Gordon Tullock's discussion of science, he characterizes (and implicitly criticizes) fields where teaching responsibilities dictate a larger number of participants than research opportunities can accommodate in the following way:

> One symptom of the existence of this condition is the development of very complex methods of treating subjects which can be readily handled by simple methods. Calculus will be used where simple arithmetic would do and topology will be introduced in place of plane geometry. In many fields of social science these symptoms have appeared.
>
> (Tullock 1966: 57)

In this case Tullock is using his economic approach to science to explain the rise of mathematical economics. Now in this particular case Tullock would not recognize a reflexivity problem since he would probably consider himself to be applying the right kind of economics to the question of how the discipline came to pay so much attention to the wrong kind of economics. On the other hand, suppose that Tullock had actually produced a formal model of the behaviour of scientists in an overpopulated field and mathematically deduced his prediction regarding their tendency to formalize. In this case the reflexivity problem would be much more obvious, though no more present, than it was in Tullock's original.

The reflexivity problem also surfaces in the contributions by Wible (particularly 1991 and 1992b). In Wible (1991) the economic approach to science is applied to the question of empirical replication in science, but the particular case he considers is replication in econometrics. Wible is quite explicit about his desire to apply the economics of science to the science of economics.

> While the rational expectations and public choice revolutions have been extremely successful at the theoretical level, there is another domain of economic activity to which the postulate of economic rationality could be applied. This category of human behaviour virtually has been ignored by economic theorists. The domain of human behaviour I have in mind is none other than positive economics itself. Economic methodologists and most others who study the professional behaviour of economists usually do not presume that economists are economically rational.
>
> (Wible 1991: 165)

There is something very curious about explaining the activity of economists on the basis of an economic theory of behaviour. Should we not then be able to explain the behaviour of the economist who is trying to explain the behaviour of economists on the basis of economic theory, on the basis of economic theory too? Where do such explanations end?[34]

Wible's most recent contribution (1992b) contains a related, and perhaps ever more unsettling, argument. In Wible (1992b) the (neoclassical) economic argument of Radnitzky and Bartley (1987) – the argument that competition in the marketplace of ideas is good for the growth of knowledge – is actually used against neoclassical economics. Knowledge requires competition, but, according to Wible's analysis, there has not been any real competition in the marketplace of economic ideas; rather than competition, economics has been dominated by the monopoly of the neoclassical approach. Thus a neoclassical-based philosophy of science is used to argue for the elimination of the neoclassical hegemony in economics. This seems a bit like throwing oneself out with one's own bath water.

Wible (unlike some of the other contributors to this literature) actually recognizes the self-referentiality and the possible methodological circularity raised by his economic approach. He ends with the following paragraph.

> After presenting the model and its applications, some possible intellectual problems arising from this point of view were raised. Specifically how far can an economic explanation of economics and other sciences be taken? The logical extreme would be that the rationality of science is completely explainable in terms of economic analysis – that economic science itself is primarily an economic phenomenon. The problem with such a position is that it would reduce all philosophies and methodologies of science to economics. Logically this would deprive economics of an independent philosophical or methodological standard of scientific objectivity. Objective knowledge would be impossible. The alternative is to recognize that economics construed as rational maximizing behaviour is incomplete and cannot be universally applied – that it can add greatly to an understanding of professional scientific conduct but not explain everything.
>
> (Wible 1991: 184)

If one stops just before the last sentence, this quotation contains a clear statement of the 'relativity' issue from the SSK. In this case it is a relativity induced by the economic argument that all science is simply the maximizing behaviour of individual scientists, rather than the relativity induced by the sociological argument that all science is socially constituted, but it is relativity nonetheless. Because of the individualism of (neoclassical) economics, the economic approach will characterize science as the product of individual rather than social interests, but the result is a scientific practice that is just as devoid of the traditional cognitive virtues as is the case for the SSK.

None of this discussion of reflexivity or relativism is meant to suggest that the economics of science is not a worthy endeavour, or that economists should be scared off by some of these potentially unsettling epistemological implications of this work. The argument is only that we should *recognize what is at stake and enter into such studies with our philosophical eyes wide open.* Economists interested in the economics of science should be knowledgeable and informed regarding the SSK, and in particular, they should be aware of the potentially quite radical implications of some of this work. If one wants to employ economics, and yet remain safely ensconced within a traditional view that allows for only one universally valid 'scientific method', then something akin to the Peirce or Bartley/ Radnitzky approaches would seem to be required. On these views knowledge has (some) objective status, but the (universally valid) way of obtaining that knowledge depends on a process that is fundamentally economic. On the other hand, if one is willing to abandon the traditional philosophy of science, and to accept a characterization of knowledge that is fundamentally local, tentative and contingent, then economics, along with a variety of other framework and discursive strategies, could be involved in the inquiry.[35] The point is that whichever of these two general approaches one chooses to pursue, there is serious philosophical work to be done; the economics of science is more than looking at first-order conditions for scientists' optimization problems and/or noting that the marketplace of ideas actually looks like a marketplace. If economists are to make any contribution to human understanding of science or scientific knowledge then they need to scrutinize the sociological literature quite carefully. Economists bring a number of tools to the project that are quite different from the tools of the sociologist; economists think in terms of optimization, information, incentives and equilibrium; economists also think of individuals creating societies rather than societies creating individuals. While the tools are different, and in some cases perhaps mutually exclusive, neither the general task nor the pitfalls entailed are necessarily different. Those involved in the SSK have travelled through much of this wilderness before us, and to neglect their signposts would surely be a folly.

CONCLUSION

In this paper I have traced the history of the SSK and discussed the main themes of its two principal schools. I have also discussed a number of places where the SSK produces narratives that sound much like what one would expect from an economic analysis of science. In addition, I have surveyed a number of attempts to explicitly apply economics to science, some by philosophers and some by economists. Finally, I examined the problem of reflexivity and discussed some of the philosophical difficulties it raises for the SSK. I argued that such problems will also be encountered by anyone pursuing the economics of science, and that while such problems are not so great as to deter entry, they need to be recognized and that there is much to learn from the literature on the SSK. In conclusion I would like to note that while the ESK (and the SSK for that matter) represents a great opportunity for those interested in economic methodology and the history of economic thought, this is not an inquiry that will come easy for most economists.

In one respect of course, the economics of science is an inquiry that *should* come easy for economists. As stated above, it seems to be an obvious next step for 'the economics of': a veritable gold mine for the Chicago and Virginia schools. There are a myriad of opportunities, not only for Becker-type economics and public choice theory, but also game theory, principal-agent analysis, incentive compatibility, and so on. For years economists have undermined and delegitimized the self-righteousness of politicians – 'you are not acting in the societal or national interest, but in your own self-interest' – now the same argument can be applied to scientists. Economics is also a discipline of 'unintended consequences' and 'invisible hands'; it is not necessary that politicians or scientists be motivated by 'higher' values in order to have the emergence of results that are consistent with such higher values. For economists, unlike for most others in modern intellectual life, the ubiquitousness of narrow self-interest in science or elsewhere, does not necessarily initiate a wringing of hands or lamentations about lost utopias; it only initiates a conversation about proper prices, compatible incentives and binding constraints.

Despite all of this, I suspect that the economics of science will be quite difficult for most economists to accept, even those normally engaged in economic methodology. The main problem is that most economists are epistemologically quite traditional. For most economists there is simply a world 'out there' and good science represents that world accurately. Such good science has something to do with letting the data decide between theories – confirmation for some authors and falsification for others – but 'the facts' in either case. This method is, for most economists, the way real science proceeds; it is the way that economics should proceed, and whatever problems the discipline has are generally a result of failing to follow this method of good science. Such views by economists are worlds away from the 'negotiation over facticity' and 'the social construction of nature' that pervades much of the SSK. There are many places in the SSK where the *a priori* distinction between the 'natural' and the 'social' is totally abandoned; the world is socially co-produced by a variety of actants (agents who may or may not be humans) who engage in negotiation over its construction; in one recent case these actants included the scallops of St Brieuc Bay who actively negotiated with researchers regarding their anchorage.[36] Such stories involving negotiation by non-human actors are unusual of course, even in the more radical versions of the SSK, but the point is simply that almost anything is up for grabs. Not all of the SSK has such a post-modernist flair, but much of it does, and such argumentation cannot be ruled out of court from the general perspective of the social construction of knowledge. As I argued above, any attempt at an ESK will require economists to take the arguments and the insights of the SSK quite seriously. This is what should be done and the prospects are exciting; it will not be easy for many economists to do.

ACKNOWLEDGEMENTS

I would like to thank Roger Backhouse, Larry Boland, Bruce Caldwell, Bob Coats, Uskali Mäki, Philip Mirowski, Warren Samuels, Paul Wendt, James Wible and Nancy Wulwick for comments on an earlier draft of this paper.

NOTES

1 The work of Merton is often characterized as a reaction to the Marxist external histories of science written during the 1920s and early 1930s (Hessen 1931, for example). The Marxist influence on the early development of the sociology of science is emphasized by Collins and Restivo (1983) and Bunge (1991, 1992).

2 It should be noted that Kuhn did not stress an ontological interpretation of this collectively constructed world. For Kuhn, unlike for some of the more radical among the recent sociologists of scientific knowledge, there always seems to be something 'out there' that is fixed and unchanged as the scientific paradigm, and thus what the scientists 'see', is transformed. When the 'duck' in the optical illusion is transformed into a 'rabbit' before our very eyes, the paper and the marks on it remain unchanged. As Kuhn stated in 'Second thoughts on paradigms':

> In *The Structure of Scientific Revolutions*, particularly chap. 10, I repeatedly insist that members of different scientific communities live in different worlds and that scientific revolutions change the world in which a scientist works. I would not want to say that members of different communities are presented with different data by *the same stimuli*. Notice, however, that that change does not make phrases like 'a different world' inappropriate. The given world, whether everyday or scientific, is not a world of stimuli.
>
> (Kuhn 1977: 309, n. 18, italics added)

3 Other philosophical influences on the SSK include L. Wittgenstein's theory of the social/conventional nature of language use and the under-determination thesis associated with the work of Pierre Duhem and W. V. O. Quine. See Bloor (1983) for a discussion of Wittgenstein in this context, and Roth (1987, esp. ch. 7) for a discussion of Duhem and Quine.

4 The literature on the strong programme (and the literature critical of it) has become rather extensive over the last two decades. Major contributions to the strong programme include: Barnes (1977, 1982), Bloor (1976, 1983) and Shapin (1982). The relationship between the strong programme and the discipline of economics is considered in Coats (1984) and Mäki (1992, 1993).

5 This of course is not to suggest that the notion of 'cause' is a philosophically

simple notion. It is only to say that the strong programme does not make any original contribution to, nor does it try to make any contribution to, the philosophical discourse on the nature of causality.

6 As Mäki states in his recent discussion of the sociology of scientific knowledge and economics:

> It is believed by Bloor that all this amounts to applying the principles of science to science itself. The program is radically pro-science. More particularly, it is based on a naturalistic methodological monism. Unlike some other currents in the sociology of science, Bloor's programme is strongly anti-hermeneutic.
>
> (Mäki 1992: 68)

7 One causality question that has been raised regarding the strong programme is the programme's failure to specify any explicit causal mechanism connecting social conditions with the formation of beliefs (see Roth 1987: chapter 8 on 'Voodoo Epistemology'). Another criticism has been that if there actually is an implicit causal mechanism in the strong programme, it is a type of 'social behaviorism' that is replete with its own philosophical problems (see Slezak 1991).

8 This alternative school – if 'school' is even the appropriate term – is fairly amorphous. It would include such disparate views as the micro-sociological approach of Collins (1985), the ethnographic approaches of Latour and Woolgar (1986), Latour (1987) and Knorr-Cetina (1981), and the 'science as practice' approach of Galison (1987) and Pickering (1984). The McMullin (1992) and Pickering (1992a) volumes contain an excellent collection of papers discussing the similarities and differences among these various views. The papers in the McMullin (1988) volume relate the literature on the SSK to other recent developments in the philosophy of science.

9 At this point the only self-consciously constructivist study in economics is Weintraub (1991). In addition to this major work on the (constructivist) history of stability theory in general equilibrium, Weintraub has also discussed the constructivist viewpoint in a number of shorter papers (1992, for example).

10 For the remainder of this paper 'economic' will mean 'microeconomic'; given our desire to explain the behaviour of individual scientist agents (or the intended and/or unintended consequences of their individual actions) macroeconomics does not seem to be particularly useful. The 'economics' that will be considered as a possible candidate for studying the economics of science is the standard neoclassical theory of rational choice. As the discussion proceeds it will become obvious that certain strains of neoclassical economics, particularly public choice theory and the microeconomics of the older Chicago school, are better suited to this particular task than other strains such as mathematical general equilibrium theory, but only neoclassical microeconomics (in some form) will be considered.

It is also important to note that 'economics' will not include Marxian economics. While this exclusion will probably not surprise (nor bother) most economists, it is important with respect to the SSK. As stated above (see note 1) there is a Marxist tradition in the SSK (or at least the sociology of science) and for Marxist social theory there is little difference between a 'sociological' explanation and an 'economic' explanation; the economic mode of production determines the social relations. Thus, in this general sense, all of the literature on the Marxist sociology of science is actually on the economics of science broadly defined. Economic explanations are so much associated with Marxian

D. WADE HANDS

explanations in the SSK that authors often reject 'economic' explanations altogether on the basis of the failure of Marxian explanations. For example, the sociologist of science Karin Knorr-Cetina uses the following argument to reject 'economic theory' as a source of inspiration for the study of science.

> In economic theory, the notion of capital is linked to the idea of exploitation defined in terms of the appropriation of surplus value, and to the corresponding concepts of class structure and alienation. Without adequate conception of exploitation and class structure, the capitalist model loses its most distinctive characteristics. But how are we to conceive of exploitation and class structure in scientific fields said to be ruled by capitalist market mechanisms?
>
> (Knorr-Cetina 1982: 108)

Needless to say, this critique of the economic approach to science has nothing to say (one way or another) about the application of neoclassical microeconomics to the study of science.

11 This distinction, the distinction between sociologists that employ economic-type arguments in the study of science and those who explicitly apply economics to science, is of course arbitrary. The distinction requires the assignment of an unobservable methodological intent to the various authors involved. Nonetheless, while it is not without problems, the distinction can be, and will be, usefully maintained in what follows.

12 It should be noted that while Latour and Woolgar's market for credibility sounds very much like the standard neoclassical characterization of a competitive market, their story is, in many respects, quite anti-neoclassical. In the standard neoclassical story of the market the actions of individuals are primary and explanatory – the behaviour of the market prices and quantities is 'explained by' and 'determined by' the actions of (ontologically primary) individual agents – and not the other way around. Latour and Woolgar are not this individualist, nor are they as linear in their explanatory thinking. For Latour and Woolgar there is a market, and there are credibility-seeking actions by individual scientists, but the latter does not necessarily cause the former. This process involves the market, the scientific culture, the individual scientists, the instruments and a myriad of other factors: all wrapped up in an amalgamated and mutually co-determining ensemble of interdependent influences. Latour and Woolgar certainly have a market in their story, but it is not the standard neoclassical market. As they say:

> This consideration is important because we certainly do not wish to propose a model of behaviour in which individuals make calculations in order to maximize their profits. This would be Benthamian economics. The question of the calculation of resources, of maximization, and of the presence of the individual are so constantly moving that we cannot take them as our points of departure.
>
> (1986: 232, n. 10)

13 Two other sociological studies of science that draw on economic analogies are Bourdieu (1975) and Hagstrom (1965). Both of these studies are discussed in Latour and Woolgar (1986) and Knorr-Cetina (1982). Bourdieu is also discussed in Mäki (1992).

14 The warning in note 11 is still applicable of course.

15 The CQ in this quotation refers to Constructing Quarks (1984).

100

16 Pickering clarifies the role of 'reality' in his response to Roth and Barrett: Pickering (1990).

17 This paper on SSK is not the place to attempt a general discussion of the relationship between economics and folk psychology. See Rosenberg (1988: ch. 2; 1992) or Hands (1993: ch. 11) for a more general discussion.

18 One of Pickering's comments is particularly telling in this regard. In his response to Roth and Barrett (R&B) he emphasizes the multifaceted and interdisciplinary nature of his work by saying: 'My model of practice – as expressed in CQ and as elaborated here – seems to me to touch upon the legitimate interests of a variety of disciplines: sociology, certainly, but also psychology, cognitive science, anthropology and even, to return to R&B, philosophy' (1990: 709).

19 I am indebted to James Wible for drawing my attention to this important early contribution of C. S. Peirce. Wible (1992b) discusses Peirce's paper in detail along with the work of Nicholas Rescher, a contemporary philosopher of science influenced by Peirce (see Rescher 1976). Peirce's work has recently appeared in the philosophical discussion surrounding the SSK (see Delaney 1992) and it is also examined in Kevin Hoover's contribution to the current volume.

20 Wible compares Peirce's paper to a 1965 paper by Frederic Scherer on the utility approach to research project evaluation, and finds the resemblance to be 'striking and uncanny' (1992b: 14).

21 The last paragraph of Pierce's paper is very interesting in this respect.

> It is to be remarked that the theory here given rests on the supposition that the object of the investigation is the ascertainment of truth. When an investigation is made for the purpose of attaining personal distinction, the economics of the problem are entirely different. But that seems to be well enough understood by those engaged in that sort of investigation.
>
> (Peirce 1967: 648)

22 Also see Delaney (1992) and Wible (1992b).

23 Radnitzky defines 'cost–benefit analysis' (CBA) quite broadly. He mentions neoclassical economics, Gary Becker in particular, but he also considers the approach to be general enough that it includes Austrian economics as well as Popper's 'situational analysis' approach to social science (see Hands 1985, for a discussion of the latter). On the question of the generality of CBA, Radnitzky says:

> Man is a chooser. *All* rational choices involve the weighing up of benefits and costs. Hence, CBA is the core of the economic approach/ rational-problem-solving approach.
>
> (1986: 127)

24 This question is also considered in Ghiselin (1987).

25 See Bartley (1984, 1990) and Radnitzky and Bartley (1987).

26 In addition to the Boland paper in this volume and the works cited therein, the argument is presented in detail in Hands (1993: ch. 11) and also in Wible (1992b).

27 Tullock's comments on the sociology of science are worth quoting:

> I have, for example, read *The Structure of Scientific Revolutions* with profit and pleasure, but it will not be further mentioned in this book. This is not because I regard it as unimportant but because it deals with different problems. In this it is typical. Most of the recent work has

been done by people whose basic orientation is sociological, while mine is economic. There is no necessary conflict between sociologists and economists, but they do ask rather different questions.

(1966: v-vi)

28 Reprinted as chapter 5 of Boland (1989).

29 The examples I have discussed do not exhaust those in the literature. Mäki (1992) discusses papers by Earl (1983) and Loasby (1986), and Diamond (1992) provides a survey of much of this literature as well as the somewhat related literature on natural science's contribution to economic growth.

30 One of the reasons the strong programme has borne the brunt of the criticism is simply that it has been around longer than most of the constructivist approaches. A second reason for the strong programme being targeted is its rather narrow and carefully delineated methodological stance; critics generally prefer targets that are clearly defined and stable over those that are ill-defined and constantly moving.

31 I am intentionally giving a rather relativist reading of the reflexivity problem here. It is certainly the case that many authors in the SSK, particularly those in the strong programme, do not see reflexivity as having such relativist implications. For these authors, science proceeds by induction; the fact that most natural scientists act consistently with their social interests, has nothing to say about the legitimacy of the sociology of science that correctly applies the inductive method to the study of the behaviour of those in the scientific community. The strong programme would admit that the sociologist's tools could be turned on the sociology of science itself; that is just not what they are interested in doing; they are interested in studying natural science.

32 The exchange between Collins and Yearley (1992a, 1992b), Callon and Latour (1992) and Woolgar (1992) offers various interpretations of the reflexivity problem. Collins and Yearley (1992a) discuss three approaches to the problem: 'reflexivity' (associated with Woolgar and others), the 'French School' (associated with Latour and others), and 'discourse analysis' (associated with Mulkay and others). Of these three approaches, the only one that is (thus far) directly relevant to economics is discourse analysis; McCloskey's much discussed work on the 'rhetoric of economics' (1985) is basically discourse analysis applied to economics. The Woolgar edited volume (1988) contains a number of different papers that wrestle with the reflexivity problem in a variety of ways.

33 Perhaps the most radical reading of reflexivity is given by Steve Woolgar. For Woolgar the primary reason for doing the SSK is its potential for radical reflexivity: the 'potential for reevaluating fundamental assumptions of modern thought' (Woolgar 1991: 25). According to Woolgar, the SSK has failed to fully exploit the radical implications of its reflexivity – or perhaps failed because it has not fully exploited the radical implications of reflexivity. For him:

the radical potential of SSK has been compromised because it has failed to interrogate its concept of hardness and thereby failed to exploit the analytic ambivalence at the heart of its practice. With a few encouraging recent exceptions, SSK has not addressed its own dependence upon conventions of realist discourse. Consequently, SSK fails to address the issue of representation at a fundamental level; it seems set to become another exemplification of the relativist–constructivist formula rather than an occasion for questioning the idea of applying formulae altogether.

(Woolgar 1991: 43)

34 A similar reflexivity occurs in Grubel and Boland (1986) where mathematical economists are characterized as an interest group that attempts to capture economic rents for its members, and also in chapter 2 of Mayer (1993) where the economics profession's emphasis on formalism is attributed to market failure within the discipline.

35 This latter approach seems to be suggested in that last line of the above quotation from Wible, and it is also one of the main themes in Philip Mirowski's contribution to this volume.

36 See Collins and Yearley (1992a) and Callon and Latour (1992).

BIBLIOGRAPHY

Barnes, B. (1977) *Interests and the Growth of Knowledge*, London: Routledge & Kegan Paul.

Barnes, B. (1982) *T. S. Kuhn and Social Science*, New York: Columbia University Press.

Bartley, W. W. III (1984) *The Retreat to Commitment*, 2nd edn. La Salle, IL: Open Court.

Bartley, W. W. III (1990) *Unfathomed Knowledge, Unmeasured Wealth*, La Salle, IL: Open Court.

Bloor, D. (1976) *Knowledge and Social Imagery*, London: Routledge & Kegan Paul.

Bloor, D. (1983) *Wittgenstein: A Social Theory of Knowledge*, New York: Columbia University Press.

Bloor, D. (1984) 'The strengths of the strong programme', in J. R. Brown (ed.), *Scientific Rationality: The Sociological Turn*, Boston: D. Reidel, pp. 75–94.

Boland, L. A. (1971) 'Methodology as an exercise in economic analysis', *Philosophy of Science* 38: 105–17.

Boland, L. A. (1989) *The Methodology of Economic Model Building*, London: Routledge.

Bourdieu, P. (1975) 'The specificity of the scientific field and the social conditions of the progress of reason', *Social Science Information* 14: 19–47.

Bunge, M. (1991) 'A critical examination of the new sociology of science: Part I', *Philosophy of the Social Sciences* 21: 524–60.

Bunge, M. (1992) 'A critical examination of the new sociology of science: Part II', *Philosophy of the Social Sciences* 22: 46–76.

Callon, M. and Latour, B. (1992) 'Don't throw the baby out with the bath school! A reply to Collins and Yearley', in A. Pickering (ed.), *Science as Practice and Culture*, Chicago: University of Chicago Press, pp. 343–68.

Coats, A. W. (1984) 'The sociology of knowledge and the history of economics', *Research in the History of Economic Thought and Methodology* 2: 211–34.

Collins, H. (1985) *Changing Order: Replication and Induction in Scientific Practice*, Los Angeles: Sage.

Collins, H. and Yearley, S. (1992a) 'Epistemological chicken', in A. Pickering (ed.), *Science as Practice and Culture*, Chicago: University of Chicago Press, pp. 301–26.

Collins, H. and Yearley, S. (1992b) 'Journey into space', in A. Pickering (ed.), *Science as Practice and Culture*, Chicago: University of Chicago Press, pp. 369–89.

Collins, R. and Restivo, S. (1983) 'Development, diversity, and conflict in the sociology of science', *The Sociological Quarterly* 24: 185–200.

Delaney, C. F. (1992) 'Peirce on the social and historical dimensions of science', in

E. McMullin (ed.), *The Social Dimensions of Science*, Notre Dame, IN: University of Notre Dame Press, pp. 27–46.

Diamond, A. D. (1988) 'Science as a rational enterprise', *Theory and Decision* 24: 147–67.

Diamond, A. M. (1992) 'Is there an economics of science?' Paper presented at the American Economics Association meetings in Anaheim, CA, January 1993.

Earl, P. E. (1983) 'A behavioral theory of economists' behavior', in A. S. Eichner (ed.), *Why Economics is Not Yet a Science*, London: Macmillan.

Feyerabend, P. K. (1975) *Against Method*, London: New Left Books.

Fuller, S. (1990) 'They shoot dead horses, don't they? Philosophical fear and sociological loathing in St. Louis', *Social Studies of Science* 20: 664–81.

Galison, P. (1987) *How Experiments End*, Chicago: University of Chicago Press.

Ghiselin, M. T. (1987) 'The economics of scientific discovery', in G. Radnitzky and P. Bernholz (eds), *Economic Imperialism: The Economic Approach Applied Outside the Field of Economics*, New York: Paragon House, pp. 271–82.

Grubel, H. G. and Boland, L. A. (1986) 'On the efficient use of mathematics in economics: some theory, facts and results of an opinion survey', *Kyklos* 39: 419–42.

Hagstrom, W. O. (1965) *The Scientific Community*, New York: Basic Books.

Hands, D. W. (1985) 'Karl Popper and economic methodology: a new look', *Economics and Philosophy* 1: 83–99.

Hands, D. W. (1993) *Testing, Rationality, and Progress: Essays on the Popperian Tradition in Economic Methodology*, Lanham, MD: Rowman & Littlefield.

Haskell, T. L. (1984) 'Professionalism *versus* capitalism: R. H. Tawney, Emile Durkheim, and C. S. Peirce on the disinterestedness of professional communities', in T. L. Haskell (ed.), *The Authority of Experts: Studies in History and Theory*, Bloomington, IN: Indiana University Press, pp. 180–225.

Hessen, B. (1931) 'The social and economic roots of Newton's "Principia" ', in N. Bukharin *et al.*, *Science at the Crossroads* (2nd edn, 1971), London: Frank Cass & Co., pp. 151–212.

Kitcher, P. (1992) 'Authority, deference, and the role of individual reason', in E. McMullin (ed.), *The Social Dimensions of Science*, Notre Dame, IN: University of Notre Dame Press, pp. 244–71.

Knorr-Cetina, K. (1981) *The Manufacture of Knowledge: An Essay on the Constructivist and Contextual Nature of Science*, Oxford: Pergamon Press.

Knorr-Cetina, K. (1982) 'Scientific communities or transepistemic arenas of research? A critique of quasi-economic models of science', *Social Studies of Science* 12: 101–30.

Knorr-Cetina, K. (1991) 'Epistemic cultures: forms of reason in science', *History of Political Economy* 23: 105–22.

Kuhn, T. S. (1962) *The Structure of Scientific Revolutions*, Chicago: University of Chicago Press.

Kuhn, T. S. (1977) 'Second thoughts on paradigms', in T. S. Kuhn, *The Essential Tension: Selected Studies in Scientific Tradition and Change*, Chicago: University of Chicago Press, pp. 293–319.

Latour, B. (1987) *Science in Action: How to Follow Scientists and Engineers Through Society*, Cambridge, MA: Harvard University Press.

Latour, B. (1992) 'One more turn after the social turn', in E. McMullin (ed.), *The Social Dimensions of Science*, Notre Dame, IN: University of Notre Dame Press, pp. 272–94.

Latour, B. and Woolgar, S. (1986) *Laboratory Life: The Construction of Scientific Facts*, 2nd edn., Princeton: Princeton University Press.

Loasby, B. J. (1986) 'Public science and public knowledge', *Research in the History of Economic Thought and Methodology* 4: 211–28.

McCloskey, D. N. (1985) *The Rhetoric of Economics*, Madison, WI: University of Wisconsin Press.

McMullin, E. (ed.) (1988) *Construction and Constraint: The Shaping of Scientific Rationality*, Notre Dame, IN: University of Notre Dame Press.

McMullin, E. (ed.) (1992) *The Social Dimensions of Science*, Notre Dame, IN: University of Notre Dame Press.

Mäki, U. (1992) 'Social conditioning in economics', in N. de Marchi (ed.), *Post-Popperian Methodology of Economics: Recovering Practice*, Boston: Kluwer, pp. 65–104.

Mäki, U. (1993) 'Social theories of science and the fate of institutionalism in economics', in U. Mäki, B. Gustafsson and C. Knudsen (eds), *Rationality, Institutions, and Economic Methodology*, London: Routledge.

Mayer, T. (1993) *Truth versus Precision in Economics*, Aldershot: Edward Elgar.

Merton, R. K. (1970) *Science, Technology and Society in Seventeenth-Century England*, New York: Harper & Row [originally published in 1938].

Mulkay, M. (1982) 'Sociology of science in the West', *Current Sociology* 28: 1–116.

Peirce, C. S. (1967) 'Note on the theory of the economy of research', *Operations Research* 15: 642–8 [originally published in 1879].

Pickering, A. (1984) *Constructing Quarks: A Sociological History of Particle Physics*, Chicago: University of Chicago Press.

Pickering, A. (1990) 'Knowledge, practice and mere construction', *Social Studies of Science* 20: 682–729.

Pickering, A. (ed.) (1992a) *Science as Practice and Culture*, Chicago: University of Chicago Press.

Pickering, A. (1992b) 'From science as knowledge to science as practice', in A. Pickering (ed.), *Science as Practice and Culture*, Chicago: University of Chicago Press, pp. 1–26.

Radnitzky, G. (1986) 'Towards an "Economic" theory of methodology', *Methodology and Science* 19: 124–47.

Radnitzky, G. (1987a) 'Cost–benefit thinking in the methodology of research: the "economic approach" applied to key problems of the philosophy of science', in G. Radnitzky and P. Bernholz (eds), *Economic Imperialism: The Economic Approach Applied Outside the Field of Economics*, New York: Paragon House, pp. 283–331.

Radnitzky, G. (1987b) 'The "Economic" approach to the philosophy of science', *The British Journal for the Philosophy of Science* 38: 159–79.

Radnitzky, G. (1989) 'Falsificationism looked at from an "economic" point of view', in K. Gavroglu, Y. Goudaroulis and P. Nicolacopoulos (eds), *Imre Lakatos and Theories of Scientific Change*, Boston: Kluwer, pp. 383–95.

Radnitzky, G. and Bartley, W. W. III (eds) (1987) *Evolutionary Epistemology, Rationality, and the Sociology of Knowledge*, La Salle, IL: Open Court.

Rescher, N. (1976) 'Peirce and the economy of research', *Philosophy of Science* 43: 71–98.

Rosenberg, A. (1985) 'Methodology, theory and the philosophy of science', *Pacific Philosophical Quarterly* 66: 377–93.

Rosenberg, A. (1988) *Philosophy of Social Science*, Boulder, CO: Westview Press.

Rosenberg, A. (1992) *Economics – Mathematical Politics or Science of Diminishing Returns?* Chicago: University of Chicago Press.

Roth, P. A. (1987) *Meaning and Method in the Social Sciences*, Ithaca, NY: Cornell University Press.

Roth, P. A. and Barrett, R. (1990) 'Deconstructing quarks', *Social Studies of Science* 20: 579–632.

Shapin, S. (1982) 'History of science and its sociological reconstructions', *History of Science* 20: 157–211.

Slezak, P. (1991) 'Bloor's bluff: behaviorism and the strong programme', *International Studies in the Philosophy of Science* 5: 241–56.

Tullock, G. (1966) *The Organization of Inquiry*, Durham, NC: Duke University Press.

Weintraub, E. R. (1991) *Stabilizing Dynamics: Constructing Economic Knowledge*, Cambridge: Cambridge University Press.

Weintraub, E. R. (1992) 'Commentary by E. Roy Weintraub', in N. de Marchi (ed.), *Post-Popperian Methodology of Economics: Recovering Practice*, Boston: Kluwer, pp. 355–73.

Wible, J. R. (1991) 'Maximization, replication and the economic rationality of positive economic science', *Review of Political Economy* 3: 164–86.

Wible, J. R. (1992a) 'Fraud in science: an economic approach', *Philosophy of the Social Sciences* 22: 5–27.

Wible, J. R. (1992b) 'Cost–benefit analysis, utility theory, and economic aspects of Peirce's and Popper's conceptions of science', manuscript.

Woolgar, S. (1981) 'Interests and explanations in the social study of science', *Social Studies of Science* 11: 365–94.

Woolgar, S. (ed.) (1988) *Knowledge and Reflexivity*, London: Sage.

Woolgar, S. (1991) 'The turn to technology in social studies of science', *Science, Technology and Human Values* 16: 20–50.

Woolgar, S. (1992) 'Some remarks about positionism: a reply to Collins and Yearley', in A. Pickering (ed.), *Science as Practice and Culture*, Chicago: University of Chicago Press, pp. 327–42.

Part II

FALSIFICATIONISM: FOR AND AGAINST

6

WHY I AM NOT A CONSTRUCTIVIST

Confessions of an unrepentant Popperian

Mark Blaug

They say that there are only three writers on economic methodology who espouse Popperianism, Terence Hutchison, Johannes Klant and myself. Who are *they*? Well, Bruce Caldwell has said it (1991a: 64; 1993: xix) and so has Wade Hands (1993: 23). I am not sure they are right but until others come forward, I for one declare myself to be an unrepentant Popperian. I know that Popper enjoys little esteem among professional philosophers of science. I know that there are real weaknesses and perhaps even damaging flaws in his position. But I still believe that much of the letter and certainly all of the spirit of this theory come closer to my deep-held convictions about the methodology of economics than any other philosophical thinker.

Mind you, this is a view shared by many other writers on the methodology of economics. Caldwell (1991a) is a Popperian of sorts; so are Lawrence Boland (1992), Roger Backhouse (1985: 2–6) and Hands (1993: 149–51); it is just that their reading of Popper differs from mine.[1] Still, our common philosophical sympathies are much greater than our differences. That is not true of Daniel Hausman (1989, 1992), whose hostility to Popper is unqualified, nor of Deborah Redman (1991). Alexander Rosenberg's (1983, 1992) position is more difficult to categorize but a fair description might be one that once was close to Popper but which is now far away from it. The same might be said of Neil de Marchi (1992a: 3–9). Likewise, Roy Weintraub (1988, 1991) has travelled from great sympathy with Popperianism all the way to constructivism and anti-foundationalism.

PRESCRIPTION VERSUS DESCRIPTION

The tension between the methodology of science and the history of science runs like a thread through the literature on the philosophy of science. There are those who believe like Popper that it is impossible to study the history of science without some notion, however crude, of the difference between science and non-science, resting ultimately on the idea that the development of 'science' is marked by 'progress', whereas 'non-science' evolves without becoming 'better' in any sense of the term. In other words, we must start with methodological views derived from general epistemic principles and, since there is no certainty of knowledge, such views are frankly normative. Nevertheless, having derived our methodological norms, we then examine the history of science to check whether our norms are practised by at least some scientists and hopefully by most. If that expectation is refuted by historical studies, we ought to be prepared to abandon our norms just as we ought to abandon scientific theories that are repeatedly contradicted by empirical evidence.

Every critic of Popper either begins or ends up by rejecting this priority assigned to prescriptive methodology. Instead, they insist on the priority of practice, that is, on starting descriptively with the history of science in the hope of eventually inferring some general methodological principles from their historical investigations. Just as Karl Popper is the patron saint of the first view, Thomas Kuhn is the patron saint of the second: the over-whelming importance of the workaday world of the practising scientist has of course been emphasized by countless historians of science but Thomas Kuhn's *Structure of Scientific Revolutions* (1962) placed it for the first time at the centre of the philosophy of science.

To a Popperian, the Kuhnian position is simply 'the inductive fallacy' all over again. How can we study the history of science without some prior notions of what is science and indeed what is good or bad science? There is simply too much science to imagine that we can study it without some principles of selection and what are these principles if not method-ology? Just as we cannot study 'data' *per se* without some preconceptions, we cannot study history without some ideas of what is or is not significant in the past.

To a Kuhnian, however, the Popperian position smacks of philosophical arrogance. Why worry about methodological canons that might never have been obeyed by practising scientists and if we think they can be obeyed, surely we must have derived that conviction from historical knowledge of past developments in science?

The tension between these two views can never be decisively resolved but it can be minimized by openly confronting it. One of the attractive features of the philosophy of science of Imre Lakatos, a disciple of Popper, is the way in which he separated normative principles of methodology from positive questions about the history of science. He argued that what he called 'scientific research programmes' inevitably evolve as time passes and that their evolution is either characterized by 'progress', because amendments of the programme involve the discovery of 'novel facts', or by 'degeneration' because the amendments are merely *ad hoc*.[2] Having expounded the idea of progress in science, he then conjectured that pro-gressive scientific research programmes succeed by gaining scientific adher-ents, whereas degenerating scientific research programmes steadily lose the support of fellow scientists. This is a conjecture about the history of science and he invited us to test his conjecture by what he called a 'historiographical scientific research programme'. No wonder then that the last fifteen years have seen a number of case studies in the history of physics, chemistry, biology and economics to test the validity of Lakatos's conjecture.[3] In my view, 'the jury is still out on this one', at least as far as economics is concerned, but clearly if I did not believe that the jury will one day return a favourable verdict, I would not be inclined to advocate Popperianism in any form, and Lakatos is clearly Popperian. This is an issue to which we will return.

Suffice it to say that some extreme critics of Popper deny that 'falsificationism' (which we have not yet defined) can ever be applied to either natural or social science, so that in their view all talk of Popperianism in economics is simply nonsense (Redman 1991: viii, 119). But Popper (1983: xxvi–xxx; also Caldwell 1991a: 67) himself gave twenty examples of the use of falsificationism in the history of science 'chosen at random' and elsewhere I have furnished numerous examples from economics (Blaug 1992: xv–xvi). None of this implies that all economists are falsificationists but it does imply that many are and that some even practice what they preach. As for those who do not, the argument so far recommends that they should try harder.

POPPERIANISM PRO AND CON

Popper begins with the logical asymmetry between 'verification' and 'falsification': nothing can ever be exhaustively verified but a single falsification suffices; in popular parlance, you cannot 'prove' anything but you can certainly 'disprove' some things. Unfortunately, the so-called Duhem–Quine thesis demonstrates that it is just as difficult conclusively to falsify a hypothesis as to verify it because every test of a hypothesis is in fact a joint test of the hypothesis in question, the quality of the data, the measuring instruments employed and a host of auxiliary hypotheses stipulating the particular circumstances of the test; in the event of a falsification, we can never assign guilt unambiguously to the central hypothesis under examination.

Popper was perfectly aware of the Duhem–Quine thesis and hence laid down a number of methodological norms or conventions to prevent endless 'immunizing stratagems' to safeguard a refuted theory. These twenty or so norms (see Blaug 1992: 19) boil down to the idea that refuted theories may be amended to avoid future refutations but only if these amendments increase the empirical content of the theory, that is, render it more falsifiable or testable. Thus, 'science', according to Popper, involves not just propositions that are at least in principle falsifiable but also propositions that are increasingly strengthened by being more severely tested. A falsifiable theory forbids some possible events or observations. Thus, we should ask of theories, not what observations are consonant with them, because that is a test all too easy to pass, but rather what events would never be observed if this or that theory were true. If there are no such events, the theory is either trivial or tautological.

Alas, in the course of amending our refuted theories in the effort to increase their empirical content, we never know when to stop and when to go on. There is no golden rule that will tell us when finally to abandon a frequently refuted and constantly amended theory but clearly it will depend on our past record in that area of endeavour and on the availability of alternative theories. But to infer present practice from past experience is to make use of induction as a form of gaining knowledge and Popper not only denies the validity of inductive logic but even denies the possibility of making inductions; induction for him is simply a psychological illusion.

The problem is aggravated if we face not one refuted but amended theory but two or more such theories, in which case we must compare them for their respective 'degrees of verisimilitude' as Popper calls it, that is, the extent to which each of them has so far resisted falsification. But Popper has reluctantly agreed with his critics that it is not possible to quantify the 'verisimilitude' of theories (see Hands 1993: 126–30), so that we are thrown back in the last analysis on a qualitative judgement in comparing rival theories. Here, as elsewhere in his writings, Popper's attack on inductivism and all notions of 'supporting' evidence for theories is so extreme as to cast some doubt on the entire enterprise of falsificationism.

The point is well made by Popper's claims on behalf of 'situational analysis'. 'Situational analysis' is his label for what we in economics know as the concept of rational choice, that is, the view that economic behaviour is simply individual maximizing behaviour subject to constraints, and indeed Popper declared 'situational analysis' to be a generalization of the method of economic analysis. What is surprising is that (1) he claimed it to be the one legitimate mode of explanation in the social sciences; (2) he admitted it was false as a universal law of economic behaviour but nevertheless insisted that it should be retained as an unexamined 'metaphysical' principle; and (3) he virtually implied, without quite saying so, that it should be retained because it had shown itself to be fruitful in the past, particularly in economics. Now, (1) contradicts his 'unity of science' thesis, the doctrine that there is no difference in the structure of explanation in the natural and the social sciences and that all sciences must validate their theories in the same way. Likewise, (2) actually endorses one particular 'immunizing stratagem' in the face of refutations of rationality, namely to retain the rationality principle and to place the blame for refutation on, say, the constraints, the limited information available to agents or any other feature of the test in question. Finally, and most damningly, (3) provides an inductive argument on behalf of rational choice models of behaviour –

they have worked well in the past and so might work well in the future – which flies in the face of everything that Popper has ever written on induction.

When I first encountered this argument in Hands (1985, 1993), I pooh-poohed it (Blaug 1985) on the grounds that it appeared in *The Poverty of Historicism* (1957) which even Popper described as one of his 'stodgiest pieces of writing'. But since then it has been restated and somewhat ampli-fied by Popper as late as 1976 (see Caldwell 1991a: 72–81) and there is no doubt that at best it lies uneasily in the corpus of his writings and at worst it blatantly contradicts it. I think that a very good defence can be made of individual rationality as a principle of explanation in economics, particularly if we recognize that what is usually involved in economic analysis is 'means-rationality', not 'belief-rationality' or 'end-rationality', that is, consistency of actions and not necessarily perfectly informed 'reasonable' actions (Hamlin 1986: 12–59). There is also no doubt that it has in some sense 'worked' well in microeconomics. Nevertheless, there is mounting evidence that economic behaviour frequently violates any and all senses of 'ration-ality' (Blaug 1992: 232–3) and it has even been argued that economic expla-nations involving rational choice are a species of 'folk psychology', explaining actions in terms of beliefs and desires, variables that cannot be measured independently of the actual choices we want to predict, so that these are not genuine explanations at all (Rosenberg 1992: ch. 5). Be that as it may, it remains true that Popper's defence of rational choice models will not wash in terms of the methodology of falsificationism.

Some lukewarm Popperians like Caldwell (1991a: 84–6), Boland (1992) and Hands (1993: 118–19, 185–8), after reviewing these and other objec-tions to Popper's methodological views, come down in the end in favour of 'critical rationalism' as the essence of Popper. By this they mean the view that scientific theories are open to criticism in all respects and particu-larly with reference to the problems which the theories in question were designed to solve. In *Postscript to the Logic of Scientific Discovery* (1983), Popper makes it clear that he now subscribes to this interpretation of his views: 'the real linchpin of my thought', he writes, 'is fallibilism and the critical approach' (quoted by Caldwell 1991a: 81; see also Hands 1993: 160–1). By 'fallibilism' Popper means the denial that there is ever certainty of knowledge or even truth: all knowledge is conjectural and provisional in that it has not yet been shown to be false; by 'the critical approach' he means what we have just labelled 'critical rationalism'.

The principal weakness of 'critical rationalism' is that it appears to be a prescriptive methodology with very little content: 'it is a view', as Wade Hands (1993: 118) puts it, 'that may be palatable by virtue of its blandness – the epistemological analog of the ethical mandate to "live the good life".' Of course, all theories must be criticized and all scientists ought to, and perhaps even do, tolerate criticism of all sorts, but criticism of what? Apart

113

from pointing out internal inconsistencies we can only criticize with meta-theoretical criteria and, according to critical rationalism, the only one we are encouraged to employ is that of assessing a theory's ability to solve the problems it has set itself.[4] This is something but it is not very much and if this is what falsificationism amounts to in the end, we can say with perfect confidence 'we are all falsificationists now'. Having trimmed the lion's claw and pulled his teeth out as well, all with the aid and assistance of the lion himself, there is not much left to argue about.

CLARIFYING LAKATOS

Many surveys of recent developments in the philosophy of science have depicted the ideas of Imre Lakatos as a dilution or even a betrayal of Popper. In fact, Lakatos is 80 per cent Popper and 20 per cent Kuhn and virtually everything that Lakatos ever said is found in Popper in some form or another. However, Lakatos's starting point, the idea that theories provide scientists with 'research programmes' which guide their daily practice, is Kuhnian. Being research programmes they consist at their centre of metaphysical beliefs, 'paradigms' *Weltanschauungen*, or Schumpeterian 'visions', and a set of pragmatic do's and don'ts for tackling the problems selected for analysis. The idea that science cannot dispense with meta-physical beliefs, but that these are kept so to speak 'out of sight', is pure Popper. Surrounding the 'hard core' of empirically irrefutable propositions ('nature is uniform is space and time'; 'everything has a cause'; 'there always are equilibrium solutions for every economic problem', etc.) is 'the protective belt' of scientific theories, which always have predictive implications about the slice of reality with which they are concerned. Apart from ironic language, this is again just straight Popper.

The next idea is also no more than what is found in Popper, namely that theories can only be appraised *ex post* and that such appraisals are never final because theories are in a constant dynamic process of change as the appearance of anomalies leads to continuous adjustments in the theoretical framework. This is what Popper called 'assessing the degree of corroboration' of a theory, which he defined as 'an evaluating report of past performance' (quoted in Blaug 1992: 25). As I said earlier, Popper agreed in the end that such reports were only qualitative in character and at best involved ordinal comparisons between two or more theories.

Now comes the one genuinely new element in Lakatos that is not in Popper and which has therefore attracted more controversy than any other feature of his methodology. For Popper, the evaluating report of a theory consisted of 'the state (at a certain time *t*) of the critical discussion of a theory, with respect to the way it solves its problems; its degree of test-ability; the severity of the tests it has undergone; and the way it has stood up to these tests' (quoted in Blaug, ibid.). All this is reduced by Lakatos to the stipulation that theories or rather 'scientific research programmes' must be altered in the face of anomalies in such a way to continually generate 'novel facts'. Programmes that do this are dubbed 'progressive' and programmes that fail to do so, that simply produce *ad hoc* excuses whenever a refutation is encountered, are dubbed 'degenerating'. Such assessments are never final in the sense that nothing prevents a programme that has been degenerating for some time from becoming progressive again.

Even this characteristic Lakatosian idea was first formulated by Popper who, as we noted earlier, restricted the use of face-saving, refutation-avoiding theoretical adjustments to those that had 'excess empirical content', meaning 'new and testable consequences' or 'the prediction of phenomena which have not so far been observed' (quoted in Hands 1993: 86). Lakatos at first adopted this latter definition of 'novel facts' but his followers soon weakened it to 'facts', possibly known already as isolated instances, that are logically implied by a theory; in other words, what is ruled out are known facts which are employed to construct a theory and then subsequently employed to support that theory (see Hands 1993: 43–4). Thus, what we have in Lakatos is an even stricter empirical criterion for 'progress of knowledge' in science than we get in Popper but it is nevertheless extremely Popperian in flavour.

But there is nothing in Popper to warrant Lakatos's idea of a 'historiographical research programme' that would attempt to falsify his own 'methodology of scientific research programmes'. That is, Lakatos conjectured that the history of science could be almost wholly written in terms of the 'rational' preference of scientists for progressive over degenerating scientific research programmes. He called a history so written 'internal history of science' and everything else 'external history', suggesting that the latter should be assigned to footnotes on the grounds that it would be swamped by the 'internal history' in the text (Blaug 1992: 35–6). This claim is so strong that even so careful a reader as Hands (1993: 61–2; also Caldwell 1991a: 101) simply could not credit that Lakatos had conflated historical appraisal and psychological acceptance. Of course, he did not because he did not confuse, as Hands does, the assertion that a research programme is progressive because it accurately predicts novel facts and the assertion that it is 'rational' for scientists to subscribe to that programme because it is progressive. The first is an issue in the methodology of scientific research programmes. The second is an issue in the methodology of historiographical research programmes. The twain may meet but they need not.

THEORETICAL AND EMPIRICAL PROGRESS

All this is no doubt very interesting but the question remains: is there any economics that looks at all like the practice of falsificationism? Do economists ever modify their theories so as to predict novel facts? Is there actual empirical progress in economics? These are questions we can no longer postpone addressing.

We may begin our discussion by drawing upon a list of twelve basic innovations in economics between the years 1900 and 1965, selected on the basis of the personal judgements of the editors of a study of *Advances in the Social Sciences, 1900–1980* in the light of the advice of a number of prominent economists (Deutsch *et al.* 1986: 374–84). The twelve innovations in economics are a subset of sixty-two basic innovations in social science over the same period, the point of the entire exercise being to demonstrate that there are such things as social science innovations and achievements that are almost as clearly defined and as operational in character as technological innovations. The innovations in economics are:

1 Theory and measurement of social inequalities (Pareto, Gini).
2 Role of 'innovations' in socioeconomic change (Schumpeter, Ogburn, Usher, Schmookler).
3 Social welfare functions in politics and economics (Pigou, Arrow).
4 Economic propensities, employment and fiscal policy (Keynes).
5 Game theory (Neumann and Morgenstern).
6 Economics of monopolistic competition (Chamberlin, Robinson).
7 National income accounting (Kuznets, Clark, UN Statistical Office).
8 Input–output analysis (Leontief).
9 Linear programming (Kantorovich, Souto, Dantzig, Dorfman).
10 Theories of economic development (Rosenstein-Rodan, Prebisch, Nurkse, Lewis, Myrdal, Hirschman, Harrod, Domar, Chenery).
11 Econometrics (Tinbergen, Samuelson, Malinvaud).
12 Computer simulation of economic systems (Klein, Orcutt).

Apart from certain oddities (growth theory as a subset of 'economic development'? Samuelson as an econometrician?), the list nevertheless raises the interesting question: in what sense were any of these advances in economics? It seems clear that progress in economics can be usefully distinguished as either theoretical progress or empirical progress or both. By 'theoretical progress' I shall mean what Lakatos termed 'heuristic progress': greater precision in the definition of terms and relationships between terms and, in general, improved conceptual clarity, frequently accompanied by analytical innovations; in short, sharper tools for that 'box of tools' that Joan Robinson once told us is economic theory. A perfect example is the Monopolistic Competition Revolution of the 1930s to which we owe our current conceptions of different market structures and forms of non-price competition, as well as the definition of such analytical terms as 'marginal revenue' and 'the tangency solution'.

'Theoretical progress' may or may not be accompanied by 'empirical progress', which is a much more elusive idea than theoretical progress. By 'empirical progress' I shall mean a deeper grasp of the inner springs of economic behaviour and hence of the operations of the economic system. It is always difficult to know whether we have actually achieved such a deeper grasp and this is one reason and perhaps the major reason why economists (like most scientists) are literally obsessed with the idea of making economic predictions. Every predictive implication of our economic theories that is borne out by events strengthens our confidence that we have caught a glimpse of how the economy actually works.[5]

This is why every 'explanation' in economics must ultimately be checked by a successful prediction. Indeed, 'explanation' is simply 'prediction' written backwards which is the so-called 'symmetry thesis' of the despised logical positivists (see Blaug 1992: 5–10). But the symmetry thesis is a much older idea and as Alfred Marshall (1961: 773) said: 'the explanation of the past and prediction of the future are not different operations, but the same worked in opposite directions, the one from effect to cause, the other from cause to effect'.

I have so far carefully avoided the use of the word 'understanding' because those who are fond of employing it do so to suggest that there is a way of gaining economic knowledge that does not involve the making of predictions. This may be accompanied by an appeal to the trappings of *Verstehen* doctrine (see Blaug 1992: 43–4; Hutchison 1992: 39–45) but more typically it denotes nothing more than the proposition that there is theoretical progress in economics without any empirical progress.[6]

This notion of theoretical progress, of greater understanding of economic relationships not necessarily accompanied by an improved ability to predict the economic consequences of our behaviour, is almost mystical and difficult to pin down. Nevertheless, it is that irrepressible conviction that we see further which seizes hold of us every time we read an older author. We can just *see* when we read *The Wealth of Nations* that Adam Smith could never figure out how ground rent could be price-determined in one sense and price-determining in another sense; at moments like this we have absolutely no doubt that there has been theoretical progress in economics. Nevertheless, as soon as we ask ourselves whether the scarcity of land in central London is responsible for high cinema prices in the West End, we realize that questions about theoretical progress are simplicity itself compared to questions about empirical progress. Can we actually explain the determination of ground rent in urban areas better than Adam Smith did?

I know of no economist who denies that the history of economic thought, right up to yesterday, is characterized by theoretical progress. Many economists, however, doubt that there has been significant empirical progress, at least in the intermediate run of the last half-century, although not many are willing to go as far as Rosenberg (1992: 224–7) in denying that economics is any better today at predicting the likely outcome of specific events than it was at the time of Adam Smith. In assessing the predictive power of economics, we need to distinguish between forecasting the magnitude of a change in the endogenous variables of our models in response to a change in one or more of the exogenous variables and predictions of the algebraic sign of such a change; what Rosenberg (ibid.: 69, 103–5) calls the difference between precise and 'generic' predictions or what Samuelson called the difference between the 'quantitative' and the 'qualitative calculus' (see Blaug 1992: 88).[7] The predictive track record of economics is much better in the realm of qualitative than quantitative predictions, which explains why those who are cynical about the scientific status of economics emphasize the claims of 'real sciences', like quantum mechanics and biochemistry, to make accurate quantitative forecasts of the significant effects with which they are concerned.

Although it is tempting to deny the need for quantitative predictions in economics, so as to defend the subject against its denigrators, it is questionable whether qualitative predictability suffices for a subject like ours. Economics has always claimed to provide guidance to policy-makers and all the great economists were clearly inspired to study economics in order to 'do good'. Since the Second World War, this aspiration to be useful has been satisfied by the wholesale invasion of governments by economists; America has her presidentially appointed Council of Economic Advisors and Britain's Chancellor of the Exchequer now has his 'seven wise men'. The price that must be paid for all this glory, however, is a measure of intellectual prostitution, the tendency to oversell the subject, and a general inclination to ignore empirical evidence that is unfavourable to whatever case economists may be making at the time (see Blaug 1992: 31–3).

Suffice it to say that the policy relevance of economics poses a little difficulty for those who are inclined to pour cold water on the predictive content of the subject.[8] One way out of the difficulty, of course, is to pour scorn on the eagerness of economists to have practical influence and instead to uphold the importance and significance of strictly abstract economic theory. It is no accident that Joseph Schumpeter (1983: 125), a great admirer of Walrasian general equilibrium theory, decried the tendency of Keynes's *General Theory* to 'sublimate practical issues into scientific ones'. But if we accept and even welcome the inevitable policy implications of much even seemingly abstract economic theory, we cannot at the same time pour cold water on the predictability of economic theories, sometimes going so far as to suggest that the very character of economics as a social science necessarily robs the subject of any capacity to predict. The late George Shackle (1972) was not at all unwilling to go down that road but others were inclined to come half-way and then inconsistently to halt. I have shown elsewhere (Blaug 1990: 107–18) that John Hicks managed throughout his long and influential career to uphold the view that economics is 'a discipline, not a science' because economic theories can neither be verified nor falsified, and at the same time to insist that all theory should be 'the servant of applied economics'. To hold that economic theory should be practically useful and yet to deny that there is any place for empirical testing in economics is, surely, inconsistent. I endorse the Marshallian dictum that economics is 'not a body of concrete truth, but an engine for the discovery of concrete truth', but if economics is to be practically relevant, there must be some concrete truths in which we can place confidence. In that case, economics is not just a discipline, a technique of thinking; it is a substantive subject, rich in empirical content.

To give up the policy-relevance of economics is to reduce the study of economics to the aim of satisfying 'idle curiosity' (see Rosenberg 1992: 49–55). It is noteworthy that those who, like Frank Hahn, extol 'understanding' rather than 'explanation' as the goal of economics are not reluctant to recommend quite specific policies to governments.[9]

ADVANCES IN ECONOMICS

Let us return to the question before us: is there empirical progress in economics? Consider our list of twelve twentieth-century innovations in economics. Which fits the bill? Take the first, the theory and measurement of social inequalities, associated with the names of three Italians, Pareto, Lorenz and Gini, and in more recent years, Simon Kuznets and Anthony Atkinson. This is an area in which theoretical progress has marched hand-in-hand with empirical progress. Despite continuous controversy between statistical and economic interpretations of income distribution, certain 'stylized facts' – such as the tendency for the upper tail of incomes to follow the Pareto 'law' and the Kuznets U-curve between income inequality and the growth of GNP (see Shorrocks 1987) – have gradually emerged from the melee. Similarly, that neglected stepchild of classical and neoclassical economics, technical progress, has slowly come into its own in the last half-century but it may be argued that the Schumpeterian research programme, despite a welter of empirical studies of process and product innovations, continues to be understudied and understaffed (see Freeman 1987). There has been undoubted progress in this area but, nevertheless, few would claim that economics has yet acquired a firm background of testable knowledge about technical change. That may be due, of course, not to the limitations of economics but to the intrinsic difficulties of the subject of innovations.

The next advance is 'social welfare functions'. Needless to say, there can be no empirical progress in the area of welfare economics. Thus the 'new' welfare economics of Hicks, Kaldor and Lerner developed in the 1930s, refining and extending the concept of Pareto-optimality into that of 'potential Pareto-improvements', is a perfect example of what we have called 'theoretical progress'. Progress in this area has a peculiar significance for a subject like economics, which was virtually borne as a justification for or at least defence of the rule of competition in a regime of private property.

However, once having expounded a rigorous Invisible Hand Theorem, it is difficult to resist the temptation to argue that what is true under perfect competition is almost true in the imperfectly competitive real world. In this way theoretical progress in welfare economics easily spills over into the appraisal of empirical progress in positive economics.

That brings us to the fourth advance in economics 1900–65, namely, Keynesian macroeconomics, which we may couple with no. 7 in the list, namely national income accounting. The Keynesian-cum-national-income-accounting Revolution is one of the stellar examples in twentieth-century economic thought of a scientific research programme that succeeded because it predicted 'novel facts' à la Lakatos, chiefly the greater-than-unity spending multiplier, and the excess of the average over the marginal propensity to consume, etc. I have elsewhere given an account of the Keynesian Revolution in these terms (Blaug 1990: 88–106; 1992: 203–5), so will say no more about it here. However, for those who want to find evidence of empirical progress in economics, the story of the Keynesian Revolution, and that of the Monetarist Counter-revolution too, will provide ample raw material.

The same is true of the Monopolistic Competition Revolution. A textbook like Scherer and Ross (1990) is simply littered with empirical evidence in the field of industrial organization, evidence which grew naturally out of the apparatus forged by Chamberlin and Robinson.

I have passed over the fifth item in the list, namely, game theory. After a promising start in the 1940s, game theory in economics died out in the 1950s, possibly because Neumann and Morgenstern failed to carry their research programme much beyond that of two-person, zero-sum games and zero-sum games have little relevance to most economic transactions. But game theory showed a remarkable recovery in the 1970s and today it constitutes virtually the dominant mathematical technique of economic theorists. As such it deserves a separate discussion and I will return to it below.

Next we have input–output analysis. It is an avowedly empirical method for writing down the production structure of a disaggregated economy but its practical fruits are still limited (see Leontief 1987). Oddly enough, despite its promise of immense practical usefulness, its greatest impact may well be theoretical: it has spawned and encouraged a vast outpouring of linear production models, which have figured heavily in both price theory and growth theory in the 1960s and 1970s (Burmeister 1987).

Linear programming, no. 9 in the list, like input–output analysis was promoted as an empirical technique but, unlike input–output analysis, its aim was to develop optimal solutions to a particular class of allocation problems. As presented by Dorfman et al. (1958), it promised to revolutionize economics by showing that the same set of mathematical tools underlies what at first appear to be widely disparate branches of economics,

such as production economics, input–output analysis, capital theo
eral equilibrium economics, welfare economics and even game the
the fullness of time, it is probably fair to say that these expectatio
theoretical revolution around the theme of 'linearities' have faded
without leaving much trace in economics. Linear programming is still .nere
of course but in management science rather than in economics departments.
It certainly was marked by theoretical progress but it is not at all clear
that much was learned from it in the way of substantive insights into the
workings of the economic system.

We leave to one side 'theories of economic development'. We have
certainly clarified our thinking about economic development over the last
forty years but how much we have really imbibed about the springs of
economic development is a nice question. Even the famous conflict between
import-competing and export-led economic development strategies has
been left up in the air; some have even questioned whether there is such
a thing as 'development economics' or whether the entire field is just
economics applied to the Third World. Nevertheless, there is little doubt
that the literature in development economics is rich in accurate descriptions
of the development problem and in that sense there has been empirical
progress even in this helter-skelter branch of economics.

I say nothing about econometrics, which cannot by the nature of the
case exhibit empirical progress.[10] As for 'computer simulation of economic
systems', it must be said we have invested a great deal in a hammer that
can still crack nothing bigger than walnuts. The present-day achievements
in GNP forecasting in industrialized countries may be summed up as
capable of doing just a little better than crude extrapolations for about a
year or two ahead as for predicting the precise moment of a downturn or
upturn in the economy, we still go wrong as often as we go right (see
Blaug 1992: 246–7).

We may now conclude that there has been much theoretical progress in
twentieth-century economics. There has also been some empirical progress
which, however limited, is perhaps enough as to refute the extreme pessimists. It would be salutory to set out precisely what we now know about
economic behaviour that we did not know in, say, 1900 or 1920 in such
fields as labour economics, development economics, industrial organization, urban and regional economics, environmental economics, international trade, public finance, financial analysis and public choice theory,
but I am not equal to the task. But can anyone doubt that the list of
substantive knowledge gained in these fields over the last century would
be a long one?

DESCRIPTIVE ADEQUACY

But what has all this to do with Popper and Lakatos? Simply this: there is no doubt in anyone's mind that this history of economic thought is characterized by theoretical progress but, as we have seen, there is doubt in the mind of some commentators that it is also characterized by empirical progress. If that doubt were to be sustained, the irrelevance of either Popper or Lakatos to economics would be self-evident. Both rely in their philosophy of science on the notion of 'progress of knowledge' and by that they did not mean a more precise definition of terms or a greater clarification of concepts; they meant an enhanced explanatory power over the domain of the subject as manifested by more accurate or more general predictions. In short, we do need to establish the fact of empirical progress in economics if Popper and Lakatos are to be given any credence at all. Given some credence, it still remains an open question whether they are 'descriptively adequate' in respect of economics, that is, whether much or little economics conforms to their precepts.

One might have thought that the Rosenberg thesis that there has been little empirical progress in economics over the last two centuries is a minority viewpoint but others too have implied almost as much. Wade Hands (1993: 44–7, 61–3), for example, scoffs at what he called the 'novel-fact fetishism' of Lakatosians; having originally denied that the Keynesian Revolution involved any 'novel facts', he now concedes that the spending multiplier qualifies but expresses amazement that anybody should bother to make the point. 'The history of great economics', he opines,

> is so much more than a list of ... novel facts. Smith's invisible hand, the Ricardian law of comparative advantage, Walrasian notions of multi-market interdependence, Marshallian welfare economics; and the basic Keynesian notion of output and employment being determined by aggregate demand: these things constitute *great* economics; such theoretical developments have given us insight and scientific *progress*, not an occasional fact.

It is clear that Hands is thinking chiefly of theoretical progress in economics and particularly so in microeconomics. It is not surprising that he couples this view with an explicit denial of the Symmetry Thesis:

> Neoclassical microeconomic theory is primarily an explanatory rather than a predictive theory, while Keynesian macroeconomic theory is primarily a predictive rather than an explanatory theory. ... My argument is simply that the so-called symmetry thesis – the proposition that explanation and prediction are merely two sides of the same coin – does not apply in economics. What makes neoclassical macro-economics most successful is its apparent ability to provide acceptable explanations of microeconomics phenomena. On the other hand,

what makes [made] Keynesian macroeconomics most successful is [was] its ability to predict the behaviour of aggregated economic variables.

(ibid.: 147)[11]

The notion that microeconomics explains without predicting, if accepted, would merely demonstrate that the explanations of microeconomics are what Hempel once called 'pseudo-explanations', that is, accounts that ascribe some unfamiliar event to a perfectly familiar generalization but which are more accurately labelled *post hoc* rationalizations'. No doubt the term 'explanation' can be employed in a variety of meanings (Blaug 1992: 7–12) but once we deny the Symmetry Thesis, statements that some branch of economics manages mysteriously to explain without predicting says little more than that the accounts in question satisfy our desire for ingenuity. Everything can be 'explained' if we place no restrictions on what we mean by 'explanation'.

Even so, the thesis that modern microeconomics is 'primarily an explanatory rather than a predictive theory' is profoundly misleading. No doubt, the scope of microeconomics is wide but it is not too much to say that it all boils down to the prediction that demand curves generally, although not necessarily, slope downwards, while supply curves generally, although not necessarily, slope upwards. There has been a simply vast amount of empirical research on demand relationships going back to the 1920s, but accelerating in the 1950s and 1960s, all of which confirms the central prediction of the modern theory of consumer behaviour: demand curves are almost certain to have negative slopes and indeed no unequivocal case of a positively sloped demand curve has ever been found (Blaug 1992: 140–7).

There has always been some question, however, about cost curves with some studies reporting constant short-run marginal cost curves for firms, while others report L-shaped long-run average cost curves (Walters 1963: 48–9; also Eatwell 1987: 165–6). In any case, orthodox theory purports to deduce short-run and long-run U-shaped cost curves from the physical characteristics of production functions, coupled with axioms of profit maximization, and if cost curves are not in fact U-shaped, this is empirical progress if ever one needed examples of it. There is also the mountain of evidence in the public finance literature on the effects of taxes and subsidies; finally, there are the results of quasi-controlled social experiments concerned with the effects of negative income taxes. In short there is really no warrant for the belief that, while macroeconomics makes refutable predictions, microeconomics makes no predictions at all.

GENERAL EQUILIBRIUM THEORY

But what makes so astute an observer of the contemporary economic scene as Wade Hands arrive at this strange contrast between micro- and macroeconomics? It is simply the conviction that modern microeconomics is dominated by general equilibrium (GE) theory and GE theory, almost everyone agrees, has no empirical content (see Rosenberg 1992: ch. 7).

In a brilliant historical study, Ingrao and Israel (1990) trace the evolution of GE theory from the pioneering efforts of Léon Walras and Vilfredo Pareto through the mathematical rebirth of the theory by Karl Schlesinger, Abraham Wald and John von Neumann in the 1920s to its emergence in the 1930s as mainstream orthodox economics in the writings of Oskar Lange, John Hicks and Paul Samuelson; this led eventually to its post-war formulation in the works of Kenneth Arrow, Gerard Debreu and Frank Hahn.

The theory was concerned from its very outset with three aspects of multi-market equilibrium: can it exist? is that existence unique? and is it both locally and globally stable? The theory has some success with respect to the first of these questions: the possible existence of general equilibrium in all markets of the economy can be demonstrated under very general assumptions, some of which, however, do not accord with any observed economic systems (such as the absence of money or any other kind of exchange intermediary, the absence of inventories or buffer stocks held by agents, and the existence of forward markets for all goods). Moreover, as far as uniqueness and global stability are concerned, the assumptions required to obtain definite results are so restrictive and patently *ad hoc* as to be unacceptable even to those deeply enamoured of GE theory. In short, after a century of more or less endless refinements of the central core of GE theory, an exercise which has absorbed some of the best brains in twentieth-century economics, the theory is unable to shed any substantive light on how multi-market equilibrium is actually attained, not just in a real-world decentralized market economy but even in the toytown economies beloved of GE theorists. Thus, GE theory has proved in the fullness of time to be a cul-de-sac: it has no empirical content and never will have empirical content; even regarded charitably as a research programme in 'social mathematics', it stands condemned as an almost total failure.

This is not to say that highly aggregated computable GE *models* (such as IS–LM) are pointless or that a GE formulation of an economic problem may not prove illuminating, but simply that Walrasian GE *theory* – the notion that the problem of multi-market equilibrium may be usefully studied as analogous to solving a set of simultaneous equations – has turned out to be an utterly sterile innovation.

Mirowski (1989) has described the whole of neoclassical economics ever since the marginal revolution of the 1870s as suffering from physics-envy, going so far as to claim that it was deliberately modelled on the energy concept of mid-nineteenth-century physics. But Walras's heroes were Newton and Laplace, not Clausius, Joule and Helmholtz, and despite some superficial references to 'energetics' in the writings of such second-generation marginalists as Pareto and Irving Fisher,[12] what constantly inspired the advocates of GE theory down to modern times was not 'scientism' but the goal of complete mathematization. GE theorists suffered from mathematics-envy rather than physics-envy: physicists faced with GE theorizing would never have dreamed of spending a whole generation on purely mathematical proofs of existence, uniqueness and stability of a virtual economic system (McCloskey 1991).

Roy Weintraub (1988) once provided a convenient defence of the empirical emptiness of GE theory by claiming that it constituted the Lakatosian 'hard core' of neoclassical economics and 'hard cores' are non-empirical by definition. In other words, the empirical implications of GE theory are to be found in 'the protective belt' comprising the neoclassical theory of consumer behaviour, the neoclassical theory of the firm, human capital theory, search theory, etc. But apart from the curious suggestion that Marshallian partial equilibrium theory is not neoclassical economics (see Salanti 1991), this interpretation of the meaning of GE theory simply endorses the half-century spent ironing out every mathematical wrinkle of Walras's research programme. More recently, Weintraub (1991) has conceded that the stability component of GE theory has run into the sand, a conclusion which he shrugged off by a hermeneutical interpretation of the concept of stability: 'stability is a feature of our models, not of the world'. It is hardly surprising that this account is accompanied by a bold statement of the constructivist credo – 'Knowledge is constructed, not found' (Weintraub 1991: 3, 109). Let us just say that this stance is extraordinarily convenient to those, like Weintraub, who are convinced of the utility of GE theory despite its unsolved puzzles.

Weintraub (1989) naturally has no use for prescriptive methodology and insists on the priority of intellectual history over all methodological preoccupations. Nevertheless, his account of GE theory never views the evolution of that theory in its historical context. Ingrao and Israel (1990) document the hostility which greeted GE theory in the years before the First World War and its virtual demise by the 1920s; as late as 1923 it was only the bowdlerized version of Walras laid down in Cassel's *Theory of Social Economy* (1918) that conveyed the essence of GE theory to English-speaking economists. By 1930, I doubt that Walras was read by more than a handful of economists in the world. It was Hicks, Hotelling, Lange and Samuelson who were responsible in the golden decade of the 1930s in bringing about the revival of GE theory. We all know Hicks's *Value and Capital* (1939) but Lange's *On the Economic Theory of Socialism* (1936–7) was probably more influential in teaching a whole generation the meaning of GE theory. Lange of course treated GE theory, as Walras did; namely, as a realistic although abstract description of price-setting in any market economy, whether capitalist or socialist (Blaug 1992: 164). It is noteworthy that by the time we get to Debreu's *Theory of Value* (1959) or Arrow and Hahn's *General Competitive Analysis* (1971), GE theory is explicitly defended as a purely formal presentation of the determination of economic equilibrium in a decentralized competitive economy, having no practical value except as a benchmark with which to evaluate other hypothetical models of the economy (Blaug 1992: 162–8).[13] All this is a remarkable paradigm-switch in the interpretation of GE theory over a period lasting only twenty-five years.

DESCRIPTIVELY ADEQUATE?

Enough has now been said to suggest that Popperian philosophy of science is not capable of describing all 'progress of knowledge' in modern economics but it does describe some of it. It is not patently inadequate as a description of what passed for economics in the twentieth century. It is perfectly possible to tell the story of macroeconomics since Keynes as driven by empirical evidence. Not everyone would agree (see Blaug 1992: 205) but why should they? As Caldwell (1991a: 68) remarks, testing a methodology against the history of a discipline is almost as problematic as testing a theory against the empirical evidence for it. Nevertheless, the anti-Popperians have been much too eager to assert the descriptive inadequacy of falsificationism in economics. They have retreated in respect of macroeconomics but they still delight in depicting the history of microeconomics as propelled forward by the sheer desire for theoretical refinements. And to be sure it is not easy to pinpoint striking examples of falsificationist practice in twentieth-century microeconomics. It is easy, however, to provide examples where the steady accumulation of empirical evidence about microeconomic phenomena has gradually, albeit not dramatically, altered our theoretical conceptions and even entire analytical structures. It seemed only yesterday that constancy of the capital–output ratio and constancy of the relative share of wages in national income were regarded as 'stylized facts' of the history of industrialized economics over the last century that any adequate theory of economic growth would have to account for; today we are inclined to deny that these are facts at all (Blaug 1990: 194–5). Similarly all the great economists of the past, including Keynes, were convinced that the rate of profit on capital showed a downward tendency over the very long run despite technical progress and yet we now think that long-run rate of profits is trendless (ibid.). Likewise, the Keynesian concept of sticky wages and prices, 'fix price' rather than 'flex price' markets to use Hicks's language, has trickled down to labour economics: in less than a generation, the notions of implicit contracts between employers and employees, 'efficiency wages' and 'insider–outsider models' of wage determination have so undermined orthodox marginal productivity theory that it hardly survives any more except in name (Blaug 1992: 175–7).

Finally, the quantity of theory of money, in the sense of a causative influence of substantial changes in high-powered money on the level of prices, is one of the best corroborated empirical propositions in economics but the strong version of that venerable theory – the 'neutrality' of money in long-run equilibrium because absolute prices vary proportionately with the money supply – is overwhelmingly refuted by all the available evidence (see Blaug 1993).

Nevertheless, there is no dearth of theory-driven developments in modern economics that seem to resist all the adverse empirical evidence piled up against them. A notorious case in point is that of experimental evidence of 'preference reversals' or intransitivity of choices which have cast doubt on the expected utility model (Schoemaker 1982: 418–22).[14] Hausman (1992: ch. 13) has documented the endless attempts on the part of economists to explain away the phenomenon of preference reversals and in particular to avoid any appeal to psychological explanations of the phenomenon. The history of job search theory (Blinder 1989: ch. 10; Kim 1992) is another example of a process of inquiry that emphasized technical refinements in the formulation of ideas rather than the search for novel facts or corroborated predictions.

We have already referred to the story of general equilibrium theory over the last forty years, which points in the same direction, but yet another example of theory-driven development is modern game theory, or what would be better called 'interactive decision theory', which is undoubtedly the flavour of the month in economics.[15] Now, despite the need to explore the meaning of rational behaviour in situations of strategic inter-actions among economic agents, which game theory has provided, game theory to date has performed poorly on both descriptive and prescriptive grounds (Blaug 1992: 240–1). Game theory is most powerful in dealing with one-shot cooperative games in which outcomes can be expressed in money or any other one-dimensional variable. Unfortunately, much economic behaviour is basically a repeated non-cooperative game with a complex informational structure in which outcomes may not be realistically measurable in one-dimensional terms. It is well known that repeated games typically exhibit an infinity of equilibria and game theory itself gives no reasons why the players will prefer one equilibrium rather than another (Bianchi and Moulin 1991: 183–4). In consequence, game theory does not provide definite predictions of behaviour in repeated-game situations, which is to say the sort of situations with which economists have tradition-ally been concerned; for example, buying and selling in highly contestable competitive markets.

Many practising game theorists will be outraged by this conclusion (but see Fisher 1989; Kreps 1990: 6–7, 30–1, 36; O'Brien 1992: 267–8, 278; and Radner 1992: 1408–9) because they minimize the enormous gulf that exists between theoretical and empirical progress. Thus, Frank Hahn (1992a) claims that 'Game theoretic approaches have turned old Industrial Organisation writings into stone age theory'. Backhouse (1992b: 4) contrasts this view with Franklin Fisher's sceptical assessment of these developments, denying that game theory has added any testable hypotheses to what Hahn calls 'stone age theory', that is, the structure–conduct–performance approach to industrial organization. Hahn (1992b: 5) in reply expresses consternation at Backhouse's endorsement of Fisher: 'Surely Backhouse doesn't believe Fisher? All one needs to do is to read the old literature on entry prevention and contrast it with the new'. To a formalist like Hahn, progress *is* theoretical progress: pouring old wine in new bottles is what better economics is all about![16]

Much if not most game theory is normative, concerned with prescribing how rational players *should* make decisions and very little has been done to develop a descriptive theory of how people actually make decisions under a variety of conditions.[17] Like traditional economic theory, game theory has been exclusively concerned with what Herbert Simon calls 'substantive' rationality and rarely with 'procedural' rationality, that is, what players do at the neglect of the question of how they decide what to do. And just as GE theory has solved the stability-of-equilibrium problem by eliminating disequilibrium trading, game theory has likewise adopted a static approach to equilibrium convergence by simply ignoring the adjustment process through which equilibrium is achieved (Binmore 1987: 180–3; 1988: 10).[18] If anything, game theory in recent years has witnessed endless conceptual proliferation which has driven it even further away from a positive description of interactive decisions. Indeed, for all its strengths, game theory feeds the economist's addiction to formalistic modelling whatever its practical relevance. As Fisher (1989: 123) has remarked: what is wrong with modern game theory applied to industrial organization is that 'There is a strong tendency for even the best practitioners to concentrate on the analytically interesting questions rather than on the ones that really matter for the study of real-life industries'.

The main contribution of game theory has been to teach us the infinite subtleties of rational behaviour, reminding us that the standard economist's account of rationality is woefully inadequate in spelling out the implicit informational structure and learning process on which equilibrium outcomes do in fact depend (Bianchi and Moulin 1991: 194). This is theoretical progress but as to empirical progress, game theory has not so far produced a single 'novel fact'.[19]

In the light of these manifestations of 'formalism' on economics – economic theory for the sake of economy theory – one can sympathize with even the most adamant anti-Popperian when they say:

> Economists are so little involved with testing because, first, many are involved with non-empirical conceptual work. . . . Second, even those who are interested in empirical theory are also relatively uninvolved with testing (in comparison with biologists or chemists) because, given the subject matter they deal with, they do not know enough to formulate good tests or to interpret the results of tests. To test a theory requires not merely that one derives a testable prediction from the theory and a set of further statements. One must also have good reasons to regard these further statements as unproblematic in the context. . . . Testing requires knowledge and simple phenomena, so that few auxiliary theories are needed to derive predictions. Facing a complex subject matter and lacking such knowledge, economists cannot effectively test their theories. If there is a cure, it can only come as a result of acquiring better experimental techniques and more detailed knowledge. This requires methodological reform. . . but not better standards of theory assessment.
>
> (Hausman 1992: 190)

Advising economists to try harder, to practise falsificationism rather than just to preach it, will only do harm, Hausman insists, because it disguises the real problem, which is to face up to the inexactness of the science of economics and to learn to live with it.

This is the depressing advice of those who would rather defend economics, such as it is, than to criticize endlessly from the sidelines. Hands (1993: 33–4) once asked why writers like myself insisted on what he disarmingly called 'the philosophic oldspeak of falsificationism' in economics. It was, he thought, to keep economics from succumbing to 'anything goes'. The problem, he went on to say, was analogous to the old dilemma in statistical inference:

> If one wishes to avoid a type-II error (accepting a false hypothesis) at any cost, the obvious solution is simply to accept nothing. The problem is that this leaves the probability of type-I error (rejecting in true hypothesis) quite high. Strict falsificationist rules certainly keep the riffraff out of science, but they also keep most of science out of science.

Maybe, but Hands and company would open the door to any and all economics: in refusing to prescribe they end up with economics just as it is. 'Economics is what economists do', Jacob Viner once said. This ironic definition of the science of economics could well serve as the rallying cry of the anti-Popperians. 'Recovering practice' is what they call it[20] but it is not much more than accepting economics as it is, for better or for worse.

THE SCOURGE OF CONSTRUCTIVISM

Encouraging this drift towards the uncritical acceptance of the whole of modern economics, warts and all, is the new anti-modernism, anti-foundationalism, post-structuralism, hermeneutical deconstructivism, discourse analysis, radical relativism, end-of-philosophy critique, call it what you will. Leading the pack, at least in economics, is McCloskey's 'rhetoric', which comes in at least two versions, a 'thick rhetoric' in which 'Methodology' with a capital M is assailed but 'methodology' with a lower-case m is tolerated, and a 'thin' rhetoric in which methodology of any sort whatever is anathematized and everything is persuasion pure and simple (see McCloskey 1988; Rothbard 1989; Blaug 1992: xvii–xx; Rosenberg 1992: 30–44; Hands 1993: 165–6). In this way, McCloskey has his cake and eats it too and while this might be regarded as inconsistent, no doubt McCloskey would regard this demand for internal consistency as another one of those hobgoblins of Popperians with their prescriptive Methodology.

Although there are endless variations in this genre, the basic theme is always that science and literature are one and the same enterprise, that all the techniques developed for analysing literary texts can be equally applied to scientific texts, that scientific ideas are just as much social constructions as are poems and novels, and in short, that the world is nothing more than a representation of words. While there is much to be said for the rhetorical analysis of the writings of economists, the upshot of all this is to undercut the empirical aspirations of economists, to pour cold water on predictive success as a central aim of economics and, in general, to supplant the goal of causal 'explanation' by that of interpretative 'understanding' (Backhouse 1992b).[21]

Not everyone in this camp is willing to go as far as Weintraub (1991: 107–8, 109–12, 126–7) does in claiming that 'equilibrium' is a term in a Wittgensteinian language game of economists, that it is 'a feature of our models, not the world', and that 'we do not justify our theories, our research programs, on the basis of the truth of those theories, the degree to which they correspond to "the reality of the economy" as it were'. Now of course, equilibrium, its existence, its stability, are features of economic models but if we did not entertain the belief that there are definite 'correspondence rules' that relate our models to the real world, we would hardly take much interest in these models, given how crude and over-simplified they are; their logical and mathematical properties are, surely, too sophomoric to hold our attention. But we can well understand how a historian of modern GE theory, whose two books on the subject contain not so much as a single critical sentence on the Walrasian tradition, would ridicule this obsession of some economists with the empirical truthfulness of economic theory (see Weintraub 1992; Hutchison 1992: 119–22).

What is wrong with Walrasian general equilibrium theory is what is wrong with most game theory, namely, 'formalism'.[22] Now 'formalism' is not the same thing as 'formalization' or 'mathematization' because it is possible to express a theory mathematically and even axiomatically without necessarily degenerating into 'formalism', which simply means giving top priority to the formal structure of modelling irrespective of its content; it is to prefer rigour and precision to relevance, and elegance and logical coherence of analysis to practical implications; it is to make a fetish of theory and to deride a vulgar appeal to the real world. The form it takes in economics amounts to a sort of 'social mathematics': words like 'price', 'markets', 'households', 'firms', etc., suggest reference to an actual economy, but when the analysis is complete we are left with a blackboard 'model' in which 'prices' are not set by economic agents, and 'households' and 'firms' are merely fictional loci for 'preferences' and 'techniques'. It is not just that the assumptions are descriptively unrealistic but that any correspondence to the real world is sacrificed for the sake of analytical tractability. The final aim is to provide the aesthetic pleasure of a beautiful theorem, to solve academic exercises that we have constructed because they are soluble by existing analytical techniques, and not to provide substantive insights into observable behaviour.

CONCLUSIONS

I have made much of Popper and Lakatos and methodology in general but the fundamental bone of contention is not about philosophy of science as applied to economics but simply the kind of economics we are going to have. Thomas Mayer (1993) has recently published a study of *Truth versus Precision in Economics*. He eschews all discussion of formal methodology but he also denies that an invisible hand always impels economists to develop the best kind of economics; in general, he argues for an empirically oriented economics against a formalistic one. As far as I am concerned, he is on the side of the angels and his book is full of illuminating illustrations of how many modern economists have sacrificed relevance for rigour, technique for substance. While familiar with the writings of philosophers of science, Mayer derives his view of best-practice economics, not from Popper or Lakatos or Kuhn, but from a lifetime of writing about monetary economics, an eminently practical branch of economics. I feel the need, on the other hand, to support my faith in an empirical science of economics by some meta-theoretical philosophical arguments. Hence, my appeal to Popper-and-all-that. If those who dislike Popperianism will take their stand with Mayer instead, I have no quarrel with them.

NOTES

1 Hutchison (1992) of course reads Popper exactly as I do.

2 I have given a more detailed account of Lakatos in Blaug (1992: 27–37).

3 For a list of English-language case studies in economics employing the Lakatosian schema, see de Marchi in de Marchi and Blaug (1991: 29–30).

4 In fact, Popper's (1983: 24–8, 64) somewhat vague discussion of the meaning of criteral rationalism includes assessing the verisimilitude of theories by examining their empirical track record.

5 See Popper's (1983: 116–17) perceptive remarks on the role of predictions in science.

6 Thus, Frank Hahn (1992a), the M. Jourdain of economics, who preaches methodology even as he professes to despise it, reflects: 'Of course Popperians, and American Popperians in particular, ask for predictions. My own view is that they will for a very long time yet be beyond us except in very special cases. Of course, all theories contain predictions, but testing these has not yet been a conspicuous success. I do not find that depressing. If I were not confined to one page I would go on to sing the praises of "understanding"'.

7 Friedrich Hayek (1992: 103) seems to have aimed at a similar distinction when he limited economics to predictions of 'trends' or 'patterns' but he never clarified his exact meaning. See Hutchison (1981: 203–32) and Caldwell (1992).

8 This is the general theme of Terence Hutchison's (1992) recent Hennipman Lectures.

9 Frank Hahn was one of the initiators of the famous letter of 364 British economists in March 1981, criticizing the Tory government for its tight budgetary policy at a time when the economy was still in severe recession. It is difficult to see how this 'Keynesian' recommendation could emanate from a mere theoretical and entirely non-predictive 'understanding' of macroeconomic relationships.

10 However, there is the encouraging appearance in the works of David Hendry and Graham Mizon of 'encompassing' in the evaluation of dynamic econometric models (Mizon 1991), which is entirely in the spirit of Popper and Lakatos.

11 Caldwell (1991a: 68–9) has made observations similar in character to those of Hands but somewhat less specific.

12 It is worth noting that Mirowski's astonishing and provocative book is in some sense totally ahistorical in that little attention is paid to the date of pronouncements; even less attention is paid to precisely what is being said, and key figures like Menger, Marshall and Wicksell are simply exempted from the central argument. This is the more curious in that the author proclaims the superiority of intellectual history over methodological concerns (see Walker 1991, Hoover 1991 and de Marchi 1992b, all of whom make this point).

13 How the fairytale portrait of economic life that is modern GE theory could ever serve as a benchmark to evaluate other economic models is of course difficult to say: even markets and trade at actual prices are excluded by definition in GE theory (see the brilliant, scathing analysis by Clower and Howitt 1993).

14 This by the way, reveals the fundamental flaw in Ludwig von Mises's 'praxeology': the notion that purposive choice as a Kantian 'a priori synthetic proposition' is more than sufficient to account for negatively inclined demand curves. This ignores the fact that a number of a posteriori auxiliary propositions are also required, such as transitivity or consistency of choices (see Blaug 1992: 77–8). To this day, this failure to recognize the limited power of a priori synthetic propositions to generate substantive implications for economic

behaviour characterizes neo-Austrian writings in defence of von Mises (Huppe 1989: 202–5).

15 As Rubinstein (1990: xi) has said: 'Many economists describe the fifties as the era of *general equilibrium*, the sixties as the era of *growth* and the seventies as the era of *economics of information*. The eighties are the years in which economics has been revolutionized by *game theory.*'

16 Tony Lawson (1992: 2) completely misconstrues Hahn's position when he ascribes his view to the influence of what he calls 'positivism'! 'Positivism, whatever else this much abused term implies, denotes a basic concern with the empirical predictability of scientific statements, and empirical predictability is the last thing that a general equilibrium theorist like Hahn would welcome.' As Hutchison (1992: 54–5, 119–50) has quite rightly observed, the term 'positivism' has become 'a kind of dustbin into which anything considered objectionable is summarily swept'.

17 However, some experimental work has been carried out, particularly in respect of the Prisoner's Dilemma game (see Rapoport 1987; see also Smith *et al.* 1991: 201–4, 212, 223–4).

18 This is of course only one of the many similarities and points of contact between GE theory and game theory. The existence of a general equilibrium was claimed by Arrow and Debreu in 1954 to be an n-person generalization of the von Neumann–Morgenstern solution to a two-person, zero-sum non-cooperative game. In 1963, Debreu and Scarf proved the existence and convergence of the Edgeworthian 'core' containing competitive equilibria by means of cooperative game theory.

19 It is interesting to note that Howard Raiffa, co-author of the pioneering text, *Games and Decisions* (1957), is troubled to this day about the prescriptive–descriptive ambivalence of game-theoretic equilibria (Raiffa 1992: 174–5; see also 209–10).

20 This is the subtitle of Neil de Marchi's recent book, *Post-Popperian Methodology of Economics* (1992a).

21 Even Marxists have succumbed to this new craze. In Resnick and Wolff (1987) everything is 'over-determined' and self-reflective; they even argue that Marx himself believed that 'anything goes'.

22 Although I have much sympathy with Woo's (1986) attack on formalization in economics, I am not convinced by his 'growth of knowledge' model of the development of formalization in science and he seems to me to overemphasize the role of mathematics in the formalization process.

BIBLIOGRAPHY

Backhouse, R. (1985) *A History of Modern Economic Analysis*, Oxford: Basil Blackwell.

Backhouse, R. (1992a) 'Should we ignore methodology?', *Royal Economic Society Newsletter* 78: 4–5.

Backhouse, R. (1992b) 'Why methodology matters. A reply to Weintraub', *Methodus* 4(2): 53–7.

Bianchi, M. and Moulin, H. (1991) 'Strategic interactions in economics: the game theoretic alternative', in de Marchi and Blaug (1991) pp. 179–96.

Binmore, K. (1987) 'Modelling rational players, part I', *Economics and Philosophy* 3(2): 179–214.

Binmore, K. (1988) 'Modelling rational players, part II', *Economics and Philosophy* 4(1): 9–55.

Blaug, M. (1985) 'Comment on D. Wade Hands, Karl Popper and economic methodology: a new look', *Economics and Philosophy* 1(2): 286–8. Also in Caldwell (1993) vol. 3: 29–31.

Blaug, M. (1990) *Economic Theories, True or False? Essays in the History and Methodology of Economics*, Aldershot: Edward Elgar.

Blaug, M. (1992) *The Methodology of Economics*, 2nd edn. Cambridge: Cambridge University Press.

Blaug, M. (1993) 'Is the quantity theory of money true?', in K. D. Hoover and S. M. Sheffrin (eds), *Monetarism and the Methodology of Economics*, Aldershot: Edward Elgar.

Blinder, A. S. (1989) *Macroeconomics Under Debate*, New York: Harvester Wheatsheaf.

Boland, L. A. (1992) 'Understanding the Popperian legacy in economics: a review essay', in W. J. Samuels (ed.), *Research in the History of Economic Thought and Methodology*, vol. 9, Greenwich, CO: JAI Press.

Burmeister, E. (1987) 'Linear models', in J. Eatwell, M. Milgate and P. Newman (eds), *The Palgrave Dictionary of Economics*, London: Macmillan, vol. 3: 202–3.

Caldwell, B. J. (1991a) 'Clarifying Popper', *Journal of Economic Literature* 29: 1–33. Also in Caldwell (1993) vol. 3: 60–92.

Caldwell, B. J. (1991b) 'The methodology of scientific research programmes in economics: criticisms and conjectures', in G. K. Shaw (ed.), *Economics, Culture and Education*, Aldershot: Edward Elgar, pp. 95–107. Also in Caldwell (1993) vol. 3: 199–211.

Caldwell, B. J. (1992) 'Hayek the falsificationist? A refutation', in W. J. Samuels (ed.), *Research in the History of Economic Thought and Methodology*, vol. 10, Greenwich, CO: JAI Press.

Caldwell, B. J. (1993) 'Introduction', in B. J. Caldwell (ed.), *The Philosophy and Methodology of Economics*, 3 vols, Aldershot: Edward Elgar.

Clower, R. W. and Howitt, P. (1993) 'Foundation of economics', *Collected Essays of Robert W. Clower*, Aldershot: Edward Elgar.

De Marchi, N. (ed.) (1992a) *Post-Popperian Methodology of Economics, Recovering Practice*, Boston: Kluwer.

De Marchi, N. (1992b) 'Review of *More Heat Than Light*, Philip Mirowski', *Economics and Philosophy* 8(1): 163–71.

De Marchi, N. and Blaug, M. (eds) (1991) *Appraising Economic Theories. Studies in the Methodology of Research Programmes*, Aldershot: Edward Elgar.

Deutsch, K. W., Markovits, A. S. and Platt, J. (eds) (1986) *Advances in the Social Sciences 1900–1980: What, Who, Where, How?* Cambridge, MA: University Press of America.

Dorfman, R., Samuelson, P. A. and Solow, R. (1958) *Linear Programming and Economic Analysis*, New York: McGraw-Hill.

Eatwell, J. (1987) 'Returns to scale', in J. Eatwell, M. Milgate and P. Newman (eds), *The New Palgrave Dictionary of Economics*, London: Macmillan, vol. 4: 165–6.

Fisher, F. (1989) 'Games economists play: a noncooperative view', *Rand Journal of Economics* 20(1): 113–24.

Freeman, C. (1987) 'Innovations', in J. Eatwell, M. Milgate and P. Newman (eds), *The Palgrave Dictionary of Economics*, London: Macmillan, vol. 2: 858–60.

Hahn, F. (1992a) 'Should we ignore methodology?', *Royal Economic Society Newsletter* 77: 5.

Hahn, F. (1992b) 'Answer to Backhouse: Yes', *Royal Economic Society Newsletter* 78: 3–5.

Hamlin, A. P. (1986) *Ethics, Economics and the State*, Brighton: Wheatsheaf.

Hands, D. Wade (1985) 'Karl Popper and economic methodology: a new look', *Economics and Philosophy* 1(1): 83–99. Also in Caldwell (1993) vol. 3: 12–28.

Hands, D. Wade (1993) *Testing, Rationality and Progress. Essays on the Popperian Tradition in Economic Methodology*, Lanham, MD: Rowman & Littlefield.

Hausman, D. (1989) 'Economic methodology in a nutshell', *Journal of Economic Perspectives* 3(2): 115–27. Also in Caldwell (1993) vol. 1: 275–90.

Hausman, D. (1992) *The Inexact and Separate Science of Economics*, Cambridge: Cambridge University Press.

Hayek, F. A. (1992) *The Collected Works IV. The Fortunes of Liberalism: Essays on Austrian Economics and the Ideals of Freedom*, P. G. Klein (ed.), Chicago: University of Chicago Press.

Hoover, K. D. (1991) 'Mirowski's screed', *Methodus* 3(1): 139–45.

Huppe, H. H. (1989) 'In defence of extreme rationalism: thoughts on Donald McCloskey, *The Rhetoric of Economics*', *Review of Austrian Economics*, M. N. Rothbard and W. Block (eds), Lexington, MA: Lexington Books, vol 3: 179–214.

Hutchison, T. W. (1981) *The Politics and Philosophy of Economics*, Oxford: Basil Blackwell.

Hutchison, T. W. (1992) *Changing Aims in Economics*, Oxford: Basil Blackwell.

— Ingrao, B. and Israel, G. (1990) *The Invisible Hand: Economic Equilibrium in the History of Science*, Cambridge, MA: MIT Press.

Kim, J. (1992) 'Testing in modern economics: the case of job search theory', in de Marchi and Blaug (1991) pp. 105–31.

Kreps, D. M. (1990) *Game Theory and Economic Modelling*, Oxford: Oxford University Press.

Lawson, T. (1992) 'Methodology: non-optional and consequential', *Royal Economic Society Newsletter*, October, 79: 2.

Leontief, W. (1987) 'Input–output analysis', in J. Eatwell, and M. Milgate and P. Newman (eds), *The Palgrave Dictionary of Economics*, London: Macmillan, vol. 2: 861–4.

McCloskey, D. N. (1988) 'Thick and thin methodologies in the history of economic thought', in N. de Marchi, 1992a, 245–57.

McCloskey, D. (1991) 'Economic science: a search through the hyperspace of assumptions?', *Methodus* 3(1): 6–16.

Marshall, A. (1961) *Principles of Economics*, C. W. Guillebaud (ed.), London: Macmillan.

Mayer, T. (1993) *Truth versus Precision in Economics*, Aldershot: Edward Elgar.

— Mirowski, P. (1989) *More Heat Than Light: Economics as Social Physics, Physics as Nature's Economics*, Cambridge: Cambridge University Press.

Mizon, G. (1991) 'The role of measurement and testing in economics, in D. Greenaway, M. Bleaney and I. Stewart (eds), *Companion to Contemporary Economic Thought*, London: Routledge, pp. 574–92.

O'Brien, D. P. (1992) 'Economists and data', *British Journal of Industrial Relations* 30(2): 253–85.

Popper, K. R. (1983) *Realism and the Aim of Science: From the Postscript to the Logic of Scientific Discovery*, W. W. Bartley III (ed.), London: Hutchinson.

Radner, R. (1992) 'Hierarchy: the economics of managing', *Journal of Economic Literature* 30(3): 1382–415.

Raiffa, H. (1992) 'Game theory at the University of Michigan, 1948–1952', in E. R. Weintraub (ed.), *Toward a History of Game Theory*, Annual Supplement to *History of Political Economy* 24, Durham: Duke University Press, pp. 165–76.

Rapoport, A. (1987) 'Prisoner's dilemma', in J. Eatwell, M. Milgate and P. Newman (eds), *The Palgrave Dictionary of Economics*, London: Macmillan, vol. 3: 973–6.

Redman, D. (1991) *Economics and the Philosophy of Science*, Oxford: Oxford University Press.

Resnick, S. A. and Wolff, R. D. (1987) *Knowledge and Class: A Marxian Critique of Political Economy*, Chicago: University of Chicago Press.

Rosenberg, A. (1983) 'If economics isn't science, what is it?', *Philosophical Forum* 14(3–4): 296–314. Also in Caldwell (1993) vol. 3: 426–44.

Rosenberg, A. (1992) *Economics, Mathematical Politics or Science of Diminishing Returns?* Chicago: University of Chicago Press.

Rothbard, M. N. (1989) 'The hermeneutical invasion of philosophy and economics', in M. N. Rothbard and W. Block (eds), *The Review of Austrian Economics*, Lexington, MA: Lexington Books, pp. 45–60.

Rubinstein, A. (1990) 'Introduction', in A. Rubinstein (ed.), *Game Theory in Economics*, Aldershot: Edward Elgar.

Salanti, A. (1991) 'Roy Weintraub's *Studies in Appraisal*: Lakatosian consolations or something else?', *Economics and Philosophy* 7(4): 221–34.

Scherer, F. M. and Ross, D. (1990) *Industrial Market Structure and Economic Performance*, 3rd edn, Boston: Houghton Mifflin.

Schoemaker, P. J. H. (1982) 'The expected utility model: its variants, purposes, evidence and limitations', *Journal of Economic Literature* 20: 529–63. Also in Caldwell (1993) vol. 2: 395–429.

Schumpeter, J. (1983) 'Review of *The General Theory of Employment, Interest and Money*', *Journal of the American Statistical Association* December 1936; reprinted in J. C. Wood (ed.), *John Maynard Keynes. Critical Assessments*, London: Croom Helm, vol. 2: 124–8.

Shackle, G. L. S. (1972) *Epistemics and Economics. A Critique of Economic Doctrines*, Cambridge: Cambridge University Press.

Shorrocks. A. F. (1987) Inequality between persons', *The New Palgrave Dictionary of Economics*, J. Eatwell, M. Milgate and P. Newman (eds), London: Macmillan, vol. 2: 821–4.

Smith, V. L., McCabe, K. A. and Rassenti, S. J. (1991) 'Lakatos and experimental economics', in de Marchi and Blaug (1991) pp. 197–226.

Walker, D. A. (1991) 'Review article: economics as social physics', *Economic Journal* 101: 615–31.

Walters, A. A. (1963) 'Production and cost functions: an econometric survey', *Econometrica* 31(1–2): 1–66.

Weintraub, E. R. (1988) 'The neo-Walrasian programme is empirically progressive', in de Marchi (1992a), pp. 213–27. Also in Caldwell (1993) vol. 3: 165–79.

Weintraub, E. R. (1989) 'Methodology doesn't matter but the history of thought might', *The State of Macroeconomics*, S. Honkapohja (ed.), Oxford: Basil Blackwell, pp. 263–79.

Weintraub, E. R. (1991) *Stabilizing Dynamics, Constructing Economic Knowledge*, Cambridge: Cambridge University Press.

Weintraub, E. R. (1992) 'Roger Backhouse's straw herring', *Methodus* 4(2): 58–62.

Woo, H. K. (1986) *What's Wrong with Formalization in Economics? An Epistemological Critique*, Newark, CA: Victoria Press.

7

TWO PROPOSALS FOR THE RECOVERY OF ECONOMIC PRACTICE

Bruce J. Caldwell

Recently I published a paper in the *Journal of Economic Literature* entitled 'Clarifying Popper' (Caldwell 1991a). The intended audience comprised everyday economists who wanted to know a little more about Karl Popper's philosophy and methodology of science and how his ideas might relate to their discipline. Much of the paper was devoted to exposition, but it also contained an argument about what I thought was valuable in Popper's work. The argument ran as follows. The part of Popper's thought that is most well known among economists, his falsificationist methodology, when strictly interpreted, is of little use to economists. Falsificationism also appears to be inconsistent with Popper's methodology of the social sciences, situational logic, a doctrine that may be of value within economics. Finally, if one emphasizes ideas found in Popper's writings on critical rationalism, it may be possible to save Popper from the inconsistency: though they apply in different domains, both falsificationism and situational logic can be used to enhance the critical environment. Because of the audience for the paper, direct references to debates in methodology were muted. One purpose of the current paper is to make them more explicit.[1] Another is to advance two proposals concerning the practice of economic methodology that, if followed, may help us to understand better the practice of economists.

MARK BLAUG'S ADVANCE (RETREAT?) FROM POPPER TO LAKATOS

There is a decent anecdote about the origins of 'Clarifying Popper'. In June 1987 I attended a conference on interpretation in economics hosted by Arjo Klamer at Wellesley College. Wellesley is one of the Seven Sisters and the men's room in the building in which we met reflected it. Since the male–female ratio among economists interested in interpretation mirrors that of the profession as a whole, there was a line in the men's bathroom at coffee break time, and it was close quarters to boot. Behind me stood

Mark Blaug, and hoping to pass the time a little less uncomfortably, I asked him an impossibly big question. I said, 'Mark, you and I have been arguing about the merits and limitations of Popper's falsificationist methodology for nearly a decade now. Where do you think our argument stands?' After about a three-second pause he said, 'We both think falsificationism is hard to put into effect in economics. You say we should abandon it, and I say we should try harder.' I was stunned. Ten years' worth of work, and he had summed it up, under duress, in two sentences. It was not the first time I was in awe in Blaug's presence, but it was doubtless the most memorable. Anyway, I resolved soon thereafter to re-read the relevant parts of the Popper corpus as well as the secondary literature in economic methodology, to see if he was right. I wrote him a couple of long letters, and he replied to them in detail. From this came a paper, and indeed, the original version of 'Clarifying Popper' looked a lot like an open letter to Mark Blaug. It took a summer of rewriting to transform it into a more standardized product.

How accurate was Mark Blaug's pithy summary? His first sentence is right: both of us agree that the problems of putting falsificationism into effect are severe, in economics and generally. But there is more to our responses to the dilemma than he gave either of us credit for, just as there is more to Popperian thought than falsificationism. It is true that at times Blaug embraces falsificationism and urges economists to alter their practices. But he also deviates from it, at least to the extent that he lauds the merits of the methodology of scientific research programmes (MSRP) and methodology of historiographical research programmes (MHRP) proposed by Popper's student, Imre Lakatos. As for me, I do not so much say 'abandon falsificationism' as I do 'embrace criticism'. Nonetheless, Blaug is right, I do not think that falsificationist principles are very helpful for criticizing economics, unless one wants to throw out virtually every economic research programme, heterodox and orthodox alike.

Let us get down to cases. There are two general instances when Blaug sounds most like a Popperian falsificationist. The first is when he is using falsificationist methodological criteria to criticize a research programme. An excellent example is the second part of his brilliant brief against Marxism (Blaug 1990: 36–56). Blaug first shows that many of Marx's predictions were hedged all around with qualifications: precious few 'bold conjectures' came from the pen of 'the socialist Böhm-Bawerk'. Of the handful of predictions that were not ambiguous, few occurred. As for later Marxists who try to revise his analysis in the light of subsequent history, all such efforts are viewed as 'immunizing stratagems' designed to protect Marxism from refutation. The second instance is when Blaug argues that falsificationism is a prescriptive ideal that economists should try to follow, hard though it may be to do. Indeed, he advocates it precisely *because* it is so easy to find confirming instances of theories in economics: economists should try to find tests that would allow us to discriminate among competing hypotheses. Blaug contrasts this aggressive and prescriptivist role of methodology with a defensive (defensive of the economics profession), descriptivist one, and he attributes advocacy of the latter to me, among others (ibid.: 3–7).

Blaug is wrong about my wanting to defend and describe the profession (I *do* want a *better* description, but I also insist on the importance of *criticizing* our practice), but let us set his caricature of my position aside for now. In the section of 'Clarifying Popper' on falsificationism, three objections to it (labelled the Philosopher's, the Historian's and the Economic Methodologist's Objections) were offered. How might they be used against Blaug the falsificationist?

The Historian's Objection is the weakest one, because it is so easy to answer. Historians of economic thought reconstruct the evolution of economic theory. If it could be shown that through time economic theory 'progressed', and did so because economists (consciously or unconsciously) had followed falsificationist principles, then Popper's prescriptions would be very useful to historians. The Historian's Objection asserts that the intellectual history of economics cannot be so reconstructed, that falsificationism is not helpful if one wishes to describe the behaviour of economists. This is a weak objection because the committed Popperian can always respond that falsificationism is a *prescriptive* doctrine. If economists have not followed it, so much the worse for their discipline. They should try harder.

Even though the Historian's Objection is easily answerable, advocates of falsificationism in economics have not felt comfortable with the standard response, probably because the most prominent ones (Blaug and T. W. Hutchison) are themselves historians of thought. In any event, something like the Historian's Objection seems to have been behind Blaug's decision, which dates back to the early 1970s, to begin moving towards Imre Lakatos's MSRP and MHRP for assessing and historically reconstructing economics (Blaug 1976; cf. Caldwell 1991a: 10–13). Blaug has recently made the link between Lakatos and the prescriptive–descriptive dilemma explicit. In his Afterword to a conference volume on Lakatos and economics, he argues that the MSRP offers reasonable prescriptive guidelines for the practice of economics, and that they should be preserved whether or not economists ever follow them. The MHRP provides an historical framework for reconstructing the history of disciplines, and he admits that for economics it may well be 'largely false' as a descriptive vehicle (de Marchi and Blaug 1991: 501–5). The Lakatosian framework, then, allows Blaug to parry the Historian's Objection: the MSRP allows him to retain his insistence on prescriptive methodology, while the MHRP permits Blaug the historian of thought to admit that economic practice often deviates from the ideal.[2]

The Economic Methodologist's Objection is a bit more formidable. The target of the objection is Popper's prohibition against immunizing stratagems, a prohibition that Blaug used so effectively against Marxist revisionists. Popper stated that the social sciences employ the method of 'situational analysis' or 'situational logic'. In using this method, the social scientist describes the 'situation' (both goals and constraints) an actor faces, assumes that the actor chooses rationally (the 'rationality hypothesis'), then makes a prediction about the actor's behaviour. If the actor fails to behave as predicted, the social scientist re-examines the description of the situation. Crucially, the rationality hypothesis is never questioned. This is what led me to argue that the method of situational logic has an immunizing stratagem as its prime directive (Caldwell 1991a: 13). It is as if the social scientist were instructed: when an actor does not behave as predicted, fiddle with the description of the situation until you get the observed behaviour to emerge, always as a rational agent's response to some set of goals and constraints.

The method of situational analysis clearly conflicts with the prohibition against immunizing stratagems. How does this relate to economics? It should be evident that much of standard microeconomics involves modelling the rational behaviour of individual agents under variously specified constraints, some examples of which were given in my paper (ibid.: 17). If this is the case, then the consequences for a falsificationist assessment of microeconomics are profound. If one takes Popper's prohibition against immunizing stratagems seriously, then not just Marxism but many parts of neoclassical microeconomics must be rejected as hopelessly 'ad hoc'. What is Mark Blaug's reply to that?

At times his response has been extraordinarily weak, as when he simply ignored situational logic (e.g. of Popper's positive contributions to the methodology of the social sciences, only his endorsement of 'methodological individualism' is discussed in Blaug 1980: 46–52), or cast doubt on Popper's grasp of the social sciences (e.g. Blaug 1985: 287). His ultimate response is more coherent, and again, Lakatos comes to the rescue. The MSRP states that all research programmes include 'hard core' propositions, initial 'givens' that are not to be questioned within the analysis. If one interprets the rationality hypothesis as a component of the hard core (as it certainly makes sense to do), then neoclassical microeconomics counts as a legitimate scientific research programme. Whether or not it counts as a *progressive* programme, either theoretically or empirically, is another matter. One gets some sense of Blaug's opinion of the issue in the conclusion of his assessment of radical economics: 'Radical economics has, I think, great failings, and I personally end as I began – an unconverted neoclassical economist. Nevertheless, a study of radical economics leaves one ultimately almost as unhappy with orthodox economics as with radical economics' (Blaug 1990: 81). Blaug's assessment of neoclassical economics brings to mind Winston Churchill's (1947) description of democracy: '... it has been said that democracy is the worst form of government except all those other forms that have been tried from time to time'.

A few comments are in order before moving to our next topic. Mark Blaug's position was strengthened by his embracing of Lakatos. Because the MSRP has a prescriptive component, Blaug was able to retain a prescriptivist role for economic methodology, an outcome he prefers. Even better (given his preference for neoclassicism), if one uses the MSRP to assess mainstream neoclassical economics, one finds that the programme is a legitimate science (though not necessarily a progressive one). Finally, by endorsing Lakatos's MHRP, Blaug is able to avoid severing the history of economics from discussions of methodology. These are no small victories. It must be added that, to his credit, Blaug developed (and when necessary, revised) his ideas while engaging in an extended and open dialogue with his critics. The transformation of his views has not been without costs, however, two of which must be mentioned. First, Blaug's current position is a retreat from Popper's prohibition against immunizing stratagems, and as such constitutes an abandonment of strict falsificationism. Second, the movement away from falsificationism undermines those of Blaug's past critiques of research programmes (like his second paper on Marxism) that rely on the prohibition against immunizing stratagems for their force.[3] These are not trivial costs.

PROPOSAL 1: SITUATIONAL ANALYSIS AND THE RECOVERY OF PRACTICE

The recent literature in methodology and related fields is filled with references to the 'recovery of practice'. The notion provides a subtitle for a recent volume edited by Neil de Marchi; paradoxically (given the argument to follow) its title is *Post-Popperian Methodology of Economics* (1992).[4] Donald McCloskey (1983: 493, 499) juxtaposes the 'official rhetoric' of modernism with the 'honorable but unexamined' rhetoric of the workaday economist. Daniel Hausman (1992: ch. 14) characterizes his own efforts as 'empirical philosophy of science', his goals being to understand and to assess the strategies of knowledge acquisition employed by neoclassical economists. Though the approaches (be they sociological, rhetorical or philosophical) differ, all wish to understand how economists 'really' practise their trade, how they persuade one another, why they embrace certain types of arguments and reject others, and so on.

It was suggested earlier that situational logic may provide a vehicle for the recovery of economic practice. It is now time to put this hypothesis into the form of a (rather carefully hedged!) proposal: *Situational analysis provides a good starting point for the reconstruction of certain fundamental aspects of economic practice, and should so be used. It can also serve effectively as a template that will allow methodologists to distinguish among the varieties of practices engaged in by economists.*

Let us unpack the hedges and qualifications. First, what exactly *is* a 'situational analysis'? As noted in 'Clarifying Popper' (p. 15), the details of how one could be done were never laid out by Popper. Luckily, his student Noretta Koertge (1975: 440) provided a more systematic restatement, a short version of which reads:

1 *Description of the Situation:* Agent A was in a situation of type C.
2 *Analysis of the Situation:* In a situation of type C, the appropriate thing to do is X.
3 *Rationality Principle:* Agents always act appropriately to their situations.
4 *Explanandum:* (Therefore) A did X.

A more extensive version (ibid.: 445) reads:

1 *Description of Problem-Situation:* A thought he was in a problem-situation of type C.
2 *Dispositional Law:* For all such problem-situations A would use appraisal-rule R.
3 *Analysis of Situation:* The result of appraising C using R is X.
4 *Description of the Agent's Competence:* A did not make a mistake in applying R to C.
5 *Rationality Appraisal Principle:* All agents appraise their situations in a rational manner.
6 *Explanandum–1:* (Therefore) A concluded that X was the rational thing to do.
7 *Rationality Principle:* People always act on the outcome of their rational appraisals.
8 *Explanandum–2:* (Therefore) A did X.

Either could be used to reconstruct the practice of economics.

Situational logic is only a 'starting point' for three reasons. First of all, the framework is clearly articulated at a very high level of generality. A lot of work would need to be done to specify the description of various 'typical' situations that are of interest to economists: is the agent a consumer, a manager of a firm, a bureaucrat? Is the agent in a game against nature or against other similarly endowed agents? Are there informational asymmetries among agents?

Second, though parts of standard microeconomics clearly fit the situational analysis mould (especially those models that describe the response of individual rational agents, like consumers or firms, to a specific change in a constraint), others do not. For example, it is not evident within the situational logic framework how one gets from the agent to the market (or other more aggregated) level, nor how to handle what the Austrians call 'the unintended consequences of human action'. To her credit Koertge recognizes that her model would have to be augmented to account for social phenomena like 'unintended consequences' (ibid.: 441). Other alterations unique to economics would doubtless be discovered as the reconstruction proceeded.

Finally, it is undeniable that certain aspects of economics are not good candidates for a situational logic reconstruction. Certain econometric investigations of social phenomena have only a tenuous relationship to microeconomic theory, and the same may be said of a number of research programmes in both theoretical and empirical macroeconomics. This is why situational analysis was described as a 'template' against which to measure different forms of economic analysis. It is *not* intended as a criterion of demarcation between 'good' and 'bad' practice. What is wanted, rather, is a device that is good at revealing the commonalities and differences that are present in our practice.

Situational analysis is not the only vehicle that could be used to reconstruct the practice of economists, of course. (We will see below that another has already been offered by Daniel Hausman, and part of my goal in making a proposal is to provoke others into offering alternatives to it). To the extent that it has merits, the advantages of using situational logic as a framework appear to be two. First, because it is based on 'folk psychological' categories, it is both a simple and an intuitively plausible device for reconstructing economic theories. Simplicity may be an especially important virtue: the mathematical formalism of much current economic theory is often intimidating, even to economists. Anything that helps to demystify our practice should be welcome. Second, by using situational analysis to recover practice, comparison with other social sciences that use similar folk psychological constructs becomes easier. Situational analysis, though modelled on the practice of economists, was intended to be a method applicable to *all* the social sciences. Different social sciences will emphasize different parts of the framework. Cross-disciplinary understanding may well be enhanced if we are able to discuss our differences in terms of a common reference point.

A final point: Noretta Koertge held out the hope that augmentation of the situational logic framework (e.g. by building-in 'supplementary theories of error, decision-making and belief formation') could increase its empirical content (1975: 447). This might occur in economics, but I think that it is equally likely that we will discover that some of the constraints of relevance for economics involve unmeasurable, subjective elements. By specifying them more precisely we may come to understand economic phenomena better, but we may also come to realize that our ability to predict is limited where such phenomena are concerned. Hayek made a similar point in his discussion of the problems of applying Popper's falsificationist principles to the 'complex phenomena' of the social sciences:

The advance of science will thus have to proceed in two different directions: while it is certainly desirable to make our theories as falsifiable as possible, we must also push forward into fields where, as we advance, the degree of falsifiability necessarily decreases. This is the price we have to pay for an advance into the field of complex phenomena.

(Hayek 1967: 29)

THE PHILOSOPHER'S OBJECTION

Thus far we have neglected the third objection to falsificationism. The Philosopher's Objection states that falsificationism is inadequate both as a methodology and as a philosophy of science. It is inadequate as a methodology because it can lead scientists to make bad decisions, and it is inadequate as an epistemology because it rules out any discussion of how evidence supports theories. These arguments have been pushed most forcefully by the philosopher of science Daniel Hausman (e.g. 1988, 1992), hence their name. It is important for economists to realize just how unpopular Popper is among philosophers of science. Popper's anti-inductivism and non-justificationism imply that all attempts to discover criteria for determining the warrant of arguments are chimerical and that consequently neither policy nor theory can be grounded on any appraisal of how well supported statements are. As one philosopher of science put it to me: 'Popper's error is to take Hume too far.' He meant by this that Popper's position comes very close to scepticism and, for most philosophers, too close.

The methodological part of the Philosopher's Objection carried over into the Economic Methodologist's Objection (where 'bad decisions' = throwing out situational analysis). The epistemological argument, though it touches on some fascinating issues, is sufficiently complex that we will forgo any discussion of it here. This is a perfect point, however, briefly to review the proposals for the recovery of practice made by Hausman in his recent book, *The Inexact and Separate Science of Economics* (1992).

In the first part of the book, Hausman provides an account of the structure of neoclassical microeconomics, including partial equilibrium theory (utility theory and theories of consumer choice and of the firm), general equilibrium theory and welfare economics. He argues persuasively that 'equilibrium theory', the components of which emerge in the course of his reconstruction (they are summarized in a diagram on p. 271), provides the framework within which neoclassical economists permit themselves to theorize. The boundaries of the structure are well defined; this is why he calls economics a 'separate' science. But the data that economists have available with which to confront their theories are not good enough to produce telling tests. Economists respond by severely limiting the domain of their discipline. Since there is more to the world than is contained in that domain, their science is also an 'inexact' one.

Hausman characterizes economists as following a variant of Mill's method *a priori*. Such approaches have been out of vogue, of course, since positivist ideas came to dominate the methodological rhetoric of economists in the 1940s. Hausman likes a qualified version of Mill's method, so he spends a chapter showing that a host of writers on economic methodology from the positivist era (Hutchison, Machlup, Friedman and Samuelson) botched their philosophy, and two more dispatching the writings of Popper and Lakatos. From Hausman's perspective, it is fortunate that these methodological writings by economists and philosophers have had little effect on economic practice. Indeed, he finds the actual methodology followed by neoclassical economists both uncontroversial and rational, with one crucial caveat that is mentioned in the last sentence of the quotation below.

> ... economists employ an uncontroversial method of theory assessment. Unfortunately, owing to poor data (relative to the state of economic knowledge), little can be learned about which theories are better confirmed. Given the initial credibility of the basic behavioural postulates of economics, it is rational to remain committed to them in the face of apparent disconfirmations. The consequence of such a defence is to leave economists unable to learn very much from typical economic data.
>
> (Ibid.: 253).

To summarize: given the problems with testing in economics, economists are rational to cling to 'equilibrium theory', even in the face of disconfirmations. But by doing so, they risk being dogmatic. Hausman offers two recommendations for changes in practice to avoid that outcome. First, economists should engage in more, and more varied forms of, empirical work: they should try to learn more from 'typical economic data'. Second, the discipline should be more open to alternative theoretical frameworks, less insistent on its status as a 'separate science' (ibid.: 253–5).

This is an excellent book, especially the first section in which the theoretical structure and strategies of neoclassical economics are revealed. In addition, Hausman's analysis of the writings of economic methodologists is more philosophically sophisticated than those of economists (like Blaug and me) who have surveyed and assessed the same literature. On methodological issues, Hausman sometimes reaches the same conclusions as Blaug and Caldwell, and sometimes he differs from them. For example, both Hausman and Caldwell share (*contra* Blaug) the same negative opinion of the prescriptions offered by the falsificationist Popper. Less obviously, Hausman's preferred method *a priori* has much in common with the method of situational logic: both direct economists to cling to their theoretical framework (whether one calls it 'equilibrium theory' or 'situational analysis', both of us are talking about theories in the same domain, namely, standard microeconomics), even in the face of disconfirmations; both embrace an immunizing stratagem. As such, it is both surprising and disappointing that, in his chapter on Popper, Hausman does not mention situational analysis even once. It would be interesting to know what this vehemently anti-Popperian philosopher thinks of Popper's social science methodology. On a final issue, and it is a critical one, Blaug the Lakatosian, Hausman the Millian, and Caldwell the Situational Logician all agree: testing is difficult in economics.

PROPOSAL 2: EPISTEMIC PESSIMISM AND THE RECOVERY OF PRACTICE

I differ from my Lakatosian and Millian comrades in my *response* to our common perception of the empirical difficulties besetting economics. Though labels are always inadequate, our differences might be characterized as follows: Mark Blaug and Daniel Hausman tend towards epistemic optimism of the empirical variety, whereas I am an epistemic pessimist.[5]

In calling them empirical epistemic optimists, I do not mean that either Hausman or Blaug are naive about the difficulties facing economists who try to do empirical work. As noted above, in his description of our practice Hausman underlines the 'poor data' economists must perforce utilize. The last third of Blaug's (1992) masterful book on methodology consists of a series of case studies of fields within economics. For all but one he is forced to conclude (and lament) that there has been precious little empirical progress in evidence.[6] Both, then, recognize the difficulties. It is their *response* to this situation that leads me to characterize them as epistemic optimists. Even in the face of the problems that they identify, Blaug and Hausman nonetheless urge economists to do more, and more kinds of, and better empirical work. They do so because they think (or hope) that this is the path to progress. And for them progress means more testing and better confirmed empirical relationships, because this leads to a better understanding of the world.

It can be mentioned in passing that the call for more and better empirical studies is a common one among methodologists. Even so, it may well be that this is something of a default position. I conjecture that the prior motivating belief is that mathematical theorizing has been taken *too far*, that the balance between theoretical and empirical work needs to be restored. In any event there are many examples of this latter type of argument. T. W. Hutchison (1977: ch. 4) wrote nearly two decades ago about 'the crisis of abstraction' in economics. More recently, Thomas Mayer (1993) pushes for a clarification of the separate domains, arguing that the 'precision' that theory provides should not be counted as more important than the 'truth' about economic phenomena that empirical studies aim to discover. As a final example, when McCloskey (e.g. 1991) demystifies the models of theorists (models are just another form of metaphor, and sometimes a form not well suited to our tasks), one of his goals is to convince the profession that formalization has gone too far. Though their approaches are very different, all of these scholars' positions lead them to arguments for more, and sometimes more kinds of, empirical work.

It is now time to lay out what I mean by epistemic pessimism. It is important to note that, at least in the variant that I endorse, epistemic pessimists (EPs) share Hausman and Blaug's view that the most important type of progress is a better understanding of economic phenomena. EPs also agree that high theory has not done much to improve our understanding. But an EP *also* has doubts about prospects for empirical work. After all, there already is plenty of empirical work going on in economics: the majority of economists do applied rather than theoretical research. To be sure, some of this is hack science. But there is also empirical work that is both sophisticated in terms of technique and significant in focus, as a perusal of the monthly list of working papers from the NBER will establish. In addition, huge data sets tracing large numbers of individuals and families through time, with data on hundreds of socio-economic variables, have been constructed. The problem is not a dearth of either data or data-massagers.

From the EP's perspective, the problem is that *none of this has led to the type of progress that optimists like Blaug and Hausman hope for.*[7] And from that (intentionally provocative and clearly unsubstantiated claim) the EP is prepared to draw an (itself admittedly premature) inference: no matter how advanced the econometric techniques and how intricate and detailed the data sets become, few robust relationships will emerge. There will always be variables that cannot be measured that will allow one rationally to question a finding, and there will always be studies that reach different conclusions when alternative plausible variables are included in a regression. As a result, differences in interpretation will always be rife.

It should be noted at the outset that this inference can never be established as true. No failure of past or present efforts will ever be enough to dissuade a convinced epistemic optimist that further efforts are unwarranted. For optimists, more (empirical or theoretical work) is always better, since it continually expands the margins of knowledge. The epistemic pessimist's inference *is* falsifiable, however. If advances in data-collection, theoretical sophistication and econometric technique have brought with them a firmer grasp of the workings of economic phenomena, the thesis is refuted. My second proposal begins with a call for the 'testing'[8] of the EP inference: *Economists should examine the recent history of their discipline to see whether and how advances in theory and measurement have improved our understanding of economic phenomena. We must answer the question:*

what do we know about the economy now that is a direct result of the manifold theoretical and empirical advances of the last half-century?

If an effort were ever made to answer this question, it would be critical to carefully distinguish among different varieties of 'progress', itself a daunting task, as the debates within the Lakatosian camp over definitions of progressivity, 'novel facts', and so on, have revealed.[9] But let us be unreasonably optimistic and assume that we *are* able to come up with a suitable categorization scheme. It seems clear that there has been a great deal of (what such a scheme might label as) various types of 'heuristic progress' within twentieth-century economics. Indeed, I suspect that the major reason that heuristic progress has been so much in evidence is precisely because we have *not* witnessed a steady improvement in our understanding and control of economic phenomena. It is only when advances in knowledge are routinely frustrated that one should expect 'progress' to become so universally measured in terms of increases in the variety or mathematical sophistication of theoretical models, or in terms of improvements in the techniques of empirical analysis, *rather than in terms of better knowledge of how the economy works*. In any event, the point is to see exactly what has taken place. This is, of course, just another recommendation for the recovery of practice.

If such a 'test' could indeed be undertaken and epistemic pessimism were to survive it, that is, if it is in fact true that there have been precious few returns (in terms of improved understanding of economic phenomena) from our sizeable investment in theoretical and empirical work, where do we go from there? Do we simply throw up our hands in despair? One could, but I think that there is a better response, namely, to try to figure out *why* economists have had so little success. The type of questions we need to ask are: what constraints do economists as scientists face? What constraints on our knowledge of the workings of the economy exist? What sorts of things do we now know, what might we someday know, and what sorts of things will we never know, due to the constraints that we have identified? The second part of my proposal is to urge us to take seriously the question: *what are the limits of our knowledge in economics?*

Again, this is not an easy question to answer. How can one 'know' what things one will never be able to know? Identifying one's own constraints is never easy, and the assessments one reaches are always provisional. Even so, I still believe that the programme is worth attempting. It is one to which methodologists and historians of economic thought, as well as applied economists and theorists, could contribute, albeit in very different ways.[10] Indeed, the programme itself could end up establishing that progress of a certain limited type *is* possible in economics, in empirical, theoretical *and* methodological work as well. But the progress would consist of discovering exactly what the *limits* of our knowledge actually are. Perhaps this is a type of progress that only an epistemic pessimist can fully appreciate.

I close this section with a final conjecture. My manner of presentation in this section has been intentionally and deliberately provocative, with the goal of stimulating thought and discussion. But even so, it should be noted that the programme that has been proposed should not seem wholly strange to economists. After all, economics is all about rational constrained choice. A programme that encourages economists to identify their own constraints should seem natural. In addition, a systematic study of the constraints that economists and other social scientists face surely makes more sense than simply presuming that our subject matter will yield to the tools of science. Yet only a very few economists in the past three generations have been epistemic pessimists. The Austrian subjectivists in general, and Hayek in particular, are exceptions. Why has this been so? The reasons are, in my view, both multiple and complex. An initial simplified conjecture is that (the insights of the methodological community notwithstanding) the grip of positivism, with its optimism and, yes, arrogance about the methods of science, has yet to be completely loosened within economics. There was a time when such optimism was not unreasonable. But after three generations that time has passed. In addition, if we are serious about the recovery of practice, it seems to me that a better understanding of the limitations faced by economists is an admirable goal to shoot for.

CRITICAL RATIONALISM

The third section of 'Clarifying Popper' examined his writings on Critical Rationalism. Though its relationship to the concerns of economists might at first appear tenuous, there were several good reasons to include reference to this part of his work. First, critical rationalism seemed to me to provide a way around the tension between falsificationism and situational logic. If Popper's essential methodological prescription is the idea that scientists must engage in *criticism* in general (rather than that they must obey specific methodological imperatives, like 'Avoid immunizing stratagems!'), then both falsificationism and situational analysis can be employed to advance the cause of criticism. In addition, since they are applicable in different domains, they need not be in conflict. Next, the non-justificationist elements of Popper's writings on critical rationalism (these were most fully developed by his student Bill Bartley; see Caldwell 1991a: 22–4) were also appealing, since they seemed to offer a response (if not an antidote) to some of the more extreme forms of anti-foundationalism that had appeared in the methodological literature in the past decade.[11] Finally, Popper's critical rationalism had provided some of the impetus for my own rough ideas about methodology: for example, that context-dependent criticism is a prime desideratum.

149

My own ideas are sufficiently rough and *ad hoc* that in the end it is probably not a good idea to attach them to Popper's. And just to emphasize that my advice is aimed at practice and is not an attempt at system-building, I will close with a quotation from the pragmatist philosopher John Dewey, taken from his appropriately titled essay, 'The need for a recovery of philosophy'.

> British empiricism, with its appeal to what has been in the past, is, after all, only a kind of *a priorism*. For it lays down a fixed rule for future intelligence to follow; and only the immersion of philosophy in technical learning prevents our seeing that this is the essence of *a priorism*.
>
> (1970: 68)

Could the author of the Preface to *The Poverty of Historicism* have put it any better?

ACKNOWLEDGEMENTS

Roger Backhouse, Wade Hands, Dan Hausman and Uskali Mäki contributed valuable comments on an early draft of this paper, but bear no responsibility for either errors remaining or opinions expressed in the final version.

NOTES

1 This goal is somewhat unusual: authors of academic papers often do not specifically identify the targets of their arguments. But especially in a volume to be used by students, the exercise can be a useful one. I see no way of parrying another possible objection (other than to acknowledge my guilt and carry on), namely, that what an *author* may have meant is quite dependent of what a *text* means, since a text's meaning is created by the interaction between the *reader* and the text. I like the Popperian philosopher Bill Bartley's formulation of the problem: 'I learnt from Popper that we never know what we are talking about, and I learnt from Hayek that we never know what we are doing' (Bartley 1984: 19). The aphorism might be decoded as follows: Hayek emphasized the 'unintended consequences' of our actions, which implies that we do not know in advance all the implications of what we do. In his discussion of 'objective knowledge' Popper argued that once a text becomes a part of 'World 3' it takes on meanings independent of, and possibly quite different from, its author's intentions, so we do not know all the consequences of what we are saying, either.

2 In my criticism of the Lakatosian framework (Caldwell 1991b), I mistakenly attacked the MSRP rather than the MHRP as being descriptively inadequate for economics. My argument should have been against the MHRP, and given Blaug's statement that the MHRP may well be 'largely false' for much of economics, my paper should be taken as an argument in support of Blaug's

conjecture. Blaug argues elsewhere that macroeconomics is an exception, more of which anon.

3 This does not mean that Classical Marxism is free from problems. Indeed, there remains a Popperian objection to it, one that can be found in the three-page Preface to his *The Poverty of Historicism* (1991). See Moseley (forthcoming) and Caldwell (forthcoming) for contrasting (though both critical) views of Blaug's critique of Marxism.

4 The title implies that Popper's work, because of its stringent normative content, has little to offer those interested in recovering practice. In a thoughtful introduction, however, editor de Marchi emphasizes that the falsificationist Popper found in some of the methodological literature in economics is a bit of a caricature. I would go further and argue that other parts of the Popperian corpus may well be useful for the task of recovery.

5 There is a third category: epistemic optimists of a theoretical variety. Examples include Hahn (1973), Gibbard and Varian (1978) and Green (1981). This is a decidedly minority view within the methodological community. Revealed preference theory suggests, however, that it is the dominant predilection among economists in general.

6 In the second edition of his methodology book Blaug includes a new chapter on macroeconomics, about which he writes, 'I hope that a reading of Chapter 12 below will convince any "reasonable economist" that the entire history of post-war macroeconomics furnishes a whole series of paradigmatic episodes of falsificationist practice...' (1992: xvi). But this misses the point. Clearly, economic theories *do* get falsified. The real question is whether any economic theory could *survive* the strictures of falsificationism, absent the sort of immunizing stratagems employed in microeconomics. (It is significant that the field in which economists are most likely to take data seriously is the branch that is most distant from standard microeconomic theory.) Blaug's examples demonstrate that each successive macroeconomic theory (from Keynesian economics through monetarism to rational expectations) has eventually faltered empirically. The lessons we might draw from this are exactly of the sort that I argue for later in my paper, namely, a better understanding of the *limits* of our knowledge in economics. In this, I think that my position comes closest to T. W. Hutchison's in his aptly titled paper, 'The limitations of general theories in macroeconomics', in Hutchison (1981: 233–65).

7 See the previous footnote for a brief discussion of Blaug's sole exception, macroeconomics. It is significant that the most 'optimistic' paper regarding the applicability of the Lakatosian framework in economics in de Marchi and Blaug (1991) was one by Roger Backhouse on macroeconomics.

8 The whole notion of 'testing' for the presence or absence of 'progress' by the examination of 'history' has been shown to be problematical by historians and philosophers of science. A good summary of the issues is Losee (1987).

9 The difficulties in coming up with agreed-upon definitions of 'progress' and other crucial terms are discussed in the introduction to de Marchi and Blaug (1991).

10 The line of inquiry that I am proposing is this: what can we say, in general and specifically, about the abilities and limitations of economists for understanding social phenomena? One need not be an EP to undertake such an investigation; clearly many economists view the presumption of steady progress as a reasonable one, and could ask the question in the context of 'What sorts of limitations have been overcome thus far?' One probably *does* have to have some leanings

towards pessimism to ask the question in the particular way that it is asked here.

In any event, certain current research programmes in economics can be characterized as trying to answer this sort of question. The case studies in Blaug's (1992) methodology book are actually a fine place to start. Studies of changes in our ability to measure economic phenomena (e.g. Berndt and Triplett 1990, which is the jubilee volume in the NBER's Studies in Income and Wealth series, which now has over fifty volumes in print), Edward Leamer's (e.g. 1983) work on the fragility of econometric inferences, and the work by Fisher and Summers mentioned at the end of Backhouse's introduction to this volume, are examples of very different approaches that nonetheless take the question seriously.

11 In the final chapter of his collection of essays on Popper, Wade Hands (1992) develops this line of argument more fully.

BIBLIOGRAPHY

Bartley, W. W. (1984) 'Knowledge is a product not fully known to its producer', in K. Leube and A. Zlabinger (eds), *The Political Economy of Freedom: Essays in Honor of F. A. Hayek*, Munich: Philosophia Verlag, pp. 17–45.

Berndt, E. and Triplett, J. (eds) (1990) *Fifty Years of Economic Measurement: The Jubilee of the Conference on Research in Income and Wealth*, Chicago: University of Chicago Press.

Blaug, M. (1976) 'Kuhn vs. Lakatos *or* paradigms vs. research programmes in the history of economics', in S. J. Latsis (ed.) *Method and Appraisal in Economics*, Cambridge: Cambridge University Press.

Blaug, M. (1985) 'Comment on Hands: Karl Popper and economic methodology: a new look', *Economics and Philosophy* 1: 286–8.

Blaug, M. (1990) *Economic Theories, True of False? Essays in the History and Methodology of Economics*, Aldershot: Edward Elgar.

Blaug, M. (1992) [1980] *The Methodology of Economics: Or How Economists Explain*, 2nd edn 1992, Cambridge: Cambridge University Press.

Caldwell, B. (1991a) 'Clarifying Popper', *Journal of Economic Literature* 29: 1–33. Reprinted in Caldwell (1993) vol. 3: 60–92.

Caldwell, B. (1991b) 'The methodology of scientific research programmes in economics: criticisms and conjectures', in G. K. Shaw (ed.), *Economics, Culture and Education: Essays in Honour of Mark Blaug*, Aldershot: Edward Elgar, pp. 95–107. Reprinted in Caldwell (1993) vol. 3: 199–211.

Caldwell, B. (ed.) (1993) *The Philosophy and Methodology of Economics*, 3 vols. Aldershot: Edward Elgar.

Caldwell, B. (forthcoming) 'Comment on Moseley: Marx's economic theory: true or false?', in F. Moseley (ed.), *Heterodox Economic Theories: True or False?* Aldershot: Edward Elgar.

Churchill, W. (1947) 'Speech', *Hansard*, 11 November, col. 206.

De Marchi, N. (ed.) (1992) *Post-Popperian Methodology of Economics: Recovering Practice*, Boston: Kluwer.

De Marchi, N. and Blaug, M. (eds) (1991) *Appraising Economic Theories: Studies in the Methodology of Research Programmes*, Aldershot: Edward Elgar.

Dewey, J. (1970) [1917] 'The need for a recovery of philosophy', in J. Dewey *et al.* (eds), *Creative Intelligence: Essays in the Pragmatic Attitude*, New York: Octagon Books, pp. 3–69.

Gibbard, A. and Varian, H. (1978) 'Economic models', *Journal of Philosophy* 75: 664–77. Reprinted in Caldwell (1993) vol. 3: 401–14.

Green, E. (1981) 'On the role of fundamental theory in positive economics', in J. Pitt (ed.), *Philosophy of Economics*, Dordrecht: Reidel, pp. 5–15. Reprinted in Caldwell (1993) vol. 3: 415–25.

Hahn, F. (1973) *On the Notion of Equilibrium in Economics*, Cambridge: Cambridge University Press. Reprinted in Caldwell (1993) vol. 3: 337–80.

Hands, D. Wade (1992) *Testing, Rationality and Progress: Essays on the Popperian Tradition in Economic Methodology*, Lanham, MD: Rowman & Littlefield.

Hausman, D. (1988) 'An appraisal of Popperian methodology', in N. de Marchi (ed.), *The Popperian Legacy in Economics*, Cambridge: Cambridge University Press, pp. 65–85.

Hausman, D. (1992) *The Inexact and Separate Science of Economics*, Cambridge: Cambridge University Press.

Hayek, F. A. (1967) [1964] 'The theory of complex phenomena', in F. A. Hayek, *Studies in Philosophy, Economics and Politics*, Chicago: University of Chicago Press, pp. 22–42.

Hutchison, T. W. (1977) *Knowledge and Ignorance in Economics*, Chicago: University of Chicago Press.

Hutchison, T. W. (1981) 'The limitations of general theories in macroeconomics', in T. W. Hutchison, *The Politics and Philosophy of Economics: Marxians, Keynesians and Austrians*, New York: New York University Press, pp. 233–65.

Koertge, N. (1975) 'Popper's metaphysical research program for the human sciences', *Inquiry* 18: 437–62.

Leamer, E. (1983) 'Let's take the con out of econometrics', *American Economic Review* 73: 31–43.

Losee, J. (1987) *Philosophy of Science and Historical Enquiry*, Oxford: Clarendon Press.

McCloskey, D. (1983) 'The rhetoric of economics', *Journal of Economic Literature* 21: 481–517.

McCloskey, D. (1991) 'Economic science: a search through the hyperspace of assumptions?', *Methodus* 3: 6–16.

Mayer, T. (1993) *Truth versus Precision in Economics*, Aldershot: Edward Elgar.

Moseley, F. (forthcoming) 'Marx's economic theory: true or false?', in F. Moseley (ed.), *Heterodox Economic Theories: True or False?* Aldershot: Edward Elgar.

Popper, K. (1991) [1957] *The Poverty of Historicism*, London: Routledge.

8

SCIENTIFIC THINKING WITHOUT SCIENTIFIC METHOD

Two views of Popper

Lawrence A. Boland

> Popper almost alone, and alone in our century, has claimed that criticism belongs not to the *hors d'oeuvre*, but to the main dish.
>
> (Agassi 1968: 317)

> The importance lent to the falsifiability criterion and the demarcation problem by Popper and others distorts his thought.
>
> (Bartley 1968: 43)

> The idea that science can and should be run according to some fixed rules, and that its rationality consists in agreement with such rules, is both unrealistic and vicious. It is unrealistic, since it takes too simple a view of the talents of men and of the circumstances which encourage, or cause, their development. And it is vicious, since the attempt to enforce the rules will undoubtedly erect barriers to what men might have been, and will reduce our humanity by increasing our professional qualifications.
>
> (Feyerabend 1970: 91)

There are two views of scientific thinking attributed to Karl Popper. The more popular among economic methodologists is not very challenging and to be useful requires only a minor adjustment to commonly held views. The less well known view considers Popper's theory of science to be revolutionary and extremely challenging and requiring a major change in attitude towards science and scientific thinking. In this paper I will explain the nature of these two views and their implications for the study of economic methodology. Also I will examine why there are two different views and why one is more popular than the other. Above all, I will try to explain why I think the less popular is the more important.

THE POPULAR POPPER

In economics, the popular view of Popper's philosophy of science is due primarily to Mark Blaug. It is the view usually known as 'falsificationism'. According to this view, scientific thinking is distinguishable from non-scientific thinking by merely noting that scientific theories are falsifiable and non-scientific theories are not. Popper's view is explicitly distinguished from a competing earlier view where scientific theories were distinguished from metaphysics using a criterion of empirical verifiability. Where scientific theories were claimed to be empirically verifiable, and thus meaningful, metaphysics was alleged to be non-verifiable and thus not meaningful. In the 1930s Popper explains the earlier view by claiming that the old distinction was designed to solve a problem of demarcating science from metaphysics. Popper then argues that the earlier view's solution is inadequate. Since scientific theories are explanations, Popper argues that for reasons of quantificational logic, if science is to be characterized as empirical knowledge, verifiability cannot be used to identify scientific theories. Specifically, every explanation involves assumptions of a strictly universal nature (e.g. 'all swans are white') and strictly universal statements can never be verified with empirical observations. However, such statements can be refuted by observation (e.g. 'Today, I saw a black swan in the zoo'). Popper offers his alternative solution, namely, that the extent to which any science is empirical, its distinguishing characteristic must be its empirical falsifiability. Based on Popper's view, the history of science can be seen not as an accumulation of verified theories (since they are impossible) but as the evolution and vicissitudes resulting from the empirical overthrow of false theories. Scientific knowledge is then considered merely a residue of failed attempts to refute, or more specifically, a collection of falsifiable but as yet unrefuted conjectural theories.

The practice of falsificationism

Based on his many observations about empirical falsifiability, many writers, both critics and friends, have saddled Popper with a 'Popperian methodology' that he is presumed to be prescribing for practising scientists. Usually it says that scientists should: (1) consider only falsifiable explanations; (2) limit scientific activity to trying to falsify existing explanations; and (3) accept those explanations that have been tested but have so far not been falsified. Some argue that this so-called methodology is not necessarily a prescription, it is better considered a hopeful description of scientific practice.

Armed with the criterion of falsifiability, Popperian methodologists are thought to be engaged in an ongoing process of appraising past and present economic thinking using this Popperian methodology as the standard. For example, a minimum condition for any theory to be considered a possible contribution to scientific knowledge is that it be empirically falsifiable. Thus, this type of Popperian methodologist is always on guard to root out and prosecute anyone who does not display a concern for falsifiability. Of particular concern are both *ad hoc* adjustments that attempt to overcome refutations and 'immunizing stratagems' designed to protect favourite theories from premature refutation.

Surely, anyone who thinks methodology must be prescriptive will not be satisfied with the nihilism and negativity that is being attributed to Popper. From the perspective of economic methodology, falsifiability by itself is no more challenging than Paul Samuelson's version of operationalism (recall that for an economic proposition to be meaningful Samuelson requires only that it be 'refutable in principle'). Furthermore, according to some observers, if methodologists can tell the scientist what not to do, should they not also be able to give some positive advice? Surely, it is easy to think that those who actively engage in refuting one theory are doing so only because they have an alternative theory in mind. All that we need are criteria to allow us to make a rational choice between competing theories.

According to the popular view of Popper, falsifiability is nothing more than one of the many criteria used to choose the best among competing explanations. Perhaps, as some say, it is the best criterion. In this sense, it would appear that Popper is offering advice to choose the most falsifiable, try to test it, reject it if it fails the test and then move on to test the next most testable theory. In this way one could see the history of science or economics as a sequence of conjectured theories offered as explanations of observed phenomena but which, when empirically rejected, are replaced by another conjecture. The only question here is whether the popular Popperian view of scientific method captures the widely believed view of the history of science, namely that since the time of Isaac Newton there has been a stable and continuous accumulation of scientific knowledge.

Falsificationism and the history of science

It was not obvious that Popper's so-called falsificationism could ever provide an adequate explanation for the apparent stability of science until Imre Lakatos came to the rescue. Lakatos presented a version of falsificationism that substitutes what he called scientific research programmes for singular theories. Lakatos explained why there can be continuity and stability while at the same time recognizing that the business of science involves conjectures, testing and refutations. History according to this view is a sequence of theories and models designed to carry out the research programme. While the research programme may change very slowly, there can be numerous conjectures and refutations of specific models and theories. The task for any historian of thought would seem to be the identification of those aspects of a programme that do not change and those that do. Apart from identifying which programmes rely on immunizing stratagems and which do not, falsification does not seem to play a big role in the explanation of any research programme. While historians of science and economic thought have found the notion of a research programme useful – since it may give them something to do while analysing and modelling various research programmes – there does not seem to be much for a so-called falsificationist methodologist to do.

THE SOCRATIC POPPER

There is a very different view of Popper's theory of science that is not well known in economics. In this alternative view, falsifiability plays a very minor role. Moreover, this view does not take for granted that the history of science is one of stability and progressive accumulation. Popper's theory of science emphasizes that science is embodied in a process which is not at all choice or endorsement but rather criticism or rejection. Theories are rejected because they do not meet available criticism – for example, the criticism may include empirical data that is thought to conflict with the theories. Where many traditional philosophers prior to Popper equated science with rationality and rational choice, Popper emphasizes the critical role of rationality. Briefly stated, science for Popper is a special case of Socratic dialogue, namely, one where we learn with the elimination of error in response to empirical criticism. Rationality is critical debate – with the emphasis on debate. Popper sometimes calls this Critical Rationalism. Given its emphasis on Socratic dialectics, I will call this view the Socratic Popper.

Problem orientation and situational analysis

In his early work Popper openly employs a problem orientation as is evident in his promotion of what he called the Problems of Demarcation and Induction. Popper both offers and recommends a problem orientation to facilitate the emphasis on criticism. It is important to recognize that the problems he identifies are tools which he has manufactured to explain past events or theories. One must be careful when reading Popper not to confuse the message with the medium.

Socratic Popperians stress the centrality of problems. Specifically, to understand any economist we have to know his or her problems. Consider, for example, one of the favourite topics of historians of economic thought, namely the question of whether some particular idea is novel. It is not enough to indicate that the idea is or was new but, according to the Socratic Popper, one would want to show that it is a solution to some

157

problem. But the new idea may not have been introduced to solve the conjectured problem literally. That is, the problem orientation is a heuristic. Every invention of an idea can be seen *post hoc* to solve a problem or answer a question. Said another way, there may not be an answer for every question but there is a question for every answer and, similarly, there may not be a solution for every problem but there is a problem for every solution.

While problem orientation is central to Popper's view of science it is also important to recognize how it is based on his view of rationality. When examining the contribution of an economic thinker, problem orientation always involves presuming that the thinker was implicitly or explicitly trying to solve a problem: achieving his or her aims by overcoming or dealing with all relevant obstacles. This orientation, sometimes called situational analysis, is second nature to every neoclassical economist. Consider the textbook consumer. A neoclassical economist sees the logic of the situation for a consumer to be one where the aim is utility maximization but the consumer faces the constraint of a limited budget as defined by available income and existing prices. The only difference for Socratic Popperians is that they would say that the economist sees the consumer attempting to solve a choice problem. But it is important to keep in mind that problem orientation is always retrospective. The consumer has already made a choice and the economist *post hoc* tries to explain how the choice was made. For example, the consumer is usually thought to be facing a limited budget and psychologically given preferences. The budget defines what can be afforded and preferences enable the consumer to compare any two alternative decisions, and specifically to determine which is better. When the consumer is deciding how much of two goods, say A and B, to buy with that budget, he or she is thought to consider every possible bundle of quantities (where a bundle consists of a pair of quantities, one for each good). If the consumer chooses to spend the entire budget, then certain trade-offs must be made. The consumer is thought to have tentatively picked one affordable bundle and then considered a second bundle which has one less unit of A and comparing how much more B could be purchased and whether the additional amount of B leaves the consumer better off or not. If the second bundle is better, the consumer is presumed to switch to that second bundle and then to use it as a basis of the next comparison – one might see this as a trial-and-elimination process. The consumer is thus thought to have solved the choice problem by determining which of many possible affordable bundles is better than any other affordable bundle. The economist's explanation thus explains why the consumer chose the bundle in question and why all other bundles would not have been chosen (i.e., all other bundles are either inferior according to the preferences or not affordable according to the limited budget, or both).

Presented this way, it should be easy for everyone to understand Popper's problem orientation.

Practising Socratic Popper

As a few writers in economics have recently noted, the essence of Popper's view of science is a matter of embracing a 'critical attitude'. While this is true, it somewhat misses the main point. The main point is that, as Socratic dialogue and critical debate, science is based on non-justificationist rationalism. Some writers think Popper is saying merely that it is impossible to justify one's beliefs. If their view were true, it would be saying that Popper is merely offering us his form of scepticism. The reason usually given for this interpretation of Popper is that he says that he has an unambiguously negative view of what can be called the problem of justification (i.e., the problem of providing a justification for any knowledge claim). What Popper is most negative about is the *necessity* to solve this problem. (Unfortunately, Popper insists on declaring some of his rejections of the necessity of solving specific problems to be 'solutions' of those problems – e.g. the problem of induction.)

The practice of a Popperian methodologist who follows the notion that science is Socratic debate will differ considerably from the activities of those methodologists who see themselves as Popperian falsificationists. Methodologists who follow the Socratic Popper will devote most of their time to fostering and encouraging criticism. Problem orientation is the most popular approach. Using situational analysis, they will provide explanations of existing criticism and critiques, usually by identifying a problem for which existing solutions are inadequate or are in dispute. If there is any appraisal activity, it will be limited to the effectiveness of existing lines of criticism. For example, one might attempt to determine the most effective way to criticize Friedman's instrumentalism or try to explain why criticizing the maximization hypothesis might not be given a sympathetic hearing by neoclassical economists.

Learning and Socratic dialectics

The Socratic aspects of Popper's view are most evident in his claim that people learn from their errors. In Popper's terms, this is not only a process of trial and error, but a process motivated by rational criticism and not by the pursuit of a rational justification. Non-justificational rationalism says that the rationality of a debate or an argument does not guarantee its truth status. More important, the combination of trial and error with the absence of guarantees means that science is inherently unstable.

To say that science is Socratic dialectics begs an explanation of the nature of Socratic dialectics, at least with reference to learning. My view is that

Plato's early dialogue 'Euthyphro' is a perfect case study. Recall that in this dialogue the situation is that Socrates is on his way to his famous trial for impiety and he encounters Euthyphro who is on his way to a trial where he is prosecuting his own father for impiety. As I see this dialogue, Socrates is attempting to deal with a problem: he does not understand why he is being tried for impiety since by his understanding of piety he has committed no crime – Socrates' understanding may be erroneous but Socrates cannot find the error. Now, Euthyphro is obviously an expert on matters involving piety and impiety – if for no other reason, only an expert would prosecute his own father. So, in this dialogue, Socrates is the student trying to learn from Euthyphro the expert. The dialogue proceeds by Socrates presenting his understanding of piety and impiety and inviting Euthyphro to point out where Socrates is in error – after all, if Socrates' understanding were correct he would not be seen to be guilty. Socrates wishes to learn where he is in error and thus lays out his understanding, step by step. Unfortunately, at each step, Euthyphro agrees with Socrates – consequently, if there is an error in Socrates' understanding, Euthyphro failed to find it. At the end, Socrates invites Euthyphro to restart at the beginning but Euthyphro declines. Thus, while there was the perfect opportunity to learn – discovering one's error – Socrates failed to learn anything. For my purposes, Plato's 'Euthyphro' illustrates all of the major ingredients of Popper's theory of learning. Trying to learn from discovering error, inviting criticism in order to learn, putting one's own knowledge at the maximum risk in doing so, and demonstrating the absence of guarantees. Of course, it is important to emphasize that the person who wishes to learn asks the questions.

My interpretation of this dialogue is not universally accepted. I have been publicly criticized for not realizing that Socrates is the teacher and Euthyphro is the student, and thus this dialogue cannot illustrate what I claim is Popper's theory of learning – discovering the errors in one's knowledge. My critics say that it is obvious that Socrates is trying to show Euthyphro the shortcomings of Euthyphro's assumed knowledge of what is pious and impious. My critics say that Socrates leads Euthyphro into a circular argument to convince Euthyphro that his understanding of piety and impiety is inadequate. But Socrates fails and thus Euthyphro does not learn. That there is a failure in learning here we all agree. But my critics claim that the evidence that learning did not take place is that Euthyphro did not see that his knowledge was in error. But as can be plainly seen, my critics invoke Popper's theory of learning in order to claim that Euthyphro did not learn! So whichever way one interprets this dialogue, it would appear that it does illustrate that one learns from discovering one's errors and fails to learn when errors are not uncovered. And either way, it illustrates the absence of a guaranteed outcome. What my interpretation captures but my critics' does not is why Socrates would go to the trouble of asking questions of Euthyphro in the first place. The motivation is that Socrates recognizes that his problem is one that Euthyphro might be able to solve. In other words, Socrates wishes to learn and that is why he asks the questions. By either interpretation, Plato's 'Euthyphro' provides a good metaphor to help understand Popper's view of the process of science; namely, science is critical theory without a method that can guarantee a desired outcome.

Science in flux

Apart from the recognition that even though Socrates follows his usual method of learning, success was not assured, the Euthyphro dialogue may not be the best way to bring out the revolutionary aspects of Popper's view of science. Another way to appreciate why Popper's view is revolutionary would be to consider the difference between how the relationship between rationality and science was viewed before and after Albert Einstein.

Looking as far back as the eighteenth century one can find people who commonly believed that if science is rational then it is stable. Rationality provides universality and universality provides stability. The key point here is that a minimum requirement for an argument to be rational is that *everyone* who accepts the truth of its premises must by both the force and definition of logic accept the truth of all validly inferred conclusions from those premises. Universality is provided by the fact that this is true for *everyone* who accepts the assumptions. When we also realize that people once thought that rational proof included infallible inductive proof, that is, proof based only on undisputed observations, there would be very little room for disagreement and hence for instability. Today, the task of the philosopher or historian of science is more often thought to involve explaining the success of science, and thus there is even less room to see instability in science.

Throughout the nineteenth century, the most obvious evidence in favour of this equation between a rational science and a stable science was Newton's mechanics. But at the beginning of the twentieth century, Einstein's theories challenged the adequacy of Newton's theories and of inductivist scientific method and openly demonstrated that science is fallible. That is, the success of science is not necessarily the result of an infallible scientific method. Moreover, recognition of a fallible science meant that a rational science cannot assure a stable intellectual foundation on which so much of Western culture depends. In this regard, then, Popper's view is revolutionary since it is probably the first to deal with the post-Einsteinian reality of science. According to the Socratic–Popper view, science should be seen to be a process which is potentially in a state of constant flux rather than one which establishes incorrigible stable truths. There are no infallible methods, no authorities and no unquestionable facts. Science is scientific thinking without scientific method.

POPPER'S SEMINAR AND THE HIJACKER

During the 1950s Popper generated a group of self-declared disciples by means of his 'Tuesday Afternoon Seminar'. Popperian-style seminars are notorious. There is much criticism, tension and above all constant interruptions. Nothing is to be protected from criticism. The rule seems to be, as noted by J. O. Wisdom, 'Thou shall not speak while I am interrupting!' Students and participants who can handle all the tension, as well as the shameless disregard for the traditional rules, will usually find such seminars very stimulating and productive.

Since Popperian seminars are almost exclusively concerned with learning and criticism, participants are warned at the outset to 'leave their toes outside the door'. That is, participants should not take criticism personally because if they do they limit their own opportunities to learn. Even when this warning is heeded, Popperian seminars often run into difficulties. Students unfamiliar with the medium will often start looking for the rules and methods required to conduct a successful seminar and tension begins as soon as it is pointed out that there are no such rules or methods other than 'everything is open to question'. Interestingly, such difficulties are virtually the same ones which Popper has faced in his struggles with the entire philosophy profession – which for most of the nineteenth century had been built on the presumption of a reliable method that would guarantee success.

Some of the early disciples of Popper and his seminar were Wisdom and John Watkins. Joseph Agassi joined the group at the beginning of 1953 when Paul Feyerabend was about to be Popper's assistant. When Feyerabend left for Vienna, Agassi became Popper's assistant. Assistants were often put in charge of constructing indexes for Popper's books. Ian Jarvie attended the seminar as an undergraduate. William Bartley joined Agassi in the seminar and somewhat later Agassi brought Imre Lakatos. With the exception of Lakatos, all of them were Popper's devoted disciples, particularly with regard to Popper's constant complaints that he had not received the recognition he was due in the philosophy profession.

The disciples were united in their appreciation for what I am calling the Socratic version of Popper's philosophy of science. Criticism and problem orientation are essential to learning and understanding. Some of the disciples thought they understood this well enough to put Popper's views into practice – they even ventured criticism of Popper's views. Their efforts have led to much acrimony, sometimes at the level of soap opera.

The all-consuming situation in the early 1960s was that while there was a rapidly growing interest in the philosophy and history of science, the name most often mentioned was not Popper's but that of Thomas Kuhn. Everyone in almost every discipline seemed to be discussing Kuhn's 'paradigms'. Some of the disciples claim that Lakatos took advantage of the situation and, in effect, hijacked Popper's seminar. Supposedly, Lakatos convinced Popper that the desired recognition could be obtained by recasting Popper's views in a form closer to Kuhn's. Thus Lakatos and Popper made much more of the growth of knowledge implications of Popper's view and much, much less of the Socratic dialectical aspects which the disciples advocated.

POPPER'S DISCIPLES VERSUS POPPER AND THE HIJACKER

While some may wish to argue about which version of Popper's philosophy of science is the 'true Popper', I think it is more important to recognize that there is more than one view. But why are there two views? What are the sources of the arguments or disagreements? Is Popper's at fault or his followers'?

Admittedly, Popper's recommended method of criticism can itself be the source of disputes. When criticizing a writer's views, Popper insists on a problem orientation whereby the critic must present the writer's problem and solution but only after making every effort to present the writer's views in the most sympathetic light. That is, the critic must make all unchallengeable improvements that can be made before launching the criticism. One would not wish to distract the debate into irrelevant side issues. In effect, the criticism must be conducted in terms that the writer can accept. This sympathetic problem orientation very often leads Popper to lean backwards to grant as much as possible to the criticized writer and this in turn leads readers to miss the rhetoric and thus to misunderstand Popper's own views.

Popper's Tuesday Afternoon Seminar itself is probably the major source of disagreements. In the early 1960s some of its participants, such as Agassi and Bartley, began publishing criticisms of Popper. The complaints from Agassi and Bartley seem to be based on apparent inconsistencies between what they thought Popper preached or practised in this seminar and what he said in his writings. Those of us who never attended the famous seminar are left only with the views Popper expressed in his writings. And if one is not aware of his sympathetic problem orientation, it is all too easy to see inconsistencies where they do not exist.

Popper's writings do not seem to stress the importance of criticism nearly as much as his disciples claim his seminar did. The participants in the seminar equate Popper's view of science with what I have called the Socratic Popper. It is not surprising then that when Lakatos developed what he called the 'methodology of scientific research programmes' as his version of Popper's view of science, the other members of the seminar were very critical. Bartley claimed that Lakatos added nothing of importance to the philosophy of science other than a few catchy phrases. Agassi claims that Lakatos did not know enough about the philosophy of science to make his pronouncements worthwhile. While almost everyone says that Lakatos made significant contributions to the philosophy of mathematics, the disciples routinely claim that Lakatos did not understand Popper and the 'methodology of scientific research programmes' of Lakatos does not represent the views of Popper. Moreover, they say, Lakatos misled Popper into a pursuit of fame at the expense of integrity, that is, at the expense of throwing the Socratic baby out with the inconveniently unmarketable dirty bath water.

THE POPULAR POPPER VERSUS THE IMPORTANT POPPER

The major question to consider is why so much is known about the Lakatos version of Popper's philosophy of science and so little about the Socratic Popper promoted by Popper's disciples. An obvious reason is that the popularly accepted version of Popper's view allows one to see Popper as a philosopher making only minor improvements in the ordinary view of science. The ordinary view is that science is a stable enterprise and its stability is based on the avoidance of irresolvable questions such as those concerned with the absolute truth of scientific theories. After all, scientific theories cannot be proven true but only false. But Popper warned that the ordinary view allows any refutation to be avoided by refusing to accept the refuting evidence. Popper's disciples call the ordinary view 'conventionalism' since according to conventionalism, theories are not to be considered true in an absolute sense but only in a sense where a theory is 'true' as defined by the conventional notions of truth. Typically, a probability calculus is substituted for an absolute notion of truth status. According to the ordinary view, it is rational to accept a theory with a high probability of being true (given currently available empirical data) and to reject any theory with a lower probability. The issue thus is not one of truth status but one of *rational* acceptance by a community of scientists.

Rationality and conventionalism

There is much more to the ordinary view than its foundation of conventionalism. While the notion of rationality underlying conventionalism presumes science is rational, the presumption of rationality implies that any belief in a scientific theory can be proven (i.e., justified) – at least to the point of demonstrating its logical consistency with conventional acceptance criteria. This is definitely not the non-justificationalist notion of rationality presumed in the Socratic version of Popper's view. But there is even more to conventionalism. An essential notion is that in science one strives to be able to choose the best theory from competing theories. Moreover, it is presumed that the criteria used in science are the best criteria.

While it may be difficult for followers of the popular Popper to see why anyone might strongly object to the commonplace notions of conventionalism, there are obvious reasons for why the followers of the Socratic Popper strongly reject conventionalism. It would be difficult to see how Socratic dialectics could be seriously pursued whenever it is allowed that one can always defend one's position by claiming that one's theories are not to be considered absolutely true but only the best available. The conventionalist defence that relies on the substitution of 'best' for 'absolutely true' seems to beg many questions. The most obvious question is whether the criteria that define 'best' are themselves really the best – such a question leads to an infinite regress, of course. Given the inherent possibility of avoiding contradictions with facts by denying the intended truth status and the impossibility of avoiding an infinite regress whenever rational acceptance is considered a substitute for truth status, how could one ever engage in a Socratic dialogue?

Conventionalism and the stability of science

According to the ordinary view of science, the everyday business of a methodologist seems to be either confined to a linguistic analysis of what economists say in their explanations or limited to a historical description of how particular economists reached their conclusions. Of course, there has always been room for a methodologist to make grand claims. Today, however, it would seem that moderation in methodology is much more common. Moderation may be the consequence of a certain complacency which also exists today. In terms of the alleged stability of science, there is an obvious consistency between stability and the presumptions of the ordinary view. Specifically, if everyone practised conventionalism, the chances of a 'science in flux' would be very small. It is very difficult to push on something so soft and forgiving. According to the ordinary view, Einstein's views can easily be seen as mere adjustments, such that Newton's views are viewed as a special case. In economics, Keynes's view need not be considered revolutionary but merely a special case of general equilibrium analysis. Of course, in economics there continues to be a problem of providing the micro-foundations of Keynesian macroeconomics which would prove that Keynes was not a revolutionary.

Interestingly, it is Kuhn's conception of a paradigm that seems to capture the essence of the ordinary view of science. But Kuhn goes further to say (in a verbal response to Lakatos at the 1970 Boston AAAS meetings) that what makes science scientific is that the scientific community is made up of scientists imbued with a scientific mentality! I am not sure Kuhn's elaborated psychologistic view, if widely known, would be widely accepted. Nevertheless, the ordinary view does see science and scientific knowledge as an entity on an historical continuum. Revolutions are rare and ordinary science is more a question of day-to-day puzzle solving. It is difficult to see how we could have the current textbook-based education system without Kuhn's view being correct. It is exactly the textbook-based education system that presents an overwhelming obstacle to the appreciation of the Socratic version of Popper's view of science that the disciples promote.

Understanding Socratic Popper

The followers of the ordinary view have considerable difficulty in understanding the disciples' alternative view of Popper. This difficulty needs to be explained and understood. The situation is very complex. As can be seen above, there are differences concerning theories of rationality, the history of science, the necessity of a scientific method, the nature of dialectics and, above all, the presumption that all true knowledge can be justified.

The presumption taken for granted by all followers of the ordinary view says that we would have to justify our knowledge before we can claim to know anything. There is widespread fear that without a method which will assure that only true knowledge claims will be justified, we would have to give knowledge claims of mysticism, fundamentalist religions and similar 'unscientific' disciples an equal status with science. There is nothing in the Socratic version of Popper that would overcome this fear. But, more important, the disciples claim that this fear could never be overcome. Proponents of the popular falsificationist Popper, however, think the requirement of falsifiability is a sufficient prophylactic. It may be sufficient but the disciples claim that it too often rules out potentially scientific notions that happen not to be at the time in a form that is falsifiable. And besides, some aspects of science such as metaphysics may not be falsifiable but they are essential. In one sense, every theory that is designed to explain observable events is an application of a particular metaphysics. After all, one cannot explain everything at once. Something must be assumed. For example, in neoclassical economics, every theory or model will assume that the decision-maker is an optimizer even though it is virtually impossible to refute this assumption. This is because the neoclassical decision-maker is presumed to maximize *something*. Since the 'something' does not always need to be specified, it is difficult to define what would constitute a refutation of the assumption of maximization.

For many centuries, rationality was viewed as a stable and reliable means to convince everyone that one's view was true, that is, to justify one's knowledge by means of irrefutable logical proof. Since the time of David Hume, the ability of rationality to deliver on this promise has been in doubt. Moreover, it is against this promise that some of Popper's disciples argue that rationality is better understood as a means of criticizing. Criticism is built upon discovering logical contradictions. After all, an empirical refutation is merely a contradiction between the theory and the available empirical data (i.e., it cannot be that both are true). Except for tautologies, rationality does not guarantee that one's knowledge is true but rationality can be a means of proving that one's knowledge is false. This asymmetry parallels Popper's distinction between verifiability and refutability. Every argument consists of (two or more) assumptions and at least one conclusion which is claimed to be true whenever all of the assumptions are true. In terms of rhetoric, it would be better to say the conclusion is true whenever one accepts the assumptions as true. In one sense it could be claimed that the conjunction of the assumptions forms a justification of truth of the conclusion statement. But, the justification is conditional on the actual truth of the assumptions. Thus, such a justification is always open to question. From a non-justification standpoint, the argument is a means of criticism. For example, if one accepts all the assumptions as true then one cannot at the same time accept statements which contradict any valid conclusion based on those assumptions. Specifically, if one had a consumer theory that said that the demand curve for a good is downward sloping when certain conditions are met, then if those conditions are met and the assumptions are all accepted as true, one could not at the same time claim to accept the existence of so-called Giffen goods. So, rationality may still retain its universality and ability to convince but the disciples argue that the ability may be limited to criticism and refutations.

The widespread presumption that a rationality-based science is a successful stable enterprise is denied by Popper's disciples. Nevertheless, since the presumption is so widespread, they cannot completely ignore it. Some of the disciples claim that the history of science appears to be stable only to those who wish to ignore the impact of Einstein's overthrow of Newton's mechanics. In the 1950s when I was a high-school student, some science textbooks led one to think that there existed an infallible scientific method which, if followed step by step, would lead to the establishment of a scientific law. The first step was the collection of data. The second was the formation of a hypothesis to explain the collected data. The third step was the formation of an experiment to test the hypothesis. If the hypothesis passed the test, the hypothesis was declared a theory. If the theory passed the tests of all other scientists, then one's theory would become a law! While today's atmosphere of moderation would not be so optimistic, the old textbook writers were quite confident. The basis for their confidence was their belief that the success of Newton's physics was sufficient proof that such a method existed and it worked. What is most disturbing for

Popper's disciples is the presumption that any success in science must be due to a practised scientific methodology. Again, the disciples take the view that methodology has no more guarantees than a Socratic dialogue. Unfortunately, proponents of the ordinary view of science seem to want more.

The foundation of the belief in the stability and reliability of science has always been a belief in the universality and certainty of a scientific method. When it turned out that Newton's mechanics failed under certain conditions, believers in scientific method chose to switch rather than fight. Specifically, they held to a view that still claimed there was an infallible method but switched to say that it never was a method for proving the truth of scientific theories but only a method for choosing the best from existing competitors. So when Einstein or Popper claim that theories are either true or false, believers in the existence of an infallible scientific method are at a loss about what to do. They still wish to believe that scientific knowledge has been accumulating in a positive, progressive and stable way. Thus, it is easier to soften the goal of science so as to maintain a belief in Newton's positive contribution than have to admit that Newton's theory is somehow false. It could be argued that the softened version of scientific method not only lacks guarantees but it also lacks a purpose other than possibly to apologize for Newton's failure.

While the ordinary view sees a scientific method providing a stable and certain science, Socratic dialectics lacks guarantees, as illustrated with the Euthyphro dialogue. And while the softened version of scientific method also lacks guarantees, at least Socratic dialectics promotes a potential for learning. The potentiality is mostly due to Socratic dialectics maintaining that theories are true or false (rather than better or worse). But by promising only potentiality while requiring that theories be absolutely true, we face a dilemma. On the one hand, since the softened version of scientific method promises very little, success is easily achieved. On the other hand, while profound learning is possible with Socratic dialectics, it may take a long time. It is always possible that by engaging in a Socratic dialogue one might discover monumental truths, but more often the dialogue is one like Euthyphro. Perhaps only one of a hundred dialogues is productive. For methodologists in a hurry, dialectics do not seem to be a promising endeavour.

THE FUTURE OF POPPERIAN ECONOMIC METHODOLOGY

Kuhn's view of science presents a very comfortable (albeit, dull) picture of a science of hard-working and level-headed scientists who rarely if ever stage a revolution. The Lakatos view appears less dull but that may be due merely to its spicy language of 'hard cores' and 'protective belts'. Both views seem to provide a clear picture of a stable science. If instead of following Kuhn or Lakatos we were to follow the disciples' version of Popper, then the picture would be much less clear. What is clear is the disciples' rejection of the substitution of a probability calculus for truth status. According to the disciples' Socratic version of Popper, theories are either true or false. With such a severe stance regarding the truth status of theories it would seem that science would always be in a state of rapid flux, possibly even chaos. So how do the disciples deal with the commonly accepted view that science seems to be rather stable?

Explaining stability away

In economics, the obvious example of a well-developed and stable research programme is neoclassical theory which in terms of its basic ideas (i.e., the principles of economics) has not changed much in the last hundred years. With this programme in mind, the Socratic–Popper view of science would seem to be of limited use. Either the Lakatos–Popper view with its emphasis on a well-protected core or the Kuhnian textbook-based view would seem to be more appropriate. But their comparative advantage may be illusionary.

Why might an ordinary methodologist think that the Socratic–Popper view of science implies a science in a constant state of rapid flux and chaos? The source of this supposition would have to be the ordinary view's notion that scientists are actively *choosing* among competing theories. According to the ordinary view, should any theory be refuted (i.e., proven false) there would then be an immediate switch to the next best theory. Such alternating refutation and theory switching would almost definitely see science in a state of flux. But the disciples say that while all theories are open to testing, a state of rapid flux or chaos is not a necessary outcome. There is nothing that forces one to choose any theory. One *may* choose to accept a theory that has not been refuted by the latest test, but there is no reason for why we *must* make a choice. The fact that there is no reason to make a choice leads to a certain type of stability, but this type of stability cannot be seen to be caused by the existence of a reliable method. It is certainly not due to the acceptance of a rationality designed to justify the currently chosen theory.

While the Socratic version of Popper's view would seem to imply a science that is in constant flux and turmoil, expecting such a state of affairs presumes too much. Most obvious is the presumption that since science is fallible it is easy to overturn. For any discipline to be rapidly changing it would seem to require all science teachers to be on the frontiers of knowledge developments. Since significant changes would involve challenging strongly held views (i.e., the accepted paradigm), peer review processes are unlikely to grant funds to someone whose views seem far out. While we give lip-service to the notion that a PhD thesis is to be not only significant but also original, any thesis that was completely original would be difficult to access on the basis of the currently accepted paradigm. Advances in any discipline are usually marginal because marginal changes are easy to understand. This notion of marginalism parallels Popper's views of social change and social policy which he calls 'piecemeal engineering'.

There are many reasons for the apparent stability of science in general and of neoclassical economics in particular. Foremost is the recognition that science is a social institution involving such things as educational institutions, research-funding institutions based on peer reviews, textbook publishers and overall the constraining influence of the sociology of any scientific community. And we must not overlook the necessity for any theory or research programme to be based on some metaphysical notions that are purposefully put beyond question or are at best very difficult to test. What some disciples argue is that the apparent stability of any science is an intended consequence of decisions made within the scientific community. The stability, apparent or otherwise, is a social artefact and not in any way a logical property of an inherent nature of scientific knowledge.

The practising Popperian methodologist

In this chapter I have tried to expose the reader to a view of Popper's philosophy of science that does not seem to be widely understood. Briefly stated, according to the Socratic–Popper view of science, criticism is the main course and falsifiability, stituational analysis, critical rationalism all belong to the hors-d'oeuvre.

In the process of writing this chapter I have acquired a new perspective on my own efforts at practising Popperian methodology. I have known for some time that I have considerable difficulty communicating with those falsificationist methodologists who see their role as that of appraising various aspects of economics. I have also known that the difficulty is due to their believing that Lakatos correctly portrayed Popper's philosophy of science as falsificationism. It is clear to me now that things are much worse. It would appear that the followers of Lakatos are totally unaware of the disciples' view of Popper.

Socratic dialectics is central to Popper's view of science. Accordingly, science is critical debate. As with any debate, there is no foolproof method, no guarantees. Problem orientation is Popper's medium for conducting debates but it is not the central message. Situational analysis is only a convenient vehicle for interpreting the rationality of the problem situation but nothing more. Critical rationalism is a means of differentiating and precluding a justificational interpretation of the rationality of the problem situation but nothing more. In all of this, falsifiability is merely a logical condition required by critical rationalism. And rationality is essential but still it is only one aspect of criticism.

Since I started working in the field of economic methodology at a time before Lakatos began promoting his version of Popper, I knew only the disciples' version of Popper. In my work falsifiability plays at most a minor role. Until my 1992 book, which is explicitly about methods of criticizing neoclassical economics, I took the criticism-based Socratic-dialectical view of Popper for granted. In the 1980s I began encountering methodologists who equated Popper with a 'falsificationist methodology'. For example, some writers such as Blaug saw a virtue in this equation and others such as Dan Hausman said the equation represented a vice. In both cases, it was difficult to figure out who this 'Popper' was they were discussing. Fortunately, in the 1990s things have begun to change. Judging by recent activities of Bruce Caldwell and Wade Hands, there are indications that the disciples' version of Popper might finally be receiving the attention it deserves in the field of economic methodology.

BIBLIOGRAPHY

Agassi, J. (1963) *Towards an Historiography of Science, History and Theory, Beiheft* 2, The Hague: Mouton.

Agassi, J. (1966) 'Sensationalism', *Mind* 75: 1–24.

Agassi, J. (1968) 'Science in flux: footnotes to Popper', in R. Cohen and M. Wartofsky (eds), *Boston Studies in the Philosophy of Science* 3: 293–323.

Agassi, J. (1977) *Towards a Rational Philosophical Anthropology*, The Hague: Martinus Nijhoff.

Agassi, J. (1988) *The Gentle Art of Philosophical Polemics*, La Salle, IL: Open Court.

Agassi, J. (1992) 'False prophecy versus true quest: a modest challenge to contemporary relativists', *Philosophy of Social Science* 22: 285–312.

Agassi, J. (1992) 'The philosopher's apprentice', unpublished manuscript.

Bartley, W. W. III (1964) 'Rationality vs the theory of rationality', in M. Bunge (ed.), *The Critical Approach in Science and Philosophy*, London: Collier-Macmillan, pp. 3–31.

Bartley, W. W. III (1968) 'Theories of demarcation between science and metaphysics', in I. Lakatos and A. Musgrave (eds), *Problems in the Philosophy of Science*, Amsterdam: North-Holland, pp. 40–64.

Blaug, M. (1975) 'Kuhn versus Lakatos, or paradigms versus research programmes in the history of economics', *History of Political Economy* 7: 399–433.

Boland, L. (1968) 'The identification problem and the validity of economic models', *South African Journal of Economics* 36: 236–40.

Boland, L. (1979) 'A critique of Friedman's critics', *Journal of Economic Literature* 17: 503–22.

Boland, L. (1981) 'On the futility of criticizing the neoclassical maximization hypothesis', *American Economic Review* 71: 1031–6.

Boland, L. (1992) *The Principles of Economics: Some Lies My Teachers Told Me*, London: Routledge.

Caldwell, B. (1991) 'Clarifying Popper', *Journal of Economic Literature* 29: 1–33.

Einstein, A. and Infeld, L. (1961) [1938] *The Evolution of Physics: The Growth of*

Ideas from Early Concepts to Relativity and Quanta, New York: Simon & Schuster.

Feyerabend, P. (1970) 'Against method: outline of an anarchistic theory of knowledge', in M. Radner and S. Winokur (eds), *Minnesota Studies in the Philosophy of Science* 4: 17–130.

Hands, D. W. (1990) 'Thirteen theses on progress in economic methodology', *Finnish Economic Papers* 3: 72–6.

Hausman, D. (1985) 'Is falsification unpractised or unpractisable?', *Philosophy of Social Science* 15: 313–19.

Kuhn, T. (1970) *The Structure of Scientific Revolutions*, Chicago: University of Chicago Press.

Lakatos, I. (1970) 'Falsification and the methodology of scientific research programmes', in I. Lakatos and A. Musgrave (eds), *Criticism and the Growth of Knowledge*, Cambridge: Cambridge University Press, pp. 91–196.

Samuelson, P. (1965) *Foundations of Econonic Analysis*, New York: Atheneum.

Sassower, R. (1985) *Philosophy of Economics: A Critique of Demarcation*, New York: University Press of America.

Wong, S. (1978) *The Foundations of Paul Samuelson's Revealed Preference Theory*, London: Routledge & Kegan Paul.

9

THE LAKATOSIAN LEGACY IN ECONOMIC METHODOLOGY

Roger E. Backhouse

INTRODUCTION

Lakatos's methodology of scientific research programmes (MSRP) played a crucial role in the upsurge of interest in economic methodology in the 1980s (see Chapter 1). Though there had been earlier explorations of the relevance of Kuhnian and Lakatosian ideas to economics, the key work was arguably the volume edited by Latsis, *Method and Appraisal in Economics* (1976). In this volume a number of distinguished economists grappled with the issues of how economic knowledge grew and how it might be appraised in a way that made earlier debates on methodology seem almost arid in comparison. For about a decade after this book, Lakatosian methodology, augmented by the Popperian falsificationism advocated by Blaug, formed the major focus of debates in economic methodology. From around the middle of the 1980s, however, interest in and support for Lakatosian ideas waned to such an extent that, referring to a conference organized in 1989 to reassess Lakatosian methodology, one of the organizers expressed the view that,

> I was personally taken aback by what can only be described as a generally dismissive, if not hostile, reaction to Lakatos's MSRP. Of the 37 participants, I estimate that only 12 were prepared to give Lakatos a further run for his money and of the 17 papers only five were unambiguously positive about the value of MSRP.
>
> (de Marchi and Blaug 1991: 500)

The judgement of many leading writers on economic methodology is that Lakatosian methodology has little to offer (see, for example, Hausman 1992; Rosenberg 1992; Hands 1993a; and several chapters in this volume). At the same time, however, many economists, as will be explained below, still find Lakatosian ideas helpful.

The aim of this paper is to reflect on the Lakatosian legacy in economic methodology, asking how far Lakatos's MSRP can be defended, focusing on a number of issues: how far have criticisms undermined Lakatosian methodology? What is its attraction for economists? Where should economic methodology be going, and how does this relate to the Lakatosian perspective? In answering these questions particular attention will be paid to the role of the methodologist.[1]

LAKATOSIAN METHODOLOGY

The methodology of scientific research programmes

Lakatos's MSRP (Lakatos 1970)[2] involves appraising scientific research programmes in terms of their ability to successfully predict novel facts.[3] A *scientific research programme* is defined by sets of rules, or heuristics, governing research within the programme. These fall into two categories. *Negative heuristics* direct researchers not to question the *hard core* of the programme – the set of assumptions regarded as irrefutable by anyone working within the programme. Thus if 'Agents optimize subject to constraints' is a hard-core assumption, the corresponding negative heuristic would be 'Do not construct theories in which irrational behaviour plays a significant role'. *Positive heuristics*, on the other hand, contain rules by which research is to be conducted. These rules lay out the strategy by which anomalies are to be dealt with, and how the research programme is to be developed. They are concerned with the programme's *protective belt*: the assumptions and procedures which need to be made to apply the hard-core assumptions to specific problems, but which can be modified without calling the programme into question. Examples of positive heuristics might be 'Explain Pareto-inefficient allocations of resources by finding missing markets', or 'Start by assuming identical agents and full information, dropping these assumptions later on'.

Research programmes are, however, not static. New facts are discovered, new problems emerge, and as a result modifications have to be made to the protective belt. Lakatos, therefore, argues that research programmes should be appraised according to the way they evolve over time. If the modifications made to a programme do no more than explain away new evidence, he terms the programme *degenerating*. If, on the other hand, modifications not only explain anomalies but also lead to the prediction of new facts – facts the modifications were not designed to explain – Lakatos calls the programme progressive. It is *theoretically progressive* if new facts are predicted. It is *empirically progressive* if these new facts are corroborated.

Finally, research programmes do not exist in isolation. There will typically exist rival research programmes. Appraisal, therefore, involves choosing between competing research programmes. Lakatos's claim is that scientists should abandon degenerating research programmes in favour of progressive ones. One of the problems with this criterion, however, is that research programmes may go through progressive and degenerating phases. One might, for example, argue that Keynesian economics was progressive in the 1940s, the novel facts it predicted including the multiplier and the consequences of fiscal policy changes, but degenerated in the 1960s, the modifications being introduced to explain inflation not leading to the prediction of new, unexpected facts. It is even possible that programmes may degenerate for a while, but later become progressive. Rational scientists need to be forward looking, and the fact that a programme is less progressive than a rival does not mean that it will continue to be so in future. It may be rational, therefore, to allow fledgling research programmes time to develop.

When taken in isolation, few components of Lakatos's MSRP were original with Lakatos. A scientific research programme is very similar to what Kuhn termed a disciplinary matrix, the collection of assumptions and procedures that define a period of normal science.[4] Lakatos has narrowed the definition slightly, and has suggested that science will be characterized by competing programmes where Kuhn argued that a single disciplinary matrix would typically be dominant at any time, but beyond that there is little difference. As for the appraisal criterion, that a programme successfully predict novel facts, this has a long history going back at least to Whewell and Herschel in the mid-nineteenth century. The Lakatosian account of how one programme supersedes another places greater emphasis on rationality than does Kuhn's account of paradigm-shifts, and the irrational, 'gestalt-shift' aspect of the process is completely absent. In both the Kuhnian and Lakatosian frameworks, however, the main force for change is the need to modify theoretical frameworks to take account of anomalies and deal with new problems.

The main source of Lakatos's ideas, however, is Popper. Though, with important exceptions discussed in Chapter 1, Lakatos became influential in economic methodology before Popper, Lakatos presented his methodology of scientific research programmes as a natural development of Popper's falsificationism. Popper, according to Lakatos's interpretation, started out as a naive falsificationist, stressing the asymmetry between confirmation and refutation of a theory (one observation is sufficient to refute a theory, whereas no finite number of observations can confirm it with complete certainty). In response to the problems inherent in naive falsificationism, however, Popper moved on to a position Lakatos characterized as sophisticated methodological falsificationism. Greater stress was laid on predicting novel facts, and less on falsifiability. Popper even wrote about metaphysical research programmes (1983: 189–93).[5]

When compared with certain of Popper's writings, Lakatos seems hardly to go beyond Popper (see, for example, Popper 1972: 240–8). The MSRP appears to represent a minor variation on what Lakatos termed Popper's sophisticated methodological falsificationism, distinguished from the latter as much by Lakatos's new terminology as by its content. Lakatos, however, altered the emphasis in some key respects. Notably, his concept of a research programme involves placing certain assumptions (the hard core) beyond criticism. Though Popper saw the heuristic power of metaphysical hypotheses, this is very un-Popperian.[6] Furthermore, though he still thinks of empirical content in a Popperian way, as the set of potential falsifiers, he places greater emphasis on corroboration than on falsification. Progressive research programmes are ones whose predictions are corroborated.

Why have economic methodologists turned against the MSRP?

Lakatos's MSRP has been criticized at a number of levels. First, there are criticisms of the concept of a research programme, perhaps the most distinctively Lakatosian aspect of his methodology. Second, there are objections to the Popperian epistemology out of which Lakatos's methodology arose, and of which it forms a part. Finally, there is the argument that it is pointless trying to provide *any* general philosophical analysis of how scientific knowledge evolves. These will be considered in turn.

(1) Perhaps the most direct criticism of the methodology of scientific research programmes is the argument that Lakatos's definition of a research programme in terms of an invariant hard core is too narrow: that research programmes in economics need to be characterized in more complex ways so as to allow for change over time.[7] A good example of such criticism is provided in Hoover (1991) who argues that the new classical economics (which most economists would think of as a coherent, well-defined research programme) cannot be characterized in terms of an invariant set of hard-core assumptions. One of the most persuasive attempts to define a research programme in Lakatos's sense is the neo-Walrasian programme outlined by Weintraub (1985). This programme, however, is defined by assumptions and heuristics that are primarily methodological (commitment to rational behaviour and the use of optimizing models) with the result that its hard core has little economic content. It is a programme held together by modelling strategy as much as anything else. As a result the neo-Walrasian research programme thus has a character very different from those postulated for physics (such as Newtonian mechanics) where the hard core typically includes some substantive hypotheses (such as Newton's laws of motion).

There are additional, though related, problems concerning the overlaps between programmes. In economics there is, for example, a strong case for speaking of a neo-Walrasian research programme, dominated by a commitment to mathematically rigorous, formal analysis of the consequences of individual optimizing behaviour. Much post-war macroeconomics clearly forms part of such a programme: macroeconomists have sought to provide rigorous micro-foundations for macroeconomic theor-ies.[8] Milton Friedman's work, first on the consumption function and later on the expectations-augmented Phillips curve, forms an indispensable part of the history of such a programme. Equally, it can be argued that there is a Chicago programme, defined along the lines outlined by Reder (1982) in terms of commitment to the assumption that the world is approximately Pareto-efficient, and that Friedman is a key figure in this programme. However, it cannot be argued that Chicago economics forms a sub-pro-gramme within neo-Walrasian economics: the commitment to formal mod-elling and mathematical rigour are missing. Friedman's 'Marshallian' methodology, stressing the importance of empirical evidence and simple models, is clearly not Walrasian. There is thus a strong case for speaking in terms of two overlapping programmes, with work conducted within one programme providing a crucial input into another programme. Research programmes are thus not self-contained enterprises. Whilst it would be possible to argue that at least one research programme is inappropriately defined, it is perhaps more persuasive to argue that this example shows the limitations of the concept of a research programme as defined by Lakatos.

This conclusion that interdependence between research programmes is an essential feature of any analysis of economics is reinforced by the argument that criticism of rival programmes is frequently important in a programme's development. Hoover (1991) has cited the importance of the Lucas critique for the new classical macroeconomics. Steedman (1991) has emphasized the importance for Sraffian economics of its critique of neoclassical theory. The conclusion both Hoover and Steedman reach is that Lakatos's methodology of scientific research programmes is unhelpful in trying to understand the relationships between different economic theories.

(2) Lakatos's methodology of scientific research programmes is also vulnerable to criticisms of the Popperian epistemology on which it is based. Two such criticisms will be considered here. The first is the argument that Popper's rejection of induction as a principle underlying knowledge is taken too far. His argument was that, however many observations we have, we can *never* be sure that the next observation is not going to disprove a theory. For Popper it followed that *all* knowledge is provisional and uncer-tain, and that we can never have evidence in favour of a theory. It can be argued (e.g. Hausman 1992) that we *do* know some things, and that it is wrong to reject induction completely.

Hands (1991a) has taken this argument further by arguing that there is a close link between prediction of novel facts as an appraisal criterion and Popper's attempts to solve the problem of induction. Popper and Lakatos are both scientific realists, wanting to show that scientific theories could, if developed in accordance with their methodologies, become closer to the truth. Popper noted that rejecting theories which fail severe tests reduces the falsity content of science, whilst the requirement that theories have interesting, testable consequences should increase its truth content. The prediction of novel facts is thus linked to the aim of increasing the 'verisimilitude', or truthlikeness of scientific theories. Popper's formal theory of verisimilitude has, however, serious flaws. Without it, Hands has argued, there is no reason to attach special significance to the prediction of novel facts – Lakatos's appraisal criterion is left hanging in the air.

The second main criticism of the Popperian framework is that it is too narrow. Mäki (1980) has criticized what he calls the Popperian dominance, by which he means not that economic methodologists advocate Popperian ideas, but that methodological discussion has been dominated by a narrow range of issues:

> epistemological questions related to rational theory choice or rational theory development, formulated in the dynamic but anti-inductivist and asocial framework of Karl Popper or Imre Lakatos, have dominated the field.
>
> (Mäki 1980: 79)

Similarly, de Marchi (1992: 3) blames the narrow range of questions with which economic methodology has been concerned on the result of the acceptance of Popper's notion that science results from following certain rules. For Popper it is adherence to certain rules that guarantees that false claims will be exposed.

Of the many issues Mäki and de Marchi see as having been neglected, one is the possible significance of the context of discovery. Fundamental to Popper's work is the idea that there is a clear distinction between the contexts of discovery and justification, and that the former forms no part of philosophy. The basis for this is the argument that the way in which an idea is discovered is irrelevant to its truth: it is relevant to psychology but not to the logical analysis of theories, discovery involving an irrational element, creative intuition, which is not susceptible to logical analysis (Popper 1934/1959: ch. 1). The sociology of science is thus neglected as being concerned simply with this irrational side of science. This view is too narrow, for three reasons. The first is that the study of algorithms and methods for generating theories is just as much a philosophical question as the study of how theories can be justified. The second is that ruling out these lines of inquiry means that methodologists are handicapped in their attempts to understand what economics is like. The third and perhaps most important reason is, it has been argued (de Marchi 1991, 1992), that the context in which ideas are discovered can be relevant to their appraisal. For example, it is impossible to evaluate the results of econometric work without knowing the beliefs and convictions of the economists undertaking the work (de Marchi 1992: 6–7).

178

(3) Finally there is the argument that it is pointless to look for general philosophical principles that can be used to appraise scientific theories. The main work on which such arguments are based is Rorty's *Philosophy and the Mirror of Nature* (1980). In this book Rorty sought to undermine the notion that philosophy was a discipline which stood above other disciplines and which could pass judgement on them. His argument that we should cease to think of ' "knowledge" as something about which there ought to be a "theory" and which has "foundations" ' (Rorty 1980: 7). This view, he argued, rested on the notion of the mind as a mirror containing representations – some accurate, some inaccurate – of reality. The notion that philosophy could provide criteria for appraising the accuracy of such representations rested on the (indefensible) assumption that philosophers had privileged access to the truth. Instead, he contended, we should think of knowledge as pertaining to a conversation – as a matter of social practice – as socially constructed.

For Rorty, such arguments undermined the project of philosophy. Others have used similar arguments to undermine what they see as the privileged status of other disciplines. It has been argued that it does not make sense to look for an account of interpretation in general, for that would imply that the literary theorist had privileged access to the meaning of texts. Meanings are socially constructed – the property of interpretive communities. Science, too, has been criticized in this way. The sociology of scientific knowledge literature approaches scientific knowledge as produced by scientists' social practices (see Chapter 5). The question of whether scientific theories are true (in the sense of corresponding to reality) is not asked, for, in the absence of any privileged access to knowledge, it is not seen as a question to which a meaningful answer can be provided.

'Constructivist' or 'post-modernist' arguments of this nature have been used to undermine the project of methodology, of which Lakatosian methodology is a part.[9] McCloskey (1986) and Weintraub (1989) have argued explicitly that methodology (in the sense of normative methodology) is a pointless exercise. The conclusion has been drawn that in writing the history of economic thought, we should not ask about whether or not there has been progress, but that we should provide accounts of the social processes underlying the construction of economic knowledge (for example, Weintraub 1991). The tension between positive and normative methodology that we find in Lakatos has been resolved by completely abandoning any normative aims.

Why does Lakatos's MSRP appeal to economists?

Given that Lakatos's methodology of scientific research programmes has been criticized so strongly, why have economists found it so attractive? One suggestion has been provided by Hands (1993b). His claim is that

'The places where Lakatos differs from Popper are exactly the places where Lakatos is likely to win the favour of economists since these happen to be areas where there is substantial tension between falsificationism and the actual practice of economics' (Hands 1993b: 68). These include: the existence of unfalsifiable, metaphysical hard cores; the preference for corroboration rather than falsification; and the importance attached to theoretical progress. Where Lakatos is closest to Popper, on the other hand, economists are most likely to part company with him. In other words, Hands is suggesting that Lakatosian ideas are likely to appeal to economists because they are 'softer' than Popperian falsificationism, and because they can be used to defend economists' existing practices.

In a similar vein, de Marchi (1991: 2–6) suggests that Lakatos's MSRP captures a number of features that are also attractive to mainstream economists: that economics is rational, rationality being defined in terms of progress, and that it is research programmes, not individual theories, that should be appraised. Citing Latsis and Rosenberg, de Marchi argues,

> Lakatos holds certain attractions for economists precisely because he offers a less bizarre-sounding replacement for Friedman's unrealism-of-assumptions methodology to justify their convictions in the face of falsifying evidence.
>
> (de Marchi and Blaug 1991: 6)

For de Marchi, as for Hands, economists find Lakatosian methodology attractive because it provides a way of defending what they do. This arises from the nature of economic theorizing as it exists in the mainstream of economics today. Economic theory is dominated by the attempt to explain a variety of economic phenomena on the basis of a very limited range of behavioural assumptions. Explaining a phenomenon involves demonstrating how it follows from the assumption of rational behaviour, any other assumption being viewed as *ad hoc*, for agents ought to behave rationally. Furthermore, given that assumptions can rarely be tested directly (experimental work being both problematic and in its infancy, and econometric testing frequently being inconclusive) the only option open to economists wishing to test theories is to derive further predictions which can be compared with other evidence. Thus when economists defend theories on the grounds that they 'work', what they usually have in mind is the prediction of novel facts in the sense of facts which were not used in the construction of the theory.[10]

This conjecture suggests that support for Lakatosian ideas should be strongest amongst theorists (for whom notions of theoretical progress and a metaphysical hard core should be attractive) and amongst those applied economists who do not wish to be critical of existing theory. This is not, however, what we find. Perhaps the clearest example of support for Lakatos is provided by Hendry, who refers to the 'distinguished contributions' of

Popper and Lakatos having 'revolutionized our understanding of "science" ' (Hendry 1993: 12). He supports his methodology of encompassing by arguing that it corresponds to a 'progressive research strategy', where this is understood in a Lakatosian sense (Hendry 1993: 440). Most economists, however, are less explicit, preferring to claim that their theories 'work'. This phrase, however, should be in a 'Lakatosian' way: that theories account for out-of-sample data, that they explain things their rivals cannot explain, and that they demonstrate connections between phenomena that had previously been thought unconnected.[11]

Another clear statement of the importance of predicting novel facts is provided by Friedman and Schwartz:

> A persuasive test of their results must be based on data not used in the derivation of their equations. That might mean using their equations to predict some kind of phenomena for other countries, or for a future or earlier period for the United Kingdom, or deriving testable implications for other variables.... Similarly, that is the *only* kind of evidence that we would regard as persuasive with respect to the validity of our own results.
>
> (Friedman and Schwartz 1991: 47; emphasis added)

This position is very close to that advocated by Friedman in his influential essay on methodology (1953).

These are only two examples,[12] but they suggest some alternatives to the conjectures made by Hands. The first is that Lakatosian ideas are expressed by economists deeply committed to economics being an empirical science, driven by data. Prediction of novel facts is used, especially by Hendry, not because it is a soft option, but because it is both feasible (in a way that naive falsificationism is not) and demanding. The second is that prediction of novel facts has a history in economics that goes back well before Lakatos. It is plausible to conjecture that economists found Lakatos attractive because the appraisal criterion he used was already, perhaps for very good reasons, well established.

THE ROLE OF THE ECONOMIC METHODOLOGIST

Before Kuhn

Prior to Kuhn's *Structure of Scientific Revolutions* (1962/1970) many of the most important writers on economic methodology saw themselves as applying standards and criteria that went beyond economics. Hutchison (1938), following the perspective provided by logical positivism, analysed the propositions of economic theory with a view to establishing their logical status, distinguishing in particular between propositions which are conceivably falsifiable and those which are not. The way in which the *ceteris paribus* condition was used in much economic theory, he claimed, rendered much pure theory unfalsifiable. He also provided a critique, extremely prescient from a present-day perspective, of the assumption of rationality. On the basis of such arguments he drew the conclusion that there were severe limitations on what pure theory could achieve. Economists, he argued, needed to go out and look at how the world worked, not simply theorize about it.

Hutchison's argument that the propositions of economic theory should be refutable was challenged vigorously by Machlup (1955). By the 1950s logical positivism had largely been displaced by logical empiricism, which emphasized the testability of a theory taken as a whole, not of its individual components. Propositions which, taken on their own, were untestable, might nonetheless form part of a theoretical system which produced testable propositions. If the theoretical system were successfully tested, the propositions embodied in it could be seen as being indirectly tested. The key propositions of economics, such as utility and profit maximization, which Hutchison criticized as being untestable, were, Machlup claimed, indirectly testable.

Though they differed sharply in their attitudes towards economic theory, Hutchison and Machlup shared important common attitudes. Methodology involved logical analysis of economic propositions, establishing whether or not they had empirical content. Though they made the assumption that methodological criteria taken from science could be applied to social science and to economics. For both Hutchison and Machlup the role of the economic methodologist was to apply logical analysis, using insights obtained from contemporary philosophy, to the propositions of economic theory. Though Hutchison drew critical conclusions where Machlup defended economic orthodoxy, both saw themselves as offering arguments that economists ought to find compelling.

Such an attitude also underlay Friedman's 'Methodology of positive economics' (1953) and the debates that arose out of it, and the interest in Popperian methodology which arose at the LSE around 1960. Friedman started from a premise about science in general: 'The ultimate goal of a positive science is the development of a "theory" or "hypothesis" that yields valid and meaningful (i.e., not truistic) predictions about phenomena not yet observed' (Friedman 1953: 7). From this starting point he proceeded to argue that the only relevant test of the validity of a theory was comparison of its predictions with experience, with the associated claims about the realism of assumptions. Friedman, as Hirsch and de Marchi (1990) have convincingly argued, was arguing as a practising economist, seeking to offer advice that would raise the quality of economic theories. His argument was, therefore, rooted in economics rather than in philosophy. He nonetheless drew freely on natural science examples to make what he saw as points about the nature of science in general.

In debating Friedman's essay, Nagel (1963) and Samuelson (1963) adopted the same point of view. Nagel, a leading philosopher of science, clearly drew on contemporary philosophy in providing a logical dissection of Friedman's claims concerning theories and assumptions. Samuelson uses set theory in an attempt to demonstrate the fallaciousness of what he termed the '*F*-twist' – Friedman's claim that the realism of a theory's assumptions is irrelevant to its worth. Economics, for Samuelson, was science, with methodological analysis involving the use of formal logic to evaluate claims about scientific propositions and the way they should be tested.

An emphasis on prediction as the criterion by which to evaluate economic theories was also characteristic of the group of economists centred on Lipsey and Archibald working at the LSE around 1960.[13] Their aims were the quantification and the testing of economic theory. As with the economists just mentioned, they started with a view of the nature of science, which was assumed to apply with minimal modifications (greater reliance on the law of large numbers) to economics (see Lipsey 1963: ch. 1).

After Kuhn

This view of the philosophy of science was challenged by Kuhn. His perspective was sociological, informed by the history of science. His account of periods of normal science separated by scientific revolutions was derived from an analysis of history. Influenced by Kuhn and, shortly afterwards, Lakatos, economic methodology came to be linked much more closely to the history of economic thought, with numerous attempts being made to establish whether the latter could be explained in terms of Kuhn's paradigms, Lakatos's research programmes, or some other pattern. Though much of this work was seeking to ascertain whether patterns believed to characterize natural science were also to be found in economics, it involved a new role for the economic methodologist. Though philosophy of science still provided economic methodologists with ideas on the nature of science, these ideas were now regarded as hypotheses to be tested rather than as statements about the nature of science that economists should not question. Economic methodology now involved looking at economics in order to understand it.

This change towards the methodologist being seen as understanding economists' practices rather than seeking to criticize them is even more marked in the constructivist literature. McCloskey claims no more than that the study of rhetoric will make economists' conversations more civilized – if they understand what they are doing, disagreements will be less ill-tempered. The implied perspective for the methodologist (if we can so call the student of economic rhetoric) is that of a therapist, the role Rorty sees for the philosopher.

Lakatos and the role of the economic methodologist

Kuhn, however, was not altogether clear on the relationship between description and appraisal: was he describing the way science was, or was he arguing that this was how it should be? Lakatos, in contrast, provided a clear explanation of how he saw the relationship between the history and philosophy of science: his methodology of *historical* research programmes (MHRP). This defined a new role for the philosopher or methodologist.

Lakatos's MHRP involves the following four stages: (1) Obtain agreement on a list of successful scientific achievements. (2) Provide a history of these scientific achievements as though they had developed in accordance with the methodology one is trying to appraise – what Lakatos calls a 'rational reconstruction' of the history. (3) Compare this rational reconstruction with the actual history. (4) If the two histories are very different, conclude that the methodology is inappropriate: that it is incompatible with the decisions made by practising scientists. This is based on the assumption that 'an acceptable definition of science (methodology) must reconstruct the acknowledgedly best gambits as "scientific" ' (Lakatos 1971: 124).

Lakatos's methodology of historical research programmes is thoroughly Popperian in inspiration. First, appraisals are ultimately based on agreement or convention – in this case agreement over a list of successful scientific achievements. There are no indubitable foundations on which we can build. Second, it is based on a process of conjecture and refutation. Philosophy provides the conjecture (a methodology) which is then evaluated through referring to history.

Certain aspects of Lakatos's MHRP are open to criticism. It does not provide, any more than does Popperian falsificationism, a clearcut formula by which to judge methodologies. The significance of differences between rational reconstructions and history is necessarily a matter of interpretation, as is the direction in which it is necessary to modify methodologies that do not fit. More seriously, it can be argued that the premises on which it rests are not satisfied in economics: it is difficult to agree on a list of undisputed scientific achievements; it has been argued that the structure of the economics profession distorts the incentives facing economists, so that it cannot be taken for granted that what is commonly regarded as best practice is directed towards discovering the truth. Against this, Lakatos's MHRP implies a role for the philosopher that is at least potentially different from the pre-Kuhnian one. Scientists' practices play a vital role in appraising methodology, which means that the philosopher is required to examine what scientists actually do. This, however, is achieved without abandoning appraisal.

TOWARDS A POST-POPPERIAN ECONOMIC METHODOLOGY

Constructivism

One reason for the decline in interest in falsificationist methodology, whether Popperian or Lakatosian, has been the set of arguments associated with constructivism or post-modernism, and in particular Rorty's critique of epistemology. These perspectives have undoubtedly taught us much about the creation of knowledge, and about new questions which arise when we view knowledge as socially constructed. However, like Blaug (Chapter 6) I am not a constructivist. There are three main reasons. (1) Constructivism is but one perspective amongst many. Arguments about the constructedness of economic knowledge must be applied to constructivism itself – the problem of reflexivity (discussed in Chapter 5). Why should one adopt this perspective rather than any other? The answer must depend on the standards by which methodological ideas are to be evaluated, and hence by the questions to which we are seeking answers (cf. Chapter 2). (2) Constructivism is a very conservative doctrine, which in economics is extremely dangerous. It seems hardly a coincidence that the first thoroughly constructivist account of a branch of the history of economic thought (Weintraub 1991) deals with general equilibrium theory, not an applied field such as labour economics or macroeconomics. General equilibrium theory is vulnerable to falsificationist criticism (of almost any variety) and constructivism provides an ideal way to defend it (see Backhouse 1992c). (3) The most powerful strand in constructivism is the sociology of scientific knowledge. This is empirically based. Detailed observation of the way scientists work is used as the basis for a thoroughgoing rejection of any guidance from philosophy. Methodologically it is an inductive approach, subject to all the problems associated with induction. If instead methodology is seen as a process of conjecture and refutation, on the other hand, there is no reason to reject guidance provided by philosophy – and philosophical ideas that are taken up will be tested against evidence from economics.

Taken together, these reasons provide a strong case for rejecting the post-modernist hostility to philosophical arguments. Furthermore, for all its defects, one of the major strengths of the Popperian perspective is that it is not vulnerable to Rorty's critique (Backhouse 1992b; Hands 1993a: ch. 11). However, though the Popperian perspective provides a viable starting point, it is necessary to go beyond Popper. I wish to suggest that Lakatos still provides valuable pointers as to how this might be done.

Positive and normative methodology

The move towards 'recovering practice' has been important in so far as it has forced methodologists to think seriously about what distinguishes economics from other disciplines, what the key features of economics are, and whether there is a coherent rationale for what economists currently do. But whilst there may be good reasons for current practice, this cannot be taken for granted, for one function of methodology is to ask critical questions about current practice. There is thus a tension which needs to be maintained between positive and normative methodology – between seeking to understand what economists do and seeking to evaluate it. This tension was largely absent from pre-Kuhnian economic methodology, and is again absent from the recent literature which abandons normative methodology. It is quite consistent to accept that there may be problems with the methodology of historical research programmes, whilst at the same time holding that Lakatos maintains this tension between positive and normative methodology.

Research programmes

Even though they are not necessarily thinking in Lakatosian terms, economists find the notion of evaluating research programmes, or sequences of theories, attractive. This is, arguably, something that should be taken seriously. What, however, is to be gained from analysing research programmes using the Lakatosian devices of heuristics, hard core and protective belt? Two answers suggest themselves. (1) Whether or not Lakatos was necessary for this, the effect of Lakatosian methodology has been to direct economists towards detailed studies of episodes in the history of economic thought, and away from making broad, under-researched, generalizations about research programmes in economics. (2) Lakatos's concepts have provided a set of questions that can form a useful starting point in analysing historical episodes.

The main conclusion to be drawn from the criticisms, discussed above, of Lakatos's concept of a research programme is that characterizing them in terms of an invariant hard core is too narrow. A broader concept of research programme, allowing for a greater variety of interaction between programmes, and for hard cores which change over time, would appear to be required. Here, it is useful to remember that, in setting out his MSRP, Lakatos attached prime importance not to the hard core, but to methodological rules. He introduced research programmes in the following way:

I have discussed the problem of objective appraisal of scientific growth in terms of progressive and degenerating problemshifts in series of scientific theories. The most important such series in the growth of science are characterised by a certain *continuity* which connects their members. This continuity evolves from a genuine research programme adumbrated at the start. The programme consists of methodological rules: some tell us what paths of research to avoid (*negative heuristic*), and others what paths to pursue (*positive heuristic*).

(Lakatos 1970: 132)

Though Lakatos went on to relate these heuristics to the concepts of hard core and protective belt, there is no need to do this. To illustrate this, Hausman's *The Inexact and Separate Science of Economics* (1992) could be seen as articulating a heuristic, or set of rules, underlying contemporary mainstream microeconomics. Though one might argue that his rejection of Lakatos's appraisal criterion had deprived the exercise of its bite, this could be seen as, in a sense, an exercise in the spirit of Lakatos. It may be true, as Hausman claims (see Chapter 10), that Lakatos provides little guidance as to the nature of the heuristics characterizing economics, but why should we expect him to provide this?

Predicting novel facts

Perhaps the most important aspect of the Lakatosian legacy, however, is his emphasis on predicting novel facts as an appraisal criterion. There are several reasons for suggesting this.

(1) It fits very closely with the way economists think of what they are doing. To understand economics, therefore, we need to understand why this is so. One explanation runs in terms of the structure of neoclassical theorizing: in the absence of hard empirical criteria, consistency with rational behaviour is used to decide what is and is not *ad hoc*. Another explanation focuses on econometrics, pointing to the relation between predicting novel facts and tests using out-of-sample data, encompassing and so on.

(2) Prediction is an appraisal criterion that will not go away. Not only do some philosophers still attach great importance to it (for example, Rosenberg – Chapter 11 and 1992) but so do policy-makers, who wish to know the consequences that will follow from the various actions they might take. In so far as the main aim of economics is the provision of guidance to policy-makers, prediction must be an important goal. Economics should accordingly be appraised, at least in part, according to its ability to predict. A merit of work in the Lakatosian tradition is that some of it distinguishes between different types of prediction. These distinctions

arise through asking what is meant by 'novelty'. Novel facts might mean, for example, facts of which no one was aware when the predictions were made; facts unknown to the person making the prediction; facts not used in making the prediction; or one of a number of other things.[14] It can be argued that each of these types of prediction has a different significance (see Backhouse 1993).

(3) Even though it may be impossible to defend prediction of novel facts as an appraisal criterion using Popper's theory of verisimilitude, this does not mean that it cannot be defended in other ways. It can be argued, for example, that predicting novel facts, in the sense of facts that a theory was not designed to predict, is especially important in a discipline where controlled experiment is not possible. Controlled experiments enable scientists to isolate phenomena. When this is not possible, theories have to be tested by applying them to new situations – by predicting facts which are novel in various senses of the term.[15]

CONCLUSIONS

The Lakatosian legacy in economic methodology is substantial, in two senses. Historically, Lakatos's MSRP played a major role in stimulating interest in economic methodology and in bringing about a change in perspective. It may be that such a shift, towards analysing heuristics and thinking about methodology in the context of the history of economic thought, would have happened anyway, but as it happened it was Lakatos who caught the imagination of so many economists. More important, Lakatos provides a number of pointers as to lines along which economic methodology might develop.

Lakatos's MSRP has, I suggest, more to offer than many critics admit. To say this is not to argue that Lakatos's MSRP provides a simple formula by which means of which economics can be analysed and appraised. The criticisms outlined earlier in this chapter make it clear that it does not. Neither does it imply that the only important questions are those that can be analysed within the Lakatosian framework. Mäki (Chapter 12) is surely right to argue that methodologists need to address a wider range of issues than those with which they have, by and large, been concerned in the last ten years. Knowledge is a multi-faceted, complex phenomenon that can be approached in many ways. There remains, however, an important range of questions concerning the nature and growth of economic knowledge, for which the concepts developed and put forward by Lakatos provide a valuable starting point.

ACKNOWLEDGEMENTS

I am indebted to Tony Brewer, Wade Hands and Dan Hausman for reading a draft of this paper and providing useful comments. They bear no responsibility for any remaining inadequacies.

NOTES

1 For other attempts along similar lines, see de Marchi's 'Introduction: rethinking Lakatos' and Blaug's 'Afterword' in de Marchi and Blaug (1991). Some of the issues are explored in Backhouse (1992a), but that paper did not go far enough.

2 Though his work on mathematics (Lakatos 1977) was arguably more original, it had very little impact on economists and will not be considered here.

3 Lakatos also provides a meta-methodology for appraising methodologies, his methodology of *historical* research programmes. This, however, is best considered in the next section.

4 This is one of the senses in which Kuhn uses the term paradigm.

5 Written in the 1950s.

6 Cf. Boland, Chapter 8.

7 These arguments are also discussed in Backhouse (1992a).

8 This is argued in detail in Backhouse (1991).

9 Hands (1993a: ch. 11) provides a survey of such positions which draws finer distinctions between different views than is possible here.

10 This is, of course, a weak sense of the term novelty. See Hands (1991b) and Backhouse (1993).

11 Lakatosian is placed in quotation marks because his appraisal criterion is not original with him.

12 de Marchi (1991) and Hands (1993b) are notable for the paucity of examples provided.

13 This paragraph draws heavily on de Marchi (1988).

14 For a list of five definitions of novel facts, see Hands (1991b).

15 An attempt is made to develop this argument more fully in Backhouse (1993).

BIBLIOGRAPHY

Backhouse, R. E. (1991) 'The neo-Walrasian research programme in macroeconomics', in de Marchi and Blaug (1991).

Backhouse, R. E. (1992a) 'Lakatos and economics', in S. Todd Lowry (ed.), *Perspectives on the History of Economic Thought*, Aldershot: Edward Elgar.

Backhouse, R. E. (1992b) 'The constructivist critique of economic methodology', *Methodus* 4(1): 65–82.

Backhouse, R. E. (1992c) 'Rejoinder: why methodology matters', *Methodus* 4(2): 58–62.

Backhouse, R. E. (1993) 'Realism and the prediction of novel facts in economics', Discussion Paper 93–01, University of Birmingham Department of Economics.

de Marchi, N. (1988) 'Popper and the LSE economists', in N. de Marchi (ed.), *The Popperian Legacy in Economics*, Cambridge: Cambridge University Press.

de Marchi, N. (1991) 'Introduction: rethinking Lakatos', in de Marchi and Blaug (1991).

de Marchi, N. (1992) 'Introduction', in N. de Marchi (ed.), *Post-Popperian Methodology of Economics: Recovering Practice*, Boston, Dordrecht and London: Kluwer.

de Marchi, N. and Blaug, M. (eds) (1991) *Appraising Economic Theories: Studies in the Methodology of Research Programmes*, Aldershot: Edward Elgar.

Friedman, M. (1953) 'The methodology of positive economics', in M. Friedman (ed.), *Essays in Positive Economics*, Chicago: University of Chicago Press.

Friedman, M. and Schwartz, A. J. (1991) 'Alternative approaches to analyzing economic data', *American Economic Review* 81(1): 39–49.

Hands, D. Wade (1985) 'Second thoughts on Lakatos', *History of Political Economy* 17(1): 1–16.

Hands, D. Wade (1991a) 'The problem of excess content: economics, novelty and a long Popperian tale', in N. de Marchi and M. Blaug (eds), *Appraising Economic Theories: Studies in the Methodology of Research Programmes*, Aldershot: Edward Elgar. Reprinted in Hands (1993a).

Hands, D. Wade (1991b) 'Reply to Hamminga and Mäki', in N. de Marchi and M. Blaug (eds), *Appraising Economic Theories: Studies in the Methodology of Research Programmes*, Aldershot: Edward Elgar.

Hands, D. Wade (1993a) *Rationality, Testing and Progress*, Lanham, MD: Rowman & Littlefield.

Hands, D. Wade (1993b) 'Popper and Lakatos in economic methodology', in U. Mäki, B. Gustafsson and C. Knudsen (eds), *Rationality, Institutions and Economic Methodology*, London: Routledge.

Hausman, D. M. (1992) *The Inexact and Separate Science of Economics*, Cambridge: Cambridge University Press.

Hendry, D. (1993) *Econometrics: Alchemy or Science?* Oxford: Basil Blackwell.

Hirsch, A. and de Marchi, N. (1990) *Milton Friedman: Economics in Theory and Practice*, Brighton: Harvester Wheatsheaf.

Hoover, K. (1991) 'Scientific research programme or tribe? A joint appraisal of Lakatos and the new classical macroeconomics', in de Marchi and Blaug (1991).

Hutchison, T. W. (1938) *The Significance and Basic Postulates of Economic Theory*, London: Macmillan.

Kuhn, T. S. (1962/1970) *The Structure of Scientific Revolutions*, 2nd edn 1970, Chicago: Chicago University Press.

Lakatos, I. (1970) 'The methodology of scientific research programmes', in I. Lakatos and R. Musgrave (eds), *Criticism and the Growth of Knowledge*, Cambridge: Cambridge University Press.

Lakatos, I. (1971) 'History of science and its rational reconstructions', in R. C. Buck and R. S. Cohen (eds), *Boston Studies in the Philosophy of Science* 8: 91–136.

Lakatos, I. (1977) *Proofs and Refutations*, Cambridge: Cambridge University Press.

Latsis, S. J. (ed.) (1976) *Method and Appraisal in Economics*, Cambridge: Cambridge University Press.

Lipsey, R. G. (1963) *An Introduction to Positive Economics*, London: Weidenfeld.

McCloskey, D. N. (1986) *The Rhetoric of Economics*, Brighton: Harvester Press.

Machlup, F (1955) 'The problem of verification in economics', *Southern Economic Journal* 22(1): 1–21.

Mäki, U. (1980) 'Methodology of economics: complaints and guidelines', *Finnish Economic Papers* 3(1): 77–84.

Nagel, E. (1963) 'Assumptions in economic theory', *American Economic Review* 53(2): 211–19.

Popper, K. R. (1934/1959) *The Logic of Scientific Discovery*, London: Unwin Hyman.

Popper, K. R. (1972) *Conjectures and Refutations: The Growth of Scientific Knowledge*, London: Routledge & Kegan Paul.

Popper, K. R. (1983) *Realism and the Aim of Science*, London: Hutchinson.

Reder, M. W. (1982) 'Chicago economics: permanence and change', *Journal of Economic Literature* 20(1): 1–38.

Rorty, R. (1980) *Philosophy and the Mirror of Nature*, Oxford: Basil Blackwell.

Rosenberg, A. (1992) *Economics – Mathematical Politics or Science of Diminishing Returns?* Chicago: Chicago University Press.

Samuelson, P. A. (1963) 'Problems of methodology – discussion', *American Economic Review* 53 (2): 231–6.

Steedman, I. (1991) 'Negative and positive contributions: appraising Sraffa and Lakatos', in N. de Marchi and M. Blaug (eds), *Appraising Economic Theories: Studies in the Methodology of Research Programmes*, Aldershot: Edward Elgar.

Weintraub, E. R. (1985) *General Equilibrium Analysis: Studies in Appraisal*, Cambridge: Cambridge University Press.

Weintraub, E. R. (1989) 'Methodology doesn't matter, but the history of economic thought might', *Scandinavian Journal of Economics*; reprinted in S. Honkapohja (ed.), *The State of Macroeconomics*, Oxford: Basil Blackwell.

Weintraub, E. R. (1991) *Stabilizing Dynamics: Constructing Economic Knowledge*, Cambridge: Cambridge University Press.

Part III

PHILOSOPHICAL PERSPECTIVES ON ECONOMICS

10

KUHN, LAKATOS AND THE CHARACTER OF ECONOMICS

Daniel M. Hausman[1]

The questions in philosophy of science that immediately occur to most people concern the assessment of the accomplishments of science. Though these are indeed central questions, there are many others that are of great importance. If one wants to understand the enterprise of economics, it is not enough to be able to state explicitly the fundamental principles of economics such as diminishing returns and to cite evidence that bears on them. As philosophers of science such as Thomas Kuhn and Imre Lakatos have emphasized, to understand science one also needs to understand the structure and strategy implicit in the interrelated work within scientific communities. Economists belonging to some particular tradition do not face phenomena armed only with some set of explicit generalizations. What makes a neoclassical or a Marxian or an institutional economist is not just learning the generalizations accepted by members of the particular tradition. Economists within a single school agree implicitly on the answers to queries such as: what questions are the right ones for economists to ask? How should one simplify these questions to make them answerable? How should economists distinguish their questions and answers from those of other social theorists? What sorts of techniques should one employ in seeking answers? What sorts of causal factors should economists emphasize and what sorts should they ignore? How should one respond to apparent disconfirmations? How should one present hypotheses to colleagues? How should one defend hypotheses from criticism? Learning economics, like learning any science, is not just learning some set of generalizations, such as the law of demand. It is a socialization process in which one learns facts, generalizations and techniques at the same time as one comes to share values, language and perspective.

Before the publication of Thomas Kuhn's *The Structure of Scientific Revolutions* (1962, 2nd edn 1970), philosophers paid little attention to the web of commitments that bind together co-workers in a common research enterprise. Philosophers of science during the previous two generations were well aware that there is more to science than its theories and laws, their testing and their use for explanation and prediction. In fact most of

195

the so-called 'logical positivists' or 'logical empiricists' knew quite a lot of science, especially, though not exclusively, physics.[2] But their ambition was to use formal logic and conceptual analysis to provide abstract characterizations of central features of science, such as confirmation or explanation. They were inclined to regard the context-sensitive shared presuppositions that constitute distinct subdisciplines as obstacles in the way of appreciating the uniform underlying 'logic' of explanation, confirmation, theory structure and so forth. For example, Carl Hempel was well aware that different disciplines are concerned with different sorts of explanatory factors, but he still hoped to identify a uniform logic of explanation that applied to all sciences. There were anticipations of themes that Kuhn emphasized, such as Sidney Morgenbesser's distinction between a theory *of* a subject matter and a theory *for* some investigator (1956: 2–4). But even philosophers such as Karl Popper, who took the metaphysical, methodological and non-testable aspects of science seriously, focused on explicit theories and offered abstract and context-independent treatments of fundamental concepts.

Kuhn's *Structure of Scientific Revolutions* was published against this intellectual background, and its effect was explosive. Not only did it throw a spotlight on fascinating features of science that had been ignored by previous philosophy, but it offered a way of avoiding the dead-end to which logical empiricism apparently had led. For analysing abstractly the logic of explanation, the logic of confirmation or the logic of theory construction seemed to have led to paradox and confusion rather than to precision and clarity. More might be learned by studying apparently successful *practices* of explaining, testing or theorizing and then cautiously generalizing. Though few philosophers of science accept many of Kuhn's specific philosophical claims,[3] his book nevertheless transformed philosophy of science.

In this chapter I shall be concerned with Thomas Kuhn's and Imre Lakatos's accounts of the broader structures, presuppositions and commitments that shape individual theories and are in turn shaped by particular theoretical achievements. Kuhn and Lakatos are not the only philosophers to have offered accounts of such 'global' theory structure, but no others have had appreciable influence in economics.[4] I shall, in passing, say something about how views of global theory structure interact with issues of theory assessment, and at the end I will also offer my own characterization of the structure and strategy of economic theorizing, but the emphasis in this chapter shall be on what Kuhn and Lakatos have to say about what unifies research communities. To simplify the discussion I shall focus exclusively on orthodox theoretical microeconomics and general equilibrium theory. In speaking of 'economics', I shall be speaking only of this part of the discipline. This is only a terminological simplification, not of course a denial that there are other important parts of economics.

NORMAL SCIENCE, PARADIGMS, ANOMALIES AND REVOLUTIONS

In *The Structure of Scientific Revolutions*, Kuhn offers a striking, compelling, but troubling picture of the structure of scientific disciplines. Work in mature science is *not* devoted to thinking up hypotheses, testing them and then passing on to the next problem or conjecture. Backyard inventors, philosophers and those who have no idea about how to study some subject matter may proceed that way. But theoretical scientists do not. After one has been sufficiently educated to do fruitful work in some branch of science, one already believes that the fundamental problems have been solved. For example, those concerned to refine the application of Newton's laws of motion and gravitation to the orbits of planets took Newton's laws for granted. They shared a commitment to a set of mathematical techniques. They shared views about what idealizations were appropriate and about what the dynamically significant properties of the solar system were. In Kuhn's terminology, they shared a '*paradigm*'. Consequently, theirs was essentially a 'mopping-up' operation in which there were puzzles to be solved (such as why the observed orbit of the moon did not match their calculations), but in which there were reasonably clear rules for how to solve the puzzles and grounds to be confident that the puzzles could indeed be solved. Such work is what Kuhn calls 'normal science', and its narrowness and complacency concerning foundations is, in his view, the key to its importance and success. Because the puzzles are so well-defined and their solutions so heavily constrained, each researcher can easily grasp what others are doing and can build on their successes and failures. Enormous efforts can be justified, because the researchers can be confident that they are not wasting their time on unanswerable or ill-conceived problems. Difficult, confusing and time-consuming debate about fundamentals can be avoided, and members of the subdiscipline can devote themselves to the precise articulation, development and testing of detailed theoretical refinements of the paradigm.

But nature resists mopping up, and the commitment to a paradigm that constitutes normal science ironically paves the way to scientific revolution. For the lavish resources that are devoted to solving narrow esoteric puzzles, which would never have been forthcoming but for the conviction that the paradigm is correct, reveal anomalies that cannot be dismissed or resolved. As these become serious, more attention and resources are devoted to them, and commitment to the paradigm itself is shaken. The subdiscipline passes into a period of crisis. Sometimes the crisis is resolved without a change of paradigm, but sometimes instead a scientific revolution occurs in which the old paradigm is replaced by a new. In *The Structure of Scientific Revolutions*, Kuhn suggests that such transformations are so radical and fundamental that rational argument and even communication between those committed to different paradigms may become impossible.

It is an exciting story, and it offers philosophers of science new ways to pose questions concerning science. But it is also, as Kuhn has conceded, an exaggerated and somewhat confused story. The story is clearly exaggerated: communication across paradigms is possible, though it is more difficult than communication between those who share the same paradigm. There may be competing normal science traditions rather than just one. Commitment to a paradigm need not be so absolute, even when there is no crisis.

More important than the exaggeration is the confusion. For Kuhn uses the word 'paradigm' in several (twenty-two according to Masterman 1970) different ways. In the 'Postscript' to the second edition of *Structure*, Kuhn distinguishes between two central meanings (see also Kuhn 1974). On the one hand, he called striking scientific achievements, such as Newton's theory of gravitation, 'paradigms'. In the 'Postscript' he says he will now speak of these as 'exemplars'. On the other hand, he used the term 'paradigm' to refer to the whole web of presuppositions and commitments that ties together work in a discipline. Paradigms in this sense, he now proposes to call 'disciplinary matrices'. One concerned to use Kuhn's categories to understand the overall structure and strategy of economics should thus focus on Kuhn's theory of disciplinary matrices.

Disciplinary matrices are the constellations of beliefs, presumptions, heuristics and values that tie together scientists working in some discipline. When Kuhn speaks of a 'discipline' or a 'community', he has in mind narrow research specialities, which involve perhaps a few dozen scientists. But, like most of those who have attempted to fit Kuhn's views to branches of economics, I shall take them as applying to a large discipline, to microeconomics as a whole.

Kuhn maintains that disciplinary matrices consist of four main components: (1) 'symbolic generalizations', (2) metaphysical and heuristic commitments, (3) values and (4) exemplars. Symbolic generalizations are fundamental laws. They are not merely empirical generalizations, and indeed they often define the terms they employ. The claim that individuals are rational, in contrast to the law of demand, might be regarded as a 'symbolic generalization' of economics. Such generalizations are held tenaciously and are not easily revisable. The basic claims of microeconomics are not quite symbolic generalizations in Kuhn's sense, because economists are not firmly committed to all of them. For example, the claim that individuals are self-interested is fundamental in much of microeconomics, but not in all of it. Most, if not all of its basic behavioural postulates are actually *denied* in some theories.

The second component of a disciplinary matrix is metaphysical or heuristic. Examples Kuhn provides include ontological claims such as 'heat is the kinetic energy of the constituent parts of bodies', and preferred models, such as 'the molecules of a gas behave like tiny elastic billiard balls in random motion' (1970: 184). These metaphysical and heuristic commitments set the standards for acceptable answers to questions. This aspect is of particular importance in understanding how economists construct simplified economic models. In studying economics, one learns the strategies for beating phenomena into mathematically tractable shape. Without knowing these strategies, one does not know economics. Furthermore, economists also have heuristic commitments against regarding aspects of human social life, such as emotion, irrationality or mistake as significant causal factors in economics.

Although Kuhn treats exemplars as a separate component of a disciplinary matrix, I think it is useful to think of these as part of the discipline's heuristics. One striking point Kuhn emphasizes is that scientists mimic past achievements. There are few explicit rules for doing science. Scientists instead imitate those whom they perceive to have made major contributions. Past achievements not only lead to symbolic generalizations and the metaphysical or heuristic commitments that dominate a discipline, but they also determine heuristic details. The importance of problem-solving in learning economics or physics shows how important exemplars are. One learns how to construct models in economics by imitation rather than by rule.

The final component in a disciplinary matrix consists of 'values'. These are general commitments to honesty, consistency, respect for data, simplicity, plausibility, precision, problem-solving, compatibility with other theories and so forth. Kuhn points out that individuals differ in how they apply these values and that such differences may contribute to scientific progress. The values of economic theorists are distinctive in the weight given to mathematical elegance, in the comparatively slight attention given to experimentation, data gathering and testing, and in the concern for policy relevance. But even with this distinctive weighting, there is plenty of potentially fruitful disagreement concerning the importance of different empirical and theoretical virtues. I am concerned here with how useful Kuhn's framework is for describing what economists do, and I shall not explore whether these facts about economics suggest a scientific failing (see Hausman 1992: chs 12 and 15).

Kuhn's account of disciplinary matrices provides a checklist of what to look for in examining the large-scale structures of economic theorizing, but the basic principles of microeconomics have a different status and role than do Kuhn's symbolic generalizations. Consequently, economics does not fit his schema very well.[5]

This fact might be taken as a criticism of economics, for Kuhn's purpose in characterizing disciplinary matrices was not only to describe scientific practices, but also to understand how larger-scale theoretical commitments contribute to the goals of science. If it could be shown that disciplinary matrices as described by Kuhn were necessary in order to acquire knowledge efficiently, then one would have reason to condemn microeconomics. But Kuhn never argues that the shared commitments of practitioners must match his account of disciplinary matrices in order for rational scientific progress to be possible, and nothing in his work justifies criticizing economics. Furthermore, his account does not have *enough* structure to enrich one's description of microeconomics. If one could fit economics easily into Kuhn's structure, how much would one have learned?

RESEARCH PROGRAMMES

In highlighting larger-scale theoretical structures, Kuhn's *Structure of Scientific Revolutions* poses a serious challenge to the views of theory assessment defended by logical empiricists and by Karl Popper (1968, 1969, 1972). Committed as they are to disciplinary matrices, scientists do not, in Kuhn's view, confront theories with data that confirm or falsify them. In 'normal science', scientists aim to solve the puzzles that arise in attempting to make reality fit the theory or disciplinary matrix, not to test theories. Kuhn singles out for criticism Popper's falsificationism:

> As has repeatedly been emphasized before, no theory ever solves all the puzzles with which it is confronted at a given time; nor are the solutions already achieved often perfect. On the contrary, it is just the incompleteness and imperfection of the existing data-theory fit that, at any time, define many of the puzzles that characterize normal science. If any and every failure to fit were ground for theory rejection, all theories ought to be rejected at all times.
>
> (1970: 146)

Kuhn is disputing the view that scientists confront individual theories with the results of testing and in case of conflict jettison the theories. The relations between theory and evidence and the methodological rules concerning how to respond to apparent falsification are determined by the disciplinary matrix.

Imre Lakatos attempts to defend a sophisticated Popperian view of theory assessment from this challenge.[6] Crucial to his response to Kuhn is a novel account of scientific 'research programmes', which has been influential in economics. In Lakatos's view, one can concede that responses to anomaly are governed by the detailed norms directing work within a research programme, much as Kuhn contends, without surrendering the Popperian view that knowledge grows from conjecture and refutation. Although Lakatos's views on large-scale theory structure are thus intertwined with his views of theory assessment, I shall separate them and focus on his views of global theory structure.

In developing his alternative, Lakatos incorporates elements from Kuhn's work, although Lakatos's account also derives from Popper's lectures on metaphysical research programmes (1983, sect. 23) and from Lakatos's earlier work on the philosophy of mathematics (1976). A *research programme* for Lakatos consists of a series of theories linked to one another by *heuristics* and a common theoretical 'core' (1970: 48f.). The heuristics that define a research programme are of two kinds. The *negative heuristic* forbids tinkering with a group of propositions, which Lakatos calls 'the hard core' of the research programme. The *hard core* consists of fundamental laws, metaphysical presuppositions, or perhaps even non-law factual assertions. Lakatos's hard core seems broader than Kuhn's symbolic generalizations, for Lakatos counts as part of hard cores what Kuhn classified as metaphysical commitments and preferred analogies. For example, Lakatos regards Descartes's metaphysical view that the fundamental properties of all matter are mechanical or geometrical as the hard core of the Cartesian research programme. Newton's three laws of dynamics and his law of gravitation constitute the hard core of the Newtonian research programme (1970: 48). Writers on economic methodology have disagreed concerning what the hard core of neoclassical theory is.

The other sort of heuristic that constitutes a research programme, the *positive heuristic* consists of hints or instructions about how to use the hard core to generate specific models and how to modify theories that face apparent disconfirmation. Lakatos gives the example of the way in which Newton first derived planetary orbits ignoring interplanetary gravitational forces and planetary volumes and then dealt successively with the complications left out of the initial derivations (1970: 50–1). The example is, however, misleading in two ways. First, although it is true that suggestions such as 'think of bodies first as point masses' belong to the positive heuristic of Newtonian dynamics, the order of theoretical development in this example is determined by the mathematical difficulties, rather than by the heuristics of Newtonian physics. Second, the positive heuristic is supposed to direct the improvement of already developed theories that confront anomalies as well as to contribute to the development of an initial testable empirical theory. The positive heuristic of economics includes suggestions such as: 'Think of choices as constrained maximization.' 'Make qualitative comparisons of equilibria.' 'Regard moral commitments as having no effect on behaviour.'

Although Lakatos plays down the role of what Kuhn calls 'values' and says little about exemplars, his account of the global structure of theoretical science resembles Kuhn. With its more vivid and salient categories, it has, however, been more attractive to writers on economic methodology than has Kuhn's account,[7] and Lakatos integrates his emphasis on heuristics into an account of scientific theory assessment.

A few words concerning Lakatos's account of theory assessment are in order here. Lakatos grants Kuhn's claim that theories always confront apparent anomalies. Those committed to a particular research programme consequently devote their efforts to modifying current models and theories, *in accordance with the heuristics of the programme*. When these modifications preserve the unrefuted content of previous theories and also make novel predictions, then the modifications are 'theoretically progressive' (1970: 33). When some of the novel predictions are not refuted, then the modifications are 'empirically progressive', and the previous theory is regarded as having been falsified (1970: 34). Scientists never test individual theories; they only compare theories (1970: 34–5), and the only relevant evidence concerns the success or failure of novel predictions (1970: 38). Research programmes as a whole are progressive when their heuristics drive empirically progressive theory modifications (1970: 112–13). They are degenerating when their heuristics are not so fruitful. But there is no clear point at which it is rational to abandon a degenerating research programme (1970: 117).

This view of theory assessment is inadequate in several ways. Here are three of them: first, Lakatos emphatically seconds Popper's denial that evidence can ever provide reason to believe that a theory is true, reliable or even close to the truth (1970: 10–12). So in the process of modifying and testing theories one cannot make use of information concerning how well supported different claims are. For example, in modifying an unsuccessful economic model, one cannot decide to retain the law of demand and to modify the assumption of perfect information on the grounds that the law of demand has been well supported, while it is questionable to assume that individuals have perfect information. Popper and Lakatos are thus calling for a revolutionary (and dubious) transformation of both science and practice. Second, Lakatos exaggerates this point by insisting that one only *compares* theories, one never *tests* them. But of what worth is the information that T' is better than T, without any knowledge at all of how good T is? Would you stake your life on some medical treatment M if you knew only that M is safer than some other treatment M', whose safety is in turn completely unknown? Third, 'progress' for Lakatos requires that theory modifications lose none of the unrefuted content of previous theories. (Otherwise T could be empirically progressive compared to T' and T' could also be empirically progressive compared to T.) But since modifications of theories in science usually come with some loss, few 'theoretically progressive' theory modifications will be possible. Lakatos's views on the appraisal of theories and research programmes are thus unacceptable.

Though not as obviously inadequate, I doubt whether Lakatos's sketch of the structure (as opposed to the appraisal) of research programmes helps one to understand the character of theoretical economics. Once one separates what Lakatos has to say about structure from what he has to say about assessment, one can see that the account of the structure of sciences is as thin as Kuhn's. All Lakatos is saying is that a research programme is unified by a common core and common principles for developing theories that include this core. Just as a social theorist might help empirical researchers to identify the salient characteristics of some religion by providing a checklist of helpful questions, so Lakatos has provided a checklist for methodologists. But there are only two questions on the list: 'What's the hard core?' 'What are the heuristics?' Whether or not these are good questions to start with, attempting to answer them will not take one far.[8]

It is also unclear how to fit economics into Lakatos's categories. Latsis, for example, argues that the hard core of the theory of the firm consists of claims that decision-makers have correct knowledge, that they prefer the best alternative, given their knowledge, that decision-makers 'act appropriately to the logic of their situation' and that the result is stable and coordinated behaviour (1976b: 22). Leijonhufvud (1976: 71) and Blaug (1976: 162) claim that the hard core of pre-Keynesian neoclassical economics includes the claim that economies tend to converge to equilibrium. de Marchi (1976: 117) argues that Bertil Ohlin took the 'mutual interdependence theory of pricing' as part of his hard core. Blaug regards the hard core of pre-Keynesian neoclassical economics as consisting of 'weak versions of what is otherwise known as the "assumptions" of competitive theory, namely rational economic calculations, constant tastes, independence of decision-making, perfect knowledge, perfect certainty, perfect mobility of factors, etc.' (1976: 161). In an extended account, E. Roy Weintraub sees the hard core of the 'neo-Walrasian research program' as consisting of six propositions (1985: 109):

HC1. There exist economic agents.
HC2. Agents have preferences over outcomes.
HC3. Agents independently optimize subject to constraints.
HC4. Choices are made in interrelated markets.
HC5. Agents have full relevant knowledge.
HC6. Observable economic outcomes are coordinated, so they must be discussed with reference to equilibrium states.

But Roger Backhouse denies that HC5 and HC6 should be regarded as part of the hard core, if one takes the neo-Walrasian research programme as providing microfoundations for macroeconomics (1991: 404–5).

Since the positive heuristics of a research programme are supposed to be rather open-ended, there are fewer disagreements about what they consist of. These different accounts of the hard core of the theory of the firm, of pre-Keynesian neoclassical economics and of neo-Walrasian economics are not necessarily inconsistent, since these might be regarded as at least partially distinct research programmes. But there are tensions between these accounts. It is not entirely clear how to resolve these disputes and, more importantly, it is difficult to see what would be gained by doing so. Attempting to apply Lakatos's view of the structure of research programmes to economics creates unnecessary and unhelpful questions.

Furthermore, in attempting to make economics fit Lakatos's scheme, one must construe its hard core as extraordinarily weak. Consider Weintraub's six hard-core propositions. The first states that there are economic agents. No one who disagreed could be a neo-Walrasian economist. So we can grant that HC1 is a hard-core proposition. But this hard-core proposition, like HC2 and HC4 completely fails to discriminate neo-Walrasian economists from Marxian or institutionalist economists or from the regulars at Harry's Bar at the corner of Main and Elm Streets.[9] It is as if one claimed that the hard core of Newtonian theory consisted of claims such as 'There are bodies', 'Some bodies move' and 'Some bodies change their state of motion'. The only propositions that even begin to distinguish neo-Walrasian economics are HC3, HC5 and HC6, two of which Backhouse (who is attempting to apply rather than to criticize Lakatos) would reject.

The emptiness of Weintraub's characterization of the hard core of neo-Walrasian economics does not result from any mistake on Weintraub's part (other than his reliance on Lakatos's framework). For there is very little that is shared by *every* neo-Walrasian theory or model.[10] The hard core cannot include the claim that preferences are complete or transitive, for there are neo-Walrasian theoretical explorations which involve incomplete and intransitive preferences (McKenzie 1979; Mas-Colell 1974). The hard core cannot include self-interest, for there are neo-Walrasian models with altruism. One cannot include diminishing returns, because there are neo-Walrasian models with fixed production coefficients. One cannot include profit maximization, for there are neo-Walrasian models (particularly as formulated by so-called agency theorists such as Fama 1980 and Jensen and Meckling 1976) without profit maximization. If one insists on characterizing neo-Walrasian economics by those features shared by *all* neo-Walrasian theories and models, then one cannot do much better than Weintraub or Backhouse.

Attempting to force neoclassical economics into Lakatos's categories hides the crucial fact that *most* neoclassical models share many things that are nevertheless not shared by all neoclassical works. The Lakatosian perspective casts this fact into the shadows, while one worries fruitlessly about which are the real hard-core propositions. Kevin Hoover (1991) makes this point vividly with regard to so-called 'new-classical macroeconomics', which has, he argues, no interesting hard core, despite the many overlapping common features of new-classical work. To clarify this point, Hoover draws on a famous discussion from Ludwig Wittgenstein's *Philosophical Investigations*, in which Wittgenstein argues that people call things 'games' in virtue of a whole set of 'family resemblances' among different sorts of games, not because all games possess anything significant in common. One cannot say that all games are competitive, or that all involve elements of skill or strategy, or even that all involve winning and losing (Wittgenstein 1953: sect. 66). Just as one can have a single cohesive rope with no single thread running its entire length, so one can have a unified research community without a significant hard core (Hoover 1991: 374).

A Lakatosian reconstruction of the global theoretical structure of economics is thus rather unenlightening. It raises difficult and empty questions concerning the individuation of research programmes and of their hard cores. It demands that one conceive of what unifies research programmes as features shared by *all* work within the given research programme. And even if the categories were readily applicable, their application would be uninformative, since this view of the structure of scientific disciplines is so thin.

THE STRUCTURE OF ECONOMICS

Kuhn's and Lakatos's visions of disciplinary matrices and research programmes do not provide any useful recipe for grasping the overall structure and strategy of contemporary economics. Let us see whether, turning from philosophy of science to economic theory itself, it might not be possible to make some more substantive assertions concerning what the discipline is like. Providing such a description is a complicated task, because the character of the discipline depends on detailed peculiarities of its domain, its dominant theory and its social role. So it is impossible to get very far in just a few pages. But I shall try at least to give some hints, which I develop at greater length in *The Inexact and Separate Science of Economics*, particularly in chapter 6, 12 and 15. Note that what follows is a description, not an evaluation.

Economics is governed by a coherent vision of its overall theoretical mission. Although the following theses are rarely explicitly stated, they are generally accepted and, more than any generalities concerning paradigms and research programmes, they define the global structure and strategy of economics.

1 Economics is defined in terms of the causal factors with which it is concerned, not in terms of a domain.
2 Economics has a distinct domain, in which its causal factors predominate.
3 The 'laws' of the predominating causal factors are already reasonably well known.
4 Economic theory, which employs these laws, provides a unified, complete, but inexact account of its domain.

Moreover, as I shall explain later, these theses have definite implications concerning what sorts of theory modifications are permissible. But first let me clarify what they assert.

1. **Economics is defined in terms of the causal factors with which it is concerned, not in terms of a domain.**[11] In one of the earliest discussions of economic methodology, John Stuart Mill maintained that economics focuses on only a few causal factors:

> Political economy [is concerned with] such of the phenomena of the social state as take place in consequence of the pursuit of wealth. It makes entire abstraction of every other human passion or motive, except those which may be regarded as perpetually antagonising principles to the desire of wealth, namely aversion to labour, and desire of the present enjoyment of costly indulgences.
>
> (1843: 6.9.3)

A century later, Lionel Robbins's classic definition states that 'economics is the science which studies human behaviour as a relationship between ends and scarce means which have alternative uses' (1935: 15). In Robbins's view economics is concerned with the causal factors (which are similar to Mill's) that constitute scarcity.

2. **Economics has a distinct domain, in which its causal factors predominate.** Mill suggests that a few causal factors are sufficient to account for the major features of a distinct domain of social phenomena:

> There is, for example, one large class of social phenomena in which the immediately determining causes are principally those which act through the desire of wealth, and in which the psychological law mainly concerned is the familiar one that a greater gain is preferred to a smaller.... By reasoning from that one law of human nature, and from the principal outward circumstances (whether universal or confined to particular states of society) which operate upon the human mind through that law, we may be enabled to explain and predict this portion of the phenomena of society, so far as they depend on that class of circumstances only, overlooking the influence of any other of the circumstances of society.... A department of science may thus be constructed, which has received the name of Political Economy.
>
> (1843: 6.9.3)

I do not know of any comparable modern defences of the existence of an 'economic realm', but what is taken to be obvious is often not defended. Economists certainly speak freely of 'economic phenomena' and of the 'economic realm', and they seem to have in mind a range of social behaviour that can be identified without a prior commitment to standard economic theory. Notice that since economics is defined by its causal factors, there can be an economic realm only if some domain of social life is in fact dominated by the causal factors or 'laws' with which economics is concerned.

Not all of what is called economic, even orthodox neoclassical economics, is concerned with a peculiarly economic realm. Inquiries in game theory, for example, which shade into work in standard economics and are carried on by many of the same theorists, often relax common motivational assumptions (such as self-interest, commodity bundles as the sole objects of preference and independence of utility functions). The strategic interactions with which game theorists are concerned consequently need not lie within the specifically economic realm or domain. But to recognize that some of economics does not concern this domain is consistent with accepting the existence of an economic realm and demanding that economic theory span it.

3. **The 'laws' of the predominating causal factors are already reasonably well known.** Mill and Robbins believe that they know the fundamental causal factors, and indeed they take them to be platitudes such as 'a greater gain is preferred to a smaller' (Mill 1843: 6.9.3) or 'individuals can arrange their preferences in an order, and in fact do so' (Robbins 1935: 78). One might question whether most economists are committed to this thesis. Certainly no good Popperian, for example, could accept it. I cannot make the case here, and I recognize that many economists will be uncomfortable with this bald formulation, but very little work in microeconomics lacks apparent confidence that the fundamental principles have already been revealed. This fact has important implications for theory assessment in economics, for such presuppositions influence the way that economists react to apparently disconfirming data.

4. **Thus, economic theory provides a unified, complete, but inexact account of its domain.** Economic theories and models explore the implications of the laws of the major causes. Since an economic phenomenon is defined in terms of the causes with which economics is concerned, or, in other words, the laws that make up economic theory, economic theory thus provides an account of all economic phenomena. And since economic causal factors predominate in the economic domain, the scope of economic theory is the entire economic domain. The theory provides a unified account of all of economics since the laws in the theory are themselves systematically interrelated in particular economic models and theories. The laws of separate subdomains of economics (such as consumer choice theory and the theory of the firm) are not united into a single theory only by arbitrary conjunction. In general equilibrium theories the 'laws' of different branches of microeconomics work together.

Since the laws of the major causes are joined together within economic theory and are thought to be reasonably well known, economic theory is regarded as *complete*. Economists (of course) recognize that causal factors left out of economic theory sometimes influence market phenomena.

Economic theory is thus inexact. It is only supposed to be complete at a high level of abstraction or approximation. It is as if one wanted a theory of an economy as seen from a distance through a low-resolution telescope. Economics is not merely imprecise, because minor 'disturbing' causes occasionally cause anomalies even at a low resolution, yet one might still reasonably hope or believe that economics theory provides the whole 'inexact truth' (Hausman 1992: ch. 8) concerning the economic realm.

The thesis that economic theory provides a unified, complete, but inexact account of the economic realm, has strategic implications. It implies that the explanatory task of economics is done when economic phenomena have been traced to the fundamental economic causal factors. Any attempt to explain the fundamental laws of economics is not a part of economics. The right approach is to deduce the consequences in the economic domain of the fundamental economic causes '... once for all, and then allow for the effect of the modifying circumstances' which are 'ever-varying' (Mill 1843: 6.9.3).

Unlike in physics or biology, the search for fundamental laws is not a part of economics, for the fundamental principles are already reasonably well known and, in any case, come from outside. They are simple generalizations that are evident to introspection or everyday experience. The task of economists is to apply the basic principles to particular problems.

Economics resembles individual theories such as Newtonian dynamics or Mendelian population genetics more closely than it resembles disciplines such as physics or biology. For an orthodox theorist, it is in effect a one-theory science. A perfected general equilibrium theory coupled with accurate descriptions of the significant circumstances would permit explanations and predictions of all economic phenomena. These explanations and predictions would not be exact, for there would be many 'disturbing causes'. Other social forces affect economic outcomes, and generalizations concerning these other forces might occasionally be incorporated into specific economic models, but in the pure science of economics a single unified theory is refined and applied. The generalizations of psychologists and sociologists are not welcome in economic theorizing.

What does this vision of economics as a separate science mean in practice? If one not only accepts this vision but also the fundamental generalizations of economics, then one will take these generalizations as defining the causal factors with which economics is concerned. The domain of economics is then the realm of social phenomena in which those causal factors predominate. In particular:

> Economic phenomena are the consequences of rational choices that are governed predominantly by pursuit of one's own consumption and profit. In effect, economics studies the consequences of rational greed.

The exact content of rationality can be left open. One can modify standard utility theory and still be doing economics. The nature of the predominant motivational 'force' is also rather loose. One can do economics with satiation and with some interdependence among preferences. But agents rationally seeking their own material welfare is what makes economics go, and theories which dethrone this motive cease to be economics. Economic theories cannot portray agents as exploitable fools.

Two central methodological rules follow governing the use of additional behavioural generalizations in economic theorizing:

1 Generalizations about choice or other economic phenomena are *ad hoc* and should be avoided unless they are derivable from microeconomic theory and further legitimate generalizations about preferences, beliefs and non-economic constraints on choices.
2 Additional generalizations about preferences, beliefs and constraints are legitimate and may be incorporated into economic theories only if they do not conflict with or threaten the central place of rational greed, the possibility of equilibrium or the universal scope of economics.

These rules identify a distinctive theoretical strategy. Further generalizations concerning constraints, beliefs and preferences are permissible, for these are the factors which, according to utility theory, govern choice. So, for example, one can add generalizations concerning time preference, as is common in theories of capital and interest. But the rational pursuit of consumption and profits must keep their places as the dominant motives in the economic realm, and equilibrium must remain possible. Notice that the rules also express not merely the *preference* for *wide* scope that is characteristic of all science, but a *requirement* that fundamental theory retain *maximal* scope, that it span the entire domain.

One sees these methodological rules at work especially in the reactions of economists to macroeconomic theories that lack explicit microfoundations. Keynes's claim that the marginal propensity to consume is less than one is regarded as '*ad hoc*' (for example, Leijonhufvud 1968: 187), unless it can be shown to follow from fundamental microeconomic theory and further generalizations about beliefs, preferences and constraints, such as Modigliani's life-cycle hypothesis or Friedman's permanent income hypothesis (see Modigliani and Brumberg 1955; Ando and Modigliani 1963; Friedman 1957). Modigliani's and Friedman's hypotheses about beliefs and preferences are not *ad hoc*, because they do not threaten the explanatory unity of the basic theory. Generalizations about wage or price stickiness are criticized as *ad hoc* on the same grounds (Olson 1984: 299).[12]

The only general methodological principle governing economics and the other social sciences for which one finds much *explicit* argument is methodological individualism – the insistence that explanatory laws in economics concern features of individual human beings.[13] The demands of methodological individualism are looser and less detailed than the rules discussed above. Although consistent with some formulations of methodological individualism, the strategy of economic theorizing is more specific and more closely tied to economic theory.

One should also mention the intermediate methodological demand that all economic explanations must be in terms of the rational choices of individuals.[14] In some ways it demands more than methodological individualism, which does not forbid explanations in terms of individual irrationality. But the insistence on rational choice models is also more permissive than some versions of methodological individualism, since rational choice explanations permit references to institutional facts among the constraints on individual choices. The limitation to rational choice explanations is implicit in the rules above and helps to explain why economists will accept some modifications and reject others. For example, to insist that further generalizations may only concern beliefs, preferences and constraints follows from the methodological preference for rational choice explanations. But to insist on rational choice explanations is much weaker than insisting on the primacy of acquisitive preferences, the possibility of equilibrium and on maximal scope.

Implicit in the theoretical practice of economics are the requirements that all economic explanations employ some subset of fundamental microeconomic theory and eschew additional behavioural postulates unless they have wide scope and are compatible with rational choice explanation, acquisitiveness and equilibrium. The only justification for these restrictions is the fruitfulness of insisting on them. I personally am unconvinced that these methodological constraints have in fact been very fruitful.

But in passing here from description to evaluation, I am straining at the boundaries of my topic, and here I must bring this chapter to an end. There is, I believe, a great deal to be learned about the character of economics from studying economics and its history. Kuhn and Lakatos may help one get started, but the serious student of economic methodology must move beyond their sparse frameworks.

NOTES

1 This chapter is largely drawn from chapter 6 of my *The Inexact and Separate Science of Economics* (1992). I am also indebted to Roger Backhouse for detailed criticisms.
2 For overviews of logical positivism, see Ayer (1936, 1959) and Hanfling (1981a, b).
3 For criticism, see Scheffler (1967), Shapere (1964) and Suppe (1977).
4 Although not yet influential, Larry Laudan's (1977) views should be of particular interest to economists because of his emphasis on conceptual problems. See also Shapere (1974, 1984, 1985).
5 For attempts to apply Kuhn's views to understand both the structure of eco-

nomic theories and the dynamics of theory change in economics, see Baumberger (1977), Bronfenbrenner (1971), Coats (1969), Dillard (1978), Kunin and Weaver (1971), Stanfield (1974) and Worland (1972).

6 Lakatos's most important essay is 'Falsification and the methodology of scientific research programmes' (1970), which was originally published in Lakatos and Musgrave (1970) and is included in volume 1 of his *Collected Works* (1978) along with most of the other essays Lakatos wrote that are relevant to the issue with which this chapter is concerned.

7 For some of the many attempts to apply Lakatos's views on research programmes to economics, see Latsis (1976a), especially the essays by de Marchi (1976) and Blaug (1976), de Marchi and Blaug (1991), Weintraub (1988), and essays by Ahonen (1989), Blaug (1987), Fulton (1984), Hands (1979, 1985, 1990), Jalladeau (1978), Rizzo (1982), Robbins (1979), Rosenberg (1986) and Weintraub (1988).

8 I should say that I think that it would be difficult to improve upon the checklists that Kuhn and Lakatos provide, as thin and uninformative as they are. Just as one can question whether, without invoking features of particular theories and disciplines, there are many informative and true things to be said about specific concepts such as explanation, so I doubt that there is much that is true and useful to be said about the structure and strategy of scientific disciplines in general. Determining how well economics or parts of economics can be described as research programmes, as paradigms, or as any other general something-or-other, tells one little about the structure or strategy of economics.

9 On some interpretations of the term 'economic agent' it is controversial whether any exists. If an economic agent is somebody who, for example, cares about nothing but wealth (not even food or sleep, except in so far as these are needed for the accumulation of wealth), then not everybody would agree that there are economic agents. But 'economic agent' is not a technical term of economics and Weintraub's HC1 is not disputed by anybody.

10 With more good sense than philosophical consistency, Mark Blaug gives substance to his characterization of the hard core of 'pre-Keynesian neoclassical economics' in the quotation above only by ignoring Lakatos's insistence that hard-core propositions must be common to (and indeed unquestioned by) *all* work in a research programme. It is not true that no pre-Keynesian neoclassical theories or models ever allowed uncertainty, limited mobility, or changes in tastes.

11 For an intriguing discussion of the way in which scientific theories define their domains see Stegmueller (1976: 93, 176–7).

12 D. Wade Hands argues that accusations of *ad hocness* by economists should be construed in a Lakatosian way: *ad hoc* claims are those which are not in accord with the positive heuristic of a research programme (1988). He is right, but the reference to Lakatos is in my view unhelpful. The relevant parts of the 'positive heuristic' are the two rules above.

13 See Hayek (1952), Kincaid (1986), Levine *et al.* (1987), Lukes (1973), Popper (1957, 1966: vol. 2), Sensat (1988), Watkins (1953, 1968) and the collection by O'Neill (1973).

14 'If an institution or a social process can be accounted for in terms of the rational actions of individuals, then and only then can we say that it has been "explained"' (Coleman 1986: 1).

BIBLIOGRAPHY

Ahonen, G. (1989) 'On the empirical content of Keynes' *General Theory*', *Ricerche Economiche* 43: 256–69.

Ando, A. and Modigliani, F. (1963) 'The life-cycle hypothesis of saving: aggregate implications and tests', *American Economic Review* 53: 55–84.

Ayer, A. (1936) *Language, Truth and Logic*, 2nd edn 1946, New York: Dover.

Ayer, A. (ed.) (1959) *Logical Positivism*, New York: Free Press.

Backhouse, R. (1991) 'The neo-Walrasian research programme in macroeconomics', in de Marchi and Blaug (1991) pp. 403–26.

Baumberger, J. (1977) 'No Kuhnian revolutions in economics', *Journal of Economic Issues* 11: 1–20.

Blaug, M. (1976) 'Kuhn versus Lakatos *or* paradigms versus research programmes in the history of economics', in Latsis (1976a) pp. 149–80.

Blaug, M. (1987) 'Second thoughts on the Keynesian revolution', mimeograph. English version of 'Ripensamenti sulla rivoluzione keynesiana', *Rassegna Economica* 51: 605–34.

Bronfenbrenner, M. (1971) 'The structure of revolutions in economic thought', *History of Political Economy* 3: 136–51.

Coats, A. (1969) 'Is there a "structure of scientific revolutions" in economics?', *Kyklos* 22: 289–94.

Coleman, J. (1986) *Individual Interest and Collective Action: Selected Essays*, Cambridge: Cambridge University Press.

de Marchi, N. (1976) 'Anomaly and the development of economics: the case of the Leontief paradox', in Latsis (1976a) pp. 100–28.

de Marchi, N. (ed.) (1988) *The Popperian Legacy in Economics*, Cambridge: Cambridge University Press.

de Marchi, N. and Blaug, M. (eds.) (1991) *Appraising Economic Theories: Studies in the Methodology of Research Programmes*, Aldershot: Edward Elgar.

Dillard, D. (1978) 'Revolutions in economic theory', *Southern Economic Journal* 44: 705–24.

Fama, E. (1980) 'Agency problems and the theory of the firm', *Journal of Political Economy* 88: 288–307.

Friedman, M. (1957) *A Theory of the Consumption Function*, Princeton: Princeton University Press.

Fulton, G. (1984) 'Research programmes in economics', *History of Political Economy* 16: 187–206.

Hands, D. Wade (1979) 'The methodology of economic research programs', *Philosophy of the Social Sciences* 9: 292–303.

Hands, D. Wade (1985) 'Second thoughts on Lakatos', *History of Political Economy* 17: 1–16.

Hands, D. Wade (1988) 'Ad hocness in economics and the Popperian tradition', in de Marchi (1988) pp. 121–39.

Hands, D. Wade (1990) 'Second thoughts on "second thoughts": reconsidering the Lakatosian progress of *The General Theory*', *Review of Political Economy* 2: 69–81.

Hanfling, O. (1981a) *Logical Positivism*, Oxford: Basil Blackwell.

Hanfling, O. (1981b) *Essential Readings in Logical Positivism*, Oxford: Basil Blackwell.

Hausman, D. (1992) *The Inexact and Separate Science of Economics*, Cambridge: Cambridge University Press.

Hayek, F. (1952) *The Counter-Revolution of Science: Studies in the Abuse of Reason*, Glencoe, IL: Free Press.

Hoover, K. (1991) 'Scientific research program or tribe? A joint appraisal of Lakatos and the new classical macroeconomics', in de Marchi and Blaug (1991) pp. 364–94.

Jalladeau, J. (1978) 'Research program versus paradigm in the development of economics', *Journal of Economic Issues* 12: 583–608.

Jensen, M. and Meckling, W. (1976) 'Theory of the firm: managerial behavior, agency costs and ownership structure', *Journal of Financial Economics* 3: 305–60.

Kincaid, H. (1986) 'Reduction, explanation, and individualism', *Philosophy of Science* 53: 492–513.

Kuhn, T. (1970) *The Structure of Scientific Revolutions*, 2nd edn, Chicago: University of Chicago Press [1st edn 1962].

Kuhn, T. (1974) 'Second thoughts on paradigms', in Suppe (1977) pp. 459–82.

Kunin, L. and Weaver, F. (1971) 'On the structure of scientific revolutions in economics', *History of Political Economy* 3: 391–7.

Lakatos, I. (1970) 'Falsification and the methodology of scientific research programmes', in Lakatos and Musgrave (1970) pp. 91–196 and Lakatos (1978) vol. 1: 8–101. Page references to Lakatos (1978).

Lakatos, I. (1976) *Proofs and Refutations: The Logic of Mathematical Discovery*, J. Worrall and E. Zahar (eds), Cambridge: Cambridge University Press.

Lakatos, I. (1978) *Philosophical Papers*, 2 vols, Cambridge: Cambridge University Press.

Lakatos, I. and Musgrave A. (eds) (1970) *Criticism and the Growth of Knowledge*, Cambridge: Cambridge University Press.

Latsis, S. (ed.) (1976a) *Method and Appraisal in Economics*, Cambridge: Cambridge University Press.

Latsis, S. (1976b) 'A research programme in economics', in Latsis (1976a) pp. 1–42.

Laudan, L. (1977) *Progress and its Problems*, Berkeley: University of California Press.

Leijonhufvud, A. (1968) *On Keynesian Economics and the Economics of Keynes*, Oxford: Oxford University Press.

Leijonhufvud, A. (1976) 'Schools, "revolutions" and research programmes in economic theory', in Latsis (1976a) pp. 65–100.

Levine, A., Sober, E. and Wright, E. (1987) 'Marxism and methodological individualism', *New Left Review* 162: 67–84.

Lukes, S. (1973) 'Methodological individualism reconsidered', in Ryan (1973) pp. 119–30.

McKenzie, R. (1979) 'The non-rational domain and the limits of economic analysis', *Southern Economic Journal* 26: 145–57.

Mas-Colell, A. (1974) 'An equilibrium existence theorem without complete or transitive preferences', *Journal of Mathematical Economics* 1:237–46.

Masterman, M. (1970) 'The nature of a paradigm', in Lakatos and Musgrave (1970) pp 59–90.

Mill, J. S. (1843) [1949] *A System of Logic*, London: Longmans, Green & Co.

Modigliani, F. and Brumberg, R. (1955) 'Utility analysis and the consumption function', in K. Kurihara (ed.), *Post-Keynesian Economics*, London: Allen & Unwin, pp. 383–436.

Morgenbesser, S. (1956) 'Theories and schemata in the social sciences', dissertation, University of Pennsylvania.

Olson, M. Jr. (1984) 'Beyond Keynesianism and monetarism', *Economic Inquiry* 22: 297–322.

O'Neill, J. (1973) *Modes of Individualism and Collectivism*, London: Heinemann.

Popper, K. (1957) *The Poverty of Historicism*, New York: Harper & Row.

Popper, K. (1966) *The Open Society and its Enemies*, vol II, 5th edn, Princeton: Princeton University Press.

Popper, K. (1968) *The Logic of Scientific Discovery* (rev. edn), London: Hutchinson & Co.

Popper, K. (1969) *Conjectures and Refutations; The Growth of Scientific Knowledge*, 3rd edn, London: Routledge & Kegan Paul.

Popper, K. (1972) *Objective Knowledge; An Evolutionary Approach*, Oxford: Clarendon Press.

Popper, K. (1983) *Realism and the Aim of Science: From the Postscript to the Logic of Scientific Discovery*, W. Bartley III (ed.), Totowa, NJ: Rowman & Littlefield.

Rizzo, M. (1982) 'Mises and Lakatos: a reformulation of Austrian methodology', in I. Kirzner (ed.), *Method, Process and Austrian Economics: Essays in Honour of Ludwig von Mises*, Lexington, MA: D. C. Heath.

Robbins, L. (1935) *An Essay on the Nature and Significance of Economic Science*, 2nd edn, London, Macmillan (1st edn 1932).

Robbins, L. (1979) 'On Latsis' *Method and Appraisal in Economics*: a review essay', *Philosophy of the Social Sciences* 17: 996–1004.

Rosenberg, A. (1986) 'Lakatosian consolations for economics', *Economics and Philosophy* 2: 127–40.

Ryan, A. (ed.) (1973) *The Philosophy of Social Explanation*, Oxford: Oxford University Press.

Scheffler, I. (1967) *Science and Subjectivity*, Indianapolis: Bobbs-Merrill.

Sensat, J. (1988) 'Methodological individualism and Marxism', *Economics and Philosophy* 4: 189–220.

Shapere, D. (1964) 'The structure of scientific revolutions', *Philosophical Review* 73: 383–94.

Shapere, D. (1974) 'Scientific theories and their domains', in Suppe (1977).

Shapere, D. (1984) *Reason and the Search for Knowledge*, Dordrecht: Reidel.

Shapere, D. (1985) 'Objectivity, rationality, and scientific change', in P. Asquith and P. Kitcher (eds), *PSA 1984*, vol. 2, East Lansing: Philosophy of Science Association, pp. 637–63.

Stanfield, R. (1974) 'Kuhnian revolutions and the Keynesian revolution', *Journal of Economic Issues* 8: 97–109.

Stegmueller, W. (1976) *The Structure and Dynamics of Theories*, trans. William Wohlhueter, New York: Springer-Verlag.

Suppe, F. (ed.) (1977) *The Structure of Scientific Theories*, 2nd edn, Urbana: University of Illinois Press.

Watkins, J. (1953) 'Ideal types and historical explanation', in H. Feigl and M. Brodbeck (eds.), *Readings in the Philosophy of Science*, pp. 723–44; reprinted in Ryan (1973) pp. 82–104.

Watkins, J. (1968) 'Methodological individualism and social tendencies', in M. Brodbeck (ed.), *Readings in the Philosophy of the Social Sciences*, New York: Macmillan.

Weintraub, E. R. (1985) *General Equilibrium Analysis: Studies in Appraisal*, Cambridge: Cambridge University Press.

Weintraub, E. R. (1988) 'The neo-Walrasian program is empirically progressive', in de Marchi (1988) pp. 213–30.

Wittgenstein, L. (1953) *Philosophical Investigations*, trans. G. E. M. Anscombe, New York: Macmillan.

Worland, S. (1972) 'Radical political economy as a "Scientific Revolution" ', *Southern Economic Journal* 39: 274–84.

11

WHAT IS THE COGNITIVE STATUS OF ECONOMIC THEORY?

Alexander Rosenberg

INTRODUCTION

Economic theory is a perplexing subject. Though I have spent the better part of my academic career thinking about its aims and methods, I have never been confident that I or anyone else for that matter really understand its cognitive status. Partly, no doubt, this is because everyone's understanding of the cognitive status of most intellectual disciplines has been subject to great disturbances over the last two decades or more. Even at the time I first began thinking and writing about the problems which economics presents for the philosophy of science, in the late 1960s, the conceptual framework within which scientific disciplines were assessed was coming under serious question. Since then matters have moved so far in the philosophy, history, sociology and psychology of science, that the very notion of 'cognitive status' has gone into eclipse.

Over the same period that philosophy's sense of certainty about what science is has disappeared, the philosophy of economics has emerged as a growth industry, and many people are now confident they understand the aims and methods of the discipline. However, my own views about the nature of economic theory have remained permanently unsettled. Since the appearance of my first book, *Microeconomic Laws: A Philosophical Analysis* (Rosenberg 1976) about the only thing that has remained fixed about my approach to this subject are the questions with which I started: questions about the cognitive status of economic theory; that is, questions about whether that theory is to be understood and assessed for adequacy along the lines of theories, in the sciences, physical, biological, behavioural. Over the period since I wrote *Microeconomic Laws*, these questions about cognitive significance have not been popular. But I have stuck with them, largely because an answer to the question can have significant ramifications for public policy, for our hopes to improve its intended effects and mitigate its unintended ones. If economics is a science, if its theories are composed of improvable regularities about human behaviour and its aggregate consequences, then its bearing on policy is as evident as the study of physiology is to human health. If not, confidence reposed in it will be repaid by frustration at best. Without some assurance about the cognitive status of the theory, there is no basis for confidence in it. Now the trouble with this question about the cognitive status of economic theory is that in the philosophy of science there is no longer any conviction about the existence of a litmus test that will indicate the cognitive status of a theory. Though some economists still pay lip-service to Popper's litmus test of falsifiability, most students of the philosophy of economics recognize that (a) economic theory is not in fact falsifiable, and (b) falsifiability is unacceptable as a test for the scientific respectability of a theory. But no adequate substitute litmus test has been found. The absence of such a test has led some students of the subject (I have in mind Donald McCloskey[1]) to conclude that there is in fact no difference in the cognitive status of economics, physics, mathematics, literary criticism or astrology, for that matter. While I recognize that there is no litmus test here, I persist in believing that there are important differences between the cognitive status of these various enterprises. It is just very difficult to establish what these differences are.

When I wrote *Microeconomic Laws* I argued that there was no conceptual obstacle to microeconomic theory's status as a body of contingent laws about the cause of choice behaviour, and its aggregate consequences. In the years since I wrote that book, I have not changed my mind on this score, but I have come to believe that this conclusion takes us only a very little way towards understanding the nature of economic theory. Treating economic theory as a contingent theory about the causes and consequences of choice behaviour will not explain the attachment of economists to the theory, because it is just not a very good explanatory theory of the causes and consequences of economic choice. Over the course of a century it has failed to explain these processes with anything like improving accuracy and precision. Economic theory seems permanently stuck at the level of generic predictions – predictions that tell us that some change will happen some time and some place, without ever telling us when and where and how much of a change will occur. Economics tells us that after a freeze a rise in orange-juice prices will occur, or that the demand for college education is not very elastic. But it never seems able to improve these predictions in the direction of exactly how much prices will rise or what the coefficient of inelasticity will be. Indeed latter-day apologists for economic theory insist that economic theory need not improve its predictive powers beyond the generic, because it is in the nature of such predictions to be suicidally self-refuting the moment they gain wide visibility. If this is true it must be cold comfort to economists. For a theory that cannot predict cannot explain – or at least we have no way of telling whether its explanations are correct.

In recent years I have begun to think that we need to seek a non-explanatory rationale for the continuing commitment of economists to neoclassical microeconomics. In this paper I report on two such rationales. First, the idea that economic theory is fundamentally a normative discipline; second, the notion that economic theory is a branch of applied mathematics. In neither case will we impose explanatory demands on economics, or predictive ones for that matter.

ECONOMIC THEORY AS NORMATIVE

Let us consider whether the rationale for economics might in the end be normative. This is not a particularly new idea in the philosophy of social science, or even the philosophy of economics. It has often been held that theories in the social disciplines are normative because they are about action or otherwise use vocabulary that is evaluative. For example, it is often held that economics is a body of prescriptions for how to be rational, and rationality is taken to be a normative concept. So viewed, of course economic theory and any normative theory for that matter is beyond the criticism that it is predictively weak or otherwise defective as empirical science. But this is of little consolation, because normative claims are also irrelevant to the explanation of actual behaviour.

But there is another more interesting way of arguing that economic theory is fundamentally part of a normative enterprise, one which really does shed light on its character – and sheds light especially on the theoretical core of microeconomics: general equilibrium theory. In what follows I shall sketch what such an interpretation looks like. The rationale I sketch helps itself to the historically most compelling of all strategies for the establishment of political philosophies: the social contract.

One hint that this may be a useful way of approaching the aims and claims of general equilibrium theory is to observe how much political philosophy and especially contractarian political theory have been influenced by economic theory in the last two decades. Many philosophers have simply taken over the jargon and the agenda of welfare economics in order to express their problems and seek solutions to them. In particular the recognition that the establishment of cooperative institutions is a public goods problem has driven philosophers to explore economists' ways of solving such problems. Perhaps philosophers' enchantment with welfare economics for their purposes reflects a belated recognition which we can also expect economists explicitly to endorse: that economic general competitive equilibrium theory is a species of formal political philosophy. (Hereafter I drop the qualifier 'competitive', since most general equilibrium models reflect the features I shall treat below.)

What is so seductive about general equilibrium theory is that it is a formal proof of an apparently surprising possibility. As Arrow and Hahn have noted, 'The immediate "common sense" answer to the question "What will an economy motivated by individual greed and controlled by a very large number of different agents look like?" is probably: there will be chaos' (Arrow and Hahn 1971: vii). This response is right and it is probably the chief source of the attractions of a centrally planned economy, one in which the planners can reconcile everyone's conflicting wants and decide on a schedule of production that meets these wants optimally, given the constraints of available resources. Let us hazard a guess that most intelligent persons thinking abstractly about the need for coordination, efficiency and equity in a society will be attracted to some form of central planning.[2]

Arrow and Hahn, however, note, in a tone of understatement and technicality, that the contrary is the case:

> a decentralized economy motivated by self-interest and guided by price signals would be compatible with a coherent disposition of economic resources that could be regarded, in a well-defined sense, as superior to a large class of possible alternative dispositions . . . . It is important to understand how surprising this claim must be to anyone not exposed to this tradition.
>
> (Arrow and Hahn 1971: vi)

Now, imagine a large number of rational agents who have already come to agreement about the advantages that each will accrue from the existence of a state with political authority to coerce each of them as necessary to enforce rules on which they have also agreed.

Having agreed on political rules, these individuals fall to arguing about what commercial institutions they will establish. What arrangement will recommend itself? Given the assumption contractarian political philosophy makes, that they are rational, and not altruistic in their preferences, and given some undeniable facts about information, incentives and scarcity, it is not difficult to establish the preferability for society as a whole of decentralized market mechanisms over centralized planning ones.

Except in the case of public goods, what seems most remarkable about a market economy is that by accepting the inevitability of surpluses and shortfalls, it does better at mitigating them than a planned economy which denies their inevitability. That is, it not only avoids shortages and surpluses more frequently, but when it does result in them, they are smaller. A market economy will be especially receptive to innovations. These it brings to market quickly. If we can prove that by arranging a scheme that will mitigate gluts and shortages to the maximum extent, we do better than we would if we simply aimed directly at eliminating them through the central collection of information and rational planning in the use of it, we shall have provided a powerful incentive for rational agents to adopt such a scheme. If we can show that there is too much information from consumers and producers for a planner to process, and too much information that consumers and producers have an incentive to hide, so that gluts and shortages will be inevitable, and that a market mechanism takes advantage of both of these facts about information, then we will have little difficulty convincing the parties to a social contract that the market is the way to go. These are the kinds of considerations that seduce intelligent young minds from socialism to capitalism. Because these considerations work, because they actually move people, we should accord them considerable respect in any account of why general equilibrium should have any claims on our attention (even as we recognize that general equilibrium's relevance to explaining market processes in the actual world is very limited).

For general equilibrium theory is the formalized approach to the systematic study of this claim about how the unintended consequences of uncoordinated selfishness result in the most efficient exploitation of scarce resources in the satisfaction of wants. It is of course an inquiry with many limitations. But at least now we can understand why economists continue to lavish attention on general equilibrium theory. It is not because they think it can be improved in the direction of a descriptively and predictively accurate explanation of economic activity, but because they believe it is already part of the best contractarian argument for the adoption of the market as a social institution.

Consider general equilibrium theory as one important component in the research programme of contractarian political philosophy. Doing so helps explain two other features of neoclassical theory: its remarkably *a priori* character, and the temptation felt by philosophers, among others, to view it as a body of prescription about rational conduct. In effect, this approach to general equilibrium theory assimilates neoclassical economics to what James Buchanan identifies as one of its subdivisions: 'constitutional economics'. Buchanan distinguishes 'orthodox economic analysis' and 'constitutional economic analysis':

> Orthodox economic analysis, whether this be interpreted in Marshallian or Walrasian terms, attempts to explain the choices of economic agents, their interactions with one another, and the results of these interactions.
>
> (Buchanan 1989: 64)

So far, we must disagree with Buchanan, for interpreted as an explanatory project, orthodox economic analysis or its core at any rate, just is not explanatory. But Buchanan goes on,

> By contrast ... constitutional economic analysis attempts to explain the working properties of alternative sets of legal–institutional–political rules that constrain the choices and activities of economic agents, the rules that define the framework within which the ordinary choices of economic and political agents are made.

... the whole exercise is aimed at offering guidance to those who participate in discussions of constitutional change ... constitutional economics offers a potential for normative advice to members of the constitutional convention.... It examines the *choice of constraints* as opposed to the *choice within constraints*.

(Buchanan 1989: 64; emphasis added)

But to decide on choice of constraints, we need information about the effects of choice within those constraints. To the extent that orthodox economics provides information about those choices within constraints, it will be a compartment of what Buchanan calls orthodox economic analysis. But, suppose that the *only* information it reliably provides is information relevant to the choice among constraints, that is, to what rules rational agents would contract, were they required to do so. Then, there would be no other role for what Buchanan calls orthodox economic analysis.

Now, the doubts about the explanatory relevance of general equilibrium theory suggest that it cannot explain choice within constraints. That is, so to speak, how the problem of justifying general equilibrium theory starts. But these doubts are irrelevant to its role in a search for optimal constraints. For in this search there is every reason to assume that agents ruthlessly maximize their utilities everywhere and always, that they dissimulate when it is to their advantage, free-ride where they can. For this is just the sort of behaviour against which a polity must protect itself. Therefore, as Hume writes (and Buchanan is fond of quoting):

Political writers have established it as a maxim that, in contriving any system of government, and fixing several checks and controls of the constitution, every man ought to be supposed a *knave*, and to have no other end, in all his actions, than private interest.

(Hume 1985)

There is a prudential requirement that for purposes of institution design we treat all agents as utility maximizers and assure ourselves that each of us is willing to live with the consequences of doing so. The prudential requirement is honoured in an especially clear and powerful way by general equilibrium theory, as its game-theoretical development reveals.

As histories of general equilibrium theory make clear,[3] it was early recognized that the existence of a general equilibrium was also the solution to an *n*-person generalization of the von Neumann-Morgenstern solution for a two-person zero-sum competitive game. Arrow and Debreu's (1954) version of this realization is particularly instructive for the assimilation of general equilibrium to a contractarian agenda. We are given two kinds of agents, price taking budget-constrained utility maximizers, and an omniscient auctioneer, whose only aim is to minimize excess demand among the other agents. The auctioneer agent announces price vectors, for

221

which the other players each announce their best response. The auctioneer chooses one which clears the markets most fully. His position is little different from Hobbes's sovereign. The auctioneer and his institution are thus shown to be the most advantageous arrangement parties to a contract about the rules for economic activity can adopt in the abstract.

For the equilibrium whose existence it establishes can be shown to be a Nash equilibrium – one in which each such egoistical agent has an optimal strategy, regardless of the strategies of other agents. The market in which an equilibrium producing price vector exists thus has an especially desirable property from the point of view of contractarian political philosophy: no one can do better by adopting another strategy and the strategies result in an informationally efficient market-clearing Pareto-optimal unique stable equilibrium.

It remains possible on this view to cavil at the abstractness of general equilibrium theory, at the demanding assumptions required to prove that there is a market-clearing price vector. But the evident desirability of such a price vector makes it worth attempting to identify the institutional constraints under which the desirable equilibrium is attainable, no matter how unbridled the egoism of Hume's knave.

But can a theory which is predictively weak, really carry the normative burden that general equilibrium is being saddled with by this interpretation? The question reflects an objection to treating general equilibrium theory as a species of political philosophy. As the solution to a set of normative problems, general equilibrium theory still needs to have some measure of relevance to actual choice. After all, 'ought' implies 'can' and if we ought to adopt institutions that approach those of the market that general equilibrium describes, then it must be the case that we can do so. But we have no assurance of this possibility unless economic theory has a certain amount of explanatory and predictive power. If the actions it counsels are beyond us it is irrelevant as moral philosophy. If rational choices are within our abilities, then the fact that we do not seem to engage in these activities fully enough to give the theory much empirical warrant must reduce its normative bearing as well.

But how much predictive power does a theory need in order to have normative bearing on institutional design? Recall the reasons Buchanan gives for adopting the prudential assumption that agents will be 'knaves', in Hume's term – self-seeking but enlightened egoists. Buchanan gives us grounds to suggest that the most we need from economic theory for purposes of political philosophy is generic prediction.

As Hume noted, 'it is a maxim that in contriving any system of government, and fixing the several checks and controls of the constitution', we should assume the worst-case scenario – that every agent seeks only his own advantage. Because we cannot be sure how people will act, and we wish to avoid the worst possible outcome for ourselves, the outcome that ensues from selfishness, free-riding and non-cooperation.

If people are at least sometimes capable of such actions, and if sometimes they actually so comport themselves, then at a minimum the theory that describes the institutions we contract for should allow for, should predict, this generic possibility. If it does more then well and good. If it can give us confidence that in some specifiable cases we need not make this worst-case assumption, all the better. But at a minimum the contractual arrangements justified must be compatible with the possibility of the operation of rational self-interest. And the theory from which the arrangements are derived should enable us to predict what the generic consequences of self-interest will be.

ECONOMIC THEORY AS APPLIED MATHEMATICS

I have suggested that there is some reason to treat economic theory as a part of political philosophy, in particular as an area of debate in social contract theory. This is a view which some economists might be eager to adopt, especially those preoccupied by welfare economics. But others are, I suspect, inclined to find it too limited an area for the influence of their discipline. Most economists will insist that their discipline is a science, and their theories the best and most powerful explanatory and predictive devices there are among the social sciences. However, anyone with much knowledge of the history of economic theory will agree that the discipline does not seek or respond to empirical data in the way characteristic of an empirical science – even a theoretically impoverished one. If social contract theory is too Procrustian a bed for economic theory, and empirical science too demanding a status, is there not some other interpretation of the aims and methods of economic theory that will do full justice to its scope and its insulation from data? More than once, students of the subject have sought an interpretation of its aims and claims that reflects adequately its mathematical character. Both detractors and defenders of orthodox neoclassical theory have found its intellectual core in its mathematical expression.[4] Let us explore this interpretation of economic theory as a branch of applied mathematics.

Economic theory assumes that the categories of preference and expectation are the classes in which economic causes are to be systematized and that the events to be explained are properly classified as actions like buying, selling and the movements of markets, industries and economies that these actions aggregate to. The theory has made this assumption because of course it is an assumption we all make about human behaviour; our behaviour constitutes action and is caused by the joint operation of our desires and beliefs. Marginalists of the late nineteenth century, like Wicksteed, saw clearly that microeconomics is but the formalization of this commonsense notion and the history of the theory of consumer behaviour is the search for laws that will express the relations between desire, belief and action, first in terms of cardinal utility and certainty, later in terms of ordinal utility, revealed preference and expected utility under varying conditions of uncertainty and risk.[5] The failure to find such a law or any approximation to it that actually improves our ability to predict consumer behaviour any better than Adam Smith could have resulted on the one hand in a reinterpretation of the aims of economic theory away from explaining individual human action, and on the other in the tissue of apologetics with which the consumer of economic methodology is familiar.[6]

The real source of trouble for economics' attempts to find *improvable* laws of economic behaviour is something that has only become clear in the philosophy of psychology's attempts to understand the intentional variables of commonsense and cognitive philosophy. 'Beliefs' and 'desires' – the terms in which ordinary thought and the social sciences describe the causes and effects of human action – do not describe 'natural kinds'. They do not divide nature at the joints.

Unlike 'gene' or 'acid' or 'electric charge', 'belief' and 'desire' – or, in economists' labels, 'expectations' and 'preferences', do not label 'natural kinds' – sets of items that behave in the same way, that share the same manageably small set of causes and effects and so cannot be brought together in causal generalizations that improve on our ordinary level of prediction and control of human actions, let alone attain the sort of continuing improvement characteristic of science. The intentional concepts are more like 'chair' or 'fish', words that may well be essential for the ordinary business of life, but are missing from any catalogue of the basic kinds recognized in scientific laws. Because of the character of our intentional variables, we cannot expect to improve our intentional explanations of action beyond their present levels of predictive power. But the level of predictive power of our intentional theory is no higher than Plato's. The predictive weakness of theories couched in intentional vocabulary reflects the fact that the terms of this vocabulary do not correlate in a manageable way with the vocabulary of other successful scientific theories; they do not divide nature at the joints, in so far as its joints are revealed in already successful theories like those of neuroscience.

The failure of microeconomic theory to uncover laws of human behaviour is due to its wrongly assuming that these laws will trade in desires, beliefs or their cognates. And the system of propositions about markets and economies that economists have constructed on the basis of its assumptions about human behaviour is deprived of improving explanatory and predictive power because its assumptions cannot be improved in a way that transmits improved precision to their consequences. Thus the failure of economics as an empirical discipline is traced not to a conceptual mistake, or to the inappropriateness of constrained maximization theories and their elegant mathematical apparatus to human action, but to a false assumption economists share with all other social scientists, indeed with everyone who has ever explained their own or others' behaviour by appeal to the operation of desires and beliefs.

Just as economists have been given no pause by previous analyses of the empirical weakness of their discipline, they are unlikely to down tools in the face of this diagnosis either. Indeed, the persistence of economists in pursuing the intentional approach that has been conventional for well over a century suggests that nothing could make them give it up. At any rate nothing which would make empirical scientists give up a theory will make economists give up their theoretical strategy. But the unwillingness to surrender this conviction leads to the conclusion that economics is not empirical science at all. Despite its appearances, and the interest of some economists in applying their formalism to practical matters, this formalism does not really have the aims, nor does it make the claims, of an unequivocally empirical theory.

The claim that microeconomic theory, or at least its core, is a branch of abstract mathematics, reflects both its differences from empirical science, and its derivational, deductive structure as fully or more fully perhaps than treating it as a portion of political philosophy.

But, what of the successes of economic theory? How can we square the claim that economic theory is a branch of mathematics with the evident applicability of such staples as the laws of supply and demand? After all, it is a fact about markets in all commodities that *eventually* price will influence demand and supply in the directions that microeconomic theories of economic action dictate. Surely that price influences demand is an economic regularity and surely it is a consequence of individual choices, preferences and beliefs. What will our view of microeconomic theory as mathematics make of the laws of supply and demand?

The fact that we can usefully employ false or vacuous general statements, up to certain limits, should be no mystery at all. Mathematics provides clear examples of the utility of both false and vacuous claims. The clearest instance of such restrictedly useful though false or vacuous general statements is Euclidean geometry. For millennia this axiomatic system was viewed as the science of space and the great mystery which surrounded it was how we can have the apparently *a priori* knowledge of the nature of the world that the science of space, Euclidean geometry, gave us. Attempts to solve this mystery drove the creative energy of seventeenth- and eighteenth-century epistemology, especially the work of Leibniz and Kant, both of whom attempted to reconcile the necessity of geometry to its applicability in a world of apparently contingent spatial properties. The result was, with Kant, a theory of knowledge that made geometry and physics synthetic truths about the world known *a priori*.

Since Poincaré and Einstein this problem has been largely resolved. Prior to the twentieth century Euclidean geometry was *equivocally* interpreted. It was alternately viewed as (a) a pure axiomatic system about abstract objects, one that constituted the implicit definitions of terms and was therefore *a priori* true, and (b) as a body of claims about actual spatial relations among real objects in the world. The equivocation between these two interpretations in part caused Kant's problem of how synthetic propositions could be known *a priori*. Once distinguished, the general theory of relativity revealed that, interpreted as a theory of actual spatial relations, Euclidean geometry is false. Of course this discovery left untouched Euclidean geometry interpreted as a body of *a priori* truths implicitly defining the terms that figure in it.

So interpreted pure geometry was left untouched by scientific developments, except of course to the extent that it was shown to be useless and inapplicable as a body of conventions, beyond certain values of distance and mass in space. In retrospect, we can explain why no one ever noticed these facts about geometry and why before the acceptance of the general theory of relativity, Euclidean geometry provided entirely satisfactory for settling empirical questions of geography, surveying, engineering, mechanics and astronomy. The reason, of course, is that for these questions we neither needed nor had the means to make measurements fine enough to reveal the inadequacies of Euclidean geometry. When we need to improve our measurements beyond this level of fineness, in contemporary cosmology, for instance, we must forgo Euclidean geometry in favour of one or another of its non-Euclidean alternatives.

One way to describe the twentieth-century fate of Euclidean geometry is to say that its kind terms proved not to name *natural kinds*: nature diverges from the predictions of an applied Euclidean geometry, because it does not contain examples, realizations and instances of the kind terms of that theory. There are no Euclidean triangles, as we came to learn only with the advent of another theory: the general theory of relativity, which not only revealed this fact but also explained the degree of success Euclidean geometry does in fact attain when applied to small regions of space.

Of course economic theory has attained nothing like the success of Euclidean geometry. But the apparent applicability of some of its claims is to be explained by appeal to the same factors which explain why we can employ, e.g., the Pythagorean theorem, even though there are no concrete Euclidean triangles or Euclidean straight lines. We can employ the laws of supply and demand, even though human beings are not economically rational agents; that is, we can employ these 'laws' even though individuals do not make choices reflecting any empirical regularity governing their expectations and their intentions. We can employ them all right, but the laws of supply and demand cannot be applied with the usefulness and exactitude of the Pythagorean theorem, just because the kind terms of economic theory are different from the real kinds in which human behaviour is correctly classified. And this difference is comparatively much greater than the difference between the kind terms of applied geometry and those of physics. There are no concrete Euclidean triangles, but we know why and we can calculate the amount of the divergence between any physical triangle and the Euclidean claims about it, because we have a physical theory to make these corrections, the very one which showed Euclidean geometry to be factually false. We can make no such improvements in the application of the laws of supply and demand; we can never do any better than apply them retrospectively or generically; we cannot specify their parameters, or their exceptions, because the axiomatic system in which they figure diverges from the facts very greatly and because we have no associated theory that enables us to measure this divergence and make appropriate corrections of it. The lack of such a theory is a difference in kind between Euclidean geometry and economic theory. They differ in applicability only by degree, the predicate of neither pick out natural kinds; but they differ in kind because for Euclidean geometry there is a theory, physics, that enables us to correct and improve the applicability of its implications. There is no such theory that enables us to improve on the applicability of economic theory.

Such a theory is of course logically possible, say a version of cognitive psychology, that provides bridges from economic variables like preference and expectation to independently identifiable psychological states. Such a theory might enable us to actually predict individual economic choices and to correct our microeconomic predictions of them, when these predictions go wrong. It would either enable us to improve microeconomics beyond the level at which it has been stuck for a hundred years, or it would show that the determinants of human behaviour are so orthogonal to the theory's assumptions about them that microeconomics is best given up altogether. But the fact is that no such theory is in the offing, or on the horizon.

What is more, even if it were available, such a psychological theory is not likely to actually deflect practising economists from their intentional research programme. And the reason is that economists and humanity in general are far more committed to viewing one another as agents, as people whose behaviour is caused by desires and beliefs, than we are committed to viewing light rays as Euclidean straight lines. Before the general theory of relativity and even after, it has been hard for non-physicists to surrender Euclid. It is even harder to surrender folk psychology. Indeed, the very prospect sounds incoherent. To surrender folk psychology is to surrender the view that there are desires and beliefs and they cause actions, but surely surrender is an action caused by desires and beliefs. The pragmatic contradiction of believing that there are no beliefs, however, is a problem for philosophy, not economic methodology.

Euclidean geometry was once styled the science of space, but calling it a science did not make it one and we have come to view advances in the axiomatization and extension of geometry as events not in science, but in mathematics. Economics is often defined as the science of the distribution of scarce resources, but calling it a science does not make it one. For much of their histories, since 1800, advances in both these disciplines have consisted in improvements of deductive rigour, economy and elegance of expression, in better axiomatizations and in the proofs of more and more general results, without much concern as to the usefulness of these results. In geometry, the fifth axiom, the postulate of the parallels, came increasingly to be the focus of attention, not because it was in doubt, but because it seemed so much more ampliative than the others.

The crisis of nineteenth-century geometry was provoked by the discovery that denying the postulate of the parallels did not generate a logically inconsistent axiomatic system. Thus the question of the cognitive status of geometry became acute. Some, following Plato, held it to be an intuitively certain body of abstract truths. Some, following Mill, held it to be a body of empirical generalizations. Others, following Kant, viewed it as a body of synthetic *a priori* truths. Matters were settled by distinguishing between geometry as a pure axiomatic system, composed of analytic truths about abstract objects with or without real physical instances; and geometry as an applied theory about the path of light rays, which was shown to be false for reasons given in the general theory of relativity. Moreover, the abstract and apparently pointless exercises of nineteenth-century geometers in developing non-Euclidean geometries turned out to have an altogether unexpected and important empirical role to play in helping us understand the structure of space after all. For they apparently describe the real structure of space in the large. Of course pure geometry, both Euclidean and non-Euclidean, has continued to be a subject of sustained mathematical interest and both have had applications undreamed of eighty years ago.

Compare the history of economic theory during the same time. Unlike physical theory, or for that matter the other social sciences, economics has been subject to exactly the same conceptual pigeonholing as geometry. Some have viewed it, with Lionel Robbins, as a Platonic body of intuitively obvious, idealized but nonetheless correct descriptions of human behaviour. Others, following Ludwig von Mises, have insisted it is a Kantian body of synthetic *a priori* truths about rationality. Others, like the geometrical conventionalists and following T. W. Hutchison, have derided economics as a body of tautologies, as a pure system of implicit definitions without any grip on the real world. Still others, following Mill, have held it to be a body of idealizations of rough empirical regularities. Finally, some loosely following Friedman, have treated it as an uninterpreted calculus in the way positivists treated geometry.[7]

But most economists, like most geometers, have gone about their business proving theorems and deriving results, without giving much thought at all to the question of economic theory's cognitive status. For them the really important question, the one which parallels the geometer's concern about the postulate of the parallels, was whether Walras's theorem that a general market-clearing equilibrium exists, that it is stable and unique, follows from the axioms of microeconomic theory. Walras offered this result in 1874, as a formalization of Adam Smith's conviction about decentralized economies, but he was unable to give more than intuitive arguments for the theorem. It was only in 1934 that Abraham Wald provided an arduous and intricate satisfactory proof and much work since his time has been devoted to producing more elegant, more intuitive and more powerful proofs of new wrinkles on the theorem.[8]

Just as geometers in the nineteenth century explored the ramifications of varying the strongest assumptions of Euclidean geometry, economists have devoted great energies to varying equally crucial assumptions about the number of agents, their expectations, returns to scale and divisibilities, and determining whether a consistent economy – a market-clearing equilibrium – will still result, will be stable and will be unique. Their interests in this formal result are quite independent of, indeed are in spite of, the fact that its assumptions about production, distribution and information are manifestly false. The proof of general equilibrium is the crowning achievement of mathematical economics. But just as geometry as a science faced a crisis in 1919 observations that confirmed the general theory of relativity, so too economic theory faced a crisis in evident fact of the great depression. For a long time after 1929 the economists lost the *conviction* that the Walrasian general equilibrium was at least a state towards which markets must, in the long run, move.

The main reaction to this crisis was, of course, Keynesianism. In so far as this theory rests on a denial of the fundamental microeconomic assumption that economic agents' expectations are rational, that they do suffer from money illusions, that they will tailor their actions to current and future economic environments, Keynesian theory represents as much of a conceptual revolution as non-Euclidean geometry did. Keynes of course did not entirely win the field, even during the period when his theory appeared to explain why the market-clearing general equilibrium might never be approached, let alone realized. One reason for this is that many economists continued to be interested in the purely formal questions of the conventional theory, quite regardless of its irrelevance to understanding the actual world. These economists were implicitly treating microeconomics as a pure axiomatic system, whose terms may or may not be instantiated in the real world, but which is of great interest, like Euclidean geometry, whether or not its objects actually exist.

More crucially for the history of economics, there never was and is not yet a theory which can play a role for economics like the role played for geometry by physical theory. Physics enables us to choose between alternative applied geometries and to explain the deviations from actual observation of the ones we reject. There is no such theory to serve as an auxiliary in any choice between an applied neoclassical equilibrium theory and a Keynesian equilibrium theory. When, in the 1970s, Keynesian theory foundered on empirical facts of joint unemployment and inflation, as unremitting as was the fact of the apparent non-market clearing equilibrium of the 1930s, the result was an eager return to the traditional theory. Economists have not forgotten the great depression, but their interest in it seems limited to showing that, after all, the Walrasian approach is at least logically consistent with it, something Keynes's earliest opponents could have vouchsafed them. In short, the theory and its development have been as insulated from empirical influences as geometry ever was before Einstein. All this suggests that, like geometry, economics is best viewed as a branch of mathematics somewhere on the intersection between pure and applied axiomatic systems.

Much of the mystery surrounding the actual development of economic theory – its shifts in formalism, its insulation from empirical assessment, its interest in proving purely formal, abstract possibilities, its unchanged character over a period of centuries, the controversies about its cognitive status – can be comprehended and properly appreciated if we give up on the notion that economics any longer has the aims or makes the claims of an empirical science of human behaviour. Rather we should view it as a branch of mathematics, one devoted to examining the formal properties of a set of assumptions about the transitivity of abstract relations: axioms that implicitly define a technical notion of 'rationality', just as geometry examines the formal properties of abstract points and lines. The abstract term 'rationality' may have far more potential interpretations than economists themselves realize,[9] but rather less bearing on human behaviour and its consequences than we have unreasonably demanded economists reveal.

Indeed, treated as a body of pure research and shorn of its intended interpretation, parts of general equilibrium theory and game theory have begun to have an impact well beyond economics, in biology. Again, there is a parallel to apparently useless nineteenth-century research on non-Euclidean geometry, which in the twentieth century proved essential to the general theory of relativity. The formalism and results of general equilibrium theory are turning out to have applications to establishing stability conditions for ecosystems undreamed of by the economists who proved the existence, uniqueness and stability theorems in economics. Their results are being taken over and reinterpreted by mathematical ecology: stripped of their intentional interpretation, they provide proofs, and stability conditions for unique stable equilibria, that modern evolutionary biology requires in the development of its own theory of balance and competition in the evolution of the biosphere.[10]

Indeed, when recognized as a part of contractarian political philosophy, rational choice and conditions of general equilibrium have emerged as crucial tools of the sociobiologist. Sociobiology hopes to explain how norms of cooperation have emerged as stable equilibria among agents acting so as to maximize genetic fitness, or its shortsighted surrogate, ordinal preference. The possibility of free-riding and the consequent failure to provide public goods at optimal levels has daunted sociobiological speculation about the emergence of culture. If the rational choice theorist can show that rational agents would choose other-regarding outcomes as maximizing ones, then both some forms of contractarianism and some forms of Darwinism about cultural evolution will have been vindicated. These results are a pay-off hardly any one could have expected. Interestingly, they reflect the compatibility of viewing economic theory both as an *a priori* discipline and an exercise in contractarian political philosophy. For the most powerful results to be hoped for in this area are proofs that a particular socially desirable strategy commends itself to a thoroughgoing fitness or utility maximizer. But such a proof would by no means show that the strategy actually emerged because it maximized fitness. Nothing could convert such a possibility into a confirmed account of how sociality emerged. For the fossil record preserves no relevant evidence. The result is always at most the demonstration of an abstract possibility, a suggestive piece of applied mathematics.

Can we expect more of a pay-off to the development of pure general equilibrium theory, or for that matter more from the derivation of theorems about strategies in parametric and strategic games? The question is no harder or easier to answer than the equivalent answer in mathematics. Can we expect pay-offs in mathematics? Yes, of course we can. Can we say in advance what they are, where they will come from and when? Emphatically not. Is this the slightest reason either to deny import to mathematics or to suggest that attention should not continue to be lavished upon it? No. On the contrary it is reason to hold it to a slack reign, to give it all the intellectual freedom it demands and leave the assessment of what is good and what is bad mathematics, to mathematicians. *Mutatis mutandis* for economic theory.

CONCLUSION

It may be asked, what is the cash-value difference between this *laissez-faire* attitude to economics and McCloskey's claim that what is good, right and true, in economics is just what pleases, convinces and sways economists?

There are two large differences between this view and McCloskey's, one conceptual and one practical. The conceptional difference is obvious. If economic theory is a branch of mathematics, then it is to be held up to the standards of that discipline. And these standards are standards for knowledge; they assume that in mathematics it is possible to acquire the truth, in some realist's sense according to which what is true may well not be what happens to convince mathematicians at any given moment. There is a fact of the matter in mathematics, and so too there must be in economics, even if this fact turns out to be as abstract in economics as it is in mathematics.

The practical difference between my view and the rhetorician's has to do with the bearing of economic theory on policy. If economics is best viewed as more akin to a branch of mathematics on the intersection between pure axiomatization and applied geometry, then our long-term perspective on the policy-bearing of economic theory must be qualified. And the vacuum that economic theory leaves in the guidance of policy must be filled by something else, something that will provide improvable guidance to policy, both private and public. That there might be an alternative to economic theory, better at policy guidance than economics, is an alternative the rhetorician declines to face. Presumably, on the rhetorician's view, the reflexive nature of economic theory – the fact that economic agents can learn the economist's theory of how they choose, is a sort of impossibility proof: no theory can do any better than the poor job McCloskey admits economics does today.[11] This pessimistic view is not one my view need share with the rhetorical approach.

As I have noted, philosophers and economists sometimes advert to the normative interpretation of microeconomic theory. As a normative discipline, microeconomics' theories are treated as hypothetical imperatives, whose consequents enjoin action on the hypothesis that you wish to be economically rational, or to encourage it in others. These theories identify incentives and disincentives for rational individuals and suggest ways of attaining, say, a government's aims, by putting these incentives and disincentives into play. If the moral of my story about microeconomic theory is right, then we cannot expect the long-term sharpening of such hypothetical imperatives to provide better and better means of manipulating individual choice. In fact, the use of these hypothetical imperatives will have to be hedged around with qualification and our expectations based on them must reflect readiness to deal with completely unanticipated consequences: not only will people fail to behave rationally, but there will be no systematic correction that we can apply to our hypothetical imperatives that will enable them to be used more reliably. And all this is for exactly the same reason that these imperatives, when treated as descriptive generalizations about what rational agents do, instead of what they ought to do, are not subject to systematic improvement by the appeal to other factors that work with them to produce action.

In this respect, microeconomic theory is worse off than Euclidean geometry. Geometry too can serve as a body of hypothetical imperatives – for the use of surveyors, and the paths of light rays so nearly reflect geometry's assumptions, that surveyors can rely on Euclidean geometry and require no corrections. Cosmologists, however, do and when they employ the imperatives of geometry to realize their measurement aims, they must add corrections that reflect the effect of massive objects on light rays. But these effects are few in number and uniform in their consequences. We can easily adjust and accommodate for them. Such adjustment and accommodation is just what we cannot do in economics. And when you add in that besides appealing to hypothetical imperatives about individual action, public policy requires also that we aggregate these imperatives to suggest governmental microeconomic policies, the problem of correction multiplies.

Thus, we should neither attach unqualified confidence to predictions made on the basis of microeconomic theory nor condemn it severely when these predictions fail. Microeconomic theory can no more be faulted than Euclidean geometry should be in the context of astrophysics.

Does this attitude leave a vacuum in the foundations of public policy which will be filled by some other theory offered to serve as the basis for hypothetical imperatives useful in public policy? Perhaps before the events of the late 1980s and 1990s, proponents of the economic theory behind central state planning might have come forward with such a candidate. But nowadays, only the most brazen Marxian economists would do so. On the other hand, if there is a connection between general equilibrium theory and contractarianism's aim of protecting all against the egoism of each, the generic powers of the theory have some bearing on policy. But it will be a relatively *laissez-faire* bearing. Until another theory turns up, if we insist on interpretations that accord economic theory empirical bearing on the way the world actually works, we should not apply it to justify policy beyond its generic powers to prove how the actual is possible, and how the possible might be actual. On the other hand, interpreted as a body of mathematical axioms, lemmas and theorems, economic theory offers us even less by way of guidance.

Either way, these interpretations create a vacuum for the real guidance of public and particularly economic policy beyond the merely generic, that alternative theories will be eager to fill. To the extent that they trade in the preferences and expectations of individuals, they will do no better than neoclassical economics. To the extent that they ignore tastes and information, they will probably do worse. Accordingly the *laissez-faire* economists were probably right, albeit for the wrong reasons. This is not the best of all possible worlds, but it is very easy to make it worse.[12]

NOTES

1 See for instance, McCloskey (1985).
2 One reason to think this is right is the large number of autobiographical admissions of neoclassical economists that they were attracted to economics by

the socialist vision. But as Stigler is infamous for noting, nothing makes an intelligent person an opponent of central planning faster than a good dose of microeconomics.

3 Cf. Weintraub (1985: ch. 6).
4 Detractors include Leontief (1982). For a recent example of a defender, see Debreu (1991).
5 Cf. Rosenberg (1980a) for a detailed account of this transformation.
6 Cf. Rosenberg (1980a).
7 Lionel Robbins (1932), T. W. Hutchison (1948), von Mises (1949), Milton Friedman (1953).
8 Walras (1954) and Wald (1954). For a contemporary version of the proof, cf. Debreu (1959).
9 I discuss at least one of these applications, in biology, below.
10 Cf., for instance, Oster and Wilson (1978) and May (1973). Game theory was introduced into evolutionary contexts as early as Lewontin (1961). An excellent introduction is to be found in Smith (1982), in which economists will recognize much of their handiwork, sometimes under different names.
11 See, for example, McCloskey (1990).
12 I develop much of this argument at greater length in Rosenberg (1992).

BIBLIOGRAPHY

Arrow, K. and Debreu, G. (1954) 'Existence of equilibrium for a competitive economy, *Econometrica* 22: 376–86.
Arrow, K. and Hahn, F. (1971) *General Competitive Analysis*, San Francisco: Holden Day.
Buchanan, J. (1989) *Explorations in Constitutional Economics*, College Station: Texas A&M Press.
Debreu, G. (1959) *The Theory of Value*. New York: Wiley.
Debreu, G. (1991) 'The mathematization of economics', *American Economic Review* 81: 107.
Friedman, M. (1953) *Essays in Positive Economics*, Chicago: University of Chicago Press.
Hume, D. (1985) *Essays, Moral, Political and Literary*, Indianapolis: Liberty Press.
Hutchison, T. W. (1948) *The Significance and Basic Postulates of Economics*. Reprinted, New York: Kelley, 1960.
Leontief, W. (1982) *Science*, 9 July, p.xii.
Lewontin, R. (1961) 'Evolution and the theory of games', *Journal of Theoretical Biology* 1: 382–403.
May, R. (1973) *Stability and Complexity in Model Ecosystems*, Princeton: Princeton University Press.
McCloskey, D. (1985) *The Rhetoric of Economics*, Madison: University of Wisconsin Press.
McCloskey, D. (1990) *If You're So Smart*, Chicago: University of Chicago Press.
Oster, R. and Wilson, E. O. (1978) *The Social Insects*. Cambridge: Cambridge University Press.
Robbins, L. (1932) *An Essay on the Nature and Significance of Economic Science*, London: St Martin's.
Rosenberg, A. (1976) *Microeconomic Laws: A Philosophical Analysis*, Pittsburgh: University of Pittsburgh Press.

Rosenberg, A. (1980a) 'A skeptical history of economic theory', *Theory and Decision* 12: 75–85.

Rosenberg, A. (1980b) 'Obstacles to the nomological connection of reasons and actions, *Philosophy of Social Science* 10: 79–91.

Rosenberg, A. (1992) *Economics – Mathematical Politics or Science of Diminishing Returns?*, Chicago: University of Chicago Press.

Smith, J. M. (1982) *Evolution and the Theory of Games*, Cambridge: Cambridge University Press.

von Mises, L. (1949) *Human Action*, New Haven: Yale University Press.

Wald, A. (1954) 'On some systems of equations for mathematical economics', *Econometrica* 19: 368–403.

Walras, L. (1954) *Elements of Pure Economics*, Homewood, Il: Irwin.

Weintraub, E. R. (1985) *General Equilibrium Analysis*, Cambridge: Cambridge University Press.

12

REORIENTING THE ASSUMPTIONS ISSUE

Uskali Mäki

ECONOMISTS AND THE ASSUMPTIONS ISSUE

The most important methodological issue in economics has been and persists to be over what is called the 'realism' of theories and their 'assumptions'. Profit maximization, perfect information, transitive preferences, diminishing returns, rational expectations, perfectly competitive markets, givenness of tastes, technology and institutional framework, non-gendered agents – these and many other ideas have been assumed by some economists and questioned by others. The issue has often been whether such assumptions are ('too') unrealistic or ('sufficiently') realistic or whether it matters at all if they are one way rather than the other.

The forms in which this issue appears in the work of practising economists can be approached from a variety of angles. From the perspective of the kind of behaviour in which economists engage themselves we may distinguish two forms: let us call them the silent form and the loud form.

The silent form is silent in that the general principles guiding an economist's attitudes and decisions are not explicitly pronounced and invoked in the practice of research and communication. For instance, an economist who prefers realistic to unrealistic assumptions in theories and models, may, without making any noise about it, simply ignore frameworks that are supposed to give rise to insufficiently realistic theories, and pursue ever more realistic models by introducing modifications within the chosen framework. In this silent form, the issue appears most of the time as the daily bread of an economist when considering which theoretical frameworks and, within such frameworks, which assumptions to adopt and which to reject in model building.

The loud form of the issue is loud in that explicit appeals are being made to general principles of scientific theorizing in defending or criticizing a theory or framework for being realistic or unrealistic. It often takes the shape of open controversy in which arguments are forwarded about the past failures and successes and the desirable future course of economic inquiry. Such an open debate occasionally bursts out as an expression of

236

deep disagreements between schools of thought or between inquirers with different mentalities. This debate has had many incarnations and it has gone through exciting episodes, including the German *Methodenstreit* in the 1880s between Carl Menger and Gustav Schmoller; the marginalist controversy in the 1940s between Richard L. Lester and Fritz Machlup; the Friedman controversy in the 1950s and 1960s; the capital controversy in the same period between the two Cambridges; and so forth. This is a recurring controversy which is generated around ever new topics.

From another perspective, that of the kinds of stakes at issue, we may also find two forms, call them antagonism and family quarrel. An *antagonism* is something that prevails between mutually incompatible frameworks of analysis, theories and approaches, traditions and schools of thought, while *family quarrels* appear within such intellectual formations. Statements about whether a given theory and its assumptions are or should be realistic occur within both antagonisms and family quarrels. Antagonisms and family quarrels differ from one another in regard to the seriousness of consequences that a challenge to a theory or framework may have. A statement made within an antagonism implies a suggested switch or a refusal to switch to another theory or approach, such as from the standard neoclassical framework to Austrian or institutionalist or post-Keynesian frameworks. On the other hand, a statement within a family quarrel implies a suggested move or a refusal to move to another version within a theory or framework, such as within the neoclassical framework.

There is considerable overlap between the two pairs of forms in which the issue appears. Antagonisms are often loud, whereas family quarrels are often silent. However, the two pairs are not identical. Advocates of radically rival approaches often refuse to engage in open controversy over fundamental principles, even though – and sometimes because – the stakes are high. This is the not-so-unlikely case of silent antagonism. On the other hand, open debate on the ways of theorizing may be sparked even though the stakes related to the basic substance of a theory are low. That is, family quarrels may sometimes be noisy, too.

It should also be noted that instead of two dichotomous forms of the issue, we rather have two continua of forms, the first having antagonism at one extreme and family affair at the other, the second having the loud form at one end and the silent form at the other. The issue may take forms that are more or less loud or silent, and closer to constituting an antagonism or a family quarrel. It is not always easy to locate actual cases on these continua. For example, since the identity of a theory or framework is not always firm and clear, it is sometimes hard to tell whether a revision means a move from one theory or framework to another or whether it constitutes a move within the original theory or framework.

In whatever form, the chronic and recurring issue has been and is being plagued by obscurity regarding the fundamental concepts that have been used in formulating the issue itself and the rival positions about it. The most importantly obscure and ambiguous concept has been that of realism itself. It has been used in a number of varying and mutually inconsistent meanings in the course of the debate both by economists and by economic methodologists. There is a pressing need to bring clarity to the discussions about the issue.

METHODOLOGISTS AND THE ASSUMPTIONS ISSUE

As suggested above, the assumptions issue is both ubiquitous and central to economics, and plagued by serious unclarities. Given these two facts, one would expect that it has to be one of the major preoccupations of the specialists in economic methodology to analyse the issue and to clarify its elements. Surprisingly, one is disappointed in this expectation. Methodologists of economists have recently paid relatively little attention to this theme. There was a lot of more or less sophisticated discussion by economists (with some help from philosophers) in the 1950s and 1960s, mostly centred around elaborating various positions in regard to Milton Friedman's statement to the effect that the 'realism' of assumptions is irrelevant. One would have expected that the new generation of methodologists of economics entering the field from the mid-1970s onwards would have taken this issue as one of their primary concerns.

One reason for the failure of methodologists to contribute to the assumptions issue may be the dominance of Popperian frameworks in recent methodological study. Both the Popperian and Lakatosian varieties of falsificationism approach theory assessment in terms of the success and failure of testable implications. A closer scrutiny of the nature and role of assumptions – their logic, semantics and pragmatics – gets easily discouraged within this framework (with the partial exception of Lakatos's methodology of scientific research programmes which does have something to say on the pragmatics of assumptions). As a consequence, we are not very much wiser about the ways of the assumptions issue than our predecessors in the 1960s, even though much more effort has been invested in the methodological study of economics in the 1980s than during any other earlier decade (see Mäki 1990).

This is not to deny that a few important contributions have been published after the mid-1970s, such as Boland (1979), Musgrave (1981), Caldwell (1992), Lawson (1992) and Hausman (1992), to mention a few. Progress has not been absent, but relative to the recent investments in economic methodology, the fruit has been scant.

TWO APPROACHES TO THE ISSUE

A popular approach to the issue is to construe it in abstract terms and to look for generalized answers. The issue is taken to be one over whether, descriptively, the assumptions of a given economic theory are realistic or unrealistic, or whether, as a general normative principle, theories in economics should involve realistic assumptions, or whether, given the current situation, theories and assumptions should be 'more' realistic. A radical position along these lines has been formulated to read as follows: 'Truly important and significant hypotheses will be found to have "assumptions" that are wildly inaccurate descriptive representations of reality, and, in general, the more significant the theory, the more unrealistic the assumptions' (Friedman 1953: 14).

This abstract construal of the issue is often accompanied by the idea that the dividing line between people holding rival views concerning the desirability of realistic or 'more' realistic assumptions distinguishes those holding a *realist* position from those who are *non-realists* (instrumentalists, conventionalists, etc.). Accordingly, the idea goes, realists prefer realistic assumptions to unrealistic assumptions, while non-realists are either indifferent or have their preferences the other way around.

I argue that the above approach is not very helpful for understanding the assumptions issue. There is a need for reorientation. The alternative approach is different: the issue should not be construed as one of realistic versus unrealistic assumptions in the abstract but rather as one over which specific assumptions are and should be unrealistic or realistic, and over rival ways in which they are or should be so. It is understood that all theories are unrealistic in a number of ways and that the issue cannot be resolved in the abstract. A more concrete (more 'realistic'!) approach is needed to understand the nature of the issue in each specific case.

With this reorientation, it also becomes possible to understand that the advocacy of more or less realistic assumptions *per se* does not yet make anybody a realist or non-realist about economic theories. Both realists and non-realists may legitimately hold theories which are unrealistic in their assumptions.

This line of thought cannot be followed without an array of refined concepts. We need a few notions for distinguishing between different kinds of assumptions in different roles, and between a number of different ways of being realistic and unrealistic. I will provide a beginner's rudimentary guide to these concepts and to the overall argument (for more detailed formulations and discussions, see Mäki 1989, 1991, 1992a, 1992b, 1992c, 1993a, 1993b, 1993c, 1993d, 1993e).

THE UNAVOIDABILITY OF UNREALISTICNESS

Amongst economists, amusing illusions about physical sciences abound. Witness the following:

> In physics the assumed premises are realistic. If there is evidence that they are not realistic, or not close approximations to reality, they will be rejected; and at every step the propositions derived from theory will be tested by experiment and observation: all propositions made are subject to the test of falsification. In general-equilibrium economics, by contrast, the assumptions are the extreme opposite of realistic. They are mad.
>
> (Neild 1984: 42)

It is easy to provide evidence to the contrary. Take Boyle-Charles's law of ideal gases in classical thermodynamics. It states that $PV=RT$, where P is the pressure, V the volume, and T the temperature of a body of gas, while R is a constant. This statement is about ideal gases, which means that it may be formulated to assume that the volume of gas molecules is zero, that the forces of interaction between gas molecules are nil, and that the gas molecules are perfectly elastic. It requires a lot of imagination to say that these assumptions are realistic.

Or consider Galileo's law of falling bodies, an example much used by economists in the assumptions controversy. The law states that $s=\frac{1}{2} gt^2$, where s is the distance travelled by a body, t is time and g is the gravitational constant. Among other things, it is assumed here that air pressure is zero, i.e., that the body falls in a vacuum; that all other gravitational forces, such as that of the moon, are nil; that all magnetic forces are zero; that the radius of the earth is infinite, that is, that the earth is flat. Most of these assumptions are unrealistic all the time; all of them are unrealistic most of the time.

We may conclude that economics is not alone in involving unrealistic assumptions. Nor is neoclassical general equilibrium theory alone within economics. Consider Marx's law of value which states that the market prices of commodities correspond to their labour values. Among other things, it assumes that there is pure competition; that there is no foreign trade; that the merchants' profits are zero; that supply equals demand; that the average organic composition of capital in the sector producing the commodity equals the average organic composition of capital in the whole economy. Again, most of the time, such assumptions cannot avoid being unrealistic.

The important thing to note here is that the heavy reliance on unrealistic assumptions is not taken by scientists themselves as a sufficient reason to judge theories or laws either as unscientific or as failures as scientific hypotheses. On the contrary, it is a ubiquitous feature of the most celebrated scientific theories that they contain unrealistic elements.

KINDS OF REALISTICNESS AND UNREALISTICNESS

We have so far used the attributes 'is realistic' and 'is unrealistic' as if they were unambiguous. They are not so, not in the least. Let us point out some typical meanings in which these terms are being used by economists and others.

Aboutness

A representation may be said to be realistic if it is about something real; it is unrealistic if it is not about anything real. For instance, it may be argued that the theory of phlogiston – or, more precisely, the concept of phlogiston in the phlogiston theory of burning – is not about anything real, since there is no such thing as phlogiston as a constituent of matter. On the other hand, the concept of oxygen is probably about a real constituent of the world. Galileo's law may be taken to be about real bodies and real gravitational attraction. The maximization assumption may be about households and business firms, provided there are such agents acting purposefully in social reality.

Observability

Some variants of realisticness and unrealisticness are related to the idea of observability. Constructs are sometimes regarded as realistic if they are about observable matters. There are those who insist that '[w]e must deal only with observable variables. To speculate about things you cannot observe is futile' (Neild 1984: 42). In a sense, this is a plea for avoiding unrealistic variables in favour of realistic ones. We know that Paul Samuelson's work on revealed preference was inspired by a principle similar to this. We also know that Newton wrestled with this issue when considering his notion of gravitational force. Yet, the postulation of gravitation, electromagnetic forces, black holes, photons, quarks and other unobservables is regarded by scientists and philosophers of science as one of the key reasons for the success of science. Unrealisticness in this sense is vital for science.

Truth

Truth and falsehood are obvious forms of realisticness and unrealisticness. In some discussions about the assumptions issue in economics, they are the only forms (e.g., Brunner 1969; Boland 1979). It is probably false to assume that the pull of the moon does not have any impact on bodies falling within the gravitational field of the earth, but it may be true to state that the latter does exert an influence expressed by g. It is not true that economic agents have perfect information, and it may be true or it may be false that they maximize in some sense.

A theory or statement has to be realistic in the sense of being about something real – but not necessarily about something observable – in order to be true or false about that something. Truth and falsehood presuppose aboutness.

Success in empirical tests

A representation may be regarded as realistic if it is testable and well confirmed by evidence in empirical tests. One may say that a theory or statement fails to be confirmed by evidence, hence is unrealistic, either because the appropriate test conditions cannot be established or because the evidence is negative in cases where the test conditions are appropriate. Bearing in mind that appropriateness is a contestable notion, we may expect that the travel of a feather in actual atmosphere does not, while the travel of a cannon-ball does, support Galileo's law; for the feather, a vacuum would have to be created. In both cases, many other forces cannot be removed, and the earth cannot be made flat. In economics, a traditional controversy has been over whether the maximization assumption is testable at all, and if it is, what would be an appropriate empirical test of it.

Truth and confirmation – and falsehood and disconfirmation – are sometimes confused with one another (e.g. Nagel 1963; Brunner 1969). However, evidence may speak against a true statement or for a false statement, or there may be no appropriate evidence at all for or against a true – or false – statement.

Plausibility

Truth is sometimes confused also with plausibility, and falsehood with implausibility. Here we have yet other meanings for our key terms. A representation is realistic in one sense if it is plausible, and unrealistic if it is implausible. Plausibility is a matter of being believed by people. (For discussions of plausibility in the context of economics, see Hirsch and de Marchi 1989; Nooteboom 1986; Mäki 1993a.) Some time ago, the assumption of the infinity of the radius of the earth used to be very plausible in relation to the vast majority of humankind: people did believe that the earth is flat. For some time now, it has been found an extremely implausible assumption.

Partiality

A concept, statement or theory is often regarded as unrealistic if it is partial, if it isolates only selected aspects of objects for representation. Galileo's law is unrealistic in this sense, since, among other things, such as omitting the colour of falling bodies, it focuses on the influence of only one factor on the behaviour of the bodies, to the exclusion of others. The maximization assumption not only omits mentioning the shoe size of economic actors, it also excludes other possible motives from consideration. One-sector models in growth theory and 2 × 2 models in the theory of international trade are prime examples of partial representations. Marshallian analysis is partial in excluding, for instance, cross-elasticities between markets, while Walrasian analysis is partial in excluding culture and gender, for example. All representations are partial in that they isolate small slices of the world from the rest of it.

Sometimes, partiality is confused with falsehood. While it is true that partial representations violate 'the whole truth', it does not follow that they therefore also violate 'nothing but the truth'. A representation may be true or false about a part of a complex whole (see Mäki 1993c).

Abstractness

Abstractness is a special case of partiality. A representation is abstract if it isolates a general feature or a universal from the particularities of the many objects that share it. The concept of the business firm is such an abstract notion, while the concept of, say, the Nokia Corporation is a concrete one. The concept of a falling body is abstract, while 'Hemmo Huimapää' is the name of a particular parachutist and hence concrete.

Practical usefulness

A representation is often regarded as realistic in one sense if it serves well the pursuit of some practical ends. Realisticness in this sense is relative to the specific practical ends at hand. The formulae of atomic theory are practically useful for attempts to fly to the moon, while they are useless, hence unrealistic – some might say as unrealistic as the formulae of the Arrow–Debreu construct – for manipulating the rate of unemployment in your economy. Galileo's law may be useful for destroying your enemy with a cannon, but it is relatively useless for controlling the travel of a feather to delight your baby.

TYPES AND FUNCTIONS OF ASSUMPTIONS

It is vital for dealing with the assumptions issue to understand that economic theories involve many types of assumptions with a variety of functions. This has been recognized by earlier commentators on the issue (see, for example, Machlup 1955; Rotwein 1959; Melitz 1967; Brunner 1969). Within the set of assumptions that are elements of versions of a theory it is helpful to distinguish between assumptions that are taken to be central to a theory and those that are regarded as less central, or between those that constitute the theory and those that do not. Let us call these two classes 'core assumptions' and 'peripheral assumptions'.

Core assumptions

Galileo's law involves the statement that bodies are attracted by the gravitational field of the earth, measured by parameter g in the formulation of the law. If it were called an assumption, it would be a prime example of a core assumption. It serves to sort out what is believed to be the most central force influencing the fall of bodies. Even more, it denotes a fact that is believed to constitute the essence of falling.

The assumption that agents maximize may be regarded as a core assumption in much of economics. It is central to the most popular economic theories, and many economists believe that the constrained strive for maximum outcomes is the most important motive force influencing agents' behaviour. Many of them think that maximizing constitutes the essence of economic behaviour.

Peripheral assumptions

In Galileo's law, the assumptions of vacuum and the absence of other attractional forces serve as peripheral assumptions. They serve to neutralize factors that are not regarded as central or essential to the phenomenon of falling bodies. In economics, assumptions such as closed economy, instantaneous and costless transferability of resources, perfect divisibility of goods and factors, homogeneous capital, full use of resources, constancy of tastes and technology, and the general *ceteris paribus* clause play a similar role. Typically, many such peripheral assumptions are false.

Alan Musgrave (1981) has suggested a typology of assumptions to deal with the issue of realisticness. He distinguishes between three types of assumptions and calls them 'negligibility assumptions', 'domain assumptions' and 'heuristic assumptions'. It seems that the way he characterizes them implies that they are to be treated as subspecies of peripheral assumptions. A few notes will suffice to clarify the typology (for a detailed critical analysis, see Mäki 1994).

Negligibility

In this case, an assumption is formulated so as to function as a statement about the negligibility of a certain factor. The assumption that the pull of the moon is non-existent is false and as such helps to isolate a non-negligible force, the gravitational field of the earth. Reformulated as a negligibility assumption it may turn into a true statement that the pull of the moon has a negligible effect on falling bodies. Similarly, the assumption that a given economy is closed may be false, but reformulated as a statement that the impact of foreign trade on certain phenomena is negligible, it may be true.

Applicability

Sometimes, some of the assumptions of a theory may be used to specify the domain to which the theory can be applied. They serve as statements about applicability. In some cases, the assumption of a vacuum may play this role: Galileo's law applies only if air pressure is nil. Similarly, an economic hypothesis may be argued to be applicable only to economies that are closed. Empirical applicability is a prerequisite for testability which in turn is presupposed by being well confirmed by empirical evidence.

Early step

Some assumptions are used as elements of an early step in a series of theories or models. Closed economy models may function as early steps preparing the way to open economy models. The assumption of the zero-ness of the pull of the moon may in some cases serve as an early-step assumption, to be replaced in later versions of Galileo's law by an assumption giving an account of the specific impact of the moon on falling bodies.

The idea of early-step assumptions (Musgrave uses the term 'heuristic assumption') is often construed as a promise of increasing realisticness as a theory develops. In some senses of the term, realisticness would indeed increase. The comprehensiveness of a theory would increase and its partiality would decrease as new factors are incorporated into it. This is sometimes accomplished by relaxing assumptions that are utterly false and replacing them by other, later-step assumptions, that are true or closer to the truth. Furthermore, a theory which takes into account a larger set of factors is often more successful in empirical tests and then also in this sense more realistic. In economics, however, it is typical that only a few steps are taken in this direction (see Lind 1992).

THE FUNCTIONS OF UNREALISTICNESS

Now that we have an idea of kinds of unrealisticness and types of assumptions, we can better understand a line of thought that may be used for justifying unrealistic elements in economic theory. Consider Galileo's law first. It is unrealistic in that it is partial. It is unrealistic also in involving assumptions that are mostly false. It denotes gravitation which is unobservable. These unrealisticnesses serve one and the same purpose, that of isolating a central force influencing the behaviour of falling bodies. A number of unrealistic peripheral assumptions are used for neutralizing what are believed to be peripheral factors in order to focus on what is believed to be the most important factor. The core assumption, concerned with the contribution of the earth's gravitation, purports to be as close to the truth as possible.

The situation is similar in economics. Unrealistic peripheral assumptions help isolate what are believed to be the fundamental relations from less relevant ones or the major causes from the minor causes of phenomena studied. As Oliver Hart puts it, '[t]hese models, since they concentrate on one issue, tend to make simplifying and hence often unrealistic assumptions about everything which is not the central focus. . . . Any theory, if it is to get anywhere, must abstract from many (even most) aspects of reality' (Hart 1984: 48). The same idea can be found in Friedman's 1953 essay. Let me cite my favourite two passages:

> A fundamental hypothesis of science is that appearances are deceptive and that there is a way of looking at or interpreting or organizing the evidence that will reveal superficially disconnected and diverse phenomena to be manifestations of a more fundamental and relatively simple structure.
>
> (Friedman 1953: 33)

Based on this principle, Friedman's maxim of theory formation prescribes that we should 'abstract essential features of complex reality' (ibid.: 7).

The core assumptions are supposed to capture, in pure form, the 'essential features' or 'the more fundamental structure', while the peripheral assumptions, such as negligibility and early-step assumptions, are there to help see the essence of the matter undisturbed by eliminating the actual disturbances or complications. Friedman's mistake was to defend the core assumption of profit maximization by appealing to an analogy between it and the vacuum assumption, which is a peripheral assumption. The correct analogy would be between it and the core assumption of the gravitational attraction of the earth (see Mäki 1992b).

While it is often the case that unrealistic peripheral assumptions can be justified as devices for eliminating or neutralizing minor factors so as to bring in brighter light the major factors, this does not always have to be the case. Sometimes the only justification appears to be an increase in formal tractability, the facilitation of proofs within a pre-given formal framework. It is not always easy to tell whether the ground is ontological, having to do with the presumed structure of reality, or more purely pragmatic, related to the manipulability of formal systems. And, of course, the relevance of various aspects of the social context of theorizing for the outcome of theorizing has to be acknowledged.

ANTAGONISMS AND FAMILY QUARRELS AGAIN

We may say that in an antagonistic controversy, core assumptions are questioned. If it is suggested that gravitation be replaced by angels or that maximization be replaced by routines, we have examples of antagonism. Rival claims about the most essential features of the domain of study or the major causes of phenomena to be explained are confronted.

In family quarrels, peripheral assumptions are challenged. One may suggest that for certain falling items, the absence of a vacuum is not negligible and that a vacuum has to be assumed as a prerequisite for empirical applicability; or that the pull of the moon has to be incorporated into the equation; or that it is time to take the next step in the series of economic models by relaxing the closed economy early-step assumption and by incorporating foreign trade and international capital movements.

As said earlier, it is not always easy to agree on which statements are to be treated as the core assumptions and which as the peripheral assumptions, that is, where the stakes are highest and where they are lowest.

Domain or applicability assumptions do not seem to conform neatly to the above rule. Sometimes, there prevails a sort of peaceful coexistence and division of labour between different theories or models. The total domain is divided between them, and unanimity about domain assumptions obtains. Each theory or model is only applied to its agreed-upon respective domain. In other cases, theories make rival claims about one and the same domain as answers to one and the same question. The stakes may then be high in challenging the respective domain assumptions.

REALISTICNESS AND REALISM

Economists usually talk about the 'realism' of their theories and assumptions. This easily misleads them to think that those who favour more such 'realism' in theories are advocates of realism as a philosophical doctrine, while those who are content with unrealistic assumptions are non-realists. In order to avoid this confusion, I have suggested that 'realism' and 'nonrealism' be reserved for denoting a variety of philosophical theses, and that 'realisticness' and 'unrealisticness' be adopted for denoting various properties of linguistic and other representations such as economic theories and their parts (Mäki 1989).

Once this terminological convention is accepted, it becomes easier to see that the use of radically unrealistic assumptions does not commit one to non-realism. A realist economist is permitted, indeed required, to use unrealistic assumptions in order to isolate what are believed to be the most essential features in a complex situation (for the whole argument, see Mäki 1993e). To count as a minimal realist, an economist is required to believe that economic reality is unconstituted by his or her representations of it and that whatever truth value those representations have is independent of his or her or anybody else's opinions of it.

INTERLUDE: REORIENTING THE ISSUE

The controversy over the assumptions of economic theories has often been construed as one between those who are in favour of realistic or at least more realistic assumptions as against those who are satisfied with unrealistic assumptions. It is one of the implications of the above suggestions that I find this construal of the controversy 'unrealistic' in the sense of being oversimplified. Since all theories contain unrealistic assumptions, the real issue can be construed as one about the *substance* of those theories and assumptions, namely *what they exclude* as supposedly irrelevant or inessential and *what they include* as allegedly relevant or essential, and *what they say about* the included items. The issue is one over rival conceptions of what Friedman termed the 'more fundamental structure' of the economy.

FOUR ILLUSTRATIONS

Let us briefly illustrate the idea with four major issues in recent economics. They are the issues of whether the Keynesian or the monetarist approach managed to focus on the crucial factors, whether to include the role of positive transaction costs in one's theory, whether to put the emphasis on equilibrium states or on processes of change, and whether to begin the construction of economic theory with an analysis of exchange or of production.

Friedman and Keynes

Take first Milton Friedman's account of the opposition between his monetarist approach and that of Keynes. We know that Friedman does not find certain kinds of unrealisticness in theories problematic; on the contrary, in his opinion theories have to be unrealistic to perform their task properly. On this, he finds himself in agreement with Keynes:

Of course, his assumptions were not in literal correspondence with reality. If they had been, he would have been condemned to pedestrian description; his whole theory would have lost its power. . . . I believe that Keynes's theory is the right kind of theory in its simplicity, its concentration on a few key magnitudes, its potential fruitfulness.

(Friedman 1972: 908)

Friedman locates the ultimate disagreement elsewhere, in *what* the rival theories say about the structure of economic reality:

I have been led to reject [Keynes's theory], not on these grounds, but because I believe . . . that it has not isolated what are 'really' the key factors in short-run economic change.

(Ibid.)

Friedman considers that Keynes did try to isolate the 'key factors', but that he ended up with excluding what Friedman would find the most essential factor.

The heart of the General Theory is an extremely simple hypothesis – that a highly unstable marginal efficiency schedule of investment and a liquidity preference function that is highly elastic at low rates of interest and unstable at higher rates of interest are the key to short-run economic movements. That is what gives investment its central role, what makes the consumption function and the multiplier the key concepts, what enables Keynes to develop his theory for 165 pages without having to introduce the quantity of money.

(Ibid.)

As we know, the monetarists insist on isolating the quantity of money as the key element in the short-run behaviour of the economy. Friedman thinks that he and Keynes agree that it is the task of theory to isolate the essential or 'key factors' and to exclude the less important items in social reality from theory. Friedman argues that Keynes's theory failed in performing this task, rather than in being (too) realistic or (too) unrealistic.

Transaction costs and institutions

Consider then the role of transaction costs in economic theory. Traditional neoclassical theories contain the false idealizing assumption that transaction costs are nil, that is, that the economy functions 'frictionlessly'. These theories isolate production costs as the relevant cost category. This helps isolate certain relations from the influence of positive transaction costs. These theories are unrealistic in a double sense at least, in containing a false assumption and in failing to encompass the role of one real feature of the economy. It may be held that those isolated relations constitute the most fundamental structure of the economy and that therefore the exclusion of transaction costs promotes the pursuit of true accounts of the essential features, transaction costs being among the inessential ones.

On the other hand, others argue that the exclusion of positive transaction costs not only is based on a false assumption about their non-existence, but also serves to eliminate an essential factor from our picture of economic reality, namely institutions or organizational structures. It therefore leads to 'blackboard economics' (Coase 1988: 19) which is 'remote from the real world' (ibid.: 15). The assumption is therefore not innocently false. For many purposes, it would be false also when construed as a negligibility assumption. If it is used to specify the domain of applicability, it appears that the respective theory and its theorems – such as the standard neoclassical allocative theorems – do not apply to actual economies (cf. Coase 1960). The standard neoclassical isolation can be argued to divert the focus of theory away from some of the essential features of the economy. For instance, the depiction of business firms as production functions, based on the idealization of frictionlessness, may be taken to divert the attention from what is essential for major explanatory purposes, captured only by depicting firms as governance structures. Thus, 'the modern corporation is mainly to be understood as the product of a series of organizational innovations that have had the purpose and effect of economizing on transaction costs' (Williamson 1983: 1537; see also e.g. Williamson 1985; North 1990).

Now it is clear, as many critics have pointed out and as acknowledged by its advocates, that any form of transaction cost economics is bound to be unrealistic itself; it has to exclude much and it has to idealize and simplify much. For instance, its standard forms exclude from consideration the role of technology and concrete social relations, items that are identified as the key factors in other theoretical orientations. Yet, it is by using these exclusions and idealizations that transaction cost economists can maintain that they have isolated what they find a fundamental factor in the economy. (On this interpretation of the issue, see Mäki 1992c.)

Equilibrium states and processes of change

Take next the issue about assumptions of knowledge and equilibrium. There is the widely used but presumably false idealizing assumption that the agents have full relevant information, that there is nothing to learn. This falsehood helps isolate equilibrium states to the exclusion of processes of change. As Robert Lucas states,

> [e]conomics has tended to focus on situations in which the agent can
> be expected to 'know' or have learned the consequences of different

actions so that his observed choices reveal stable features of his underlying preferences. We use economic theory to calculate how certain
variations in the situation are predicted to affect behavior, but these
calculations obviously do not reflect or usefully model the adaptive
process by which subjects have themselves arrived at the decision rules
they use. Technically, I think of *economics as studying decision
rules that are steady states of some adaptive process*, decision rules that
are found to work over a range of situations and hence are no longer
revised appreciably as more experience accumulates.

(Lucas 1987: 218; emphasis added)

On the other hand, those wishing to focus on phenomena of change are
critical of the assumptions picturing the maximizing agent: 'Strict adherence
to optimization notions either requires or strongly encourages the disregard
of essential features of change . . .' (Nelson and Winter 1982: 31; cf. p. 94).
To the above statement by Lucas, Sidney Winter responds by making a
case for a diametrically opposite position.

To be willing to limit the aspirations of economic science to the
study of the steady states of adaptive processes is presumably to view
vast realms of apparent rapid change as either unimportant or illusory;
it is to join with the writer of Ecclesiastes in maintaining that 'there
is no new thing under the sun'. I, on the other hand, side with
Heraclitus in arguing that 'you could not step twice into the same
river, for new waters are ever flowing on you'. It is the appearance
of stability that is illusory; just look a little closer or wait a little
longer.

(Winter 1987: 245–6)

Winter here comes to formulate the issue as one between two rival claims
as to the essential truth about the economy. Either change is regarded as
illusory, or stability is. Both equilibrium and process theories are based on
isolations and therefore involve unrealisticness, yet can be used to pursue
allegedly realistic accounts of what are believed to be the essential features
in the object of study. (For qualifications, see Mäki 1993b.)

Exchange and production

As a final example, consider the historically significant dividing line between
approaches building upon models of exchange and those beginning with
pictures of production. One set of theories focuses on preferences and the
allocation of given resources through exchange, while the other approach
puts stress on the use of labour in the production process. The first kind
of theories are expressions of catallactics, while the second manifest the
plutological approach (Hicks 1976). As Baranzini and Scazzieri suggest,

'[i]n the case of economics, an initial concentration of attention on certain aspects of exchange or production, respectively, often led to the formulation of "ideal" models of the economy in which what is essential in one model appears to be of secondary importance, or altogether irrelevant, in the other model' (Baranzini and Scazzieri 1986: 5). Thus Ricardo built upon

> the assumption that producibility rather than scarcity is the dominant feature of a modern economy. Utility and scarcity are excluded from Ricardo's ideal model of the economy, as well as from his theory of value ... [whereas] Jevons's 'ideal' model is a pure allocation economy in which both scarcity and utility play a crucial role.
>
> (ibid.: 6–7)

We may say that what the authors call the two 'ideal models' of the economy, are based on early-step assumptions that help exclude either production or exchange from consideration. Again, the clash between the two traditions is not one between classes of realistic and unrealistic theories but rather between rival claims of factors that are found as dominant or of primary importance for the functioning of the economy.

COMMENTS ON THE ILLUSTRATIONS

Attempts to classify the above controversies as antagonisms or family quarrels are bound to be challengeable, while it may be easier to measure their loudness at any given period of time. Yet, it would seem possible to say that some of them, such as the production versus exchange and equilibrium versus process debates, are closer to antagonisms than family quarrels. No mere peripheral assumptions are at stake. As for the monetarist controversy, even though the debate between the Keynesians and the monetarists was relatively loud, Friedman made the attempt to construe it as a family quarrel by suggesting that both positions can be formulated within one and the same framework; as we know, the attempt is controversial itself. It is also problematic to decide whether the assumption of zero or positive transaction costs has a peripheral status even though it has major implications concerning whether institutions will be included or excluded; those who suggest that transaction cost economics is just another variant of neoclassical theory imply that it is a peripheral assumption, hence the controversy between the two classes of theory would be just a family quarrel. All such judgements depend on prior, explicit or implicit, and always contestable, distinctions between core and peripheral assumptions.

It is another difficult question whether there are any grounds for denying or granting forms of realism (as distinct from realisticness) in the case of any given theory or approach. Could it be that in order to count as a realist, an economist is not allowed to exclude certain entities (such as institutions and processes?) from theoretical consideration? To answer such questions, much more concrete analyses are needed than has been customary in methodological debate (for a suggestion, see Mäki 1993b).

CONCLUSION

In all four cases and numerous others similar to them, the issue is not about realisticness versus unrealisticness in the abstract; each of the rival approaches produces theories and models that are inescapably unrealistic. The issue is rather about the functions of unrealisticness in the orientation of theorizing, either driven by ontological considerations as to how to draw a line between what is believed or hypothesized to be essential and what is believed or hypothesized to be inessential in the economy, or driven by pragmatic considerations of formal tractability, without forgetting about the social conditioning of theorizing such as economists' pursuit of intellectual credibility within the economics profession with current fashions taken as given (on this last point, see Mäki 1992d).

The argument should not be mistaken for a legitimation of all kinds of unrealisticness in any parts of the structure of any economic theory. The argument suggests that the basic issue should be reconceptualized and relocated. The issue over assumptions should not be construed as one over realisticness in the abstract but instead as one over the functions of specific kinds of realisticness and unrealisticness and the lack thereof in the context of concrete theories, that is, over what is included and what is excluded by each particular theory and framework. This is also how practising economists seem to construe the issue. This is evidenced by statements to the effect that 'in economics the wrong things are often, nay, usually, abstracted from; and the *ceteris paribus* clause often includes the very variable that should be the main object of research' (Wiles 1984: 308).

The task for economists and economic methodologists then is to develop principles that could be used for assessing and choosing between rival claims to realisticness based on theories that involve unrealistic ingredients. We cannot simply follow rules such as that of choosing the theory that appears more realistic than its rivals in being more encompassing or in containing fewer false assumptions. We need principles for assessing theories on the basis of how close they come to capturing the essential aspects of the economy for given explanatory purposes.

One response to this need is to appeal to the predictive success of theory. This is what Friedman seems to be suggesting when he says that 'this question can be answered only by seeing whether the theory works, which means whether it yields sufficiently accurate predictions' (1953: 15). The problem with this suggestion is, of course, that simple predictive success is not always very reliable in this role, not even in sciences that have in fact indicated remarkable predictive capabilities. A classical example of this is, in the sixteenth century, the predictive superiority of Ptolemaic geocentric astronomy over its young challenger, Copernican heliocentrism, even though the latter was decisively closer to revealing the fundamental structure of the planetary system. The difference between Copernican theory and economics, however, is that the former has indicated predictive progress, while the occurrence of such progress is controversial in the case of economics (see Rosenberg 1992). It may be that we cannot base the appraisal of economic theories on considerations of predictive power only. Other principles seem to be in operation, and other principles may have to be put into operation to get what we want. Much work remains to be done in the articulation of such principles.

ACKNOWLEDGEMENTS

I wish to thank Roger Backhouse and Bruce Caldwell for comments.

REFERENCES

Baranzini, M. and Scazzieri, R. (1986) 'Knowledge in economics: a framework', in M. Baranzini and R. Scazzieri (eds), *Foundations of Economics. Structures of Inquiry and Economic Theory.* Oxford: Basil Blackwell, pp. 1–87.

Boland, L. (1979) 'A critique of Friedman's critics', *Journal of Economic Literature* 17: 503–22.

Brunner, K. (1969) ' "Assumptions" and the cognitive quality of theories', *Synthèse* 20: 501–25.

Caldwell, B. (1992) 'Friedman's methodological instrumentalism: a correction', *Research in the History of Economic Thought and Methodology* 10: 119–28.

Coase, R. M. (1960) 'The problem of social cost', *Journal of Law and Economics* 3: 1–44.

Coase, R. M. (1988) *The Firm, the Market and the Law*, Chicago: University of Chicago Press.

Friedman, M. (1953) *Essays in Positive Economics*, Chicago: University of Chicago Press.

Friedman, M. (1972) 'Comments on the critics', *Journal of Political Economy* 80: 906–50.

Hart, O. (1984) 'Comment', in P. Wiles and G. Routh (eds), *Economics in Disarray*, Oxford: Basil Blackwell.

Hausman, D. (1992) *The Inexact and Separate Science of Economics*, Cambridge: Cambridge University Press.

Hicks, J. (1976) ' "Revolutions" in economics', in S. Latsis (ed.), *Method and Appraisal in Economics*, Cambridge: Cambridge University Press, pp. 207–18.

Hirsch, A. and de Marchi, N. (1989) *Milton Friedman. Economics in Theory and Practice*, Ann Arbor: University of Michigan Press.

Lawson, T. (1992) 'Realism, closed systems and Friedman', *Research in the History of Economic Thought and Methodology* 10: 149–69.

Lind, H. (1992) 'A case study of normal research in theorectical economics', *Economics and Philosophy* 8: 83–102.

Lucas, R. E. (1987) 'Adaptive behavior and economic theory', in R. M. Hogarth and M. W. Reder (eds), *Rational Choice. The Contrast between Economics and Psychology*, Chicago: Chicago University Press.

Machlup, F. (1955) 'The problem of verification in economics', *Southern Economic Journal* 22: 1–21.

Mäki, U. (1989) 'On the problem of realism in economics', *Ricerche Economiche* 43: 176–98. [Reprinted in B. Caldwell (ed.), *The Philosophy and Methodology of Economics*, Aldershot: Edward Elgar.]

Mäki, U. (1990) 'Methodology of economics: complaints and guidelines', *Finnish Economic Papers* 3: 77–84.

Mäki, U. (1991) 'Realism and the nature of theory: a lesson from J. H. von Thünen's *Isolated State* for economists and geographers', mimeo.

Mäki, U. (1992a) 'On the method of isolation in economics', in C. Dilworth (ed.), *Intelligibility in Science, Idealization IV*, Amsterdam: Rodopi, pp. 319–54.

Mäki, U. (1992b) 'Friedman and realism', *Research in the History of Economic Thought and Methodology* 10: 171–95.

Mäki, U. (1992c) 'Issues of isolation in transaction cost economics', mimeo.

Mäki, U. (1992d) 'Social conditioning of economics', in N. de Marchi (ed.), *Post-Popperian Methodology of Economics*, Boston: Kluwer, pp. 65–104.

Mäki, U. (1993a) 'Two philosophies of the rhetoric of economics', in W. Henderson *et al.* (eds), *Economics and Language*, London: Routledge, pp. 23–50.

Mäki, U. (1993b) 'The market as an isolated causal process: a metaphysical ground for realism', in B. Caldwell and S. Boehm (eds), *Austrian Economics: Tensions and New Directions*, Boston: Kluwer, pp. 35–59.

Mäki, U. (1993c) 'Isolation, idealization and truth in economics', forthcoming in B. Hamminga and N. de Marchi (eds), *Problems of Idealizaiton in Economics*.

Mäki, U. (1993d) 'Scientific realism and some peculiarities of economics', *Boston Studies in the Philosophy of Science*, forthcoming.

Mäki, U. (1993e) 'Why a realist economist needs unrealistic assumptions', mimeo.

Mäki, U. (1994) 'Types of assumptions and their truth', mimeo.

Melitz, J. (1967) 'Friedman and Machlup on the significance of testing economic assumptions', *Journal of Political Economy* 73: 37–60.

Musgrave, A. (1981) ' "Unreal assumptions" in economic theory: the F-twist untwisted', *Kyklos* 34: 377–87.

Nagel, E. (1963) 'Assumptions in economic theory', *American Economic Review, Papers and Proceedings* 53: 211–19.

Neild, R. (1984) 'The wider world and economic methodology', in P. Wiles and G. Routh (eds), *Economics in Disarray*, Oxford: Basil Blackwell.

Nelson, R. and Winter, S. (1982) *An Evolutionary Theory of Economic Change*, Cambridge, MA: Harvard University Press.

Nooteboom, B. (1986) 'Plausibility in economics', *Economics and Philosophy* 2: 197–224.

North, D. (1990) *Institutions, Institutional Change and Economic Performance*, Cambridge: Cambridge University Press.

Rosenberg, A. (1992) *Economics – Mathematical Politics or Science of Diminishing Returns?*, Chicago: University of Chicago Press.

Rotwein, E. (1959) 'On "The methodology of positive economics" ', *Quarterly Journal of Economics* 73: 554–75.

Wiles, P. (1984) 'Epilogue: the role of theory', in P. Wiles and G. Routh (eds), *Economics in Disarray*, Oxford: Basil Blackwell.

Williamson, O. (1983) 'The modern corporation: origins, evolution, attributes', *Journal of Economic Literature* 19: 1537–68.

Williamson, O. (1985) *The Economic Institutions of Capitalism*, New York: Free Press.

Winter, S. G. (1987) 'Comments on Arrow and Lucas', in R. M. Hogarth and M. W. Reder (eds), *Rational Choice. The Contrast between Economics and Psychology*, Chicago: Chicago University Press.

13

A REALIST THEORY FOR ECONOMICS

Tony Lawson

INTRODUCTION

The aim in what follows is basically two-fold. I want first to sketch a brief overview of, and to argue for, a philosophical perspective recently systematized as transcendental realism or, in the context of the social realm specifically, as critical realism. I intend, second, to indicate why and how I think that the perspective in question can facilitate a more relevant economics than is currently available or is even possible within the confines of the (relatively unquestioned) explanatory norms and criteria of the contemporary economics discipline.

WHAT IS, AND WHY, A REALISM?

The first issue to address, clearly, is what is a realist theory anyway? In fact any position can be designated a *realism* in the philosophical sense of the term that asserts the existence of some disputed kind of entity (such as black holes, causal laws, class relations, economic equilibria, probabilities, etc.). Clearly on this definition we are all realists of a kind, and there are very many conceivable realisms. The question of interest in any context, then, is what sort of realism is at issue?

This philosophical conception of realism is clearly closely bound up with *ontology*, i.e., with enquiry into the nature of *being*, of what exists, including the nature of the objects of study. Indeed, it is a forthright concern with ontology, a concern in particular to elaborate the broad nature of, or of features of, natural and social reality that explains, in what follows, the explicit usage of the term realism in labelling perspectives distinguished. Most generally, then, the term realism is utilized here to denote specific accounts of the nature of reality, whether natural or social.

But why bother with realism so understood? Surely economists can and should avoid wasting their time reflecting on such matters as 'realism' and 'ontology', and, accepting the goals, criteria, methods and procedures as laid down in standard economic textbooks and recent articles, etc., just get on with the job? Even accepting that contemporary economics has proven to be notoriously unsuccessful over the last fifty years or so, is not the proper solution just to try that little bit harder?

Imagine a situation in which an instrument of some sort has been found to be useful for a specific task. Let us suppose that a big stick is used successfully to beat and thereby to clean a dusty old mat. Imagine also that the inference is automatically made that if such an instrument is found to be useful for one job it must be useful for any related jobs. Specifically, let us suppose that it is inferred from the success of the big stick in helping to clean the dusty old mat that it must also be of use in cleaning a dusty glass window – and that the window is duly beaten.

No doubt many will find such an inference and act preposterous. But why? Presumably because we know enough of the nature of glass windows and big sticks to infer that (a) beating the window with a stick is unlikely to prove to be a successful way of cleaning it (to say the least); while (b) alternative more promising ways of cleaning the window can easily be devised.

Imagine, furthermore, that the 'stick-cleans-window' theory is put to the test and consequent upon repeated instances of broken glass the inference repeatedly drawn is that it is necessary to 'try that little bit harder' – perhaps on the grounds that it is the wrong windows so far that have been beaten, and/or it is simply imagined that success is (always) just around the corner. No doubt the perpetrator of the theory would be dismissed as a rather unreflective dogmatist. Certainly, he or she is unlikely to be retained for long as a window cleaner.

Now this example in outline, I suggest (except the bit about the window cleaner not being retained), is quite analogous in relevant respects to the situation that is found in contemporary orthodox economics. Specifically, or so I shall argue, contemporary orthodox economists have noted that certain methods of scientific analysis have, like the big stick, been found to be of worth in some important application and they thereby infer that the methods in question must be equally appropriate to any task that appears related. In particular it is supposed that certain methods of reasoning, aims and criteria that have proven to be efficacious in *particular* natural science contexts, must thereby be equally appropriate to all other scientific contexts including, specifically, the analysis of society and economy. Such an inference is, of course, questionable, and it is the, in practice largely unquestioned, reliance upon this inference, I believe, that is fundamental to understanding the failure of contemporary economics for the last fifty years or so. The solution I shall suggest, however, warrants something more than an endeavour to try a little bit harder.

Now the point I am wanting to emphasize in all this, of course, is that just as insights into the nature of glass should be brought to bear upon the choice of materials that are to be used in the attempt to illuminate the window, so insights into the nature of social reality should be brought to bear upon the modes of reasoning and techniques employed in the endeavour to illuminate the economy. And while focusing upon the nature of social material just means giving attention to questions of *ontology*, any theoretical insight into the nature of social material so sustained constitutes a *realist* theory.

The case for realist analysis as understood here, then, derives precisely from its direct opposition to the unsound epistemological reductionism of contemporary economic orthodoxy. Instead of deciding upon methods and techniques, etc., in advance of doing social analysis, solely because they are perceived to have proven successful in some alternative domain, a realist perspective has it that methods of social science, in their design, etc., should also take account of (including being continually modified by) insights elaborated (which may also be continually revised) concerning the nature of social material. It is thus, in short, a concern continually to tailor or adapt methods to insights available concerning the nature of the object of analysis that characterizes an explicitly realist approach, or orientation, to economics.

THE 'BIG STICK' OF CONTEMPORARY ECONOMICS

But is there really a 'big stick' analogue within contemporary economics? Even granted the often noted incapacity of orthodox 'economic theory' or 'applied economics' to explain or otherwise illuminate real-world phenomena, surely it is impossible to lay the 'blame' for this at the door of any one particular and erroneously universalized method or mode of analysis? Actually, I think it is possible. The 'culprit' I suggest, the big-stick analogue, is essentially a mode of explanation that I shall refer to here as deductivism, or at least the conception of science upon which it depends.

Deductivism

To explain some event, thing or phenomenon, etc., (i.e., the 'explanandum') is to provide an account (the 'explanans') whereby the initial phenomenon is rendered intelligible. According to deductivism (as I shall use the term here) to be able to explain something is to deduce it, or a statement of it, from a statement of initial and boundary conditions plus universal laws of the form 'whenever event (type) x then event (type) y'. The explanation of laws, theories and sciences similarly proceeds by deductive subsumption.

Now the feature of deductivism as a mode of explanation that I want specifically to focus upon here is its dependency upon supposed universal laws of the form 'whenever event (type) x then event (type) y'. Science, according to the perspective in question, supposedly is, or turns upon, precisely the elaboration of such universal constant event conjunctions. Notice that this formulation of laws should be interpreted quite generally. 'Event x' can be a composite of many events, for example, and the relationship between events elaborated can be probabilistic (so that y can be interpreted as the average or limit, etc., of a series) or deterministic. Notice too that the formulation in question does not in any way depend upon the criterion or method of its elaboration or assessment – whether inductivist, falsificationist, verificationist, etc. The crucial point here being emphasized is that in all cases of analysis or explanation of the sort in question the identification or elaboration of some constant conjunction of events is required.

I do not think that it is contentious to observe that deductivism so understood characterizes contemporary economics. Just as the persistent search for event regularities of a probabilistic kind characterizes econometrics, for example, so the positing of strict constant event conjunctions is a condition of axiomatic–deductive 'economic theory'.[1] Nor is the supposed universality of deductivism ever really questioned in the contemporary orthodox programme. Those few, typically non-orthodox, economists who occasionally voice a degree of concern about the almost universal contemporary reliance upon the noted methods are usually (mis)interpreted as not agreeing with certain substantive premises or axioms of the theory, or some such. Criticism of the mode of reasoning *per se* is something that cannot, apparently, be comprehended. As Hahn (1985: 9) writes:

> Opponents of [economic] theory often argue that it is tautologous because it consists of logical deductions from axioms and assumptions. If one is kind to such critics one interprets them as signalling that they do not care for these axioms or these assumptions. In any case all theory in all subjects proceeds in this manner.

Now if deductivism is here being interpreted as the 'big stick' of social science it is clearly beholden on me that I make a case for doubting its general relevance in that sphere and, conditional upon that case having been made, desirable that I elaborate in its place a more sustainable, and perhaps widely relevant, alternative form or mode of social scientific explanation. A first question to address then is what is, and what is the relevance of, the conception of reality presupposed by deductivism and specifically the view of science on which it depends? Specifically, if a legitimate usage of the big stick presupposes something sturdy like the old mat that needs a beating what conception of social material is presupposed by the wielding of methods and techniques that are premised upon the deductivist conception of explanation and implicit ideal for science, and can it be regarded as universal or at least widely attaining? Clearly, if the image of science in question turns, as I have noted, upon the identification of regularities of the form 'whenever event x then event y' – let us refer to systems in which such constant conjunctions of events arise as *closed* – then a precondition of the universality, or wide applicability, of deductivism is that reality is, if amongst other things, characterized by a ubiquity of such spontaneous closures.

Empirical realism

Are there, then, grounds for supposing that event regularities of the kind in question are pervasive? Historically, in fact, encouragement for the conception of science and explanation in question stems from a version of *positivism* that is rooted in Hume's analysis of causality – or at least from Hume's arguments as they are usually interpreted. Now positivism as I shall interpret the term here[2] is first of all a theory of knowledge, its nature and limits. Specifically, it is a claim that human knowledge takes the form of sense-experience or impression. But any theory of knowledge presupposes some ontology. For it must be supposed, even if only implicitly, that the nature of reality is such that it could be the object of knowledge of the required or specified sort. The positivistic conception in question, of course, implicitly entails an account of reality as consisting of the objects of experience or impression constituting atomistic events. Indeed, because on this perspective reality is essentially defined as that which is given in experience, then, following the usual practice of referring to the domain of experience as the *empirical* I shall, for obvious reasons, follow Kant, Bhaskar and others in referring to the perspective on reality sustained as *empirical realism*.

Now the point to emphasize here is that, from the perspective in question, science, *if* it is to be at all possible, must take the form of elaborating regularities of the type 'whenever event x then event y'. For if particular knowledge is restricted to atomistic events given in experience then the only possibility for general, including scientific, knowledge is the elaboration of event regularities of the noted form. It is such constant event patterns, or regularities of the form 'whenever event x then event y', of course, that constitute the Humean or positivist account of causal laws. If, moreover, the successes of science are perceived to be widespread then it follows on this account that Humean causal laws must also be ubiquitous.

If, then, I am going to argue against deductivism as a universally applicable form of explanation, it is clearly necessary that I elaborate an alternative theory of ontology to empirical realism (i.e., to the claim that reality is exhausted by atomistic events and their constant conjunctions) which at least allows of a different conception of science to the search for the noted event regularities. It is also necessary, of course, given the intention of my project, that I establish that this alternative conception is, while the former is not, appropriate to the analysis of (features of) the social realm. It is these tasks then that I turn to address in what follows.

TRANSCENDENTAL REALISM: AN ALTERNATIVE CONCEPTION OF REALITY, SCIENCE AND EXPLANATION

Before elaborating a theory of *social* ontology specifically, however, it is necessary to outline first a more adequate account of the nature of the material of the natural realm as well. For it is important to recognize at the outset that even in this realm spontaneous event regularities of the form 'whenever event x then event y' are hardly ubiquitous but, instead, arise only in rather special circumstances.

At a very general level the alternative conception to empirical realism that I want to sustain here – a conception that, as we shall see, does apply, albeit at a very high level of abstraction, to the natural and social realms alike – is a perspective that has recently been systematized under the heading of *transcendental realism*.[3] Now according to this account, and in contrast to empirical realism, the world is composed not only of events and our experience or impression of them, but also of (irreducible) structures and mechanisms, powers and tendencies, etc., that, although perhaps not directly observable, nevertheless underlie actual events that we experience and govern or produce them. Thus not only does the autumn leaf pass to the ground and not only do we experience it as falling but, according to the perspective in question, underlying such movement and governing it are real mechanisms such as gravity. Similarly the world is composed not only of such 'surface phenomena' as skin spots, puppies turning into dogs, and relatively slow productivity growth in the UK, but also of underlying and governing structures or mechanisms such as, respectively, viruses, genetic codes and the British system of industrial relations. In short, three domains of reality are, from this perspective, distinguished, namely the *empirical* (experience and impression), the *actual* (events and states of affairs – i.e., the actual objects of direct experience) and the *non-actual* or, metaphorically, the '*deep*' (structures, mechanisms, powers and tendencies).

Now not only is it the case that these domains are ontologically distinct, according to transcendental realism, but in addition, and crucially, they are unsynchronized or out of phase, as it were, with one another. Thus, while experience is out of phase with events, allowing the possibility of contrasting experiences of a given event, so events are typically unsynchronized with the mechanisms that govern them. As an example of the latter structure/event non-correspondence, autumn leaves are not in phase with the action of gravity for the reason that they are also subject to aerodynamic, thermal and other forces or mechanisms. Events, in other words, are multiply determined by various, perhaps countervailing, factors so that the governing causes, though necessarily 'appearing' through, or in, events, can rarely be read straight off. These contrasting perspectives of empirical realism and transcendental realism can be summarized diagramatically as follows:

Empirical realism

Domain	Objects	
actual	events state of affairs	different realms 'fused'
empirical	experience impression perception	

Transcendental realism

Domain	Objects	
'deep'	structures mechanisms powers tendencies	different realms 'out of phase' with one another
actual	events states of affairs	
empirical	experience impression perception	

Transcendental realism differs from empirical realism then in viewing the world as composed, in part, of objects that are structured and, to adopt Bhaskar's term, intransitive – *structured* in the sense of being irreducible to the events of experience,[4] *intransitive* in the sense of existing and acting independently of their identification. From the transcendental realist perspective, clearly, empirical realism thus involves two closely related philosophical mistakes in particular. The first lies in the use of the category of experience to define the world. This entails giving an epistemological category an ontological task and in doing so commits in a particular way a more general error that Bhaskar refers to as the 'epistemic fallacy'. This 'fallacy' consists of the view that statements about being can be reduced to, or analysed solely in terms of, statements about knowledge, that matters of ontology can always be translated into epistemological terms. The second error consists of the view that its being experienced, or being open to possible experience, is an essential feature of reality, as opposed to an accidental property of some things or phenomena, etc. Empirical realism

263

then neglects, if amongst other things, the causal criterion for ascribing something as real, acknowledging as real only what is experienced. One consequence of these 'mistakes', it will be argued below, is an inevitable failure or inability to distinguish the conditions under which experience is in fact significant to science.

Now a crucial feature of the transcendental realist perspective that is of relevance here is that it supports a quite different conception of science to the constant conjunction view underpinning deductivism, a conception that gives rise in turn to an alternative mode of explanation. Specifically, according to transcendental realism science is not, as in positivism, confined to, or even dependent upon, the seeking out of constant event conjunctions. Indeed, it is primarily concerned not with events at all. Instead, the concern is with identifying and illuminating the structures and mechanisms, powers and tendencies, that govern or facilitate the phenomena of experience. Explanation then entails providing an account of those structures that have contributed to the production of, or facilitated, some already identified phenomenon of interest.

Note also that the alternative conceptions of science and explanation now elaborated entail a contrasting mode of inference to those presupposed in empirical realism. A restricted focus upon the positivistic or Humean generalizations about conjunctions of events facilitates at most, and in practice has endlessly encouraged, debates or worries concerning the relative advantages and limitations of methods of induction versus those of deduction, of the correct application/interpretation of falsificationism,[5] and so on. Indeed, it is the sterility of such discussion that seems to have encouraged the view expressed by Hahn amongst others that methodological analysis has in fact got the subject nowhere. It is important to recognize then that the essential mode of inference presupposed by the transcendental realist perspective is neither induction nor deduction but one that can be styled *retroduction* or *abduction* or 'as if' reasoning. It consists in the movement (on the basis of analogy and metaphor amongst other things) from a conception of some phenomenon of interest to a conception of some totally different type of thing, mechanism, structure or condition that is responsible for the given phenomenon. If deduction is, for example, to move from the *general* claim that 'all ravens are black' to the *particular* inference that the next one seen will be black, and induction is to move from the *particular* observation of numerous black ravens to the *general* claim that 'all ravens are black', retroductive or abductive reasoning is to move from the observation of numerous black ravens to a theory of a mechanism intrinsic to ravens which disposes them being black. It is a movement, paradigmatically, from a 'surface phenomenon' to some 'deeper' causal thing.

If, then, the *aim* of science according to the transcendental realist perspective is to illuminate structures that govern surface phenomena it follows that *laws*, or *law-statements*, must express not event regularities but precisely such structures and their modes of activity. And if, moreover, with the activity of any structure rarely precisely manifest in events, we refer to this activity as a *tendency* rather than an actuality, it is necessary to be clear what exactly this ambiguous term is intended to designate. It should be apparent, in fact, that a statement of a tendency is not a *counterfactual* statement about, nor even a claim concerning long-run or average, etc., outcomes at the level of, events. Indeed, it is not a claim about *events* at all. Rather it is a *transfactual* statement about a structure or thing and its activity. It is not, in other words, a *conditional* statement about something actual or empirical but an *unconditional* statement about something non-actual and non-empirical. It is not a statement of logical necessity subject to *ceteris paribus* restrictions, but a statement of natural necessity without qualifications attached. It is not about events that would occur if things were different but about a power that *is* being exercised (if triggered) whatever events ensue.

According to transcendental realism, then, science is concerned with identifying and illuminating structures and mechanisms, etc., that act independently of the process of their identification. But if this is the aim of science, *where* does our knowledge come from and *how* does it come about? Clearly, if, as with transcendental realism, an intransitive dimension (i.e., one of objects existing independently of our knowledge of them) is acknowledged, it is possible to understand how a changing knowledge of (possibly) unchanging objects is possible. But if the objects of the world are not merely given in (and so effectively constituted through) sense experience, and specifically if structures and mechanisms act independently of their identification, of being known, how does our knowledge of them arise? Where does it come from? Now, if knowledge is not merely given in experience, it is hardly intelligible that it is created out of nothing, as it were. It must, then, come about through a transformation of pre-existing knowledge-like materials. In other words, it is necessary also to recognize a *transitive* dimension to knowledge including science, a dimension of *transitive* objects of knowledge, including facts, observations, theories, hypotheses, guesses, hunches, intuitions, speculations, anomalies, etc., which facilitate, and come to be actively transformed through, the laborious social practice of science. Knowledge, in other words, is a produced means of production (of further knowledge) while science must be recognized as an ongoing transformative social activity. Knowledge is a social product, actively produced by means of antecedent social products – albeit on the basis of a continual engagement, or interaction, with its (intransitive) object. Of course, if this is the *nature* of knowledge and its mode of production the aim of the knowledge process, or science, remains the production of knowledge of objects which, for the most part, exist and act independently of our, or at least of any individual, knowledge of them. Specifically, the primary aim of science is the production of knowledge of mechanisms that, in combination, produce the phenomena that are actually manifest.

In summary, two perspectives on science and explanation have been elaborated and contrasted. While the first, rooted in positivism, depends upon, and, in its claim to universality, presupposes the ubiquity of, spontaneous event regularities, the second, associated with transcendental realism, does not. Rather the latter turns on the elaboration of socially produced and fallible accounts of structures, mechanisms, powers, and tendencies that have produced, or contributed in a significant way to the production of, some identified phenomenon of interest – mechanisms, etc., which, if triggered, are operative in open and closed systems alike.

Finally, while I have attempted to draw the contrasts between the two positions as starkly as possible, two points of qualification warrant attention. First, although the positivist conception of science in which deductivist explanation is rooted follows necessarily once the empirical realist perspective is accepted, it by no means follows *a priori* that the event regularities on which it turns cannot occur even if the transcendental realist ontology proves to be the most sustainable characterization of reality. The widely accepted view that science is successful, at least in the natural realm, entails that if empirical realism were true then event regularities are, or have been, ubiquitous. But if transcendental realism is true, while this conclusion no longer follows necessarily, neither can it be rejected *a priori*. The point is, of course, to provide further argumentation or analysis turning on actual experience (see below).

The second qualification to make is that, while I have no doubt written about transcendental realism above in a rather positive tone, the case for it in preference to empirical realism (as well as for transcendental realist explanation in preference to deductivism) still needs to be made. Although I have doubtless indicated my belief in the superior adequacy of the transcendental realist perspective and conception of science and hence explanation, I have not as yet provided any explicit argument for accepting it as the more satisfactory position. In consequence, I turn to consider next the case for the transcendental realist perspective in general, and the illegitimacy of accepting positivism and so deductivism as universal conceptions.

THE CASE FOR TRANSCENDENTAL REALISM

How then is it possible to choose between the contrasting perspectives and, of most immediate interest, the generalized conceptions of science and explanation in question? In fact the inadequacy of the positivistic or Humean conception of science (and so of empirical realism as a theory of ontology and deductivism as a generalized form of explanation) is immediately apparent once we examine the nature of the conditions under which the sought-after event regularities of positivistic science actually obtain.

We are concerned here with both social and natural realms. Let me consider first of all, however, the situation in the natural sciences and, specifically, two observations the relevance of which has been well brought out by Bhaskar. The first of these is that, outside astronomy at least, most of the constant-event conjunctions that are held as significant, that are interpreted as laws, only in fact occur under the restricted conditions of experimental control – i.e., typically they do not occur spontaneously. The second observation is that the results or 'laws' supported in controlled experimental activity are nevertheless frequently successfully applied outside the experimental situation.

Now these observations raise certain problems for those accounts which tie laws to constant conjunctions of events. For, if scientific laws, or significant results, only occur in such restricted conditions as experimental set-ups then this bears the rather constricting implication that science and its results, far from being universal, are effectively fenced off from most of the goings on in the world. In other words, most of the accepted results of science are not of the form 'whenever event x then event y always follows' after all, but are of the form 'whenever event x then event y always follows, as long as conditions e hold', where conditions e typically amount to a specification of the experimental situation. This also bears the rather counter-intuitive implication that any actual regularity of events that a law of *nature* supposedly denotes does not generally occur independently of human intervention. In addition to such problems the constant conjunction view of laws leaves the question of what governs events outside of experimental situations not only unanswered but completely unaddressed. In doing so, it also leaves the observation that experimentally obtained results *are* successfully applied outside experimental situations without any valid explanation.

In order to render Bhaskar's observations intelligible it is necessary to abandon the view that the generalizations of nature consist of event regularities, and to accept instead the transcendental realist account of the objects of the world, including science, as intransitive and structured. That is, experimental activity and results, and the applications of experimentally determined knowledge outside experimental situations, can be accommodated only through invoking something like the transcendental realist ontology of generative structures, powers, mechanisms and necessary relations, etc., that lie behind and govern the flux of events in an essentially open world. As already noted, the fall of an autumn leaf does not typically conform to an event regularity, and precisely because it is governed in complex ways by the actions of different juxtaposed and counteracting mechanisms. Not only is the path of the leaf governed by gravitational pull, but also by aerodynamic, thermal, inertial and other mechanisms. On this transcendental realist view, then, experimental activity can be explained as an attempt to intervene in order to *close* the system, in order, in other words, to insulate a particular mechanism of interest by holding off all other potentially counteracting mechanisms. The aim is to engineer a closed system in which a one-to-one correspondence can obtain between the way a mechanism acts and the events that eventually ensue. In other words, on this view, experimental activity can be rendered intelligible *not* as creating the rare situation in which an empirical law is put into effect but as intervening in order to bring about those special circumstances under which a non-empirical law, a power, a tendency, or way of acting of some mechanism, etc., can be empirically identified. The law itself, of course, is always operative – if the triggering conditions hold, the mechanism is activated whatever else is going on. In this transcendental realist view, for example, a leaf is subject to the gravitational tendency even as I hold it in the palm of my hand. Through this sort of reasoning, then, transcendental realism can render intelligible the application of scientific knowledge outside experimental situations. The context or *milieu* under which any mechanism will be operative is irrelevant to the law's specification. Once activated the mechanism is operative whatever empirical pattern ensues.

In short, although the traditional conception of science is the seeking of constant conjunctions of events, in practice such event regularities that have been elaborated have been restricted in the main to situations of experimental control. Transcendental realism, unlike empirical realism, can render this situation intelligible. And it follows from the transcendental realist perspective that the traditional Humean conception rests upon an inadequate analysis and illegitimate generalization of what emerges as a special case – wherein a single and stable (set of) aspect(s) or mechanism(s) is physically isolated and thereby empirically identified.

Now a premise of the above argument was the observation that outside astronomy, universal event regularities are forthcoming only in situations of experimental control. The question then is what about astronomy and, specifically, the celestial closure so successfully utilized by Newton? Surely the fact, as well as the spectacular nature, of this particular closure is sufficient to justify the Humean insistence on the actuality of causal laws? This is not so. First of all it is possible from (and it seems only from) the transcendental realist perspective to provide an explanation of the celestial closure – that it arises because of rather *peculiar* conditions that hold in the case of the planets, in that both their intrinsic states as well as the extrinsic forces acting upon them are essentially constant, at least over the time period with which most people are usually concerned, i.e., over human life-spans. Properly interpreted, Newtonian mechanics posits theories of how bodies (tend to) act, and, for this science, celestial phenomena function merely as evidence of the postulated tendencies. Thus, if the intrinsic or extrinsic states of the planets in our solar system were not so stable but were to change in some way – perhaps a massive meteorite were to pass through the solar system – then such a mechanics would entail a consequent disruption of the familiar celestial phenomenal patterns. There is no problem in all this for transcendental realism. Second, and just as much to the point, it must be recognized that, despite its spectacular nature, this closure, as a spontaneous phenomenon, represents a relatively rare situation. Indeed, it is no doubt precisely the spectacular nature of the celestial closure that, at least in some part, accounts for a general failure from Laplace onwards to realize that the situation is relatively unique – a failure to appreciate that the celestial closure is far from being indicative of the phenomenal situation that can be expected to prevail more or less everywhere. This failure, in turn, appears to be largely responsible for the widespread, if tacit, acceptance, formerly in philosophy, and currently in the social sciences in particular, of the ubiquity of constant conjunctions of events in nature, and thus of the doctrine of the actuality of 'causal' laws.

It will not have gone unnoticed that most of the discussion on this point has referred to the situation in the 'natural' sciences. However, it is not difficult to reason that the transcendental realist perspective must carry over to the social realm. To see this it is necessary only to consider two often noted problems of contemporary economics. The first is that significant event regularities of the sought-after kind have yet to be turned up in the social realm. The second is that many economists appear to share the intuition that human agents possess the capacity of real choice even if these same economists are unable to reconcile this insight with their understanding of scientific explanation (see Lawson 1994a). Now if choice is real any agent could always have done otherwise, each agent could always have acted differently than he or she in fact did. Clearly, a necessary condition for this is that the world, social as well as natural, is open in the sense that events really could have been different. Put differently, if under conditions x an agent chose in fact to do y, it is the case that this same agent could really instead have done not y. Choice to repeat presupposes that the world is open and actual events need not have been. But the possibility of choice not only presupposes that events could have been different. It also entails that agents have some conception of what they are doing and wanting to achieve in their activity. That is, if choice is real then human actions must be intentional under some description. Intentionality in turn is bound up with knowledgeability. For agents must have knowledge at least of the conditions that render their intended acts, when they are, as feasible. In turn again, of course, knowledge presupposes sufficient endurability in the objects of knowledge to facilitate their coming to be known. Now if event regularities, or at least significant ones, do not, as widely reported, generally occur in the social realm, then the enduring objects of knowledge must lie at a different level – at that of structures

269

which govern, but which are irreducible to, events of experience including human activities.

At a very general level, then, the transcendental realist ontology carries over to the social realm. Now in the natural realm it was observed that constant event conjunctions appear to be spontaneously occurring (at least outside astronomy) only in conditions of experimental control. Of course the feasibility of experimental control in the social realm is rather limited. Are there, then, *any* grounds for expecting significant constant event conjunctions to be a feature of the social domain? If natural and social realms are similar in that both are characterized by structures underlying the events of experience, they are dissimilar in that social, unlike natural, structures depend for their existence on human agency. If the human race were to disappear tomorrow so too would the social structures on which they depend. Human agency and social structure then presuppose each other. Neither can be reduced to, identified with, nor explained completely in terms of, for each requires, the other. The simple point that warrants emphasis here is that because social structure is human-agent dependent it is only ever manifest in human activity. Thus, given the open nature of human action, the fact that any agent could always have acted otherwise, it follows that social structure can only be present in an open system. In consequence, it would seem, any economic laws must usually be manifest merely as tendencies and only rarely – usually in cases where they are consciously brought about (e.g., the occurrence of annual holidays) – as empirical regularities, so that the Humean project in its economic guise must, certainly *as a general approach*, be recognized as quite misguided.

The nature of the argument further examined – transcendental argument from experience

It is important to be clear what the nature of the argument is here, and what is, and is not, being (and can, and cannot, be) claimed with regards to the status of the results being supported. To this end it is worthwhile emphasizing just how the *aim* of the transcendental realist project differs from that of the programme initiated by Hume.

Hume's programme in fact appears most intelligible as an attempt to demonstrate that, or how, existing knowledge is justified. It was produced of an age which believed in scientific certainty. Eventually, of course, the idea of scientific certainty, so fundamental to the Humean project, collapsed. However, to the extent that this has been acknowledged within economics, the absence of a clear or explicit elaboration of an ontological dimension or, more precisely, a domain of intransitive objects existing, at least in part independent of our knowledge of them, yet expressible (fallibly) within knowledge typically encourages some kind of voluntaristic dualism. That is, it encourages a view whereby our beliefs, because they are no longer regarded as being determined by the world, are interpreted as completely cut off from it as free creations of the mind, or as taking the form merely of rhetoric, or some such thing. It is significant here, then, to appreciate that transcendental realism starts out neither by taking general scientific knowledge to be certain nor by neglecting a realm of knowable intransitive objects. Rather, instead of inquiring what science or the knowledge process must be like for general knowledge to be justified, the question put is what 'must' the world, or aspects of it, be like for recognized scientific, amongst other social, practices and human capabilities, etc., to be possible? In this, the form of argument or reasoning involved is that species of retroduction which, following Kant, can be referred to as *transcendental* – thus explaining the use of this term in the label of the perspective formulated. That is, the insights obtained, the support for the transcendental realist perspective sustained, have resulted from an analysis taking the form of an inquiry into the conditions of the possibility of certain especially significant generalized scientific practices and human capabilities that are experienced – scientific experimental practices in the natural realm as well as the capacity of human intentionality and choice in the social.

Now if the mode of reasoning employed here is essentially Kantian it warrants emphasis that in several respects Kant's project has not been accepted precisely. First, there has been no attempt to adopt Kant's idealist and individualist mode wherein such reasoning is directed only to informing us about ourselves. Second, it is necessary to recognize that the premises of transcendental argument are always contestable, never indubitable. Of course, the actual premises emphasized (concerning experimental practices and results, and the nature of human agency) are chosen because, if amongst other things, at the present stage of knowledge they appear reasonably secure. But knowledge is always fallible, and by accepting premises such as these or others, the realist cannot avoid supporting, for example, current conceptions of scientific practices and other relevant features of experience. But this merely means that the philosophical, or meta-theoretical, moment of analysis which this reasoning represents is not above or outside, it cannot be divorced from, substantive scientific research. It deals with the same reality. Of course, merely by starting the analysis with premises concerning natural scientific practices there may already be a siding with science against religion, magic and so on, at least to the extent that such activities or presuppositions are incompatible.

Third, the transcendental argument to claims of 'necessity' (in this case to the acceptance of the ontology of causal structures, powers, tendencies and generative mechanisms, etc.) is, like all cognitive claims, also fallible and corrigible. It is for this reason that inverted commas are used to encase the term 'must' in setting out the transcendental question above. In other words the question really posed is, if now stated in less conventional fashion: what claims about the nature of reality are viable in the sense that they render intelligible the generalized phenomena of experience taken as premises?

The use of the term transcendental to describe the theory of ontology so inferred is, in this light, both comprehensible yet, I think, questionable. It is comprehensible precisely because the theory of ontology, the realist perspective in question, derives support from transcendental argument from experience. It is questionable because it is at least conceivable that other conceptions might (eventually) similarly derive support via transcendental argument from (the same or alternative) accepted features of experience – facilitating different, perhaps competing, accounts equally qualifying for the ascription of 'transcendental realism'. A better label then would be one that captured the structured, intransitive nature of the ontology elaborated above – perhaps 'structural realism' or 'transfactual realism'. However, I persist with the transcendental realism label here because it is now so ingrained in the (fast growing) literature and because, for the time being at least, there is no comparably viable alternative theory of ontology on the scene. But this usage may have to be temporary. If, in due course, competing 'transcendental realist' accounts are so derived they will have to be selected amongst on the basis of their relative explanatory powers, according to their relative capacities to illuminate a range of generalized features of experience.

The upshot, then, is that the transcendental realist perspective defended above, even with respect to the experimental sciences, cannot be conclusively established via this sort of reasoning. The results obtained are provisional, not a novel species of foundationalism. If, following Kant, they are regarded as *a priori*, this cannot be so understood in any absolute manner; merely in the sense of explaining the possibility of some other forms of knowledge. In short, the results obtained must be recognized as conditional and hypothetical.

Nevertheless, these considerations by no means undermine the realist project described here. While the premises adopted to initiate the transcendental arguments do seem secure from the standpoint of current experience, it is, as noted, difficult, at present at least, to conceive of any rival account of science, or of any conception of the way the natural and social world are, that can accommodate the relevant features of our experience so well, or even at all. Moreover, the transcendental realist case as set out is bolstered, and fear of arbitrariness in the choice of premises is diminished, with the realization that the premises actually chosen as starting points for the transcendental argument are not only secure from the standpoint of current understandings but constitute central features of those accounts that, arguably, are most opposed to the theory of transcendental realism being supported here – empiricism in the natural and social sciences and rationalistic orthodox 'pure theory' in economics. Thus, while Flew (1979), for example, in his dictionary of philosophy entry on *empiricism* observes that 'one common feature has been the tendency to start from experimental sciences, as a kind of prototype or paradigm case of human knowledge ... [with] ... the acquisition of knowledge ... limited by the possibilities of experiment and observations' (1979: 105), orthodox or mainstream economics often even stylizes itself, if misleadingly, as the science of human choice and intentionality. Presumably if the intelligibility of essential features of positions and perspectives most clearly opposed to the one here stylized as transcendental realism actually appears to presuppose or warrant something like the account of nature, science and human capabilities here defended, the transcendental realist account here being sustained can be regarded as that much more secure.

A THEORY OF SOCIAL ONTOLOGY

Let us take stock. I have argued that the deductivist mode of explanation, as with the wooden cleaning device, is limited in its legitimate scope of application, and I have attempted to *situate*, to elaborate the conditions of, its relevance. It turns out that, outside astronomy at least, this mode of explanation is restricted, in the main, to situations of experimental control, giving little reason to expect any significant scientific applications in the social realm.

What, though, can be said about social analysis and specifically the conduct of economics? Have I not, first of all, fallen into the same mistaken epistemological reductionism that I am attempting to criticize by arguing that the transcendental realist ontology and mode of explanation apply to the natural and social realms alike? Two points need to be emphasized. First, I have not argued *a priori* for transcendental realism in either the natural or social realms. Unlike with the 'big stick' story I have not argued the case for some conception in a specific context on the basis of its apparent relevance in a different context. The case for the transcendental realist ontology and its associated conception of science has been made separately for the natural and social realms alike. In the former instance the premise of the transcendental argument has been the experimental experience; in the latter example of the social realm the argument has turned upon rendering intelligible the fact of human choice and the more or less total absence of any scientifically significant event regularities being upturned in economics so far. As it happens, the transcendental realist ontology, and the associated mode of explanation, receive support in both cases. But this, it warrants re-emphasis, is a *conclusion* of ontological inquiry or transcendental argument, not its premise. Second, the transcendental perspective here supported has been elaborated at an obviously rather high level of generality or abstraction. Although analysis at this level has been found to be sufficient to undermine the positivist project that characterizes contemporary economics, the perspective set out is insufficiently concrete to illuminate very much about the character of legitimate research in the social realm including its particularities. In order to say more the specific nature of the fabric of society and economy must be elaborated; it is necessary to turn to the question of social ontology explicitly.

Unfortunately, the elaboration of a theory of social ontology in accord with, that is conditioned by an explicit acknowledgement of, the transcendental realist perspective, a project that in recent years has been systematized under the heading of *critical realism*, would, if embarked upon in any great depth, take much more space than is available here. In any case the results of the project in question are in a state of continuous transformation and development. I content myself, then, with briefly sketching what I take to be the two most enduring and significant of the basic tenets of the framework.

The first is often referred to as the transformational model of social activity. A starting point here is the insight, emphasized especially by Hayek and other 'Austrian' economists, that society and economy depend upon human beings and their conceptions. Certainly, if the human race were to disappear tomorrow, social structures including the economy would disappear with it. But it is important to avoid the mistake, committed in hermeneutics, of conflating the insight that society is concept-dependent with the error that it is concept-determined (see Lawson 1994a, 1994b, 1994e). Social structure cannot be read straight off agent conceptions: not only does social structure almost always possess a material dimension, but individual conceptions are almost always to some degree inadequate as accounts of the social structures (rules, relations, positions, etc., – see below) which depend upon, but are irreducible, to them. An important consideration here is that social structure is dependent upon not only individual concepts but equally individual activities and praxis. It is through human actions that social structures come about and endure when they do, whether or not individual agents have a conscious or reflective awareness that, or precisely how, this is so. Thus, irrespective of whether or not individuals are, for example, discursively aware of the rules of grammar of their language, the existence and endurability of such rules are undoubtedly dependent upon the speech acts in which agents engage.

Social structure, then, depends on human conceptions and action. But, and as again already emphasized above, social structure, such as the rules of language, etc., is equally a condition of intentional human action. At issue, then, is a specific conception of the nature of the relationship between human agency and social structure. Because social structure depends upon human agency it cannot be treated as fixed. At the same time neither can it be treated as the creation of individuals, for individual intentional action presupposes its prior existence. Structure then can be neither *reified* nor interpreted as a *creation* of individuals. Rather the relevant conception here must be of *reproduction* or *transformation* – individuals reproduce or transform social structure which, at the moment of any individual act only, can be treated as given. More specifically, individual agents draw upon existing social structure as a typically unacknowledged condition for acting and through the action of all individuals taken in total social structure is, typically unintentionally, reproduced or transformed. Of course, if the transformation of social structure is rarely the reason that agents have for acting in the way they do, they will always have some conception of what they are doing in their activity. Human acts are always intentional under some description. The point, though, is that whatever the motivations and intentions of each and any individual, human action in total is always reproductive/transformational. In short, social structure is neither created by, nor independent of, human agency, but rather is the (typically) unmotivated condition of all our motivated productions, the non-created but drawn upon and reproduced/transformed condition for our daily economic/social activities. This is the transformational conception of social activity.

The second feature to elaborate here is a conception of the material of social reality as highly *relational*, and society and economy as comprising *totalities*. Now it is fundamental here to distinguish first two types of relations: *external* and *internal*. Two objects or aspects, etc., are said to be *externally* related if neither is constituted by the relationship in which it stands to the other. A barking dog and postman, or two passing strangers, provide examples. In contrast, two objects are said to be *internally* related if they are what they are by virtue of their relationship to the other. Thus, husband and wife, landlord and tenant, employer and employee, magnet and its field, are examples that come to mind. In each case you cannot have one without the other; each, in part, is what it is and what it does by virtue of the relation to the other in which it stands.

Now of particular significance to social science are the internal relations that hold between social *positions*. If it is the case that prime ministers or presidents, say, exercise different rights, tasks, obligations, practices, duties and powers from the rest of us, or that, say, teachers exercise different practices and tasks, etc., from students, it is equally the case that the relevant rights, tasks and obligations, etc., exist independently of the particular individuals taking these roles. At issue then is a system of relationally defined position-practices, i.e., a system of positions, with associated practices, obligations and powers, etc., defined in relation to other such positions, and into which agents essentially slot. According to critical realism all social structures and systems – the economy, the state, international organizations, trade unions and households, etc., – depend upon, or presuppose, internal social relations of this form.

Corresponding to the conception of external and internal relations, clearly, two polar reductionist conceptions of social ontology are feasible

– that of atomistic, externally related items, including wholes, and the other of organic internally related totalities. *A priori*, of course, there is no reason to suppose that one or the other, or any given combination, will be of relevance in any particular substantive enquiry. All such questions or issues are determinable only in the context of specific empirical analysis. *A posteriori*, however, the social world does seem to be characterized by a high degree of internal-relationality, of complex combinations of internally related structures or totalities.

THE CONDUCT OF ECONOMICS

What, then, are the implications of all this for the doing of economics? Clearly this again is too big an issue to elaborate in any great depth here (but see Lawson 1994a, 1994d). However, there are certain matters which in some schematic fashion can, and indeed should, be addressed or summarized here.

The first point to make, or to reiterate, of course, is that the legitimate concern of science, including economics, has been found to be not primarily recording events and their constant conjunctions (as in positivism), but identifying and elaborating the structures and mechanisms, etc., that underlie the phenomena of experience and govern them. In consequence, explanation must be recognized as precisely the (socially produced and fallible) accounting for the previously unknown mode of production of some identified event or phenomenon of interest.

The second point to make or, rather, issue to consider, is again an obvious one. I have argued that universal constant conjunctions of events are rare even in natural science and more so in the social realm. But if this is so how can economic mechanisms be identified? This is the question that is bound to be asked. The point that warrants emphasis is that just because universal constant conjunctions of the form 'whenever event x then event y' are unlikely to be pervasive it does not follow that the only alternative is an inchoate random flux. These two possibilities – strict[6] event regularities or a completely non-systematic flux – merely constitute the polar extremes of a potential continuum. Although the social world is open, certain mechanisms can come to dominate others over restricted regions of time–space, giving rise to rough-and-ready generalities or partial regularities, holding to such a degree that *prima facie* an explanation is called for. Thus, just as autumn leaves do still fall to the ground *much* of the time, so women are *concentrated* in secondary sectors of labour markets, and productivity growth in the UK over the last century has *frequently* been slower than that of otherwise comparable industrial countries. Such 'stylized facts' can serve both to *initiate* investigation and also in the assessment of the relative *explanatory* powers – the relative abilities to illuminate a range of empirical findings – of competing hypotheses that may, in due course, be constructed.

Notice that none of this is obviated by the claim that the object of understanding may be an internally related totality. If 'holistic' conceptions are necessitated for an account that has explanatory power, then so be it.

Notice also that a consequence of the possibility of a continuum of outcomes (i.e., ranging from closed systems of constant conjunctions of events to an inchoate random flux) is that economic explanation (that is, the account of it that can be sustained via transcendental realist analysis) must, in effect, be divided into two distinct moments or separate modes of activity. The discussion above, in fact, has been referring to a mode of inference that should really be termed *pure* or *abstract* explanation – the identification of underlying structures and mechanisms. A necessary condition for this activity is that certain mechanisms do at some time and place dominate others, so that rough or partial empirical regularities are discernible. However, it is equally clear that a second mode of inference, which is appropriately termed *applied* or *concrete* explanation, is also called for. For, to the extent that the concrete phenomena of experience are relatively unique or novel, being conjunctures or resultants of numerous countervailing tendencies, their explanation entails drawing upon antecedently established knowledge of relatively enduring structures and mechanisms (rather than revealing them), and investigating the manner of their joint articulation in the production of the novel event in question.

Now nothing yet has been said explicitly about the event-analogues of the social realm, the social phenomena to be explained. What then are these? What form do they take? It follows from the outline above, of course, that social structures govern, so that the event-analogues of the social realm are precisely *social activities*. On the transcendental realist conception, then, the object of economics is primarily to identify the structures governing, the conditions surrounding, facilitating as well as being transformed through, some human activities of interest. Social explanation entails providing an understanding of certain practices and activities of interest, that is identifying and understanding the unacknowledged conditions of these practices, their unconscious motivations, the tacit skills drawn upon, as well as unintended consequences. While society and economy are the skilled accomplishments of active agents, they remain to a degree opaque to the individuals upon whose activities they depend. The task of economics, then, is to describe all that must be going on (whether or not adequately comprehended by the agents involved) for some manifest social phenomenon, for some set of practices or activities, to be possible.

As an example, consider the productivity growth in the UK over the last hundred years which, as noted, has quite frequently been less than that of industrial countries that are comparable in many other respects. Now the activities involved here include those bearing upon the rate of introducing new techniques of production, levels of staffing of machinery, the ability of an organization to respond flexibly to change, and so forth. In Britain, however, there are definite differences in the structures drawn upon in these activities compared with, say, the countries of the continent of Europe. For in Britain, unlike other countries, the legality of collective worker organization was recognized before the introduction of mass-production techniques, when work was organized upon a craft-system basis. In consequence, norms, relationships, and practices associated with this highly localized, sectional, organization of work became built into the British industrial system. Once legitimized, this craft-oriented basis has tended to be reproduced. For the UK, unlike many other countries in the last hundred years, has not experienced fascist government with its associated prohibition on trade union organization and activities, it has not been defeated in world wars and, until relatively recently, has been able to turn to protected imperial markets to offset the otherwise revolutionizing forces of (increasing) worldwide competition. For such reasons, if amongst others, the UK's craft-oriented practices, localized system of collective bargaining, relatively strict demarcation lines, and other such structures which work to inhibit flexibility, have been subject to less (pressure for) transformation than would otherwise have been expected.

Needless to say, this summary is much too brief to provide more than an overview. (For a more detailed account of all this, see Kilpatrick and Lawson 1980). Nor does the transcendental realist account stand or fall according to the accuracy of this (or indeed of any other) substantive analysis. All that is intended is an indication of the sort of reasoning that is legitimized, encouraged or supported. Of course, once a hypothesis, or a set of competing hypotheses, of mechanisms is formed, such hypotheses can then be further assessed or selected amongst, their relative adequacy can be established, on the basis of the empirical support for any further contrasting claims that are entailed. The hypothesis entertained above, of course, entails that the more decentralized the bargaining structure, the more there will be a tendency for lower productivity growth. This has implications that can be empirically assessed both within a country like the UK, as well as across countries and time (again see Kilpatrick and Lawson 1980). And so on.

The economy as an intrinsically dynamic process

A comment should also be included here on the dynamic nature of society and economy that is articulated by realist analysis, and the implications of this conception for economic explanation. Now it is clear from the transformational conception of social activity elaborated above that change, or at least the potential for change, is always present. Social structure can never be regarded as given or fixed, it can never be reified. There is always fluidity and movement. Even when, over a restricted region of time and space, a structure might be held to have been reproduced 'intact' as it were (and, of course, given the holistic nature of much social structure all reproduction doubtless entails some change – just as change will rarely be total) this is always on the basis of intrinsically dynamic and always potentially transformative, human practice. In the event, any structure is, at any level, only ever relatively enduring, being geohistorically moored. Like everything else it is spatially situated and becomes and begoes in time.

Change then (as with continuity) is endemic to social life. Systems and structures are constantly evolving. On the conception here elaborated, then, a social thing, e.g., the market, is not to be regarded as something that exists *and* as something that experiences change, as if its existence and change were two entirely separate aspects of it. Similarly, change cannot be *reduced* merely to contrasting states of affairs such as the structure of market prices on different days, or voting patterns in succeeding general elections. Rather social items such as markets and political systems must be understood as processes, as reproduced structures of interaction, with change recognized not as an external happening, the result of an external or exogenous stock, but as an integral part of what the system or object in question is.

It follows, then, from this transformational conception of social activity that if change, or at least the potential for change, is always present, then the analysis of change *per se* is of no greater (or less) significance to social explanation than the understanding of continuity and reproduction. Both (relative) change and (relative) continuity need to be addressed and accounted for in science. *Ex-post*, of course, certain structures are found to exhibit greater continuity than others. However, this does not license any conclusion to the effect that the relatively more enduring structures are somehow more natural, normal or given. Put differently, there is no ontological asymmetry between relative continuity and relative change – it is a mistake to regard any social structure or system, etc., as something that would somehow reproduce itself unless obstructed from doing so. In consequence there is equally no epistemic or logical asymmetry between the explanation of relative continuity and relative change. Tradition or fashion, routine or novelty, habit or deliberation, imitation or invention, preservation or innovation, convention or subversion, are all in principle open to, and require, social explanation. In the social world, change and continuity are on equal terms, both as real possibilities and as phenomena that can and should be accounted for, i.e., explained in, the laborious social practice of science.[7]

Turning to the question of *analysis* of change, nothing that has been said under this heading of *change* conflicts with or undermines the discussion of the explanation above. One point, however, should be briefly emphasized. The recognition that social structures are inevitably geo historically restricted or space–time dependent entails that economics must necessarily be historical and geographical in character. It follows that the process of *abstraction* which is always involved in thought and science (see Lawson 1989a) is not restricted just to determining an appropriate level of generality (i.e., that level appropriate to identifying the cause of some phenomenon of interest) but applies also to determining an appropriate *extension* to the analysis, to setting limits in time and space on the history and spatial interaction of any particular focused upon thing or aspect. Moreover, because the features, etc., abstracted *from* will, for some questions, have a significant bearing, it also follows that all analysis and explanation is partial and unfinished, warranting reworking according to changes in questions and focus of interests, as well as developments in understanding. Clearly, a significant skill in scientific labour lies in choosing the bounds (extension), as well as level (generality) of, abstraction appropriate to the illumination of the item(s) of (current) interest.[8]

Now the preceding discussion is, I think, sufficient to justify the optimistic assessment made at the outset that the perspective opened up by realist analysis and critique, though serving to undermine contemporary mainstream economics, is empowering in its implications generally for economics as science, i.e., it is capable of facilitating a more relevant economics, *it is a realist theory for economics*. It has been found that the traditional Humean conception of science underpinning deductivism presupposes rather special conditions that are unlikely often to arise in the social realm. It is the failure to realize this that, in large part, explains the endeavour of economists to persevere with existing methods and to continue to try that little bit harder – a strategy that seems doomed to perpetual failure. However, once the critical realist perspective is accepted, and it is recognized that the social realm, just like the natural one, is structured and intransitive, and that the aim is to understand aspects of this structured domain, then it follows that economics, in principle, can be just as illuminating and revelatory as any other science.

As a final point, something should be said about the possibilities for policy analysis and intentional social change that the realist perspective elaborated above throws up. The essential point here is that while the traditional constant conjunction view of science entails the goal of *control* along with the amelioration of events and states of affairs, the critical realist perspective offers instead the policy goal of human *emancipation*. For while on the former account the point is to fix certain event(s) x in order to determine/control other event(s) y, on the critical realist understanding the aim must be to transform structures in order to enhance the scope for realizing human potential, to broaden opportunities. In the latter case, in other words, the aim must be to replace structures that are unwanted, unneeded and restrictive by those that are wanted, needed and empowering.

Of course the proposed policy concern for structural transformation is hardly new. Indeed, although government policy-makers and the like usually project the rhetoric of event conjunctions and ameliorations, the real focus, as recently experienced in the UK, is more often than not on questions of structural change. Thus, for example, recent UK policy deliberation has focused upon questions of changes to industrial relations (and especially labour) law, of whether to join (or, more recently, to leave) the European Exchange Rate Mechanism, of methods of funding and controlling schools and hospitals, of whether to legalize Sunday trading, and so on. The point here, then, is to acknowledge the critical realist rationale for such deliberation and action, and in doing so to abandon the traditional Humean rhetoric that can serve only as a misleading straitjacket.

FINAL COMMENTS AND CONCLUSION

In summary, the essential components of the argument can, I think, be most usefully drawn together if, instead of attempting a straightforward overview, I very briefly go through aspects and implications of the above discussion that bear upon that most favourite of economists' pastimes: the activity of event prediction. What are the implications of the above discussion for the continued endeavours of economists to forecast?

If the predictive goal in question is the successful forecasting of events then clearly an implication is that such a goal is likely to be only rarely if ever attainable, at least in an unqualified form. Prediction of non-experimental events rests upon the spontaneous occurrence of constant event conjunctions which, in the social realm, are not only not in evidence but appear to be an unlikely eventuality. This insight does not obviate the possibility of predicting tendencies, of course. I refer only to the (unconditional) prediction of events. There may, certainly, be a predictable *tendency* for, say, leaves and profits to fall even when, in specific instances, leaves and profits actually rise.

Not only is event prediction typically infeasible, but, if the above account is correct, it is in any case not required for a successful economics. For it can now be seen that the primary aim of science is not the illumination/prediction of events at all but the identification and comprehension of the mechanisms and tendencies, etc., that underpin and govern them. And this understanding is all that is required for policy analysis and effective action. It is not, for example, the prediction of the pattern of spots on a patient's skin that is the ultimate goal of medical research but the identification of the virus or agent that causes it and the production of an effective antidote. As an example that is closer to home, perhaps, it can be noted that Keynes, in chapter 12 of *The General Theory*, suggests how the prices of financial assets and interest rates, influenced as they are by such factors as uncertainty, whim, sentiment and chance, may be more or less anything. The conditions which encourage or facilitate the (unwanted) instability of financial markets, however, are issues that Keynes is nevertheless able to identify – and policy is formulated accordingly (see Lawson 1994d).

Finally, if event prediction is neither possible nor needed, it must also be added that in any case it is hardly wanted. For, as we have seen, its possibility, turning as it does on the existence of constant conjunctions of events, would mean either that the future was already determined, or, if exogenous variables could be fixed by us, open to social *control*. Either way the situation would be inconsistent with the possibility of generalized human choice and freedom. Although it is not the reason why critical realism is the most justified account, an advantage of the latter perspective is that human emancipation emerges as a real possibility. From this perspective, as elaborated above, it follows that policies and strategies can be formulated not with the objective of merely fixing events and states of affairs in order to control the future, but with the aim, instead, of replacing structures that are unwanted with others that are needed and empowering; to facilitate, in other words, a greater or more desirable or equally distributed range of human opportunities. Put differently, the possibility of rational, intentional, emancipatory, real change is not a potential that, as in positivism, appears in contradiction to the explanatory function of science including economics. Rather, transcendental realism, or critical realism as elaborated for the social realm, provides a perspective on science, society and economy that is not only both explanatorily powerful but also able to sustain the intuition that human social history is explicable and yet made.

ACKNOWLEDGEMENTS

For helpful comments on an earlier draft I am grateful to Leslie Turano.

NOTES

1 Notice that although many economic theorists never confront their 'models' with the data of experience this does not detract from the observation that they adhere to the deductivist explanatory form in question. Indeed, their economic 'theorizing' is usually sustained on the promise of obtaining models that can be confronted with data *eventually* – as a result of 'trying that little bit harder' to overcome current problems. Thus, for example, although Hahn, a theorist who traditionally has preferred highly 'abstract' or simple theories, frequently disclaims the 'positivist' label, there is little doubting that even here there is a promissory reliance upon results rooted in the positivist position. In particular, Hahn does not deny the existence of 'empirical regularities' awaiting discovery. Rather he sees the problem facing economics as being merely an epistemological or practical one – that event regularities will be difficult to uncover. In stressing this problem, of course, Hahn falls back on one or other, or both, of the two

extenuating circumstances regularly alluded to by mainstream economists. That is, Hahn explains the failure to discover event regularities so far, as due either to their complexity or to their existing at some level deeper than that so far examined. In the former case he notes, for example, that 'there are very many elements which enter into an explanation of an event. This in turn hinders prediction and falsification' (1984: 5). As an example of the second response, Hahn writes: 'For I do not want to deny that there are empirical regularities of human economic behaviour awaiting discovery. But I claim that these will be, as it were, much deeper down and more elementary and closer to the form in which axioms are postulated then are complex, institutional and history dependent "facts" of the econometrician' (1984: 332).

2 For elaborations of the term that are similar to, or which include, this interpretation, see, for example, entries on positivism in Outhwaite and Bottomore (1993); Bullock *et al.* (1988) or Gould and Kolb (1964).

3 Further elaborations of this perspective, which, of course, derive from and are heavily influenced by the writings of Bhaskar, can be found, for example, in Bhaskar (1978, 1979, 1987, 1989); Fleetwood (1993); Lawson (1989a, 1989b, 1992, 1994a, 1994b, 1994c, 1994d, 1994e); Outhwaite (1987); Peacock (1993), Pratten (1993), Rotheim (1993) and Runde (1993).

4 Notice that this understanding of the term structure is to be distinguished from the econometric interpretation as a putative relationship at the level of, and between, (measurable) events.

5 An emphasis that is clearly in evidence even in this volume.

6 Including probabilistically formulated event regularities.

7 This discussion has necessarily been pitched at a rather general level. In addition, the emphasis, albeit implicitly, has been primarily on reproductive or metamorphic change whereby a structure, organization, system or thing does, or at least *can*, remain essentially the same sort of thing despite continuously undergoing some alteration or transformation in its form. The intention has been to emphasize the pervasiveness of (endogenous) change in social life (as everywhere else). In a more sustained analysis, of course, specific types of change warrant elaboration, including, explicitly, changes in the nature or types of things, and their causes and conditions. An obvious example is the quantity/quality type of transformation. This is the process whereby, as some aspect of something gets bigger (or smaller), more numerous (or less numerous), hotter (or colder), etc., a point is reached at which a qualitative transformation takes place (e.g., money, through accumulation, into capital; a pressure group, through increased membership, into a movement, etc.). Similarly, the manner of emergence of new or different forms of structure, etc., due to crises resolution of contradictory (i.e., internally related and simultaneously supportive and antagonistic) processes, also warrants attention. Although such forms of change cannot be further elaborated here, they are clearly consistent with the general transformational conception outlined in the text. The point, though, is that even if the discussion here is pitched at a rather high level of generality, it should at least serve to indicate the nature, possibilities and richness of the perspective opened up through critical realist analysis compared with those of the Humean orthodoxy.

8 Of course the level of generality and the extension involved will usually be related. If, for example, the explanation of some phenomenon requires abstraction at the level of the capitalist firm, the latter already places limits on the stretch of time and space under consideration.

BIBLIOGRAPHY

Bhaskar, R. (1978) *A Realist Theory of Science*, 2nd edn, Brighton: Harvester. [1st edn, Leeds, 1975.]

Bhaskar, R. (1979) *The Possibility of Naturalism*, Brighton: Harvester.

Bhaskar, R. (1987) *Scientific Realism and Human Emancipation*, London: Verso.

Bhaskar, R. (1989) *Reclaiming Reality*, London: Verso.

Bullock, A., Stallybrass, O. and Trombley, S. (eds) (1988) *The Fontana Dictionary of Modern Thought*, 2nd edn, London: Fontana.

Fleetwood, S. (1994) 'Hayek III: recognition of the necessity of social rules of conduct', in S. Frowen (ed.), *Hayek the Economist and Social Philosopher: A Critical Retrospect*, Basingstoke: Macmillan.

Flew, A. (1979) *A Dictionary of Philosophy*, London: Pan Books.

Gould, J. and Kolb, W. L. (1964) *A Dictionary of the Social Sciences*, London: Tavistock Publications.

Hahn, F. (1984) *Equilibrium and Macroeconomics*, Oxford: Basil Blackwell.

Hahn, F. (1985) 'In praise of economic theory', The 1984 Jevons Memorial Lecture, University College London.

Keynes, J. M. (1973) *The Collected Writings of John Maynard Keynes*, Vol. VII, *The General Theory of Employment, Interest and Money*, Royal Economic Society.

Kilpatrick, J. A. and Lawson, T. (1980) 'On the nature of industrial decline in the UK', *Cambridge Journal of Economics* 4(1): 85–102.

Lawson, T. (1989a) 'Abstraction, tendencies and stylised facts: a realist approach to economic analysis', *Cambridge Journal of Economics* 13(1): 59–78. Reprinted in T. Lawson, G. Palma and J. Sender (eds), (1989) *Kaldor's Political Economy*, London and San Diego: Academic Press. Also reprinted in P. Ekins and M. Max-Neef (eds) (1992) *Real Life Economics: Understanding Wealth Creation*, London: Routledge.

Lawson, T. (1989b) 'Realism and instrumentalism in the development of econometrics', *Oxford Economic Papers* 41(1): 236–58. Reprinted in N. de Marchi and C. Gilbert (eds), (1990) *History and Methodology of Econometrics*, Oxford: Oxford University Press.

Lawson, T. (1992) 'Realism, closed systems and Friedman', *Research in the History of Economic Thought and Methodology* 10: 149–169.

Lawson, T. (1994a) 'Critical realism and the analysis of choice, explanation and change', *Advances in Austrian Economics*, vol. 1, no. 1.

Lawson, T. (1994b) 'Realism and Hayek: a case of continuous transformation', in M. Colonna, H. Hagemann and O. F. Hamouda (eds), *Capitalism, Socialism and Information: The Economics of F. A. Hayek*, vol. II, Aldershot: Edward Elgar.

Lawson, T. (1994c) 'Realism, philosophical', in G. Hodgson, M. Tool and W. Samuels (eds), *Edward Elgar Companion to Evolutionary and Institutional Economics*, Aldershot: Edward Elgar.

Lawson, T. (1994d) 'Expectations and economics', in S. Dow and J. Hillard (eds), *Keynes, Knowledge and Uncertainty*, Aldershot: Edward Elgar.

Lawson. T. (1994e) 'Development in Hayek's social theorising', in S. Frowen (ed.), *Hayek, the Economist and Social Philosopher: A Critical Retrospect*, Basingstoke and London: Macmillan.

Outhwaite, W. (1987) *New Philosophies of Social Science: Realism, Hermeneutics and Critical Theory*, Basingstoke and London: Macmillan.

Outhwaite, W. and Bottomore, T. (eds) (1993) *The Blackwell Dictionary of Twentieth-Century Social Thought*, Oxford: Basil Blackwell.

Peacock, M. (1993) 'Hayek realism and spontaneous order', *Journal for the Theory of Social Behaviour* 23(3): 249, 264.

Pratten, S. (1993) 'Structure, agency and Marx's analysis of the labour process', *Review of Political Economy* 5(4): 403–26.

Rotheim, R. J. (1993) 'On the indeterminacy of Keynes's monetary theory of value', *Review of Political Economy* 5(2): 197–216.

Runde, J. (1993) 'Paul Davidson and the Austrians: Reply to Davidson', *Critical Review*, 7(223): 1218.

14

PRAGMATISM, PRAGMATICISM AND ECONOMIC METHOD

Kevin D. Hoover

No man is an *Island*, entire of itself; every man is a piece of the *Continent*, a part of the *main*; if a *clod* be washed away by the *sea*, *Europe* is the less, as well as if a *promontory* were, as well as if a *manor* of thy *friends* or of *thine* own were; any man's *death* diminishes *me*, because I am involved in *Mankind*; . . .

(John Donne, *Meditation XVII*)

PRAGMATISM AND ECONOMICS

The kinematics of intellectual history would make a field in its own right. There may be some universal laws governing the speed and trajectories with which the ideas of one field permeate another. Casual observation of the introduction of a sequence of philosophies (those of Popper, Kuhn and Lakatos) into methodological discussions in economics suggests that it takes ten to twenty years to make the transition between fields. The rule is borne out in the introduction of pragmatism into economics with a long lag from its revival in philosophy. References to W. V. O. Quine's (1951) pragmatic assault on the dogmas of empiricism are common among economic methodologists (e.g., Cross 1982; Caldwell 1982; McCloskey 1985). Pragmatic philosophy is implicit in the now ten-year-old rhetoric programme in economics. E. Roy Weintraub's (1990, 1991) recent assault on economic methodology is grounded in his readings of Richard Rorty (1979, 1982) and Stanley Fish (1980). Rorty is a self-described disciple of the early American pragmatist John Dewey; while not given to donning philosophical labels, Fish is a literary critic whose general perspective is nearly identical to Rorty's.[1] Abraham Hirsch and Neil de Marchi (1990) interpret Milton Friedman as an implicit disciple of Dewey.

'Who are the pragmatists?' and 'what is pragmatism?' are not wholly settled questions. A list such as given by Weintraub (1990: 268) is not uncommon: Dewey, James, Peirce, Rorty and Wittgenstein. But names on such lists, just like the names in the calendar of saints, are often merely honorific. Lacking direct familiarity with their works, the peculiar virtues

286

of the philosophers, as well as the saints, are unknown or preserved only in a confused and poorly recalled intellectual folklore. While the philosophy of Charles Sanders Peirce has undergone a revival, to most philosophers and those economists with some interest in philosophy he is still merely a two-dimensional figure belonging to the history of thought; vaguely perceived as the founder of pragmatism; but neither philosopher nor economist could generally say much about his doctrines.[2] Despite Dewey's (1938: 9) view that his own pragmatic *Logic* is but a direct extension of Peirce's logic, Dewey's disciple, Rorty (1982: 161), dismisses Peirce as just another Kantian, whose '. . . contribution to pragmatism was merely to have given it a name, and to have stimulated James.'[3] Peirce was a polymath and a frustrated genius. In contrast to Rorty, many regard Peirce as the greatest American philosopher of all time.[4] Hirsch and de Marchi (1990: 18, 115, 145) are rare among economic methodologists in even briefly referring to Peirce's central doctrines. The only extended treatment I know of is James Wible's (1992) paper on Peirce's analysis of the economics of research.

In 1902, reflecting on the quarter-century since he coined the term in the company of the Metaphysical Club (of Cambridge, Massachusetts), Peirce defined 'pragmatism' according to the maxim: 'Consider what effects, that might conceivably have practical bearings, we conceive the object of our conception to have. Then, our conception of these effects is the whole of our conception of the object' (5.1).[5] Peirce perceived that there was a risk that this bald statement could be mistaken for the stoical maxim that the end of man is action (5.3). While Peirce never wavered from the importance of action in a wide sense for the definition of pragmatism, he equally became less and less committed to worldliness. He acknowledged a sphere of intellectual action, and, in particular, did not interpret his doctrine as, for example, ruling out immaterial concepts such as the incommensurables in the Weierstrassian interpretation of the differential calculus. There are scattered throughout Peirce's writings numerous other definitions of 'pragmatism', related to this one in more or less subtle ways.

Peirce acknowledged a common spirit animating the works of William James, Josiah Royce, F. C. S. Schiller and John Dewey. Yet, he feared that their versions of pragmatism would push the doctrine into the direction of a mere practicalism (5.412). In his lectures, *Pragmatism*, James sounds a Peircian note:

> The pragmatic method is primarily a method of settling metaphysical disputes that otherwise might be interminable . . . . The pragmatic method . . . is to try to interpret each notion by tracing its respective practical consequences. What difference would it practically make to any one if this notion rather than that notion were true? If no

practical difference whatever can be traced, then the alternatives mean practically the same thing, and all dispute is idle. Whenever a dispute is serious, we ought to be able to show some practical difference that must follow from one side or the other's being right.

(James 1907/1949: 45–6)

But James does not stop here. To his description of the pragmatic method he adds a theory of truth: '... any idea that will carry us prosperously from any one part of our experience to any other part, linking things satisfactorily, working securely, simplifying, saving labor, is true for just so much, true in so far forth, true *instrumentally*' (James 1907/1949: 58). Here James parts company with Peirce. For Peirce, pragmatism was a doctrine about meaning not about truth, on which his views differ considerably from James (see 'Peirce's theory of inquiry', below). Peirce never denied that James, his close friend and generous patron, or the other pragmatic philosophers had legitimate claims on his terminology, that their doctrines were generically related to is own. But he worried that the radical empiricist, instrumentalist turn of the pragmatic philosophers opened the doors to popular abuse: pragmatism came to mean the crudest sort of practicalism; 'whatever works is true' came to be seen as the pragmatic creed. So Peirce sought a new terminology: the word 'pragmatism', he noted, was

> met with occasionally in literary journals, where it gets abused in the merciless way that words have to expect when they fall into literary clutches. Sometimes the manners of the British have effloresced in scolding at the word ill-chosen – ill-chosen, that is, to express some meaning that it was rather designed to exclude. So then, the writer, finding his bantling 'pragmatism' so promoted, feels that it is time to kiss his child good-bye and relinquish it to its higher destiny; while to serve the precise purpose of expressing the original definition, he begs to announce the birth of the word 'pragmaticism', which is ugly enough to be safe from kidnappers.

(5.414)

My theme then is that as philosophers and economists we should repair to Peirce and declare a new pragmaticism. Modern pragmatists are clearly the successors to James and Dewey. As such their pragmatic credentials are secure. They do a great service, especially in advocating the importance of the situated subject and the richness of human experience. But, as I hope to make clear, they also expose us to risks – particularly, to the risk of intellectual Balkanization – that a more Peircian pragmatism would help us to avoid. We must be careful, however, not to claim too much. Although there are genuine differences between Peirce and, say, Rorty or Fish, many of the differences reduce to matters of tone and emphasis. But tone and emphasis are part of what makes the difference between noise and music, prose and poetry. It is not the least important fact about Peirce that he valued good poetry above the science that was his life's work (1.315).

THE PRAGMATIC CHALLENGE IN ECONOMICS AND PHILOSOPHY

Perhaps the clearest appeal to modern pragmatism available in economics is Weintraub's (1990) article advocating reading Methodology out of the economics profession.[6] Weintraub distinguishes between methodology, which is the collection of procedural issues that arise in the ordinary discourse of a well-defined field, and Methodology, which is '. . . a special project in economics: the attempt to govern appraisal of particular economic theories by an account of theorizing in general' (Weintraub 1990: 266). The Methodology project in economics is likened to the theory project in literary criticism, and is dismissed on grounds similar to those that Stanley Fish and others apply to literary theory. The Methodologist, according to Weintraub, seeks knowledge that is somehow more basic than the knowledge of economists practising economics and uses this knowledge to reform the practice of economists. The problem is, in Weintraub's view, that there is no such knowledge, because there is no privileged position outside the practice of economics, that is nonetheless relevant to economics, from which the Methodologist might appraise and instruct economists. Weintraub (1990: 268; 1991: 111) puts the objection in another way. The Methodologist appeals to Truth, which is supposed to stand in correspondence with Reality. But how could we have access to such a Truth, that seems to abandon the human practice of inquiry? 'The pragmatist instead believes that we construct our world out of the ideas we create' (Weintraub 1990: 268), in much the same way that we construct constellations somewhat freely out of stars that are not, in fact, grouped that way by Nature or Reality. For the moment, at least, let us set aside the accuracy of this characterization of the practitioners of economic methodology (here I abandon Weintraub's typographical convention without prejudice). What is important is that the pragmatic objection that Weintraub raises imports the more general perspective of modern pragmatism into economics.

Rorty's (1979) attack on epistemology since Descartes is of a piece with Weintraub's attack on methodology. The advocates of the theory of knowledge, in Rorty's view, insist that knowledge is representation of reality to the mind's eye (hence the idea of the 'mirror of nature'), and that truth is the correspondence between representation and reality. The difficulty, according to Rorty, is that there is no detached observer, no polished glass in which one might observe the reflection of reality. Instead, man is an interpreter of interpretations, with no hope of securing a neutral standpoint from which to compare interpretations with independent reality.

The only standard of truth must be the coherence of our interpretations, including their coherence with our values and purposes in the world. Newton's physics is judged superior to Aristotle's not because there is a closer correspondence between it and reality, but because it enables us to better cope with life (Rorty 1979: 269). In the place of epistemology, Rorty advocates hermeneutics, which treats knowledge as a vast network of mutually interpreting beliefs. Additions to knowledge can then be seen as relatively minor adjustments in this network. The adequacy of such a network cannot be judged from any independent standpoint; for there is none. Rather, it must be judged holistically, according to how the beliefs cohere and support one another.

The central difficulty with any holistic or coherence theories of truth, as Rorty (1979: 317) clearly observes, is that they appear to license individuals to construct private wholes, paradigms, practices, Wittgensteinian language games, and so forth, without any constraint. This problem forms the core of Fish's (1980) analysis of literary theory. Fish poses a puzzle. One might think that the question of which literary theory to employ is, which is right? Empirical evidence, however, suggests that alternative theories of interpretation always work. Fish (1980: 1) argues that this is because '... the field of inquiry is *constituted* by the questions we are able to ask because the entities that populate it come into being as the presuppositions – they are the discourse-specific entities – of those questions'. But if the theories themselves constitute the only reality of literature, then is relativism not given free rein? Fish (1980: 11) answers this fear with this observation:

> the act of recognizing literature is not constrained by something in the text, nor does it issue from an independent and arbitrary will; rather it proceeds from a collective decision as to what will count as literature, a decision that will be in force only so long as a community of readers or believers continues to abide by it.

Although what is in the text is, in Fish's view, constituted by the interpretation, it is nonetheless not freely chosen for any individual, but 'there' for every member of the community bound together by the same interpretive theory.

The text is for Fish – as knowledge is for Peirce, Dewey and Rorty – a social construction. Fish christens the societies formed around literary theories' *interpretive communities*. On the one hand, different theories constitute different interpretive communities; and different communities generate different, and perhaps mutually incomprehensible, interpretations. Relativism of a sort appears to be unavoidable. On the other hand, interpretive communities stabilize texts within their limits; and stabilized texts may be subjected to principled debate. Individual interpretation is constrained. The interpretive community imposes an ethical norm on its members: a *passé* interpretation may be ruled out because 'nobody reads that way any more' just as *outré* behaviour might be censored because 'civilized people simply do not act that way'. Fish (1980: 172) writes: 'The notion of interpretive communities thus stands between an impossible ideal [of a text neutral with respect to alternative interpretive theories] and the fear [of interpretive anarchy] which leads so many to maintain it.' Weintraub (1990) imports Fish's notion of an interpretive community into economics: he regards general equilibrium theory, Keynesian macroeconomics, macroeconometrics, new classical macroeconomics and other areas of specialization as interpretive communities.

Interpretive communities for Fish create the text and facilitate principled debate, and they define a community with a definite limit:

> communication occurs only *within* . . . a system (or context, or situation, or interpretive community) and . . . the understanding achieved by two or more persons is specific to that system and determinate only within its confines . . . such an understanding is enough and . . . an understanding that operates above or across situations . . . would have no place in the world even if it were available, because it is only in situations – with their interested specifications as to what counts as a fact, what it is possible to say, what will be heard as an argument – that one is called on to understand.
>
> (Fish 1980: 304)

Weintraub (1990: 267) takes essentially the same view. The reason that Methodology cannot succeed in reforming the practice of economists is not only that it does not, indeed cannot, occupy a privileged position, but also that it does not belong to the same interpretive community as the economists whose practices it hopes to reform. General equilibrium theory cannot be successfully criticized from the perspective of an 'epistemological theory of probabilistic knowledge', and neoclassical economics cannot be successfully criticized from a Hegelian historiographic tradition. Both critical perspectives are 'outside' economics, and therefore do not participate in the same interpretive communities as their objects of criticism. Methodology is impossible, and therefore cannot matter:

> One never in fact refutes or disallows an argument in economics by an argument in Methodology. An economic argument, like an explanation of the rate of inflation, is always appraised from within economics; there is no independent basis for appraisal: Philosophy does not construct theories of inflation.
>
> (Weintraub 1990: 272)

KEVIN D. HOOVER

PEIRCE'S THEORY OF INQUIRY

To see the way in which Peirce's pragmaticism improves on modern pragmatism, we must first give a brief, and necessarily superficial, sketch of some of the main points of Peirce's own theory of inquiry. Peirce's hope for pragmatism was that it would bring an end to those disputes among philosophers that empirical evidence could not resolve. Once the meanings of the terms under dispute were stated in terms of their consequences, it should turn out either that nothing were at stake or that there were some (empirical) means of answering the now clarified question (5.6). Taken as a means of resolving disputes, the pragmatic theory of meaning is incomplete. Once disputed questions are clarified, resolution still wants evidence. Peirce's theory of inquiry fills out this aspect of pragmatism.[7]

For Peirce the life of science – and the life of philosophy as well, for he hoped for a scientific philosophy – was the life of inquiry. Peirce was a systematic philosopher. His account of scientific inquiry cuts across virtually every aspect of his philosophical system. A brief summary of the main points might be helpful. Inquiry begins, for Peirce, in disputes between people or in the intellectual unease within an individual mind that we call doubt. Inquiry aims at assuaging doubt or at, as Peirce calls it, the 'fixation of belief' (5.358ff.). That inquiry ends when doubts are satisfied might suggest that Peirce adheres to a view that would popularly be considered 'pragmatic', that whatever works to put our minds at ease is as close to truth as we can hope to come. Pragmatism and relativism are sometimes bracketed together because of this view. But Peirce takes great pains to contradict it. For him the workaday sense of 'truth' is indeed the coherence of our beliefs. If coherence were all there was to it, the door would be open to relativism. Relativism usually begins with the observation that different people are deeply committed to apparently contradictory beliefs. Peirce notices, however, that human nature being social, the coexistence of contradictory beliefs is bound to raise exactly the doubts that start any inquiry. Truth then must have another sense: ultimately fixed belief, belief that resolves all doubts and resolves all contradictions. No one can know that they possess such a truth; it nonetheless serves as a regulatory ideal for inquiry. Inquiry could not possibly converge to such a truth unless, in Peirce's view, it was really there to converge to. Peirce's doctrine of scholastic realism is thus a fundamental element of his theory of inquiry. Etymologically and doctrinally pragmatism is fundamentally related to action. The sharp end of Peirce's theory of inquiry is then found in his logic: the guide for the inquiring mind. Let us now consider the main points of Peirce's theory of inquiry in greater detail.

Belief and doubt

Doubt is itself parasitic on belief; where there was not first belief, there can be no doubt. The source of all doubt is surprise. Surprise is a disappointment of our expectations, a contradiction of our beliefs (5.512).

> Peirce defines 'belief' in accordance with his pragmatic maxim: The essence of belief is the establishment of a habit; and different beliefs are distinguished by the different modes of action to which they give rise. If beliefs do not differ in this respect, if they appease the same doubt by producing the same rule of action, then no mere difference in the manner of consciousness of them can make different beliefs, any more than playing a tune in different keys is playing different tunes.
>
> (5.398)

A belief has three properties: we are aware of it; it appeases a related doubt; and it establishes a habit or rule of action (5.397). Peirce was aware that the terms 'belief' and 'doubt' carry emotive baggage more appropriate to religion than to everyday life (5.394). Thus, while he recognized that belief and doubt have psychological correlates and are active in the imagination, he was at pains to deny that they were essentially momentary modes of consciousness or feelings (2.148, 2.210, 5.417). Rather, belief is a mostly unconscious continuing mental habit, a kind of self-satisfaction, and doubt is the privation of a habit; to have a belief is to be prepared to adopt the formula believed in as the guide to action or conduct (5.27–32, 5.417). 'A belief that will not be acted on ceases to be a belief' (7.356).

Inquiry for Peirce begins with surprise, doubt and hesitancy, which together thwart action. Inquiry aims at peace of mind and restoration of a firm basis for action. Peirce begins with doubt, but rejects the Cartesian project of universal doubt as the foundation for true knowledge:

> We cannot begin with complete doubt. We must begin with all the prejudices which we actually have.... These prejudices are not to be dispelled by a maxim, for they are things which it does not occur to us *can* be questioned. Hence this initial scepticism will be a mere self-deception, and not real doubt; and no one who follows the Cartesian method will ever be satisfied until he has formally recovered all those beliefs which in form he has given up.... A person may, it is true, in the course of his studies, find reason to doubt what he began by believing; but in that case he doubts because he has a positive reason for it, and not on account of the Cartesian maxim. Let us not pretend to doubt in philosophy what we do not doubt in our hearts.
>
> (5.265)

Descartes's project of radical doubt aims to establish a detached vantage point (a privileged position) from which to evaluate all knowledge. Like Peirce, Fish (1980: 360) rejects Cartesian scepticism: 'The project of radical doubt can never outrun the necessity of being situated . . .'. Peirce clearly agrees with the modern pragmatists that man is situated and cannot get behind the beliefs that organize his understanding of the world (5.440; cf. Fish 1980: 361). Equally, Peirce would understand why all literary theories work: they do not begin with genuine doubt, but recover the prejudices (Fish's 'interests') that motivated them in the first place.

For Peirce, the Cartesian project goes off the rails even before it leaves the station. Descartes advocated the strategy of doubting everything as a way of uncovering the bedrock of an absolutely indubitable belief, thinking that no inquiry could be secure that did not possess this firm foundation.[8] Peirce argues that it is enough to begin inquiry from less than absolutely indubitable premises, from premises that are merely free from any actual doubt: 'If the premises are not doubted at all, they cannot be more satisfactory than they are' (5.376). Such indubitable beliefs are beyond criticism: 'You cannot criticize what you do not doubt' (2.27; cf. 5.515, 5.523); and doubt presupposes previous belief (5.512). Aristotle's law of non-contradiction, 'not (A and not-A)', is an example of an indubitable proposition. Indubitability is a contingent fact. Any experienced inquirer knows that beliefs once firmly held sometimes come to be doubted and discarded. Peirce does not exempt even the simplest arithmetic or the laws of logic from the possibility of being doubted at some point (7.109). Even mathematical proofs of centuries' standing having sometimes come to be regarded as wrong (5.577). Peirce praises Hegel for trying to cast doubt where none existed before (2.192).

Peirce is as hard on radical empiricists as he is on Cartesian rationalists:

> One proposes that you shall begin by doubting everything, and says that there is only one thing that you cannot doubt, as if doubting were 'as easy as lying'. Another proposes that we should begin by observing 'the first impressions of sense', forgetting that our very precepts are the results of cognitive elaboration. But in truth there is but one state of mind from which you can 'set out' – a state in which you are laden with an immense mass of cognition already formed, of which you cannot divest yourself if you would; and who knows whether, if you could, you would not have made all knowledge impossible to yourself? Do you call it *doubting* to write down on a piece of paper that you doubt? If so, doubt has nothing to do with any serious business. But do not make believe; if pedantry has not eaten all the reality out of you, recognize, as you must, that there is much that you do not doubt, in the least. Now that which you do not at all doubt, you must and do regard as infallible absolute truth.
> (5.416)

Locally infallible, indubitable beliefs are the basis upon which any other beliefs are criticized. Here Peirce anticipates Fish (1980: 360, 361) who argues that doubt is possible only within a perspective not currently subject to doubt, so that current beliefs are privileged.[9] But Peirce examines the limits of infallibility. Common sense relies on the indubitable beliefs of everyday (even primitive) life (5.511, 5.523). Such indubitable beliefs are, however, necessarily vague (5.446). For Peirce, a belief is *vague* to the extent that the law of non-contradiction does not apply to it (5.505, 5.448).[10] As reasoning advances and becomes more subject to self-control, beliefs are formulated more precisely. Because their vagueness is reduced, the range of contradictory beliefs, including ones induced by experience, is increased, and the more subject to doubt they become. There is, for Peirce, then, no difference in kind between commonsense beliefs and scientific beliefs. Scientific beliefs are more doubtful, because they rest on more minutely drawn distinctions; yet both science and common sense are the products of the long experience of many people (2.147, 5.522, 5.498).

That common sense is the closest science comes to unshakeable foundations is evident from Peirce's observation that physical dynamics, as it was understood by its founders and not including the law of the conservation of energy, as not a science that aimed at novel facts, but one that analysed truths that all men acknowledged from experience. Virtually the whole of Lagrange's statistical mechanics, he argues, is based on working out the implications of Archimedes' principle of the lever which is presumed in our ordinary conception of equal weight. Such universal, commonsense experiences may not, he notes, be true to microscopical exactitude (this, it should be noted, before the development of quantum mechanics), but are nonetheless presupposed by anyone who devises a scientific experiment. In one of his relatively few references to economics Peirce writes:

> The analytical economics of Adam Smith and of Ricardo were examples of [the sort of science that is founded upon the common experience of all men]. The whole doctrine in its totality is properly termed the Philosophy of Common Sense, of which analytical mechanics and analytical economics are branches.
>
> (8.199)

In this, Peirce would also appear to anticipate the *apriorism* of Mises and the Austrian school (see Hoover 1988: ch. 10).

Reasoning in science and ordinary life share in Peirce's view, a foundation in common sense. Yet Peirce replaces the simple commonsensism of Thomas Reid and the Scottish school by distinguishing science from the ordinary life. Science is a 'critical' discipline, and yet another reformulation of the pragmatism is as 'critical commonsensism'. The background of indubitable beliefs makes criticism possible. Any belief may be criticized, but, as Fish recognizes, not all beliefs can be doubted or criticized at once (5.514).[11] Critical, scientific inquiry further strips belief and doubt of their emotive correlate: while not a false, paper doubt, a feigned hesitancy may be as much doubt as the advance of scientific inquiry demands (5.394, cf. 7.606). Science progresses partly by raising and entertaining doubts where they do not exist practically. Science may, therefore, be of little relevance with respect to the 'vital questions' of life. Peirce argues that experience is complex and that science is insufficiently grounded in the vital interests of life for it to provide much practical guidance. Rather, he believes, customary beliefs have adapted to the interests and experiences of life so as to provide much better guides to practical matters (1.661–77; Peirce 1992: Lecture 1; cf. 5.60 and fn. 15 below).

Truth

Peirce's theory of belief provides him with a dual-faceted theory of truth. Truth for Peirce is a property of propositions (5.569). It is therefore inextricably linked with representation. On the one hand, truth is thus a matter of *correspondence* between the proposition and the facts of the world (5.553–4). It is a matter of mirroring, but the quicksilver is provided by the indubitable beliefs that the inquirer brings to bear on the world, and not by any privileged representation detached from the situated subject. Peirce rejects metaphysical truth as a source of confusion. And, although he never stops using the term 'truth', he suggests that we could just as well replace it with 'belief unassailable by doubt' and be done (5.416). Peirce's notion of truth is thus hardly different from Dewey's (1938: 7 *passim*) 'warranted assertability' or Weintraub's (1991: 112) 'contingent truths'.

On the other hand, truth also is a regulatory ideal for inquiry. Although he does not often feel the need to make such a distinction, he does not hesitate to speak of *Truth*. Truth in this sense is also not a claim to a privileged representation. Truth is what agrees with the ultimate propositions of a community of inquirers in the fullness of time (5.416, 5.565, 5.569, 7.187). Truth is 'that at which inquiry aims' (5.557). Ultimate truth is therefore a *coherence* of the beliefs, including the experiential or perceptual beliefs; and, as always with Peirce, beliefs are mediated by other beliefs; there is no getting behind them (5.440).

Truth in either its correspondence or coherence dress is, for Peirce, parasitic on belief. A central human predicament is how to obtain stable beliefs. Peirce considers four methods of fixing belief (5.358–87).

The *method of tenacity* amounts to believing whatever one will, brooking no objections, and avoiding doubt-inducing experiences. Of the advocate of this method, Peirce writes:

It would be an egotistical impertinence to object that his procedure is irrational, for that only amounts to saying that his method is not ours. He does not propose to himself to be rational, and, indeed, will often talk with scorn of man's weak and illusive reason.

(5.377)

Peirce thus would appear to license private truth. He observes, however, that the method of tenacity is unstable:

The social impulse is against it. The man who adopts it will find that other men think differently from him, and it will be apt to occur to him, in some saner moment, that their opinions are quite as good as his own, and this will shake his confidence in his belief.

(5.378)

Peirce argues that this social impulse is strong and irrepressible:

Unless we make ourselves hermits, we shall necessarily influence each other's opinions; so that the problem becomes how to fix belief, not in the individual merely, but in the community.

(5.378)

The government, the church or some similar social institution may fix the belief of the community using the *method of authority*: official beliefs are enforced through sanctions, coercion, incitement of the passions, and even violence and terror (5.379–82). The method of authority is far more stable than the method of tenacity, and, indeed, to Peirce's mind has much to recommend it, having built many of the great edifices of civilization and marked off the great epochs of history. But the method of authority is always in danger of failing because it cannot practically be sufficiently totalitarian. Some ideas will escape regulation, and some people will, at least in private, rise above the condition in which one opinion cannot influence another. Indeed, Peirce argues that an even 'wider sort of social feeling' than that which destabilizes the method of tenacity undermines the method of authority: people come to see that other nations and other centuries held different beliefs; that their own beliefs are an accident of their situation; and that they would have to place a high value indeed on their own beliefs for those observations not to induce some doubts.

Having broken the fetters of authority, the individual in a community may employ the *a priori method* of fixing belief: he believes whatever is agreeable to reason (5.382–3). Plato, for example, found it agreeable to reason that the celestial spheres should be proportioned to the lengths of string that produce harmonious chords. *A priori* beliefs are unlikely to be completely idiosyncratic precisely because they arise in communities. Nevertheless, *a priori* beliefs are not stable as fashions of opinion change.

Awareness of the cycle of intellectual fashions raises doubt in the method itself.

For Fish, interpretive communities form to provide needed constraints on interpretation. Some or all of these communities employ essentially the *a priori* method. In Peirce's view those who abandon the *a priori* method must seek a source of constraints external to ourselves – 'something upon which our thinking has no effect'. Peirce suggests that the *method of science* provides such a constraint (3.84–5). The fundamental hypothesis of the method of science is: 'There are real things, whose characters are entirely independent of our opinions about them.' These real things are subject to laws which may be ascertained through reasoning and experience, leading ultimately to one True conclusion. It is important to note that Peirce does not here abandon his denial of a privileged position behind one's beliefs. To maintain that there is a truth is not to claim that one is in possession of it. The method of science, in Peirce's view, is a method that in the fullness of time would attain the truth, but provides no guarantee for the present.[12] The method of science, in Peirce's view, is more stable than the other methods. Although it cannot be proved that there are reals, it cannot be disproved either; there is then, unlike with the other methods, no intrinsic disharmony in the foundation of the method. Furthermore, the disharmonies of the methods of tenacity and authority and the method *a priori* arise from a bedrock belief that there is a fact of the matter; otherwise, why should the fact that other people hold opinions different from our own or that intellectual fashions change concern us all? The social impulse that undermines the other methods does not undermine science. What is more, the method of science is used in everyday life wherever we know how to apply it. At its homeliest level it is common sense; and, in some settings, is one of those things that is not actually doubted. Finally, when carried on at a more refined level, the method has been a triumph, and not raised living doubts about its efficacy.[13] For Peirce, the method of science is the method of pragmatism, and the method of pragmatism is *critical commonsensism* (5.497–590). Rorty (1979: 176) similarly identifies pragmatism with common sense.

Realism

Pragmatism and the method of science, for Peirce, are closely tied up with realism. Peirce's metaphysics is complex and mostly beyond our present purposes. Brief mention of a few points is essential, nonetheless, to understanding the role of realism in Peirce's theory of inquiry.

Peirce's phenomenology involves three categories.[14] *Firstness* is Peirce's name for the category of existence out of relation to anything else. The qualitative impression of a particular shade of blue in isolation from all context is an example of firstness. *Secondness* is existence relative to other things. Secondness is epitomized by resistance; as Rorty (1979: 375) puts it, by the 'obduracy of things'. Experience for Peirce is the sum of ideas irresistibly borne in upon us: experience is largely secondness (7.437; cf. 2.138). As with experience, so with truth: 'The essence of truth lies in its resistance to being ignored' (2.139); truth is what is *so* regardless of what anyone thinks about it (2.135); 'truth crushed to the earth shall rise again' (5.408). *Thirdness* is mediation between things. Thirdness is expressed in generalizations, laws and universals. Peirce's categories can be summarized as first, second, third: presentness, struggle, law.

Realism for Peirce is the doctrine that asserts the existence of generals; that is, the secondness of thirdness. Peirce opposes *scholastic realism*, the belief that general principles are really operative in nature, to nominalism (5.101). *Nominalism* is the doctrine that only the particular is real, while types or universals are mental constructions (see, e.g., Goodman and Quine 1947). Goodman's view, endorsed by Weintraub, that worlds are made by theories in the same way as constellations are constructed by stargazers, is a classic example of what Peirce means to reject in opposing realism to nominalism. The adjective 'scholastic' acknowledges the affinity of Peirce's doctrine to those of certain medieval philosophers, philosophers who took indubitable beliefs as their starting point (5.312). In contrast, nominalists begin with Ockham's razor and Cartesian doubt.[15]

Realism has two important consequences for Peirce's theory of inquiry. First, it makes logic possible. For logic is the generalization and codification of procedures of inquiry that, given the way the world really is, lead us to truth – i.e., to unassailable belief. Logic would have nothing to codify if generality did not exist. Peirce rejects the non-existence of the general with the observation:

> to suppose a thing sporadic, spontaneous, irregular, is to suppose it departs from the ordinary course of things. That is blocking the road of inquiry; it is supposing the thing inexplicable, when a supposition can only be justified by its affording an explanation.
>
> (1.156)

A failing of nominalism, in Peirce's view, is that it constantly assumes things to be inexplicable, which is a poor theory on which to base any inquiry (1.170).

The recognition of the social impulse to doubt our own beliefs when confronted with the beliefs of others undermines the stability of the three methods of fixing belief other than science. For Peirce, the recognition that our beliefs may be wrong is not simply a social fact, it is also a consequence of realism. The second way in which realism is important to Peirce's theory of inquiry is that it provides the foundation for his doctrine of *fallibilism* (1.159–62). Peirce observes that laws cannot explain diversity; a Laplacian dream is one of unchanging regularity. But diversity is ubiquitous. Therefore, there must be exceptions to laws, and the best grounded of our beliefs must sometimes turn out to be false.[16] Thus realism at once raises the possibility of grounded knowledge and puts us on guard against complacency and the hubris of thinking that we know the final truth.

Logic

Logic in Peirce's view follows up the positive plank of realism, and looks for the conditions that would make our reasonings be secure (2.1).[17] Logic encompasses all of rational inquiry: 'Logic is the doctrine of truth, its nature and the manner in which it is discovered' (7.321). As such, logic is the study of the method of science as a means of fixing belief. Logic is a branch of ethics: it tells us how we ought to reason (2.7). Logic requires a notion of good and bad inferences; it is, therefore, a critical study (5.108). There is no need for logic in ordinary life; for by habit or natural instinct, people draw sufficiently correct conclusions to ensure survival (2.3). Once, however, one moves into unfamiliar fields, logic comes into its own (2.4, 5.368).

Inference, which is the machinery of logic, is the process by which one belief determines another belief, habit or action (7.354). A successful inference is one that leads from true premises to true conclusions. In one sense, then, Peirce is an empiricist with respect to logic. Since the object of inference is to carry the inquirer from the known to the unknown, and since all reasoning refers to the future, one cannot know that the conclusion of an inference is in fact true in advance, at the very point when an inference is demanded and useful (2.146, 5.365, 5.461, 7.102). Consequently, useful inferences cannot be *sui generis* or *ad hoc*. Logic is therefore a product of thirdness: conclusions justified in one case are justified in analogous cases (5.108). The study of logic is, therefore, largely the study of *leading* or *guiding principles*, general rules by which one belief determines another (4.62–4, 5.367, 5.440–1).

Valid inference is inference according to leading principles which are in fact true. Peirce is not embarrassed by appealing to facts rather than form in justifying inference: it is facts, after all, that are pragmatically useful (2.214, 7.325). Material validity, therefore, is prior and decisive. The interest in leading principles, however, is not in the particular case, but in whether they are true or false in general (5.367). As generalizations, rules or habits governing the determination of truth, leading principles are all propositional and, therefore, representational. This opens up the possibility of a formal validity, a study of the circumstances in which leading principles cannot be false (7.461). Peirce, as noted earlier, does not exempt logic or mathematics from either the pitfall or the promise of thirdness: like all beliefs, leading principles are subject to fallibilism, they may be false; like all subjects, leading principles, the objects of critical logic, exemplify diversity. Logic or critical inquiry, in Peirce's view, evolves.

Peirce divides inference into explicative inference, which derives conclusions from premises known or presumed to be true, and ampliative inference, which justifies conclusions on the basis of particular facts. Explicative inference includes classical deductive logic, mathematics, and probabilistic and statistical deductions; the last two being deductions with probabilities as their subject matter (2.694, 2.785). Perhaps Peirce's most original contribution to logic was the recognition that ampliative inference could be further divided into induction and abduction.

Abduction (also known as hypothesis, presumption and retroduction) takes the general form:

> The surprising fact, C, is observed;
> But if A were true, C would be a matter of course,
> Hence, there is reason to suspect A is true.
>
> (5.189, cf. 2.264)

Kepler's laws of planetary motion are a paradigm of abduction: the particular measurements of centuries of astronomers would have their observed patterns if planetary orbits were elliptical; therefore there is some reason to think that they are elliptical. Similarly, Planck's inference of the quantum theory from the observed spectra of irradiating bodies is again a paradigmatic abduction. Abductions are not disguised deductions. As such they would clearly be invalid, committing the fallacy of affirming the consequence. Indeed, there is no guarantee of the truth of an abductive inference; in most cases the inference will be false. Abduction is thus a weak form of inference; but 'abduction is Originary in respect of being the only kind of argument which starts an idea' (2.96, cf. 2.777, 5.145). Abduction is a type of inference because it is governed by leading principles subject to critical logic, and because it carries some measure of determinative force over our beliefs. Considerations of economy of money, time, thought and energy are the important guides to abductive/inductive inquiry (2.780, 5.600; also see Peirce's early paper applying marginal analysis to science, 'Note on the economy of research' (1876) (7.139–61) and Wible 1992).

Although abductions are typically easy to doubt, Peirce notices that the subjective likelihood of an abduction sometimes becomes objective (by which he means 'indubitable'). Sense perception illustrates this well. Peirce argues that sense perception is a limiting case of abduction, an abduction immune to immediate criticism (5.181, 5.183). Perceptions are a sort of compelled interpretation (5.291, 5.584–6, 7.622, 7.627). Perceptions can be criticized, but only at one remove. The beliefs that they compel may be judged to be illusory or false when confronted with other beliefs. In recognizing the interpretive content of the most neutral observation, Peirce anticipates many elements in modern epistemology as well as recent pragmatism. There is no unmediated knowledge, no getting behind one's perceptual beliefs.

Induction for Peirce is the experimental testing of a theory (5.145). It cannot originate ideas; it can only measure the degree to which a theory, a prior abduction, fits the facts. The conflation of induction and abduction is, Peirce believed, the greatest source of confusion in science (7.218). Induction is not sterile. Peirce himself spent thirty years making exacting gravitational measurements for the United States Coast Survey. This experience may account for his observation that the validity of induction consists in its being a method that if persisted in will lead to the ultimate correction of errors (2.769, 5.170). This point is familiar to the econometrician: in a well-formulated regression, the standard errors of coefficient estimates shrink as sample size grows. Of course, the interpretation of the regression is parasitic on a prior abduction. If the functional form does not correspond to the underlying process that generated the actual data, then the coefficients, no matter how accurately measured, do not measure anything of interest.

THE WEB OF BELIEF

Rorty (1979: 170ff.) holds up Willard Quine's account of the structure of theories as a paradigm of modern pragmatism. He dissents from Quine's account only in that he sees no reason to prefer, as Quine does, science to arts, politics or religion as successors to philosophy (Rorty 1979: 171). The power of Peirce's theory of inquiry can be seen by using it to analyse Quine's account of the relationship between theory and experience.

In his famous article, 'Two dogmas of empiricism' (1951), Quine argues that statements are confirmed or disconfirmed as a corporate body rather than individually. Quine likens all belief and knowledge to

> a man-made fabric which impinges on experience only along the edges. Or, to change the figure, total science is like a field of force whose boundary conditions are experience. A conflict with experience at the periphery occasions readjustments in the interior of the field. Truth values have to be redistributed over some of our statements. Reevaluation of some statements entails reevaluation of others, because of their logical interconnections – the logical laws being in turn simply certain further elements of the field. Having reevaluated one statement we must reevaluate some others, which may be statements logically connected with the first or may be the statements of logical connections themselves. But the total field is so underdetermined by its boundary conditions, experience, that there is much latitude of choice as to what statements to reevaluate in the light of any single contrary experience. No particular experiences are linked

with any particular statements in the interior of the field, except indirectly through considerations of equilibrium affecting the field as a whole.

(Quine 1951: 42–3)

The consequences of Quine's 'field-of-force' model is the rejection of reductionism: 'any statement can be held true come what may, if we make drastic enough adjustments elsewhere in the system', and '. . . no statement is immune to revision' (Quine 1951: 43). Together, these conclusions are often referred to as the Quine/Duhem thesis, after Pierre Duhem, the French physicist who early in the century advocated similar views. A further consequence of Quine's model is that no statement is analytically true in the sense of being beyond rejection. At best, analyticity expresses one's relatively firm resolve to maintain a statement in the face of even the most recalcitrant experience – a matter of degree, not of kind.

Quine believes that theories should be judged on a pragmatic standard. As a physicist, Quine (1951: 44) believes '. . . in physical objects and not in Homer's gods' and considers '. . . it a scientific error to believe otherwise'. Nevertheless, both the gods and physical objects are on the same 'epistemological footing'. The pragmatic standard, Quine believes, only suggests that '. . . the myth of physical objects is epistemologically superior to most in that it has proven more efficacious than other myths as a device for working a manageable structure into the flux of experience' (Quine 1951: 44). To use Fish's terminology, physics and Homeric religion form different interpretive communities. Rorty's dissent from Quine is merely a challenge to Quine's assumption that the values of science are the only ones worth pursuing. His question to Quine might be: efficacious for what purpose?

'Efficacy' in Quine's usage must mean something like the relative ease of accommodating recalcitrant experience into the field of force. It is similar to Peirce's suggestion that it is considerations of economy – of time, money, thought and energy – which dictate which hypotheses should be inductively tested, and, therefore, which hypotheses should become part of our current beliefs. To account for a pragmatic standard of efficacy, both Peirce and Quine must be able to make sense of disconfirming or recalcitrant experience. Peirce's theory of inquiry suggests, as we shall presently see in more detail, that, if Quine's field-of-force metaphor is taken seriously, an adequate account of recalcitrance compels us to reject the Quine/Duhem thesis in its usual form.

As already observed, Peirce maintains a mixed coherence/correspondence theory of truth (see subsection 'Truth', above). Truth is correspondence to reality that is mediated through perceptual judgements. But perceptual judgements are simply another class of abductive inference. Thus there is no appeal to privileged observations outside or behind one's beliefs nor to an unattainable standard of truth. Seen as a coherence theory, Peirce's theory of truth involves commitments of belief in the process of interpretation (i.e., introducing a new belief into the system) and in the process of revision (i.e., establishing coherence among all beliefs). Quine's 'field' model must involve both these processes if it is to account for recalcitrant experience.

The field of force in Quine's metaphor has an interior and a periphery. Experience impinges at the periphery and compels revision, either there or on the interior. Peripheral statements or beliefs are those which are more 'germane' to sense experience (Quine 1951: 43). Each instance, every impingement, requires interpretation of what counts as an instance. This is equivalent to Peirce's rule of predesignation in abductive/inductive inquiry (2.735–40). Since perceptual judgement, for Peirce, is a limiting case of abduction, perceptual categories are limiting cases of predesignation: a perceptual judgement must be made – i.e., one must believe that some percept fits into certain perceptual categories – before any experience is registered at all. Fish and Weintraub make similar points when they assert that interpretations constrain and constitute the facts rather than the other way round (Fish 1980: 293 passim; Weintraub 1991: 150, 151).

The peripheral statements in Quine's field model interpret experience and account, in part, for the compulsive force of recalcitrant experience by introducing new beliefs into the field that must be dealt with.[18] Although in Peirce's view the beliefs produced by the abductive inference of perceptual judgement are fallible, they cannot be immediately criticized. One cannot get behind one's beliefs; rather all criticism must be based on other beliefs (2.141, 2.142, 7.662; cf. 5.181, 7.437, 7.626). The result for Quine is that on the field of a particular theory, perceptual beliefs (at least) are fixed at any given time. They can be determined veridical or non-veridical with regard to other beliefs, but they cannot be ignored.

The idea of a periphery/interior split makes sense only if interior statements do not provide interpretation of experience – i.e., are not beliefs about perceptual categories and are not germane to sense experience. If they did interpret experience directly, there would be little sense in saying that sense experience impinges upon the periphery rather than on the interior statements directly. Interior statements like 'the earth is spherical' or 'John and James are brothers' are not disconfirmed by complexes of bare sensations. Instead, a peripheral statement defines a recalcitrant experience – e.g., a ship never getting to India by sailing west or John and James being of different racial types. The experience is believed because of a perceptual judgement, and is seen to involve these interior statements because of beliefs in certain logical links. The germaneness of peripheral statements to sense experience thus distinguishes them far more radically from the theoretical interior statements than Quine imagines: single peripheral statements serve to interpret experience for interior statements as well as for themselves.

If any experience impinges at the periphery at all, the immediate, uncriticizable nature of perceptual judgement ensures that a new belief is introduced into the field of force. With the introduction of this new belief, the stage of revision is reached. Even though it is the peripheral statement which determines immediately whether or not an experience is recalcitrant, both Peirce and Quine recognize that there is some latitude in resolving the inconsistency. The perceptual belief can be accepted and the theory disconfirmed or modified or it can be explained away as hallucination or error.

The compulsive force of recalcitrant experience derives, in part, from the necessary introduction of new beliefs into the field whenever experience is interpreted through (perceptual) judgement. This compulsion is not enough to determine that the experience be recalcitrant. It is only recalcitrant if a logical inconsistency exists between the new belief and other beliefs in the field. Given such an inconsistency, what is it that compels revision of some beliefs in order to remove it? Lewis Carroll (1895) demonstrated in 'What Achilles said to the tortoise' that, if a logical rule is taken as just another premise of an argument, nothing compels the conclusion. Similarly, if logical laws are '. . . simply certain further statements of the system, certain further elements of the field', then nothing requires, as Quine claims, that '. . . truth values *have* to be redistributed over some of our statements' (Quine 1951: 42; emphasis added). If logical laws did not occupy a preferred position, recalcitrant experience would have no compulsive force. At one level, of course, logical laws *could* be further statements of the system. There can be no objection to altering the law of excluded middle to simplify quantum mechanics (Quine 1951: 43). At another level, however, either the law of excluded middle applies to quantum mechanics or it does not. The notion of recalcitrant experience in Quine's field model requires that some beliefs about logical rules remain fixed and unrevisable relative to the field. This point is implicit in Quine's emphasis on the redistribution of truth values.

Some methodological beliefs stand outside the field in the sense that they are rules governing the manipulation of statements in the field in the face of recalcitrant experience. To be outside the field is to be immune to revision. Quine's two principles – that any statement can be held true come what may and that no statement is immune from revision – are only true in a relative sense. Peirce agrees that any belief may be revised. Revision of infallible methodological beliefs, however, is a matter of committing or not committing oneself to them. It may turn out in practice that everyone agrees on the most general methodological beliefs, but it cannot be the case that they must agree. Revision of some indubitable beliefs – methodological rules or perceptual categories – may be possible, but only once their primacy has been called into doubt, either by logical considerations or success at developing new perceptual categories. Revision of ordinary beliefs can be compelled only if the class of infallible or indubitable beliefs is taken as given. Conversely, if these are given, particular ordinary beliefs must be revised in the face of recalcitrant experience. Without infallible, indubitable beliefs, there is no pragmatic standard of efficacy at all.

PRAGMATICISM, COMMUNITY AND PRIVILEGE

The central point about Quine's field model generalizes beyond the scientific context in which he first formulated it. Rorty (1979: 202) recognizes that Quine's periphery/core distinction (beliefs that express facts versus beliefs that do not) rests on his ontological commitments. Rorty would prefer a broader set of interests and values. But, as Fish (1980: 296) observes, judgements about whether or not those interests or values are furthered can only be made if we assume standards of judgement that are locally indubitable: '... assumptions are not all held at the same level and ... a challenge to one proceeds within the precinct of others that are, at least for the time being, exempt from challenge'. Science, Peirce believed, differed from philosophy as it was practised in his day (and no doubt in ours as well) in that it does not set up the individual as the ultimate judge of truth:

> In sciences in which men come to agreement, when a theory has been broached it is considered to be on probation until this agreement is reached. After it is reached, the question of certainty becomes an idle one, because there is no one left who doubts it. We individually cannot reasonably hope to attain the ultimate philosophy which we pursue; we can only seek it, therefore, for the *community* of philosophers. Hence, if disciplined and candid minds carefully examine a theory and refuse to accept it, this ought to create doubts in the mind of the author of the theory himself.
>
> (5.265)

Modern pragmatism seems to echo Peirce's notion of community. To examine the parallel, consider the problem of individuation and membership in a community.[19] Fish's interpretive communities are plural, because they are offered as a solution to the problem of why people may differ radically in their understanding of texts without abandoning principle. But communication across interpretive communities is blocked. Who is a member of any particular interpretive community is also a question of interpretation. 'The only proof of membership is a nod of recognition from someone in the same community, someone who says to you what neither of us could ever prove to a third party' (Fish 1980: 173). Both Fish (1980: 171) and Weintraub (1991: 7) recognize that the individual might belong to more than one community. Nevertheless both emphasize not the potential interconnectedness but the independence of the interpretive community. Where Fish stresses the lack of communication between communities, Weintraub stresses the idleness of criticism from beyond the borders of the community. Rorty's (1979: 189) position is similar to Weintraub's: philosophers of mind cannot reinforce or diminish '. . . the confidence in our own assertions which the approval of our peers gives us'. And who are our peers? Rorty (1979: 190, fn. 22) denies that philosophers have anything to say even on who to regard as part of the larger human community; at the same time, he suggests that novelists and poets do. Such an anti-philosophic position might seem a strange one for a professional philosopher to take. One should recall, however, that Rorty (1979: ch. 8) seeks an 'edifying' philosophy, and prefers the more poetical and novelistic philosophers, Nietzsche, Heidegger, Wittgenstein and Sartre, to epistemologists. To the extent that a philosopher succeeds in saying something that matters on the question of community, he is an edifying philosopher, which is as close to a poet or novelist as makes no difference. Weintraub's distinction between Methodology and methodology can work similarly. Had Kaldor's criticisms of general equilibrium connected with the practice of general equilibrium theorists, they would have had to have been reclassified as methodology. The term 'Methodology', then, simply becomes an aspersion to be cast on criticisms that fail to connect. Social privilege, a station from which to decide who is in and who is out, what is Methodology and what is methodology, seems to have replaced epistemological privilege in the pragmatist account of knowledge. Despite his quite specific listing of economists whose criticisms misfire because they come from outside economics and are, therefore, Methodological, Weintraub might take the view that it is really only the practitioner, and not even the non-Methodological commentator like himself, who can ultimately judge which criticisms connect and which arguments are persuasive. To make this move, however, is to render the distinction between Methodology and methodology entirely orthographical. For the arguments of philosophers of science and professional economic methodologists do sometimes appeal to economists and help to shape their economics (Samuelson's use of Percy Bridgman's operationalism is one example, and is even cited by Weintraub 1990: 268).[20] Weintraub's argument would then have to be that in particular cases these appeals are materially wrong-headed. But that amounts to saying, use good arguments, not bad ones. And who could quarrel with that?

Rorty's disdain for Peirce appears to be rooted in Peirce's architectonic approach to philosophy and inquiry: system-builders do not appeal to Rorty's humanism.[21] But Peirce's humanist credentials are, in fact, secure: after all, Peirce believed such things as '. . . nothing is truer than true poetry' (1.315). Still, he did not regard system-building as opposed to humanist values:

I know very well that science is not the whole of life, but I believe in the division of labour among intellectual agencies. The apostle of Humanism says that professional philosophists 'have rendered philosophy like unto themselves, abstruse, arid, abstract and abhorrent'. But I conceive that some branches of science are not in a healthy sate if they are *not* abstruse, arid and abstract, in which case, like Aristotelianism which is this gentleman's [F. C. S. Schiller's] particular *bête noire*, it will be as Shakespeare said (*of it* remember)

> 'Not harsh and crabbed, as dull fools suppose,
> But musical as is Apollo's lute,' etc.

(5.537)[22]

A division of labour presupposes a common enterprise. For Peirce there is a difference between the systematic and the unsystematic, but no unbridgeable gulf between them. Rorty confuses the desire for a privileged framework, a thing Peirce's theory of belief cannot allow, with the urge to generalize and systematize inquiry. Is there any reason why an edifying philosophy needs to be unsystematic, local or parochial?

Rorty (1979: ch. 7) identifies epistemology with commensuration. He looks for a world without any cultural need for constraints, one in which the commensurability of different systems of belief is not sought (Rorty 1979: 315–16). By 'commensurability' Rorty (1979: 316) means that conflicting beliefs could '. . . be brought under a set of rules which will tell us how rational agreement can be reached on what would settle the issue on every point where statements seem to conflict'. Peirce's pragmatism, unlike Rorty's (1979: 317) philosopher-king, does not set up to know everyone else's common ground from an ultimate and privileged perspective. The pragmatist is instead like a surveyor: he climbs a high hill to gain perspective, to map out other people's common ground from a better vantage point; he is, nevertheless, bound to the earth, and his vision is always more or less limited; yet, relative to the valley and the foothills, his station is genuinely detached and locally privileged.

Rorty prefers conversation to adjudication of competing beliefs. But he also concedes that good conversation requires norms. He even admits that hermeneutics is parasitic on epistemology, that to use a hermeneutical approach when epistemology will do is at best bad taste and at worst madness; and that hermeneutics is intrinsically oppositional, needing epistemological projects for its own self-definition (Rorty 1979: 366). This seems little different from Peirce's observations that some of our beliefs are indubitable, that none is infallible, and that doubt requires prior belief. It is, therefore, difficult in the end to say whether Peirce and Rorty occupy common ground after all. There is perhaps a pragmatic difference, a difference in how true followers of Peirce and true followers of Rorty would behave. Peirce believes that the object of inquiry is to seek the common ground on which the truth of abductions can be inductively decided. Rorty believes that we should be prepared to be unable to find that common ground. Peirce replies that, while it may be true that such common ground does not exist, to operate on that assumption is to block the road of enquiry and to abandon reason. The true social impulse is against this assumption. Rorty (1979: 318) appeals for civility in the face of a recognition that we share neither common goals nor common ground. Tolerance, however, requires humility; and Rorty provides us with no basis for humility. True intellectual humility arises from the faith that there is a truth; the acknowledgement that others, as well as we, seek it; and the recognition that we may not have already found it. Without true humility, we run the risk of slipping into Peirce's method of tenacity for fixing belief.

The danger of the method of tenacity is often thought to be relativism. But that is wrong: the deeper danger is Balkanization. Relativism arises when one recognizes that the beliefs of others may be as good as one's own beliefs. There is, however, as Peirce observed, no reason to accord any respect to the beliefs of others unless one senses that perhaps the others might just be right after all, unless one senses that there is a fact of the matter. Relativism, for Fish (1980: 319; cf. Rorty 1982: ch. 9), '. . . is a position one can entertain, it is not a position one can occupy'. He claims that one cannot get sufficient distance from one's own beliefs to put them on a par with the beliefs of others (cf. Fish 1980: 316). Surely, this is right as far as it goes; it follows from the indubitability of some of our beliefs. But, for Peirce, experience and the social impulse make us doubt some of our beliefs, not because we are sure that others are right, but because we recognize that others believe differently, and that there is a fact about the matter, so that adjudication is possible and necessary. Fish acknowledges the fear of relativism, and looks for constraints in the interpretive community. If the social impulse is limited, and humility does not extend beyond the bounds of the interpretive community, widening the search for common ground, then the interpretive community runs the risk of slipping into the corporate solipsism of Peirce's method of authority or *a priori* method for fixing belief.

That Fish's analysis appears persuasive is largely because it is applied to literature. Fish speaks of interpretations making texts and interpretive communities generating the constraints on interpretations that at once provide the common ground within a community and demarcate one community from another. But there is one aspect of the text that is common to all communities: the ink on paper.[23] The object of literary critical interpretation – in most cases and for the most part – is exhausted in the sense that an interpretation cannot be checked against new information related to the text but not available when the interpretation was formulated.[24] That is, there is nothing analogous to sense perception in Quine's web of scientific belief to introduce recalcitrant experience that we *must* deal with. The irresolvability of literary and some historical disputes (not excluding natural and economic history) arises from their particularity and givenness. Theoretical accounts are counterfactual: they are constructed out of conditionals (if *A* then *B*), and the theory is asserted to hold even in those cases where the antecedent (*A*) does not occur. In these disputes, there may be no new evidence. We cannot provide alternative antecedents to generate discriminating facts. The parallel situation arises frequently in empirical economics. Consider the fitted or predicted values from a regression or a test to establish what caused *x* at time *t* in a stochastic environment. When all is said and done, the estimated result may be nothing but a low probability drawn from the far tail of the distribution. The only evidence relevant to discrimination is new data, although even that is not finally conclusive. This is, of course, a paradigm of Peirce's account of induction as a method of establishing a numerical fact that must succeed, but only if persisted in indefinitely (5.145, 5.170).

The absence of a common and irrepressible experience in literary criticism (although not necessarily in literary production) distinguishes it from science. Lacking such an experience, there is nothing to block the move to solipsistic interpretive communities or to undermine the authoritarian possibilities of a narrowed social impulse.[25] For Fish, you are a member of my interpretive community and can understand me because you already accept my interpretation. There is nothing to shatter our mutual complacency, except perhaps boredom (on which see Rorty 1979: 136; Peirce 5.520). For Peirce, experience destroys complacency:

> In all the works on pedagogy that ever I read ... I don't remember that any one has advocated a system of teaching by practical jokes, mostly cruel. That, however, describes the method of our great teacher, Experience. She says
>
>> Open your mouth and shut your eyes
>> And I'll give you something to make you wise;
>
> and thereupon she keeps her promise, and seems to take her pay in the form of tormenting us.
>
> (5.51)

That the practical jokes are at the expense of us all is socially broadening. Ultimately, Peirce would not deny the existence of interpretive communities; but he would insist that their borders are extremely porous. As Dewey (1938: 50) puts it: 'In an intellectual sense, there are many languages, though in a social sense there is but one.' Perhaps the most unintentionally telling anecdote of the title essay of Fish's (1980) *Is There a Text in This Class?* is that of the student who originally asks that protean question to the misapprehension of her instructor. Fish takes the story to illustrate that interpretations are made, not discovered, and belong to particular interpretive communities. But the student is finally able to bring the instructor around to at least comprehend her own interpretation. In a pragmatic (or pragmaticistic) sense, we are all insiders to the only interpretive community that matters.

And therefore never send to know for whom the *bell* tolls; it tolls for *thee*.

(John Donne, *Meditation XVII*)

ACKNOWLEDGEMENTS

I am grateful to Roger Backhouse, Denis Donoghue, James Hartley, Abraham Hirsch, Christopher Hookway, E. Roy Weintraub and Nancy Wulwick for comments on an earlier draft.

NOTES

1 Fish (1980) hardly mentions philosophers, the main exceptions being John Searle and John Austin. Nonetheless, the pragmatic cast of Fish's work is brought sharply home to anyone who reads his *Is There a Text in This Class?* (1980) side by side with Rorty's *Philosophy and the Mirror of Nature* (1979) as I have recently done.
2 Peirce's surname sounds like 'purse' and is not to be confused with the more common 'Pierce'.
3 Whether Dewey is, as Rorty believes, a true pragmatist or a Peircian pragmaticist is a question that goes well beyond the scope of this essay.
4 For example, Karl Popper (1972: 212) refers to Peirce as '. . . the great American mathematician and physicist and, I believe, one of the greatest philosophers of all time'. Nicholas Rescher (1978: ix) says of Peirce: 'More than any other student of the nature of science, he pries into the thing we always wanted to know but were afraid to ask.' A full-length biography has just become available (Brent 1993).
5 In keeping with the common practice of Peirce scholars, references to Peirce's *Collected Papers* will be made according to the format (volume number, paragraph number, e.g., 5.51). Partly because of his personal style, but more because of the vicissitudes of his life, Peirce's writings are scattered and fragmentary. A number of only partially satisfactory anthologies are available as introductions to Peirce's thought; see Peirce (1923, 1955, 1966, 1972). Recently, Peirce's complete Cambridge lectures of 1898 have been published (Peirce 1992).
6 I single out Weintraub because his article (1990) and most recent book (1991) give clear statements of connection with Rorty, Fish and Nelson Goodman (who is not generally considered a pragmatist). I use Weintraub's recent work instrumentally and avoid a systematic discussion of Weintraub's views because the book and the article have been the subject of a vigorous exchange between Roger Backhouse (1992a,b,c,d) and Weintraub (1992a,b).
7 Both Rorty and Peirce lament the fact that disputes can take on an unproductive life of their own:

It would be foolish to keep conversation on the subject going once everyone, or the majority, or the wise, are satisfied, but of course we *can*.

(Rorty 1979: 159)

[The pragmatist] is none of those overcultivated Oxford dons – I hope their day is over – whom any discovery that brought quietus to a vexed question would inevitably vex because it would end the fun of arguing around it and about it and over it.

(Peirce 5.520)

8 Peirce's views would in a number of respects appear to be closely related to those of Popper – particularly Popper's fallibilism and conventionalism; see Freeman (1983) and Popper (1983) for a detailed discussion.

9 Rorty (1979: 275, fn. 16) takes the milder view that less controversial, but not privileged, beliefs can control more controversial ones. This is merely a difference in tone, for neither Peirce nor Fish hold that indubitable beliefs are anything more than *locally* infallible or *temporarily* privileged.

10 A belief is *general* to the extent that the law of excluded middle does not apply.

11 In a similar vein, see Rorty's (1979: 180) discussion of Wilfrid Sellars.

12 Peirce asserts that scientific belief will ultimately converge on Truth – i.e., on stable, fixed belief. He does not provide a completely compelling argument for his view. It may be motivated from his own experience as an experimentalist in which he observed the way that precise measurements, repeated using different methods, tend to converge to some central or limiting value. It is also clear that he regards the assumption of convergence as the only one that can motivate the scientific enterprise – i.e., not block the path of research. It is thus implicit in the life of the scientist, but is not an independent justification of that life.

13 Some believe that Peirce has his tongue firmly in cheek in discussing the methods other than science: these methods are straw men that allow him to present a Whiggish account of the development of method towards its final flowering in science. It is, however, difficult to read his essay 'The fixation of belief', and to doubt that he is serious in noting the advantages of the other methods: his analysis is wholly consistent with his general theory of belief. For a similar view on Peirce's sincerity in this regard, see Hacking (1983: 59). Incidentally, Hacking's evaluation of Peirce is strikingly different from Rorty's; Hacking writes: 'Peirce and Nietzsche [a Rorty hero] are the two most memorable philosophers writing a century ago.'

14 The names of Peirce's fundamental categories do not derive from simple enumeration, reflecting a lack of imagination, which would be beyond belief given Peirce's forays into improvements in scientific and philosophical nomenclature. Rather, 'firstness', 'secondness' and 'thirdness' are derived from Peirce's studies of the logic of relatives and his conclusion that the properties these terms designated must be represented as monadic, dyadic and triadic relations. Peirce has an almost cabalistic attachment to the number three. It is hardly surprising to discover that, having been brought up a Unitarian, Peirce in adulthood joined the trinitarian Episcopal Church (Brent 1993).

15 Peirce does not deny the heuristic value of Ockham's razor: it may be the most economical way for science to proceed. In practical contexts, however, it may be useless. The living beliefs of an experienced sea-captain may save the ship in a storm; whereas Ockham's razor may simply be a fancy way of spelling Shipwreck (5.60).

16 Peirce elsewhere denies that laws are ever exact (6.201–2). He endorses some-

thing like Lucretius's belief that objects are normally subject to law, but from time to time swerve ever so slightly off their destined track. Peirce is in a sense ahead of science. He advocates *tychism*, the doctrine that the universe is *fundamentally* stochastic (i.e., the randomness is 'really' there and not just an artefact of our ignorance, as might be maintained by advocates of pre-quantum thermodynamics). He also realizes that irregularity at one level may, as in the gas laws, become an element of regularity at a higher level (1.157). In all this, Peirce predates quantum mechanics, which made these Peircian doctrines commonplaces of scientific practice.

17 For a fuller discussion of Peirce's logic, see Harris and Hoover (1980).

18 Quine's metaphor of the interior and periphery appears to echo Lakatos's (1970) famous metaphor of the hardcore and protective belt of research programmes (see Hoover 1991 for a detailed criticism of Lakatos's methodology). The relationships between Lakatos and pragmatism are beyond the scope of the present paper.

19 Similar problems of individuation and communication arise in Lakatos's methodology of scientific research programmes; see Hoover (1991).

20 Abraham Hirsch has pointed out to me (private communication) that the dismissal of Friedman's monetary theories by many economists on the grounds that he has no adequate causal account of the transmission mechanism (the so-called 'black box' argument) is a good example of the influence of methodological considerations in the thinking of practising economists.

21 Rorty (1982: 161) refers to Peirce's 'undeserved apotheosis'. Peirce's '. . . contribution to pragmatism was merely to have given it a name, and to have stimulated William James. Peirce himself remained the most Kantian of thinkers – the most convinced that philosophy gave us an all-embracing ahistorical context in which every other species of discourse could be assigned its proper place and rank.' Rorty's assessment is strange in several ways: it does not appear to have been shared by either James or Dewey, whom Rorty sees as reacting to Kantianism; it stands in sharp contrast to Rorty's earlier (1961) warm appreciation of Peirce as an intellectual kindred spirit to Wittgenstein; and it seems odd to charge Peirce, who stresses the evolution of knowledge, a kind of intellectual Darwinism, with preferring an ahistorical context.

22 An editor's note to this passage points out that Peirce has mistaken Milton for Shakespeare.

23 It is not strictly true that communities must share texts in this sense: consider the Roman Catholic, Protestant and Jewish bibles or the recent controversy over the 'corrected' edition of James Joyce's *Ulysses*.

24 The qualification 'in most cases and for the most part' is necessary, for example, because in some cases scholarship adds to fragmentary texts or because some literary theories appeal to historical, biographical or social information that may not be exhausted in the intended sense.

25 That Peirce was aware of the dangers of such a move is evident in his discussion of intellectual repression (5.386); that the risks remain live is evident in Fish's (1992) discussion of the First Amendment to the United States Constitution.

BIBLIOGRAPHY

Backhouse, R. E. (1992a) 'How should we approach the history of economic thought, fact, fiction or moral tale?', *Journal of the History of Economic Thought* 14(1): 18–35.

Backhouse, R. E. (1992b) 'Reply: history's many dimensions', *Journal of the History of Economic Thought* 14(2): 277–84.

Backhouse, R. E. (1992c) 'The constructivist critique of economic methodology', *Methodus* 4(1): 65–82.

Backhouse, R. E. (1992d) 'Rejoinder: why methodology matters', *Methodus* 4(2): 58–62.

Brent, J. (1993) *Charles Sanders Peirce: A Life*, Bloomington and Indianapolis: University of Indiana Press.

Caldwell, B. (1982) *Beyond Positivism: Economic Methodology in the Twentieth Century*, London: Allen & Unwin.

Carroll, L. (1895) 'What Achilles said to the tortoise', *Mind* 4: 278–80.

Cross, R. (1982) 'The Duhem/Quine thesis, Lakatos and the appraisal of theories in macroeconomics', *Economic Journal* 92(366): 320–40.

Dewey, J. (1938) *Logic, The Theory of Inquiry*, New York: Henry Holt.

Fish, S. (1980) *Is There a Text in This Class? The Authority of Interpretive Communities*, Cambridge: Cambridge University Press.

Fish, S. (1992) 'There's no such thing as free speech and it's a good thing too', *Boston Review* 17(1): 3–5, 23–6.

Freeman, E. (1983) 'Charles Peirce and objectivity in philosophy', in E. Freeman (ed.), *The Relevance of Charles Peirce*, La Salle, IL: Hegler Institute.

Goodman, N. and Quine, W. V. O. (1947) 'Steps toward a constructive nominalism', *Journal of Symbolic Logic* 12: 105–22.

Hacking, I. (1983) *Representing and Intervening: Introductory Topics in the Philosophy of Natural Science*, Cambridge: Cambridge University Press.

Harris, F. and Hoover, K. D. (1980) 'Abduction and the new riddle of induction', *The Monist* 63(3): 329–41.

Hirsch, A. and de Marchi, N. (1990) *Milton Friedman: Economics in Theory and Practice*, New York: Harvester Wheatsheaf.

Hoover, K. D. (1988) *The New Classical Macroeconomics: A Sceptical Inquiry*, Oxford: Basil Blackwell.

Hoover, K. D. (1991) 'Scientific research program or tribe? A joint appraisal of Lakatos and the new classical macroeconomics', in N. de Marchi and M. Blaug (eds), *Appraising Economic Theories: Studies in the Methodology of Research Programmes*, Aldershot: Edward Elgar.

James, W. (1907/1949) *Pragmatism: A New Name for Some Old Ways of Thinking; Together with Four Related Essays from the Meaning of Truth*, New York: Longmans, Green.

Lakatos, I. (1970) 'Falsification and the methodology of scientific research programmes', in I. Lakatos and A. Musgrave (eds), *Criticism and the Growth of Knowledge*, Cambridge: Cambridge University Press.

McCloskey, D. N. (1985) *The Rhetoric of Economics*, Madison: University of Wisconsin Press.

Peirce, C. S. (1923) *Chance, Love and Logic*, with a supplementary essay by John Dewey, M. R. Cohen (ed.), London: Kegan Paul, Trench, Trubner; New York: Harcourt, Brace.

Peirce, C. S. (1931–58) *Collected Papers of Charles Sanders Peirce*, vols 1–8, A. W. Burks, C. Hartshorne and P. Weiss (eds), Cambridge, MA: Belknap Press.

Peirce, C. S. (1955) *Philosophical Writings of Peirce*, J. Buchler (ed.), New York: Dover Publications.

Peirce, C. S. (1966) *Selected Writings (Values in a Universe of Chance)*, P. P. Wiener (ed.), New York: Dover Publications.

Peirce, C. S. (1972) *Charles S. Peirce: The Essential Writings*, E. C. Moore (ed.), New York: Harper & Row.

Peirce, C. S. (1992) *Reasoning and the Logic of Things: The Cambridge Conferences Lectures of 1898*, K. L. Ketner (ed.), Cambridge, MA: Harvard University Press.

Popper, K. R. (1972) [1979] *Objective Knowledge; An Evolutionary Approach*, revised edn, Oxford: Clarendon Press.

Popper, K. R. (1983) 'Freeman on Peirce's anticipations of Popper', in E. Freeman (ed.), *The Relevance of Charles Peirce*, La Salle, IL: Hegler Institute.

Quine, W. V. O. (1951) [1961] 'Two dogmas of empiricism', in *From a Logical Point of View*, 2nd edn, Cambridge, MA: Harvard University Press.

Rescher, N. (1978) *Peirce's Philosophy of Science*, Notre Dame, In: University of Notre Dame Press.

Rorty, R. (1961) 'Pragmatism, categories and language', *Philosophical Review* 70(2): 197–223.

Rorty, R. (1979) *Philosophy and the Mirror of Nature*, Princeton: Princeton University Press.

Rorty, R. (1982) *The Consequences of Pragmatism (Essays: 1972–1980)*, Minneapolis: University of Minnesota Press.

Weintraub, E. R. (1990) 'Methodology doesn't matter, but history of thought might', in S. Honkapohja (ed.), *The State of Macroeconomics*, Oxford: Basil Blackwell.

Weintraub, E. R. (1991) *Stabilizing Dynamics: Constructing Economic Knowledge*, Cambridge: Cambridge University Press.

Weintraub, E. R. (1992a) 'Comment: thicker is better', *Journal of the History of Economic Thought* 14(2): 271–6.

Weintraub, E. R. (1992b) 'Roger Backhouse's straw herring', *Methodus* 4(2): 53–7.

Wible, J. R. (1992) 'Cost–benefit analysis, utility theory, and economic aspects of Peirce's and Popper's conception of science', unpublished typescript. Department of Economics, Whittemore School of Business and Economics, University of New Hampshire, June.

Part IV

ECONOMICS AS DISCOURSE

15

HOW TO DO A RHETORICAL ANALYSIS, AND WHY

Donald N. McCloskey

Start with an example, taken from a book with which I largely agree, the first edition of Richard Posner's *Economic Analysis of Law*:

> Our survey of the major common law fields suggests that the common law exhibits a deep unity that is economic in character.... The common law method is to allocate responsibilities between people engaged in interacting activities in such a way as to maximize the joint value ... of the activities.... [T]he judge can hardly fail to consider whether the loss was the product of wasteful, uneconomical resource use. In a culture of scarcity, this is an urgent, an inescapable question.
>
> (Posner 1972: 98f.)

The argument in the passage is carried in part by the equivocal use of economic vocabulary: 'allocate', 'maximize', 'value', and 'scarcity' are technical words in economics, with precise definitions, but here they are used also in wider senses, to evoke a sense of scientific power, to claim precision without necessarily using it. The sweetest turn is the use of 'uneconomical', which is not a technical word in economics, but encapsulates the argument that in their courtrooms the judges follow economic models because to do otherwise would be 'wasteful'. The 'economical/uneconomical' figure of speech supports the claim that economic arguments (arguments about scarcity) are pervasive in the law. The claim is hammered home by treble repetition (technically, *commoratio*): first in this word 'uneconomical'; then in the reference to a culture of scarcity (a nice echo of 'a culture of poverty', that, from the other side of the tracks); and finally in the repetition of 'urgent, inescapable'.

People involved mutually in automobile accidents or breaches of contract are said to be 'engaged in interacting activities'. The interaction, however, does not extend to the political or moral systems of the society. A rancher and a railroad 'interact', but a judge does not 'interact' with people who think that big enterprises like railroads are blameworthy. A vocabulary of 'engaging in interacting activities' makes an appeal to the character of Scientist or Observer (technically, an 'ethical' argument).

Again, the passage uses the metaphor of 'deepness' in unity, as do other arguments trying to change the way we categorize the world. A critical legal theorist will tell you that the 'deep' structure of law is an apology for capitalism. The legal economist will tell you, as here, that the 'deep' structure is on the contrary a celebration of capitalism.

As I say, I come down on Posner's side. But that does not make him, or me, or Milton Friedman, immune from rhetorical scrutiny. The rhetorical reading is at least richer than the reading invited by the passage itself, which claims to merely represent the World.

WHY 'RHETORIC'?

Science is writing with intent, the intent to persuade other scientists, such as economic scientists. The study of such writing with intent has been called since the Greeks 'rhetoric'. Until the seventeenth century it was the core of education in the West and down to the present it remains, often unrecognized, the core of humanistic learning. A science like economics should be read skilfully, and if so the reading needs a rhetoric, the more explicit the better. The choice is between an implicit and naive rhetoric or an explicit and learned one, the naive rhetoric of significance tests, say, or the learned rhetoric that knows what it is arguing and why.

Rhetoric could of course be given another name – 'wordcraft', perhaps, or 'the study of argument'. The book that in 1987 began the 'rhetoric of inquiry' was subtitled 'Language and argument in scholarship and public affairs'. Yet it revived the old R word in the main title, *The Rhetoric of the Human Sciences*. Why? The word 'rhetoric' after all is used by newspapers as a synonym for the many words in English that sneer at speech: ornament, frill, hot air, advertising, slickness, deception, fraud. Thus the *Des Moines Register*, 'Senate campaign mired in rhetoric'.

But the newspapers vulgarized, too, the word 'pragmatism' shortly after its birth, by understanding it as unprincipled horse-trading. They defined 'anarchism' as bomb-throwing nihilism. They defined 'sentiment' as cheap emotionalism, 'morality' as prudery and 'family values' as social reaction. They defined 'science' as something no scientist practises. Scholarly usage should not be decided by the newspapers, or else their view will be all we have. We need a scholarly word for wordcraft. The ancient and honoured one will do.

The point of a 'rhetorical' analysis is merely to read with understanding. Attending graduate school will educate an economist to read some, supplying her with an implicit rhetoric for understanding. But the rhetoric in graduate school is incomplete and the understanding partial, a beginning but not the whole of economic science. What distinguishes good from bad economists, or even old from young economists, is additional sophistication about the rhetoric. Robert Solow or Milton Friedman or Herbert Stein do not know anything of classical rhetoric – they grew up at the nadir of rhetorical education – but they can spot when a formal assumption is being used well or badly, and can sense when this or that verbal device is appropriate. And the wordcraft that the best economists exercise by instinct can be taught, at least a little.

Classical rhetoric was merely a list of terms with some thinking attached. A classical architecture without terms for architrave, echinus, guttae, mutule, quoin and triglyph cannot see the Old Capitol in Iowa City (a Doric temple with Corinthian capital) as anything other than vaguely pretty (Summerson 1963: 16, 47–52). Likewise we need terms to describe scientific argument, or else we are reduced to the vague and unexamined aesthetics of 'deep', 'rigorous', 'elegant', 'convincing' in seeing an economic argument. Gerard Debreu, for example, uses such terms in defending abstract general equilibrium analysis on the grounds that it 'fulfills an intellectual need of many contemporary economic theorists, who therefore seek it for its own sake'; 'simplicity and generality' are 'major attributes of an effective theory'; 'their aesthetic appeal suffices to make them desirable ends in themselves for the designer of a theory' (Debreu 1984). The aesthetics here is vague, unlearned, inexplicit. Debreu's is a dress-designer's vocabulary for scientific argument.

A rhetorical vocabulary is more rigorous, though it is still merely a list with some thinking attached. Literary thinking is like that. The best introduction to the schools of criticism is called *Critical Terms for Literary Study* (Lentricchia and McLaughlin 1990), listing among others Structure, Narrative, Figurative Language, Author, Value/Evaluation, Determinacy/Indeterminacy, Canon, Ideology and Rhetoric. The best way to understand the Rhetorical school 427 BC to the present is to supply oneself with a copy of Richard Lanham, *A Handlist of Rhetorical Terms* (1991) and an example of using it on a familiar text, such as George A. Kennedy, *New Testament Interpretation Through Rhetorical Criticism* (1984). The best comprehensive modern treatment is Edward P. J. Corbett, *Classical Rhetoric for the Modern Student* (1992), which is a thoughtful list of terms with readings attached. The best use of rhetorical criticism to make an argument is Wayne C. Booth, *Modern Dogma and the Rhetoric of Assent* (1974), but coherent as it is it does not approach the axiomatic style of modern economics. Booth, too, works with the mere handlists dating back to Aristotle and Cicero.

That's encouraging for beginners like you and me. By contrast, to do a useful piece of economic analysis one needs to have finished the course. The non-economists imagine it's enough to have some first-week idea of what 'oligopoly' means. Economics is in fact a good example of the 'hermeneutic circle': one needs to know the argument overall to understand the details and the details to understand the argument. But many literary techniques, and in particular the techniques of rhetorical analysis, come piecemeal, item by item, and can be put to use at once even by tyros. In this they are like some of the empirical methods of economics, such as national income analysis. Obviously a master like Booth or Lanham (compare Kuznets or Denison) is going to do a better job than you or me. But even you and I can start.

I am not suggesting that educated people come equipped to do a rhetorical analysis without study. The results of attempting to are as embarrassing as criticizing economics without knowing any. The point is simply that in rhetorical analysis even students can do useful work almost immediately. A rhetorical analysis can start with any part of 'writing with intent' and proceed. It is like unravelling a sweater: start with a loose bit of yarn and keep pulling. A student is unlikely to find a literary sweater that a professor of English cannot unravel blindingly quicker. But sciences like economics are frayed sweaters waiting to be unravelled, the better to be understood, and in some respects a professor of economics is likely to know better where to pull.

Here then is A Partial and Preliminary Handlist of Rhetorical Terms for Students of Economic Literature.

ETHOS

Ethos, the Greek word simply for 'character', is the fictional character an author assumes. It is the same as Latin *persona* or the modern 'implied author'. No one can refrain from assuming a character, good or bad. An author without good character will not be credited. The exordium, or beginning, of any speech must establish an ethos worth believing. An established ethos is the most persuasive of scientific arguments and scientists are therefore very busy establishing it. Consider for example the implied authors created by these opening lines in the *American Economic Review*'s issue of March 1989:

> Two decades of research have failed to produce professional consensus on the contribution of federal government civil rights activity to the economic progress of black Americans.
>
> (Heckman and Payner 1989: 138)

The implied authors here are policy-oriented, precise but awkward (look at the nominal phrase 'federal government civil rights activity'), aware of the longer trends in scholarship, scholarly (with a Latinate vocabulary), dignified yet decisive, men who will succeed where others have 'failed'. The reader has to be an economist for the sentence to have these effects, just as the listener had to be a fourth-century Athenian for Demosthenes' appeals to ethos to have their effects.

322

Or:

> After a period of intensive study of optimal indirect taxation, there
> has been a renewed interest in recent years in the problem of optimal
> income taxation, with particular emphasis on capital income taxation
> and economic growth.
>
> (Howitt and Sinn 1989: 106)

Here the implied authors are modest (contrast the ringing 'Two decades
of research have failed' above or the unconscious arrogance of 'Consider . . .
the setting' below), concerned to fill gaps rather than assault once more the
great questions of the age, academic rather than political ('renewed interest',
as there might be renewed interest in the satellites of Jupiter), but again
Latinate in vocabulary, anonymous, American academic writers.

Or:

> Consider the following stylized setting.
>
> (Lewis and Sappington 1989: 69)

These are mathematical, uninterested in facts, followers of a certain fashion,
pretending to be direct but staying firmly in the lecture room, unaware of
how funny the first sentence sounds to most economists. The writers
of course need not be aware of every effect their writing has on the
audience, no more than poets need be.

Or finally:

> There is good reason to think that the market for single-family homes
> ought to be less efficient than are capital markets.
>
> (Case and Shiller 1989: 125)

And these are candid, direct, practical, better writers than 'After a period
of intensive study', interested in explaining an empirical phenomenon, up-
to-date in financial theory.

Everyone makes an appeal to *ethos*, if only an *ethos* of choosing never
to stoop to such matters as *ethos*. No speech with intent is 'non-rhetorical'.
Rhetoric is not everything, but it is everywhere in the speech of human
arguers.

It is a commonplace that formal complexity, for example, is a claim to
the *ethos* of the Deep Thinker, a powerful one in modern economics. But
any figure of speech can be pointedly reversed for ironic effect. Thus,
complexity has been used in the literature on British economic 'failure' as
the opposite of an authoritative *ethos*, as evidence of disauthority. A paper
by the historical economist Stephen Nicholas in 1982 tries to cast doubt
on calculations of total-factor productivity change in Victorian Britain.
After a lucid prose survey of the debate on failure from Landes down to
1982, Nicholas 'explains' the calculation of total factor productivity. He
says,

it is assumed [note at once the style borrowed from mathematics] that the economic unit is a profit maximizer, subject to a linear homogeneous production function and operating in perfectly competitive product and factor markets. Given these limiting assumptions, the marginal productivity theory of distribution equates marginal products to factor rewards. It follows by Euler's theorem ... [etc., etc.]

(Nicholas 1982: 86)

To most of his readers he might as well have written '*it is assumed that the* blub-blub *is a* blub *maximizer,* blub-blub blub-blub-blub *and* blub *in perfectly* blub *and* blub blub. *Given these limiting assumptions, the* blub blub blub blub blub blub blub. *It follows by* blub blub ...'. The audience that can understand the argument is the audience of people who already understand it, leaving one to ponder why the argument was necessary. The people who do not understand it gain only the impression that 'limiting assumptions' are somehow involved (they are not, by the way). The rhetorical form of the passage is explanation; its effect in the pages of the *Economic History Review* is to terrify the onlookers, convincing them that the 'neoclassical' analysis makes a lot of strange and unconvincing assumptions. By the mere statement of the 'assumptions' said to underlie the 'neoclassical' calculation, one can cast doubt on the calculation in the eyes of all historians and many economists.

In replying to a sharp rebuttal by Mark Thomas in a later issue of the *Review*, Nicholas repeats the turn. The last sentence of his exordium makes the argument explicit: '*The long list of restrictive assumptions* cautions the economic historians that, at best, the Solow index is a crude measure from which to draw conclusions about historical change' (Nicholas 1985: 577; emphasis added). The *ethos* here is of the Profound Thinker Defending the Innocents from Other Profound (but Irresponsible) Thinkers.

POINT OF VIEW

The implied author, in other words, chooses a vantage point, such as Huck in *Huckleberry Finn*, a first-person narrator who in this case is portrayed as not knowing what is happening beyond his sight; or the author in *Anna Karenina*, who can hear aloud what people are thinking and can travel from Moscow to St Petersburg without a ticket. In the modern novel the suppression of the authorial 'I' has resulted in a technique peculiar to literature, 'represented speech and thought'. Grammarians call it 'unheralded indirect speech', the French *style indirect libre*. Any page or two of Jane Austen serves, as in *Persuasion*: 'Sir Walter had taken a very good house in Camdenplace, a lofty dignified situation, such as becomes a man of consequence' (1818 [1965]: 107; Sir Walter's words ['dignified ... a man of consequence'] in Austen's mouth); 'Could Anne wonder that her father and sister were happy? She might not wonder, but she must sigh that her father should feel no degradation in his change' (108; Anne's words ['sigh . . . no degradation'] in Austen's mouth).

The parallel technique in science might be called 'represented Reality' or 'unheralded assertion' or *style indirect inévitable*. The scientist says: It is not I the scientist who make these assertions but reality itself (Nature's words in the scientist's mouth). The audience applauded Fustel de Coulanges's inaugural lecture at the University of Paris; he put up his hand for silence: 'Do not applaud me. It is not I who speaks, but the voice of History speaking through me.' Redoubled applause. Scientists, including economic scientists, pretend that Nature speaks directly, thereby effacing the evidence that they the scientists are responsible for the assertions. It's just there. The result is similar in fiction: 'We (as readers) cannot question the reliability of third-person narrators . . . . Any first-person narrative, on the other hand, may prove unreliable' (Martin 1986: 142). Thus Huck Finn, a narrator in the first person, misapprehends the Duke and we the readers know he does. The scientist avoids being questioned for his reliability by disappearing into a third-person narrative of what really happened.

The sociologist Michael Mulkay notes in the epistolary arguments of biologists a Rule 11: 'use the personal format of a letter . . . but withdraw from the text yourself as often as possible so that the other party continually finds himself engaged in an unequal dialogue with the experiments, data, observations and facts' (1985: 66). The technique is similar in history: 'the plot of a historical narrative is always an embarrassment and has to be presented as "found" in the events rather than put there by narrative techniques' (White 1973: 20). It is widespread in economics, of course.

STYLE

The Romans divided rhetoric into Invention (the finding of arguments), Arrangement and Style (they included a fourth and fifth category, memory and delivery, too, but these have faded). 'Style versus content' is a rhetorical commonplace of our post-rhetorical culture, most common since the seventeenth century. But the modern premise that content can be split from expression is mistaken. The two are yolk and white in a scrambled egg. Economically speaking, the production function for thinking cannot be written as the sum of two subfunctions, one producing 'results' and the other 'writing them up'. The function is not separable.

Tony Dudley-Evans and Willie Henderson, for example, have studied intensively the style of four articles from the British *Economic Journal* over a century of publication. 'Taxation through monopoly' by C. F. Bastable (1891), for example, 'strikes one immediately as having been written for a highly educated reader [the implied reader] who happens also to be interested in economic matters' (1987: 7). And Bastable, they note, 'frequently uses "and", "but" and "again" in initial position' (an ornament in modern English). Again, he in initial position uses 'elegant adverbial phrases', such as 'So much is this the case' or 'Alike in classical and medieval times' (ibid.: 8). Alike in his scientific and his journalistic work, 'Bastable based his writing not upon shared technical knowledge but on a shared understanding of an educated culture more widely defined' (ibid.: 15).

The style of John Muth's influential article of 1961 on rational expectations makes an ethical and emotional appeal, an appeal to his character as a Scientist and to the self-image of his audience. The word 'I' occurs twice only, in keeping with scientific conventions of impersonality. About a third of the sentences have their main clause in the passive voice. Amidst much that is self-confident and even cocky, Muth adds phrases of scientific modesty: 'as a first approximation', 'I would like to suggest', 'it is rather surprising', 'it often appears'. He introduces bits of 1950s-style philosophy of science, 'purely descriptive hypotheses', 'observed phenomena', 'prediction of the theory', and 'consistent with the relevant data'. Above all, he is obscure. He doubtless did not intend to be, but the paper is unreadable, and was for a long time unread. The obscurity of the style was necessary for its later success as an authoritative text. St Augustine, as the literary critic Gerald Bruns has noted, viewed the obscurity of the Bible as having 'a pragmatic function in the art of winning over an alienated and even contemptuous audience' (Bruns 1984: 157). Obscurity is not rare in religion and science. Bruns quotes Augustine (who might as well be justifying the obscurities of a mathematical economist proving the obvious): 'I do not doubt that this situation was provided by God to conquer pride by work and to combat disdain in our minds, to which those things which are easily discovered seem frequently to be worthless' (ibid.: 157).

APPEALS TO AUTHORITY

Economic style appeals in various ways to an ethos worthy of belief. For example, a text claiming authority uses the 'gnomic present', as in the sentence you are reading now, or in the Bible, or repeatedly in the historian David Landes's well-known book on modern economic growth, *The Unbound Prometheus*. Thus in one paragraph on p. 562: 'large-scale, mechanized manufacture *requires* not only machines and buildings ... but ... social capital ... [t]hese *are* costly, because the investment required *is* lumpy ... the return on such investment *is* often long deferred'. Only the last sentences of the paragraph connect the rest to the narrative past: 'the burden *has tended* to grow ... *has become* a myth'.

The advantage of the gnomic present is its claim to the authority of

General Truth, which is another of its names in grammar. The gnomic present is Landes's substitute for explicit social scientific theory (of which he is innocent), a function the gnomic present serves in sociology and in much of the literature of economic development, too.

Note the tense in Landes's essay at p. 563, for example, after some *aporia* (rhetorical doubt) concerning whether it is true or not, 'Where, then, the gap between leader and follower *is* not too large to begin with ... the advantage *lies* with the latecomer. And the more so because the effort of catching up *calls* forth entrepreneurial ... responses.' That in general and as an economic law the advantage *lies* with the latecomer is offered as a deductive conclusion. And in truth it does follow deductively from the earlier assertions, themselves expressed in the gnomic present (for instance, p. 562, 'There *are* thus two kinds of related costs ...').

The disadvantage is that it sidesteps whether it is asserting an historical fact (that in fact the return on 'such investment' in 1900 was by some relevant standard long deferred) or a general truth (that in economies of the sort we are talking about most such returns will be long deferred), or perhaps merely a tautology (that the very meaning of 'social capital' is investment of a generally useful sort with long-deferred returns). The one meaning borrows prestige and persuasiveness from the other. The usage says: 'I speak as a historian, the voice of History, who is telling you of the facts, this being one of them; but I am also a social scientist in command of the best and timeless theorizing on the matter; and if you don't like that, consider that what I assert is anyway true by definition.'

METAPHOR

The ancients spoke of 'figures' as all the surface of prose, dividing it into 'figures of ornament' (such as the parallelism in the present sentence) and 'figures of argument'. The most well known of the figures of argument is metaphor, which since the philosophers Max Black (1962a, b) and Mary Hesse (1963) thirty years ago has been recognized as synonymous with the scientist's 'model'. In trying to explain family size, for example, Gary Becker alighted on a metaphor of children as ... well ... durable goods. A child, you see, is very like a refrigerator: it is expensive to procure, delivers a stream of returns of a long period of time, has an imperfect secondhand market, and so forth. That the list of similarities eventually become dissimilarities – 'Children, like durable goods, are *not* objects of affection and concern' – is one reason, as Black argued, that 'metaphorical thought is a distinctive mode of achieving insight, not to be construed as an ornamental substitute for plain thought' (1962: 267).

An example is a book, *The Zero-Sum Solution* (1985), by Lester Thurow, an economist and dean of the business school at MIT. The book is sporting. 'To play a competitive game is not to be a winner – every competitive

game has its losers – it is only to be given a chance to win.... Free
market battles can be lost as well as won, and the United States is losing
them on world markets' (1985: 59). One chapter is entitled 'Constructing
an efficient team'. Throughout there is talk about America 'competing',
and 'beating' the rest of the world with a 'world-class economy'. Thurow
complains that more people don't appreciate his favourite metaphor, and
calls it a 'reality': 'For a society which loves team sports ... it is surprising
that Americans won't recognize the same reality in the far more important
international economic game' (ibid.: 107). In more aggressive moods he
slips into a military uniform: 'American firms will occasionally be defeated
at home and will have not compensating foreign victories' (ibid.: 105).
Foreign trade is viewed as the economic equivalent of war.

Three metaphors govern Thurow's story: this metaphor of the international zero-sum 'game'; a metaphor of the domestic 'problem'; and a
metaphor of 'we'. *We* have a domestic *problem* of productivity that leads
to a *loss* of the international *game*. Thurow has spent a long time interpreting the world with these linked metaphors. The we-problem-game metaphors are not the usual one in economics. The metaphor of exchange as a
zero-sum game, in fact, has been favoured by anti-economists since the
eighteenth century. The subject is the exchange of goods and services. If
exchange is a 'game' it might better be seen as one in which everyone
wins, like aerobic dancing. No problem. Trade in this view is *not* zero
sum.

The example is not meant to suggest that metaphors are somehow
optional or ornamental or unscientific. I disagree with Thurow's argument
here. What is wrong, however, is not that he uses a metaphor – no scientist
can do without metaphors – but that his metaphor is inapt, as could be
showed in various ways statistical and introspective. The novice's mistake
is to suppose that a rhetorical criticism is merely a way of unveiling Error.
If we snatch away the veil of ornament, the novice thinks, we can confront
the Facts and the Reality direct. The numerous books called 'Rhetoric and
reality', such as Peter Bauer's collection of essays, commit the mistake.

True, devices of rhetoric such as metaphors *can* be veils over bad arguments. But they can also be the form and substance of good arguments. I
agree, for example, with most of Gary Becker's metaphors, from criminals
as small businessmen to the family as a little firm. Becker is an economic
poet, which is what we expect of our theorists.

TROPES

The Greek word for 'figure' is 'trope', meaning 'turn'. The Four Master
Tropes, also called the perspectival tropes, are Metaphor ('The White House
laid an egg today'), Synecdoche (part for whole: 'The Presidency', one man
standing for the whole administration), Metonymy (associated item stand-

ing in: 'The White House' for the Presidency), and Irony (saying X and meaning not-X: 'The White House had a wonderful day').

Robert M. Solow's famous paper, 'Technical change and the aggregate production function' (1957), illustrates the tropes in action. Solow was trying to understand the rising income of Americans from 1909 to 1949. He wished to know in particular how much was caused by more machinery, buildings and other physical 'capital' and how much by other things – chiefly the increasing ingenuity of people. He began:

> In this day of rationally designed econometric studies and super input–output tables, it takes something more than the usual 'willing suspension of disbelief' to talk seriously of the aggregate production function .... The new wrinkle I want to describe is an elementary way of segregating variations in output per head due to technical change from those due to the availability of capital per head .... Either this kind of aggregate economics appeals or it doesn't. Personally I belong to both schools .... It is convenient to begin with the special case of neutral technical change .... In that case the production function takes the special form $Q = A(t)f(K, L)$ and the multiplicative factor $A(t)$ measures the cumulated effect of shifts over time.

The argument depends at once on a metaphor. The 'aggregate production function' which Solow introduces asserts that the making of our daily bread is like a mathematical function. The jumble of responsibility, habit, conflict, ambition, intrigue and ceremony that is our working life is supposed to be similar to a chalked curve on a blackboard.

The L and K in the equation are metonymies. The L reduces the human attentiveness in making bread to mere hours of work. The hour is an emblem. It is no more the substance of the matter than the heart is of emotions or a bottle is of the wine. The K reduces the material inheritance of the workplace to a pile of shmoos. Solow is aware of the boldness of the figure, though defending it as conventional: he 'would not try to justify what follows by calling on fancy theorems on aggregation and index numbers', referring in a footnote to Joan Robinson's exploration of 'the profound difficulties that stand in the way of giving any precise meaning to the quantity of capital'.

The identification of $A(t)$ with 'technical change' is a synecdoche, and on it the paper turns. The notation says that the multiplier A depends on time, rising as the technologists get smarter. But Solow admits that 'slowdowns, speedups, improvements in the education of the labor force, and all sorts of things' will also cause it to rise. Critics of the calculation, such as Evsey Domar, Theodore Schultz and Solow himself, have called it a mere 'measure of our ignorance'. Calling it 'technical change' as Solow does apologetically though persistently is a bold synecdoche indeed, taking the part for the whole and running with it.

IRONY

Irony is called the 'trope of tropes', because it plays off the others. Observe Solow's ironical bow to 'rationally designed econometric studies' (he knew as did part of his audience that the rationality was in doubt, though in 1957 the econometricians were humourlessly unaware). He describes his notion as a mere 'wrinkle' and as 'elementary', so elementary a wrinkle that no one had thought of it before, and after Solow an intellectual industry arose to exploit it. He protects himself from criticism by mocking the sobersides: 'Personally I belong to both schools'. The synecdoche of 'technical change' is protected by ironical quotation marks when in doubt, though the marks fall away as doubt fades.

Irony is the most sophisticated of the master tropes. As the historian Hayden White puts it:

> It presupposes that the reader or auditor already knows, or is capable of recognizing, the absurdity of the characterization of the thing designated in the Metaphor, Metonymy, or Synecdoche used to give form to it.... Irony is in one sense metatropological, for it is deployed in the self-conscious awareness of the possible misuse of figurative language.... Irony thus represents a stage of consciousness in which the problematical nature of language itself has become recognized. It points to the potential foolishness of all linguistic characterizations of reality as much as to the absurdity of the beliefs it parodies. It is therefore 'dialectical', as Kenneth Burke has noted.
>
> (White 1973: 37)

The most sophisticated economists and the most sophisticated novelists favour irony. Irony presupposes an existing conversation from which one can score; in this and in other ways it is mature. The economist George Stigler, for instance, wrote as follows about the guiding metaphor of why people purchase things: 'It would be of course bizarre to look upon the typical family – that complex mixture of love, convenience, and frustration – as a business enterprise. Therefore, economists have devoted much skill and ingenuity to elaborating this approach' (Stigler 1966: 21). The jest protects and persuades.

STORY

The word 'story' is not vague in literary criticism. Gerald Prince used some ingenious mental experiments with stories and non-stories to formulate a definition of the 'minimal story', which has:

> three conjoined events. The first and third events are stative [such as 'Korea was poor'], the second is active [such as 'then Koreans educated themselves']. Furthermore, the third event is the inverse of the

first [such as 'Then Korea was rich']. . . . [T]he three events are conjoined by conjunctive features in such a way that (a) the first event precedes the second in time and the second precedes the third, and (b) the second event causes the third.

(Prince 1973: 31)

Prince's technique isolates what it is about the tales that we recognize as stories. Is this a story?

A man laughed and a woman sang.

No, it does not feel like one – in the uninstructed sense we learned at our mother's knee (of course in a more instructed way, after Joyce and Kafka, not to speak of writers of French detective fiction, anything can be a story). The following sounds more like a story:

John was rich, then he lost a lot of money.

At least it has the claim of sequence or consequence, 'then'. And it has the inversion of status ('rich . . . poor'). But it doesn't quite make it. Consider:

A man was happy, then he met a woman, then, as a result, he was unhappy.

Right. It feels like a complete story, as 'generally and intuitively recognized' (Prince 1973: 5). Contrast:

John was rich and he travelled a lot, then, as a result, he was very happy.

Something is screwy. What is screwy is that his status is not inverted from what it was.

One can use Prince's examples to construct stories and non-stories in economics. Test the pattern:

Poland was poor, then it adopted capitalism, then as a result it became rich.

The money supply increased this year, then, as a result, productivity last year rose and the business cycle three decades ago peaked.

A few firms existed in chemicals, then they merged, and then only one firm existed.

Britain in the late nineteenth century was capitalistic and rich and powerful.

The pattern is story/non-story/story/non-story.

Stories end in a new state. If a 5 per cent tax on petroleum is said by some Congressman or journalist to be 'designed' to fall entirely on producers

331

the economist will complain, saying, 'It's not an equilibrium'. 'Not an equilibrium' is the economist's way of saying that he disputes the ending proposed by some untutored person. Any descendant of Adam Smith, left or right, whether by way of Marx or Marshall, Veblen or Menger, will be happy to tell you a better story.

Many of the scientific disagreements inside economics turn on this sense of an ending. To an eclectic Keynesian, raised on picaresque tales of economic surprise, the story idea 'Oil prices went up, which caused inflation' is full of meaning, having the merits that stories are supposed to have. But to a monetarist, raised on the classical unities of money, it seems incomplete, no story at all, a flop. As the economist A. C. Harberger likes to say, it doesn't make the economics 'sing'. It ends too soon, halfway through the second act: a rise in oil prices without some corresponding fall elsewhere is 'not an equilibrium'.

From the other side, the criticism of monetarism by Keynesians is likewise a criticism of the plot line, complaining of an ill-motivated beginning rather than a premature ending: where on earth does the money you think is so important *come* from, and why? Our jargon word is 'exogenous': if you start the story in the middle the money will be treated as though it is unrelated to, exogenous to, the rest of the action, even though it's not.

There is more than prettiness in such matters of plot. There is moral weight. Hayden White has written that 'The demand for closure in the historical story is a demand . . . for moral reasoning' (White 1981: 20). A monetarist is not morally satisfied until she has pinned the blame on the Federal Reserve. The economist's ending to the story of the petroleum tax falling entirely on producers says, 'Look: you're getting fooled by the politicians and lawyers if you think that specifying that the refiners pay the tax will let the consumers off. Wake up; act your age; look beneath the surface; recognize the dismal ironies of life.' Stories impart meaning, which is to say worth. A *New Yorker* cartoon shows a woman looking up worried from the TV, asking her husband, 'Henry, is there a moral to *our* story?'

The sense of adequacy in storytelling works in the most abstract theory, too. In seminars on mathematical economics a question nearly as common as 'Haven't you left off the second subscript?' is 'What is your story?' The story of the gasoline tax can be put entirely mathematically and metaphorically, as an assertion about where the gasoline tax falls, talking of supply-and-demand curves in equilibrium thus:

$$w^* = -(E_d/(E_d + E_s))T^*$$

The mathematics here is so familiar to an economist that he will not need explanation beyond the metaphor. But in less familiar cases, at the frontier of economic argument, the economist will need an explanation. That is, he will need a story. Like the audience for a biologist explaining moulting glands in crabs, at the end of all the mathematics he will ask insistently *why*. In seminars on economic theory 'What is your story?' has become a technical phrase. The question is an appeal for a lower level of abstraction, closer to the episodes of human life. It asks for more realism, in a fictional sense, more illusion of direct experience. It asks to step closer to the nineteenth-century novel, with its powerful and non-ironic sense of Being There.

DECONSTRUCTION AND OTHER TERRORS

When Richard Posner wanted in a recent book to terrify his lawyer-readers about reds in the English department, you can imagine the school of criticism he began with: 'Deconstruction and other schools of criticism' (1988: 211). Deconstruction, by merest chance the most frightening version of literary criticism that could be brought before conservative readers, is 'least well understood by lawyers, and . . . is therefore an appropriate starting point . . .' (ibid.: 211). Ho, ho.

Deconstruction, for all the calls to arms against it from the ignorant (and proud of it), constitutes only a tiny part of criticism. It is not even the most *recent* of fashions in literary theory (feminism and the new historicism are, with the new economic criticism on the horizon). It is merely one of a score of partially overlapping ways to do literary criticism. A partial list in historical order would include rhetorical, philological, Aristotelian, belletristic, hermeneutic, historical, new critical, psychoanalytic, neo-Aristotelian, mythological, neo-rhetorical, Marxist, reader-response, deconstructive, linguistic, feminist and new historicist criticism. In the same way you could divide economics into Good Old Chicago School, eclectic econometric macro, nouvelle Chicago, highbrow general equilibrium, policy-oriented micro.

But the journalistic interest in the word is so great that it cannot be ignored even in a brief list (a good treatment for economists is Rossetti 1990, 1992). One insight that the deconstructionists are properly to be credited with is the notion of verbal 'hierarchy'. The point is simply that words carry with them a ranking with respect to their opposites, as the word 'infidel' calls to mind 'Muslim'; and 'black' calls to mind 'white'. A sentence will achieve some of its effect through playing on these rankings. Noticing the hierarchies exposes the politics (so to speak) in writing.

In economics long ago, for example, Wesley Clair Mitchell wrote, 'it must never be forgotten that the development of the social sciences (including economics) is still a social process. Recognition of that view . . . leads one to study these sciences . . . [as] the product not merely of sober thinking but also subconscious wishing' (quoted in Rossetti 1992). The passage contains at least these half-spoken hierarchies ready for liberating deconstruction (reading back to front, the terms in square brackets being

333

those implied but not mentioned): sober/subconscious; thought/wishing; product/[mere ephemera]; sciences/[mere humanities]; study/[beach reading]; one/[you personally]; leads/[compels]; view/[grounded conviction]; sciences/[mere] processes; development/[mere chaotic change]; must/[can]. The first term of each is the privileged one – except that in the pairs leads/[compels] and view/[grounded conviction] they are in fact polite self-deprecation, with ironic force: Mitchell is on the contrary claiming the commanding heights of compelling and grounded conviction, not the soft valleys of mere gently leading 'views'. Literary people speak of 'deprivileging' the superior term in such pairs, which in economics would be, for example, 'microfoundations/macroeconomics' or 'general/partial' or 'rigorous/informal'.

In the vernacular, the economist Mitchell is playing mind games on us readers, and we'd better watch out. Mitchell, of course, is not special. It is easier to see the mind games played by writers long ago than in our own time, but you can depend on it that writing with intent plays them.

The deeper point that deconstruction makes is that among the mind games in which all writing participates is the claim that the writing *is* the world. The realistic novel is the plainest example, but scientific writing is another (for which see again Mulkay 1985). For example, the phrase 'it is obvious that' conveys certitude in mathematics and in economics. One eight-page article in the *Journal of Political Economy* (Davies 1989) uses expressions such as 'It is obvious that', 'obviously', it is evident', 'doubtless', 'easily seen', 'needs no discussion', 'we may expect' some forty-two times. But nothing is 'obvious' on a printed page except that certain marks have been made on a white field. The 'easily seen' is evoked in the mind's eye.

WRITING AS PERFORMANCE

The point is not peculiar to deconstruction. In a way it is one of the chief findings of humanism. Books do not 'reproduce' the world. They evoke it. Skilful fiction, whether in the form of *Northanger Abbey* or *The Origin of Species*, 'stimulates us to supply what is not there', as Virginia Woolf remarked of Austen. 'What she offers is, apparently, a trifle, yet is composed of something that expands in the reader's mind and endows with the most enduring forms of life scenes which are outwardly trivial' (1953 [1925]: 142). Remarking on her remark in turn, the critic Wolfgang Iser put it this way: 'What is missing from the apparently trivial scenes, the gaps arising out of the dialogue – this is what stimulates the reader into filling the blanks with projections [the image is of the reader running a motion picture inside his head, which is of course why novels can still compete with television] .... The "enduring form of life" which Virginia

Woolf speaks of is not manifested on the printed page; it is a product arising out of the interaction between text and reader' (Iser 1980: 110–11).

As Arjo Klamer (1987) has shown for the postulate of economic rationality, scientific persuasion, too, is like that. Persuasion of the most rigorous kind has blanks to be filled at every other step, whether it is about a difficult murder case, for example, or a difficult mathematical theorem. The same is true of a debate about economic policy. What is unsaid – but not unread – is more important to the text as perceived by the reader than what is there on the page. As Klamer puts it (1987: 175), 'The student of the rhetoric of economics faces the challenge of speaking about the unspoken, filling in the "missing text" in economic discourse.'

The running of different motion pictures in our heads is going to produce different texts as perceived. Todorov asks: 'How do we explain this diversity [of readings]? By the fact that these accounts describe, not the universe of the book itself, but this universe as it is transformed by the psyche of each individual reader' (Todorov 1975 [1980]: 72). And: 'Only by subjecting the text to a particular type of reading do we construct, from our reading, an imaginary universe. Novels do not imitate reality; they create it' (ibid.: 67f.). Economic texts also are made in part by the reader. Obscure texts are often therefore influential. The crafty John Maynard Keynes, for example, most influentially in *The General Theory of Employment, Interest and Money*, left many opportunities for readers to run their own internal motion pictures, filling in the blanks.

The argument can be pushed. An economist expositing a result creates an 'authorial audience' (an imagined group of readers who know this is fiction) and at the same time a 'narrative audience' (an imagined group of readers who do not know it is fiction). As the critic Peter Rabinowitz explains (1968 [1980]: 245), 'the narrative audience of "Goldilocks" believes in talking bears'. The 'authorial' audience realizes it is a fiction.

The difference between the two audiences created by the author seems less decisive in economic science than in explicit fiction, probably because we all know that bears do not talk but we do not all know that the notion of 'marginal productivity' in economics is a metaphor. The narrative audience in science, as in 'Goldilocks', is fooled by the fiction, which is as it should be. But in science the authorial audience is fooled, too (and so incidentally is part of the literal audience, the actual readers as against the ideal readers the author appears to want to have). Michael Mulkay, again, has shown how important is the inadvertent choice of authorial audience in the scholarly correspondence of biochemists. Biochemists like other scientists and scholars are largely unaware of their literary devices, and become puzzled and angry when their literal audience refuses to believe in talking bears (Mulkay 1985: ch. 2). They think they are merely stating facts, not making audiences. Small wonder that scientists and scholars disagree, even when their rhetoric of 'What the facts say' would appear to make disagreement impossible. Science requires more resources of the language than raw sense data and first-order predicate logic.

It requires that which may be called the Rhetorical Tetrad. Fact and logic also come into the economics, in large doses. Economics is a science, and a jolly good one, too. But a serious argument in economics will use metaphors and stories as well – not for ornament or teaching alone but for the very science. Fact, logic, metaphor and story.

The reasons to do a rhetorical analysis of an economic text are various: to understand it, to admire it, to debunk it, to set it beside other works of persuasion in science, to see that science is not a new dogma but is thoroughly and respectably part of the culture. The tools are ancient. They need be mastered only at the level of an elementary book such as Corbett to begin to be useful. In the bibliographies attached here I give some suggestions for beginning study. Rhetorical sophistication is an alternative to reading scientific texts the way the implied reader does, a reader who believes, for example, in talking bears. If we are to get beyond nursery school as scientific readers we need such a rhetoric applied to economic science.

BIBLIOGRAPHY

Literary, philosophical and social-constructivist theory: an introductory list

Abrams, M. H. (1981) *A Glossary of Literary Terms*, 4th edn, New York: Holt, Rinehart & Winston.

Aristotle (1991) *Rhetoric*, trans. George A. Kennedy, New York: Oxford University Press.

Austin, J. L. (1955) [1965, 1977] *How to Do Things with Words*, 2nd edn, J. O. Urmson and M. Sbisà (eds), Cambridge, MA: Harvard University Press.

Barnes, B. and Edge, D. (eds) (1982) *Science in Context: Readings in the Sociology of Science*, Cambridge, MA: MIT Press.

Bazerman, C. (1988) *Shaping Written Knowledge: The Genre and Activity of the Experimental Article in Science*, Rhetoric of the Human Sciences, Madison: University of Wisconsin Press.

Bazerman, C. and Paradis, J. (eds) (1991) *The Textual Dynamics of the Professions*, Rhetoric of the Human Sciences, Madison: University of Wisconsin Press.

Black, M. (ed.) (1962a) *The Importance of Language*, Englewood Cliffs, NJ: Prentice-Hall.

Black, M. (1962b) *Models and Metaphors*, Ithaca: Cornell University Press.

Booth, W. C. (1974) *Modern Dogma and the Rhetoric of Assent*, Chicago: University of Chicago Press.

Brooks, P. (1985) *Reading for the Plot: Design and Intention in Narrative*, New York: Vintage.

Bruns, G. L. (1984) 'The problem of figuration in antiquity', in G. Shapiro and

A. Sica (eds), *Hermeneutics: Questions and Prospects*, Amherst: University of Massachusetts Press, pp. 174–96.

Collins, H. (1985) *Changing Order: Replication and Induction in Scientific Practice*, London and Beverly Hills: Sage.

Corbett, E. P. J. (1992) *Classical Rhetoric for the Modern Student*, 3rd edn, New York and London: Oxford University Press.

Frye, N. (1957) *An Anatomy of Criticism*, New York: Atheneum.

Frye, N. (1964) *The Educated Imagination*, Bloomington: Indiana University Press.

Gibson, W. (1980) [1950] 'Authors, speakers, and mock readers', *College English* 11 (February), pp. 1–6. Also in J. P. Tompkins (ed.), *Reader-Response Criticism*, Baltimore: Johns Hopkins University Press, pp. 1–6.

Goodman, N. (1965) *Fact, Fiction and Forecast*, 2nd edn, Indianapolis: Bobbs-Merrill.

Hesse, M. (1963) *Models and Analogies in Science*, Notre Dame: University of Notre Dame Press.

Iser, W. (1980) 'The interaction between text and reader', in Suleiman and Crosman (1980), pp. 106–19.

Kennedy, G. A. (1984) *New Testament Interpretation Through Rhetorical Criticism*, Chapel Hill: University of North Carolina Press.

Lanham, R. (1991) *A Handlist of Rhetorical Terms*, 2nd edn, Berkeley, Los Angeles and Oxford: University of California Press.

Lanham, R. A. (1994) *The Electronic Word: Democracy, Technology, and the Arts*, Chicago: University of Chicago Press.

Lentricchia, F. and McLaughlin, T. (eds) (1990) *Critical Terms for Literary Study*, Chicago: University of Chicago Press.

Lodge, D. (1990) *After Bakhtin: Essays on Fiction and Criticism*, London and New York: Routledge.

Martin, W. (1986) *Recent Theories of Narrative*, Ithaca: Cornell University Press.

Mulkay, M. (1985) *The Word and the World: Explorations in the Form of Sociological Analysis*, Winchester, MA: Allen & Unwin.

Nelson, J., Megill, A. and McCloskey, D. N. (eds) (1987) *The Rhetoric of the Human Sciences: Language and Argument in Scholarship and Public Affairs*. Series on the Rhetoric of the Human Sciences, Madison: University of Wisconsin Press.

Perelman, C. (1982) *The Realm of Rhetoric*, Notre Dame: University of Notre Dame Press.

Petrey, S. (1990) *Speech Acts and Literary Theory*, New York and London: Routledge.

Polanyi, M. (1962) *Personal Knowledge: Towards a Post-Critical Philosophy*, Chicago: University of Chicago Press.

Prince, G. (1973) *A Grammar of Stories*, The Hague and Paris: Mouton.

Rabinowitz, P. J. (1968) [1980] ' "What's Hecuba to us?" The audience's experience of literary borrowing', in Suleiman and Crosman (1980), pp. 241–63.

Ruthven, K. K. (1979) *Critical Assumptions*, Cambridge: Cambridge University Press.

Saussure, F. de (1983) [1916] *Course in General Linguistics*, trans. by R. Harris, London: Duckworth.

Suleiman, S. R. and Crosman, R. (eds) (1980) *The Reader in the Text: Essays on Audience and Interpretation*, Princeton: Princeton University Press.

Todorov, T. (1975) [1980] 'Reading as construction', in Suleiman and Crosman (1980), pp. 67–82.

Toulmin, S. (1958) *The Uses of Argument*, Cambridge: Cambridge University Press.

Vickers, B. (1988) *In Defence of Rhetoric*, Oxford: Oxford University Press.

White, H. (1973) *Metahistory: The Historical Imagination in Nineteenth-Century Europe*, Baltimore: Johns Hopkins University Press.

White, H. (1981) 'The value of narrativity in the representation of reality', in W. J. T. Mitchell (ed.), *On Narrative*, Chicago: University of Chicago Press, pp. 1–24.

The rhetoric of economics

Amariglio, J. (1988) 'The body, economic discourse, and power: an economist's introduction to Foucault', *History of Political Economy* 20: 583–613.

Ashmore, M., Mulkay, M. and Pinch, T. (1989) *Health and Efficiency: A Sociology of Health Economics*, Milton Keynes and Philadelphia: Open University Press.

Bazerman, C. (1993) 'Money talks: the rhetorical project of *The Wealth of Nations*', in Henderson, Dudley-Evans and Backhouse, (1993), pp. 173–99.

Berger, L. A. (1990) 'Self-interpretation, attention, and language: implications for economics of Charles Taylor's hermeneutics', in Lavoie (1990a), pp. 262–84.

Brown, V. (1993) 'Decanonizing discourses: textual analysis and the history of economic thought', in Henderson, Dudley-Evans and Backhouse (1993), pp. 64–84.

Collins, H. M. (1991) 'History and sociology of science and history and methodology of economics', in N. de Marchi and M. Blaug (eds), *Appraising Economic Theories: Studies in the Methodology of Research Programmes*, Aldershot: Edward Elgar, pp. 492–8.

Cosgel, M. (1990) 'Rhetoric in the economy: consumption and audience', unpublished manuscript, Department of Economics, University of Connecticut.

Cosgel, M. and Klamer, A. (1990) 'Entrepreneurship as discourse', unpublished manuscript, Departments of Economics, University of Connecticut and George Washington University.

Davis, J. B. (1990) 'Comment on Rossetti's "Deconstructing Robert Lucas"', in Samuels (1990), pp. 244–50.

Dudley-Evans, T. and Henderson, W. (1987) 'Changes in the economics article', Department of Extramural Studies, University of Birmingham, Birmingham, England.

Dudley-Evans, T. and Henderson, W. (eds) (1990) *The Language of Economics: The Analysis of Economic Discourse*, ELT Documents No. 134, Oxford: Modern English Publications, in association with the British Council.

Elshtain, J. B. (1987) 'Feminist political rhetoric and women's studies', in Nelson, Megill and McCloskey (1987), pp. 319–40.

Fish, S. (1988) 'Comments from outside economics', in Klamer, McCloskey and Solow (1988), pp. 21–30.

Folbre, N. and Hartmann, H. (1988) 'The rhetoric of self-interest: ideology and gender in economic theory', in Klamer, McCloskey and Solow (1988), pp. 184–203.

George, D. (1990) 'The rhetoric of economics texts', *Journal of Economic Issues* 24 (September): 861–78.

Henderson, W. (1982) 'Metaphor in economics', *Economics* (Winter): 147–53.

Henderson, W. (1993) 'The problem of Edgeworth's style', in Henderson, Dudley-Evans and Backhouse (1993), pp. 200–22.

Henderson, W. and Hewings, A. (1987) *Reading Economics: How Text Helps or Hinders*, British National Bibliography Research Fund Report, No. 28, British Library Publications Sales Unit, Boston Spa, West Yorkshire.

Henderson, W. and Hewings, A. (1988) 'Entering the hypothetical world: assume, suppose, consider, and take as signals in economics text', Department of Extra-mural Studies, University of Birmingham, Birmingham, England.

Henderson, W., Dudley-Evans, T. and Backhouse, R. (1993) *Economics and Language*, London: Routledge.

Hewings, A. and Henderson, W. (1987) 'A link between genre and schemata: a case study of economics text', *English Language Research Journal* 1: 156–75.

Hirschman, A. O. (1991) *The Rhetoric of Reaction: Perversity, Futility, Jeopardy*, Cambridge, MA: Harvard University Press.

Klamer, A. (1983) *Conversations with Economists: New Classical Economists and Opponents Speak Out on the Current Controversy in Macroeconomics*, Totawa, NJ: Rowman & Littlefield.

Klamer, A. (1984) 'Levels of discourse in new classical economics', *History of Political Economy* 16 (Summer): 263–90.

Klamer, A. (1987) 'As if economists and their subjects were rational . . .', in Nelson, Megill and McCloskey (1987), pp. 163–83.

Klamer, A. (1988a) 'Economics as discourse', in N. de Marchi (ed.), *The Popperian Legacy in Economics*, Cambridge: Cambridge University Press, pp. 259–78.

Klamer, A. (1988b) 'Negotiating a new conversation about economics', in Klamer, McCloskey and Solow (1988), pp. 265–79.

Klamer, A. (1990a) 'The textbook presentation of economic discourse', in Samuels (1990), pp. 129–54.

Klamer, A. (1990b) 'Towards the native's point of view: the difficulty of changing the conversation', in Lavoie (1990), pp. 19–33.

Klamer, A. (1991) 'The advent of modernism in economics', unpublished manuscript, Department of Economics, George Washington University, Washington DC.

Klamer, A. and McCloskey, D. N. (1988) 'Economics in the human conversation', in Klamer, McCloskey and Solow (1988), pp. 3–20.

Klamer, A. and McCloskey, D. N. (1989) 'The rhetoric of disagreement', *Rethinking Marxism* 2 (Fall): 140–61.

Klamer, A. and McCloskey, D. N. (1992) 'Accounting as the master metaphor of economics', *The European Accounting Review* 1 (May): 145–60.

Klamer, A. and Leonard, T. (1992) 'Economic metaphor', unpublished manuscript, Department of Economics, George Washington University, Washington, DC.

Klamer, A., McCloskey, D. N. and Solow, R. M. (eds) (1988) *The Consequences of Economic Rhetoric*, New York: Cambridge University Press.

Lavoie, D. C. (ed.) (1990a) *Economics and Hermeneutics*, London and New York: Routledge.

Lind, H. (1992) 'A case study of normal research in theoretical economics', *Economics and Philosophy* 8 (April): 83–102.

McCloskey, D. N. (1983) 'The rhetoric of economics', *Journal of Economic Literature* 31 (June): 482–517.

McCloskey, D. N. (1985a) 'The loss function has been mislaid: the rhetoric of significance tests', *American Economic Review* 75 (May): 201–5.

McCloskey, D. N. (1985b) *The Rhetoric of Economics*, Madison: University of Wisconsin Press.

McCloskey, D. N. (1986) *The Writing of Economics*, New York: Macmillan.

McCloskey, D. N. (1988a) 'The rhetoric of law and economics', *Michigan Law Review* 86 (February): 752–67.

McCloskey, D. N. (1988b) 'Thick and thin methodologies in the history of eco-

339

nomic thought', in N. de Marchi (ed.), *The Popperian Legacy in Economics*, Cambridge: Cambridge University Press, pp. 245–57.

McCloskey, D. N. (1990a) 'Agon and Ag Ec: style of persuasion in agricultural economics', invited address, *American Journal of Agricultural Economics* 72 (December): 1124–30.

McCloskey, D. N. (1990b) *If You're So Smart: The Narrative of Economic Expertise*, Chicago: University of Chicago Press.

McCloskey, D. N. (1991a) 'The essential rhetoric of law, literature, and liberty' [Review of Posner's law as literature, Fish's doing what comes naturally and White's justice as translation]', *Critical Review* 5 (Spring): 203–23.

McCloskey, D. N. (1991b) 'Voodoo economics: some scarcities of magic', *Poetics Today* 12 (Winter): 287–300.

McCloskey, D. N. (1993a) 'In defense of rhetoric: the rhetorical tradition in the West', *Common Knowledge* 2(2): 23–32.

McCloskey, D. N. (1993b) 'Some consequences of a conjective economics', in J. Nelson and M. Ferber (eds), *Beyond Economic Man: Feminism and Economics*, Chicago: University of Chicago Press.

McCloskey, D. N. (1993c) 'The lawyerly rhetoric of Coase's "The Theory of the Firm" ', *Journal of Corporate Law*, Spring, pp. 1–22.

McCloskey, D. N. (1994) *Knowledge and Persuasion in Economics*, Cambridge: Cambridge University Press.

McCloskey, D. N. and Nelson, J. (1990) 'The rhetoric of political economy', in J. H. Nichols Jr. and C. Wright (eds), *Political Economy to Economics – and Back?* San Francisco: Institute for Contemporary Studies Press, pp. 155–74.

McCloskey, D. N. and Nelson, J. (eds) (forthcoming) *A Handbook on Rhetoric of Inquiry*, London: Basil Blackwell.

Mäki, U. (1993) 'Two philosophies of the rhetoric of economics', in Henderson, Dudley-Evans and Backhouse (1993), pp. 23–50.

Mayer, T. (1993) *Truth versus Precision in Economics*, Aldershot, England and Brookfield, Vermont: Edward Elgar.

Mehta, J. (1993) 'Meaning in the context of bargaining games – narratives in opposition', in Henderson, Dudley-Evans and Backhouse (1993), pp. 85–99.

Milberg, W. (1988) 'The language of economics: deconstructing the neoclassical texts', *Social Concepts* 4(2): 33–57.

Milberg, W. (1991) 'Marxism, post-structuralism, and the discourse of economics', *Rethinking Marxism* 4(2): 93–104.

Milberg, W. (1992a) 'The rhetoric of policy relevance in international economics', unpublished manuscript, Department of Economics, New School for Social Research.

Milberg, W. (1992b) 'The rhetoric of policy relevance in international economics', unpublished manuscript, Department of Economics, New School for Social Research.

Milberg, W. and Pietrykowski, B. A. (1990) 'Realism, relativism and the importance of rhetoric for Marxist economics', unpublished manuscript, Department of Economics, New School for Social Research.

Miller, C. R. (1990) 'The rhetoric of decision science, or Herbert A. Simon says', in H. W. Simons (ed.), *The Rhetorical Turn: Invention and Persuasion in the Conduct of Enquiry*, Chicago and London.

Mirowski, P. (1989) *More Heat than Light: Economics as Social Physics, Physics as Nature's Economics*, New York: Cambridge University Press.

Resnick, S. and Wolff, R. (1988) 'Marxian theory and the rhetoric of economics', in Klamer, McCloskey and Solow (1988), pp. 47–63.

Rossetti, J. (1990), 'Deconstructing Robert Lucas', in Samuels (1990), pp. 225–43.

Rossetti, J. (1992) 'Deconstruction, rhetoric, and economics', in N. de Marchi (ed.), *The Post-Popperian Methodology of Economics: Recovering Practice*, Boston: Kluwer and Neijhoff, pp. 211–34.

Samuels, W. J. (ed.) (1990) *Economics as Discourse: An Analysis of the Language of Economists*, Boston, Dordrecht and London: Kluwer.

Summers, L. (1991) 'The scientific illusion on empirical macroeconomics', *Scandinavian Journal of Economics* 93(2): 129–48.

Tribe, K. (1978) *Land, Labour and Economic Discourse*, London: Routledge & Kegan Paul.

Weintraub, E. R. (1991) *Stabilizing Dynamics: Constructing Economic Knowledge*, Cambridge: Cambridge University Press.

Economic examples and other works cited

Austen, J. (1965) [1818] *Persuasion*, New York: Houghton Mifflin.

Bauer, P. (1984) *Reality and Rhetoric: Studies in the Economics of Development*, Cambridge, MA: Harvard University Press.

Case, K. E. and Shiller, R. J. (1989) 'The efficiency of the market for single-family homes', *American Economic Review* 79 March: 125–37.

Colander, D. and Brenner, R. (1992) *Educating Economists*, Ann Arbor: University of Michigan Press.

Davies, G. R. (1989) 'The quantity theory and recent statistical studies', *Journal of Political Economy* 97(3): 854–62.

Debreu, G. (1984) 'Economic theory in the mathematical mode', *American Economic Review* 74 (June): 267–78.

Heckman, J. J. and Payner, B. S. (1989) 'Determining the impact of anti-discrimination policy on the economic status of blacks: a study of South Carolina', *American Economic Review* 79 (March): 138–77.

Howitt, P. and Sinn, H.-W. (1989) 'Gradual reform of capital income taxation', *American Economic Review* 79 (March): 106–24.

Klamer, A. and Colander, D. C. (1990) *The Making of an Economist*, Boulder: Westview.

Landes, D. (1969) *The Unbound Prometheus: Technological Change and Industrial Development in Western Europe from 1750 to the Present*, Cambridge: Cambridge University Press. (Reprinting, with additions, his book-length essay 'Technological change and development in Western Europe, 1750–1914', in *Cambridge Economic History of Europe*, vol. VI, Cambridge: Cambridge University Press, 1965.)

Lewis, T. and Sappington, D. E. M. (1989) 'Inflexible rules in incentive problems', *American Economic Review* 79 (March): 69–84.

Muth, J. F. (1961) 'Rational expectations and the theory of price movements', *Econometrica* 29 (July): 315–35.

Nicholas, S. (1982) 'Total factor productivity growth and the revision of post-1870 British economic history', *Economic History Review* 2nd ser. 25 (February): 83–98.

Nicholas, S. (1985) 'British economic performance and total factor productivity growth, 1870–1940', *Economic History Review* 2nd ser. 38 (November): 576–82.

Posner, R. A. (1972) *Economic Analysis of Law*, Boston: Little, Brown.

Posner, R. A. (1988) *Law and Literature: A Misunderstood Relation*, Cambridge, MA: Harvard University Press.

Solow, R. M. (1957) 'Technical change and the aggregate production function', *Review of Economics and Statistics* 39 (August): 312–20.

Stigler, G. (1966) *The Theory of Price*, 3rd edn, New York: Macmillan.

Summerson, J. (1963) *The Classical Language of Architecture*, Cambridge, MA: MIT Press.

Thurow, L. (1985) *The Zero-Sum Solution: Building a World-Class American Economy*, New York: Simon & Schuster.

Woolf, V. (1953) [1925] *The Common Reader. First Series.* New York and London: Harcourt Brace Jovanovich.

16

METAPHOR AND ECONOMICS

Willie Henderson

Metaphor is a topic of some methodological significance, the exploration of which raises questions concerning the relationship between the literal and non-literal use of language and hence the problem of the relationship between language and the world. Although re-assessed in literary and philosophical circles since the mid-1950s, it is only recently that the attention of the economics profession has been drawn to metaphor (McCloskey 1986; Mirowski 1989). McCloskey has tended to concentrate attention upon viewing metaphor in economics through literary theory, sometimes seeing metaphor and narrative as having alternative roles in the context of economic argument, sometimes linking metaphor with questions of style examined at the level of the sentence. Mirowski, in his exploration of metaphor within the context of nineteenth-century economics writing, has tended to see metaphor at many different levels of the text, i.e. as a universal feature of written language and also in terms of specific analogies drawn from nineteenth-century physics. The problem with any investigation of metaphor within the context of a given discourse community, such as economics, is that of deliminating the non-literal from the literal as well as that of assessing the role metaphor plays in the construction of the discourse. Metaphor can be viewed simply as textual decoration; as a useful teaching device; as a central organizing principle of all language; as a way of viewing and constructing a new problem; as a fundamental basis for argument and of storytelling. Given this range of possibilities, it is hard to imagine that any one lens for viewing metaphor will be able to focus all aspects of metaphor's role in economic argument.

This chapter is concerned with exploring ways of looking at metaphor and with ways of exploring metaphor's role in the development of economic thought. It is divided into two broad sections. The first introduces metaphor and the tropes and provides a brief outline of the history of metaphor. In this section broad links are made between metaphor and economics. The second section examines the interactions between economics discourse and metaphor in two contexts: that of the textbook and that of metaphor in the context of research and research literature. The process

343

of appraising metaphor, raised earlier in the chapter, is also explored in the second section.

WHAT IS METAPHOR?

Metaphor has been extensively discussed since the days of Aristotle. In understanding metaphor there are two problems to be faced: that of distinguishing the non-literal from the literal and that of exploring the various forms that the non-literal use of language can take. Aristotle tended to concentrate on the former problem, his successors in the classical world tended to concentrate on the latter. Modern approaches to metaphor concentrate on the non-literal and give pride of place to it. This reverses the tradition of the early Enlightenment when metaphor was banished along with other 'wild imaginings' in an attempt to establish a scientific discourse based upon observation and reason. A broad review of metaphor in economics, therefore, needs to address the questions of the demarcation and identification of what is taken to be metaphorical language as well as of the function and assessment of metaphor (Cooper 1986).

Metaphor and transference

For Aristotle (384–322BC), metaphor is a use of words in which the meaning proper to one word is 'carried over' to another word; thus Aristotle's example, 'Achilles is a lion' in which the attributes of that which is not a lion are associated with the attributes of a lion. In defining metaphor, Aristotle uses metaphor: *metaphora* in Greek is made up of the words, '*meta*', meaning 'over' and '*pherein*', meaning 'to carry'.[1] Implicit in Aristotle's theory is the notion that ordinary, everyday meanings are not themselves metaphorically derived. A stable, literal language is taken as the point from which the metaphorical is to be measured: the literal is where language and the world most directly correspond, 'a point at which nothing is being "carried over" from another level or domain of meaning' (Hinman 1982: 182). Aristotle's analysis operated at the level of the noun. Modern views on metaphor extend its range beyond that of the noun, to include verbs ('I burn with anger') and prepositions ('I will see you *in* an hour'). In modern writings on metaphor, the non-literal tends to be seen as an organizing principle of all language.

A metaphor is a use of language in which what is said is not literally what is meant. 'Achilles' is not a 'lion', but we can find ways of making sense of the sentence, by seeing the one thing (a person) in terms of the other (a lion). 'Lion' is not a definition of 'Achilles' and 'Achilles' is not a definition of 'lion'. A metaphor is neither a definition nor a set of synonyms. The explication, suggested by some recent literary criticism, of the sense in which he is a lion, is both tedious and necessary. We are imagined as spelling out the metaphor in terms of a series of comparisons until we arrive at the sense in which 'Achilles' is a 'lion'. An obvious point is that the metaphor suppresses aspects: e.g. 'Achilles' does not have four legs. The spelling out is to avoid the literal force of the '*is*'. We have to interpret the sense in which he is and is not a 'lion'. A problem with this example is that with such a metaphor an explicit series of comparisons seems unlikely. If we take 'lion' to imply brave, then the phrase, in modern English is either a cliché or idiomatic and in both cases there is no genuine metaphorical problem. However, ambiguity remains if 'brave' is not necessarily implied or if we reflect on the anthropomorphism of 'brave' as a predicate of 'lion'. Obviously what are being compared are essentially domains of language; language normally associated with the properties of men and of lions, which, in this case, might include the idea of kingship or nobility. If the sentence is embedded in text, then the surrounding discourse will also have a part to play in leading us towards an interpretation. A problem with the process *itself* is that is seems to imply that a non-literal use of language can be translated into a series of literal uses from which the sense of the metaphor can be established. This takes away from metaphor any independent source of meaning or of creative ambiguity. This 'almost understood, but not quite' quality of metaphor in poetry or fiction (the 'tension' of the metaphor) is part of its force.

The notion of transference can be illustrated using a modern economic example. 'Investment in education is investment in the creation of human capital' is a sentence in which transference of associations across two categories takes place: 'human' and 'capital', which might be taken as exclusive categories in an elementary natural classification system. Human capital, if taken literally, might refer to slavery. Capital might be taken literally as machines. The transference across the (alleged) natural categories makes it possible to rework the notion of education. Education is, in this metaphor, not consumption but investment and if the metaphor proves useful, the application of the senses in which it is 'investment', through the application of capital theory and its associated language and techniques, will spell out the comparison implicit in the view that education is investment. If the metaphor is so successful in its implications that we slip into the assumption that education is nothing but investment in human capital and forget that elements such as individual preferences, objectives and general cultural values have a part to play in the development of an educational system, then we are being used by the metaphor rather than using it. Once a metaphorical extension of meaning has taken place, the words themselves are changed in the process. Does 'capital' have any literal meaning? In most economics writing the concept is already metaphorically extended.

Metaphor and other tropes

There are, however, other uses of language in which the words used do not mean what they are ordinarily taken to mean. These include simile, in which one thing is said to be like another, and analogy, metonymy in which something associated with a person or object is used to stand for the person or object and synecdoche in which a part of something is used to stand for the whole of it. Aristotle devoted some time to considering some of these other tropes.

Analogy, in which a similarity of relations, A is to B as C is to D, is of the essence, was included by Aristotle under the general term metaphor. Aristotle, in reviewing the study of 'likeness', also mentions a situation in which similarity of functions, 'as one is to another so another is to another' is also regarded as analogy (*Topics*: 108b, 7–12). The former, for example, applies to proportionality in geometry and the latter applies to situations in which we are moving by comparison from aspects that are known to those that are unknown (though Aristotle illustrates with respect to knowns). This is comparison and inference and the conclusions are reached by induction. Analogy spells out specific aspects of a comparison which other figures of speech, such as simile and metaphor, also either explicitly or implicitly make. In all of his writing, political, philosophical and scientific, Aristotle made considerable use of analogy. For an example from his scientific thinking, see the sustained use of a 'carpenter and timber' analogy with respect to exploring and illustrating relations and actions concerning the generation of offspring (*Generation of Animals*: 730b, 5–30). He used a negative analogy to express his views on the unnatural nature of usury: money grows out of money but not in the way that offspring grow out of their natural parents. Argument by analogy is argument and is (potentially) open to counter-argument in a way in which simple-sentence literary metaphors are not.

Aristotle held that a metaphor was a collapsed simile and his successors gave pride of place to it. This has tended to be taken to support the view that a metaphor can be translated into a simile without loss of meaning. The view that a metaphor is an implicit comparison and simile an explicit comparison suggests that it is appropriate to think of translating from one to another. However, the lack of explicitness in metaphor suggests that in the translation some aspects of (possible) meanings are likely to be lost. This can be both an advantage and a disadvantage with respect to the development of ideas. An economics example can be used to illustrate this point. What effective difference does it make to say that 'the economic agent is a utility maximizer', as opposed to 'the economic agent acts *like* a utility maximizer'? The literal force of the 'is' is potentially dangerous if it leads us to forget that such a sentence is not a definition of what it is to be human. When undergraduates object to this view of human motivation, it is likely to be their literal interpretation of the 'is' that they are objecting to. If, on the other hand, they see no objection then the danger is that they will be used by the metaphor. 'Be' is a forceful verb. With metaphor we must be careful that it does not over-deliver meanings. Simile makes one aspect of metaphorical meaning explicit and that is the idea of comparison. The difference could be that the simile forces us to make the comparison and so might help us evaluate the statement: in what sense, in what contexts or circumstances, in which discourse? Historically, the metaphor is based upon a scientific analogy with frictionless surfaces and other schematic concepts in classical mechanics. Institutionalists, of course, reject the metaphor in whichever form.

Modern authorities would hold the view that the discussion of the theory of metaphor encompasses all of the other related tropes. McCloskey correctly states that economists are constantly extending the range of application of economic theory by observing that 'situation x is just like situation y', e.g. conscription is just like a tax on labour; marriage is just like a customs union or, Black's example, 'marriage is a zero-sum game' (Black 1979: 29); local authority rates are a tax on home ownership. This is metaphor as a means of reconstructing the way a topic is viewed in terms of something that is already well known (Crider and Cirillo 1991: 181). If we carry with us the question 'in what sense', then there is something to be gained in being able to recognize the rhetorical force of such statements. The metaphor becomes a vehicle for applying established insights and vocabularies to the new (transformed) situation.

Metonymy is a process of non-logical deletion. According to Lodge, a sentence such as 'the hulls of the ships crossed the deep ocean' can be turned into a metonymy by removing 'of the ships' and 'ocean' to give: 'the hulls crossed the deep'. The ships cannot cross without the hulls and the hulls 'stand-for' the ships (Lodge 1977: 76). Lakoff takes metonymic models to apply to language situations in which a 'stands-for' relationship holds. He extends the idea to situations whereby a 'sub category' is used to gain understanding of a whole category (Lakoff 1990: 79). Where the subcategory is subsequently equated with the category as a whole, the result is stereotype. Where a subcategory is used as part of an explanatory sequence to avoid pedantically spelling out an explanatory sequence, the result can puzzle. This is essentially shorthand and this metonymic modelling of a larger 'structured scenario' is likely to be found in, for example, the later portions of textbooks when the longer structured scenario has already been familiarized. It is also likely to be found in research contexts. Lodge is of the view that we cannot talk about metonymy without discussing metaphor, not because metonymy is part of a general class of tropes to which they both belong, but because it is opposed to metaphor. Lakoff sees the possibility of overlap.

Other types of metaphor

However, if we are to take the rhetorical analysis of economics seriously, we need to be able to identify examples of metaphor when we come across them in text. It is not clear that all types have the same cognitive implications, even if we are prepared to refer to them by the term metaphor. In any review, however brief, of additional items (paradox, personification, idiom, irony and allegory) some effort must be made to link the trope with purposeful activity in construction or evaluation of written economics. What is of interest is not the classification, but the relationship with the surrounding discourse and the meanings which emerge as a result of interpretation within an economics context.

Thales's 'All things are water' is a paradox which, according to Pepper, constituted a root-metaphor up to the time of Socrates (Pepper 1942: 92). Aristotle (*Topics*: 104b, 10–25) mentions Heraclitus' paradoxical belief 'that all things are in motion'. Paradox is not unknown in economics writing. Some of Ricardo's contemporaries found his writing paradoxical. De Quincey has one of his characters, Philebus, view Ricardo 'as obscure and as ambitiously paradoxical' (1824: 473). The 'paradox of value' is an obvious example of economics paradox though more extended than a single-sentence metaphor. The relationship with metaphor is obvious, 'Achilles is a lion' is a paradox as is, to those uninitiated in economic discourse, 'money is a good like any other'.

Personification is a device often resorted to in order to talk about abstract forces or processes or to make us feel more at home in a hostile world. The personification of 'demand' is a recurrent feature of writing in microeconomics. This is explored below. Personification is also found in the field of macroeconomic policy. Lakoff and Johnson, in their work on the ubiquity of metaphor in the way that English constructs time, space and other aspects of daily life, point out the extent to which everyday discussion about inflation, including policy-discussion, resorts to the personification of inflation as adversary (Lakoff and Johnson 1980: 33–5). Their argument is that metaphor must be considered as an organizing principle for sets of language use, for example, 'warfare' as a metaphor for all situations to which we are opposed (inflation as 'the enemy'; 'attacking' an argument; 'defending' a position). Lakoff and Johnson use evidence from their social experience of language use, rather than from a detailed study of political or policy texts relating to the economy. Inflation as 'the' enemy in such texts are just as likely to be ideologically, or theory, derived. Inflation could be 'an' enemy and unemployment could be 'the' enemy. The point about 'warfare' would still stand but the particular selection of ideas would embody an alternative view as to the objectives of policy. Personification of inflation, in this sense, is not inevitable, but the result of rhetorical choices.

Dammann (1977–8: 133) warns us off idiomatic expressions, i.e. conventional expressions with a meaning that is different from their literal meanings including those that look like similes, such as 'as drunk as a newt'. No amount of knowledge about newts helps us to understand the phrase. 'The economic engine is running smoothly' would, however, be a (trivial) metaphor not because of the word 'running' but because of the use of the words 'economic engine'. We are very familiar with the extended sense of the word running and no image of a runner or an implied set of comparisons come to mind. However, the words 'economic engine' refer to one intellectual construct, 'the economy' in terms of another noun, 'the engine' and so carry the full weight of the mechanistic interpretation of economic activity.

And then there is irony in which the intended meaning is the opposite of the literal meaning. Irony is to be found in those parts of economic discourse intent upon the improvement of economic conditions through policy intervention. The term 'developing countries' is, for example, along with other terms such as 'balanced growth' and 'investment in human capital', ironic if, despite all efforts to promote development, such countries are not growing. However, this exemplification of irony is already beyond the strictly classical notion. In classical rhetorical discussion, irony is consciously contrived or intended.

A more significant use can be made of a rhetorical awareness of irony: development economics has always made classifications. Seers, for example, was concerned that the problems of development and the problems of describing the problems of development (theory production), kept slipping away from each other. He suggested research into typologies as a way out: more classification rather than less! If concepts to be used in classification are over-refined or treated as technical concepts, then change in the world is likely to move ahead before changes are made in typologies: 'developing countries' do not have a unique set of defining characteristics though they may share certain family traits. Whatever the case, change will be more rapid in 'developing countries' than in the analysis of the classification. It is ironic that a subject which must be concerned with the process of change should have, in the past, done so through a set of classifications that tended to stereotype that change. A sense of irony can add to our critical capacity to evaluate ideas about economic life. It is not, however, clear that it is best considered under metaphor: according to Dammann, to misunderstand irony is to misunderstand a context within which a statement is made. It is not about misunderstanding the difference between the literal and the metaphorical (Dammann 1977–8: 133–4).

McCloskey also includes allegory in his list of tropes and has defined it as 'long-winded metaphor' and refers to it in the context of stories (McCloskey 1986: 504). It is essentially a genre that makes extensive and sustained use of particular metaphors and analogies. Successful allegory consists of two meanings – the literal and, through personification and symbol, the figurative. To interpret one and ignore the other reduces the meaning. Mandeville's *Fable of the Bees* (1714, 1957) is the most obvious example in poetic writing of an allegorical work with some direct economic intent. Adam Smith objected to Mandeville's notion that 'private vices were public benefits' in a passage in which he analyses the argument outwith its satirical intent though the *Fable* seems to have had some influence upon Smith's view of cooperation based upon 'self-love' (Robinson 1964: 23). Keynes makes two passing references to Mandeville in *The General Theory* as well as incorporating the *Fable* on a sustained basis into chapter 23. Even if the attempt is 'somewhat forced' (Robinson 1964: 20), the *Fable* was given, in this context, a new interpretive framework as a result.

Identifying metaphor in economics

Edgeworth's *Mathematical Psychics*, despite its sustained use of metaphor, is not strictly speaking allegorical though it certainly exhibits features that would identify it as having been influenced, perhaps, by the Romantic movement (Henderson 1993: 219). Works that contributed to the critique of growth in the 1960s adopted both allegory and parable as a means of developing and communicating economic argument, suggesting that the genre of allegory is not yet a redundant one. Kahn argues that the whole of general equilibrium theory is nothing other than a sustained allegory. However, allegory in works on economics in the 1960s, is added to the mathematics in order to make the works more memorable!

The 'internal' demarcation of different tropes does not necessarily yield unambiguous classification and interpretation. Take the seemingly harmless term 'the market' as used in microeconomics. Is it a fiction like 'the Crown' in British constitutional discussions, or a metonymy in which a part of economic life stands for the whole of it, or is it a powerful personification? What is the force of the 'the' and how do 'a market', 'the market', 'market' and 'markets' differ in the meanings that they deliver? Answers will depend partly upon the contexts within which the individual term is used: some writings advocating privatization will use it to confuse an ideal (the perfect market) and likely social experience. It is as well to remember that 'market' is a noun used to sum up a bundle of social and economic conditions in the world (only some of which are known in detail) as well as the theories used to understand those conditions. Brown (this volume) sets out three different theories relevant to the understanding of markets. Such a plurality is unlikely to be implied by 'the' market. Metonymic stereotyping is a distinct possibility in which one category of 'market', the perfect market, is equated with all categories. The definite article carries with it the notion of an ideal ('the student . . .', 'the reader . . .') and so adds to the process of eliminating alternative possibilities. If we look at 'the market' and see a place where, as a result of associations set up in textbook discussions, 'competition' leads to the harmonization of interests, rather than a place where (say) 'power' is exercised and there are (potential) winners and losers, another useful vision is forced out. The same is true with respect to the term 'the economy': this too can be used to imply the existence of a single entity that is separate and distinct from society. Those interested in integrating economic aspects of life into a wider view of social life and who wish to conceptualize social life and 'the market' in terms of 'power' and 'legitimation', will inevitably wish to challenge the concrete meanings carried by the combination of concrete noun and definite article. Others will see this as tilting at windmills. The classification is less important than the realization that in elementary economic texts the summarizing concept of 'the market' has a strategic role in the construction of an economist's discourse.

Problems are therefore bound to arise with respect to how one or another author uses and identifies metaphor in a corpus of economics writing. Hoover's criticism of Mirowski's work on metaphor in neoclassical economics is based partly on what terms are taken to be metaphorical (Hoover 1991: 142). Mirowski, according to Hoover, sees almost 'every term in every context' as metaphor. Hoover prefers a more restricted view. This is a particular example of a general problem with metaphor identified by Booth: metaphor has now been identified in so many ways that 'there is no human expression' . . . that would not be metaphoric in someone's definition' (Booth 1978: 50). Specification of a theoretical framework as well as skills in tropological recognition are essential in any analysis that focuses on written discourse. When it comes to the construction of economic argument, however, not every trope included under metaphor carries equal significance, some like the deliberate use of irony or the use of idiom, either technical or familiar, may have stylistic rather than cognitive implications. Metaphor, simile and analogy are more likely to have generative implications. But there is also the question of what theory of metaphor is relevant, for this will, in part, determine the terms upon which assessment of metaphor takes place. Hoover's criticism is that Mirowski holds that metaphor is a commitment to a complete mapping of one subject upon another. Most theoreticians would hold, with Hoover, that a complete mapping would involve taking the metaphor literally, in which case it would no longer be metaphor. Discussion of this point will be postponed until later. Before that we discuss how metaphor was viewed in intellectual history before and after the Renaissance.

A BRIEF HISTORY OF METAPHOR

Metaphor and the Enlightenment

What metaphor is taken to signify has changed from society to society. It is essential to keep in mind what Booth has called the 'explosion of meanings' associated with the term (Booth). Medieval scholars viewed the world as a 'book written by God' which could, like any book, ' "mean" more than it apparently "said" ' (Hawkes 1972: 17). In such a world, 'lion', for example, signified 'the resurrection' as the lion, after three days, was held to breathe life into its still-born cubs. The domain of language associated with the word 'lion', under such circumstances would differ from that of the time of Aristotle or from that available today. The medieval scholars also held that the universe was ordered according to a hierarchical structure and proceeded from this to argue, by analogy, that what was in human society reflected what was in nature: an ordered heaven implied an ordered earth (West 1965: 11). In the later Enlightenment, 'Providence' taught humankind moral, particularly economic, lessons. These views of the world are not ours, though they become our views if we apply (say) Newtonian mechanics or quantum theory to assist us in the study of society.

Puritan England, with its desire for plainness in all aspects of life, including speech, reacted against the elaborate metaphors found in Shakespearian English (Hawkes 1972; Weimann 1974–5). Aristotle's identification of clarity with logic found its fruit in the cultural outcomes of plain style. In the intellectual movement from revelation to reason, metaphor along with other wild imaginings of the medieval type, became suspect. Logical speech came to be seen as such speech as 'attracts no attention to itself as speech' (Hawkes 1972: 28). The views of philosophers such as Hobbes and Locke altered the way in which seventeenth-century prose, both in science and in arts, came to be written. Hobbes (1588–1679), in his search for clarity, warns against metaphors as part of his description of the 'abuses of speech': the use of words 'in other senses than they are ordained for' (i.e. metaphors) lead to the possibility of deception (Hobbes 1651: 19). Locke (1632–1704), who displays an understanding of the pleasure of metaphor, and who, like Hobbes, uses metaphors with skill, later holds that, 'If we would speak of things as they are', then the, 'figurative application of words eloquence hath invented, are for nothing else but to insinuate wrong ideas, move passions, and thereby mislead judgement . . .'.[2] Metaphor puts ideas together to please the imagination. Judgement separates out ideas in order 'to avoid being misled in similitude and by affinity to take one thing for another' (Locke 1991: 72). Locke, however, felt that a 'wary reasoning from analogy leads us often to the discovery of truths and useful productions which would otherwise lie concealed' (Locke 1991: 365). 'Wary', presumably, because the inferences do not necessarily follow.

The Royal Society took a similar line, rejecting tropes and calling for plain style or, according to Thomas Sprat, 'a close, naked, natural way of speaking... preferring the language of artisans, countrymen, and merchants, before that of wits and scholars' (West 1965: 112). The separation of literary metaphor from 'wary reasoning from analogy' was almost complete. Later, behind the Royal Society stood the influential figure of Newton (1642–1729) whose mechanics were to dominate science and have a profound influence on social science (see Ingrao and Israel 1990).

Adam Smith (1723–90), whose 'invisible hand' metaphor is one of the most famous, and most infamous, in the history of economic thought, also had something to say about metaphor. His *Lectures on Rhetoric* propose a psychological approach to the study of communication. He contests the Classical view of figures of speech and suggests that:

> When the sentiment of the speaker is expressed in a neat, clear, plain and clever manner, and the passion or affection he is possessed of and intends, by sympathy, to communicate to his hearer, is plainly and cleverly hit off, then and then only the expression has all the force and beauty that language can give it. It matters not the least whether the figures of speech are introduced or not.
>
> (Smith 1983: 26)

Smith held that a system of rhetoric could not ignore tropes but he held a very low opinion of the exercise of classification: "Tis however from the consideration of these figures, and the divisions and subdivisions of them, that so many systems of rhetoric both ancient and modern have been formed. They are generally a very silly set of books and not at all instructive...' (Smith 1983: 26). For Smith it is the context and aptness of figures that gives them force and beauty and not the mere fact of being a figure. Despite his criticism of tropes, Smith used them in many different contexts:

> Money, therefore, the great wheel of circulation, the great instrument of commerce, like all other instruments of trade, though it makes a part and a very valuable part of the capital, makes no part of the revenue of the society to which it belongs...
>
> (*Wealth of Nations*: book 2, ch. 2)

Although he makes no reference to Smith, Cohen's idea that the maker and the appreciator of metaphor are drawn together by the achievement of intimacy (Cohen 1976: 6) might help us appreciate Smith's notion of 'sympathy'. What is being focused upon in such ideas is an appeal to the special interests of the audience: in policy discussion, for example, an appeal could be made to the electorate in terms of an elaborate set of metaphors based upon the notion of the national cake: slicing the existing cake; making the cake bigger. Such metaphors try to reconcile 'multiple interests' (Crider and Cirillo 1991: 184) in terms of the audience's own interests.

Recent views on metaphor

There was a reaction to such negative views in the course of the nineteenth century when the poets Shelley, Keats, Wordsworth and Coleridge re-emphasized the imaginative power of metaphor to create meaning.[3] In stressing the power of the imagination, the Romantics demoted reason. Reason in science was seen 'almost as an antidote to the imagination' (Medawar 1984: 45). By the middle of the century, Mill recognized, somewhat nervously, the role that imagination played in the formation of hypotheses (Medawar 1984: 115–35).

The idea of the creative power of metaphor was not new. Vico (1669–1744), Italian philosopher of history and jurist, had held that through work, man created the world and that metaphor was not the decoration of facts but the means whereby facts were experienced. Vico had stressed the relativism of human nature and of understanding and underlined the role of critical interpretation in the analysis of human society. The modern view of metaphor is consistent with that of Vico: metaphor changes perceptions and so is constitutive of experience. McCloskey has drawn the attention of economists to Vico's ideas. It is through the work of economists that economic language has made and fashioned the economist's world. In the philosophical writings of Nietzsche, according to Hinman, the very distinction between the literal and the figurative is obliterated: for Nietzsche, literal language is nothing other than metaphors that we have forgotten, root metaphors that structure experience and which are often not recognized as metaphors. Such a view eliminates any notion of truth based upon correspondence; with respect to root metaphors there is no 'privileged' point of view from which the metaphor can be assessed (Hinman 1982: 197). For philosophy, Pepper identified four that stood the test of time: formism (the root metaphor being 'similarity'), mechanism ('machine'), organicism ('the organic process') and contextualism ('the historic event') (Pepper 1942: 141). The latter three are to be found in most of the major schools of economics and may constitute a basis for their classification.

Although economists in the late nineteenth century used metaphor, more particularly, analogy, the theory of metaphor held by the wider academic community tended to be dominated by the thought of the English empirical tradition. The notion that logical positivism was influenced by the linguistic ideas associated with plain style, with the possibility of a clear, unambiguous language for reporting on the world, is widely held to be the case. Positivism, in an effort to cope with the ambiguity of aspects of social science, distinguished between means and ends as well as between the context of discovery (where ideas are developed) and the context of justification (where ideas are tested). However, with the insight that metaphor generates a whole language field, it is difficult to see how the divisions suggested can actually be sustained. Although metaphor and language are necessarily bound together, Burrell holds that the decorative view of metaphor is sustained by a 'world view'. Fowler provides an interesting language-led description of the elements: 'Cumulatively, consistent structural options, agreeing in cutting the presented world to one pattern or another, give rise to an impression of a world view . . .' (Fowler 1977: 76). When metaphor is seen as 'mere decoration' then it can be removed, and in excising it ambiguity is removed: what is in the world and what is in human language will coincide (Burrell 1973: 258). This is the 'one real-world' view, or the 'successively closer approximations to nature' view of the relationship between language and what really exists (Kuhn). It is a view that many economists hold and which modern notions of metaphor challenge.

The current view of metaphor is that it is a universal aspect of ordinary talk with a significant role in all aspects of language including academic language. Cicero noticed that even 'rustics use metaphor' but it is only in the last forty years that the university of metaphorical usage has begun to be studied. Metaphors shape and extend what can be said through comparisons and associations. The force of the comparisons are not simply a matter of pre-existing comparisons. Metaphors, particularly, but not only, in literature have the power to create the comparisons. Both in science and art, metaphor works to change meanings. In this progressive and generic sense it throws light upon new areas of inquiry. As with any light, metaphor is capable of both illuminating dark areas and of casting shadows. The dark side of metaphor is that it suppresses aspects of a topic (and this can be an advantage as well as a disadvantage) or dismisses them as inconsistent with the prevailing construction, as well as expressing salient points compatible with the inherent comparisons that are being made. In discussing a new area of inquiry with the vocabulary properly derived from another area it sets down a language, modified with the passage of time, within which discussion takes place.

METAPHOR IN ECONOMICS

Loewenberg holds that not all metaphors are the same and distinguishes between 'single-phrase metaphors' (viz., 'Achilles is a lion') and 'extended metaphors' (analogy, model and theory) and holds that generalizations that apply to the former do not necessarily apply to the latter (Loewenberg 1973: 32). The substantive use of metaphor in economics is more likely to be associated with extended rather than single-sentence metaphor and this is the justification for introducing Loewenberg at this point. The explication of a single-sentence metaphor, by the process of comparison, has already been shown to be unconvincing. Indeed, the idea of comparison is not an essential aspect of the metaphor's meaning but such explorations may be an essential aspect of extended metaphors. These have research and other implications that go beyond their immediate literary effect. In both practical and theoretical terms the appraisal of metaphor is likely to be undertaken in different ways because of the different contexts. Metaphors in literature are likely to be judged by their emotional impact or by the strength of the pictures that they paint. In science, the judgement is more likely to be in terms of the usefulness or 'fruitfulness' of a metaphor or even in terms of 'truth' and 'falsity'; although there is a contradiction, for a metaphor, if taken literally, is (usually) false.

Extended metaphors, which must be taken to include root metaphors, though Loewenberg makes no specific reference to them, unlike simple 'single-sentence' metaphors, need to be explicated by further comparisons and counter-analogies. This is, of course, the purpose of Locke's 'wary reasoning'. A root metaphor provides a sustained basis for the organization of discussion of a topic, for the selection of terms that are used to discuss the topic and for the selection of any subsidiary metaphors that are likely to be applied to the topic (Pepper 1942: 91–6). In the face of the web of language, a critical, self-reflecting approach to any study is essential if we are to avoid being used by the now decayed metaphors adopted by scholars in the past. In re-examining metaphor 'the only probe we possess is a still more accurate employ of language' (Burrell 1973: 258).[4]

Metaphor and the language of economics

In economics the power of metaphor to develop a way of talking might be best illustrated by referring to the pedagogic writing in the textbook with respect to the development of notions of equilibrium. The language of supply and demand is built on the transference of the idea of balance and equilibrium, forces and pressures (leading to the directional metaphors: 'upwards' and 'downwards') on price and equilibrium. Prices and goods are the key elements in the market. The outcome of this approach is the elimination of individual economic agents from direct influence in the market, by exploitation of the tense and mood structures available in English and by the personification of demand. The 'point of view' is that of the neutral scientific observer, rather than that of the agents involved. Thus, in the simple supply-and-demand model 'prices rise' rather than 'prices are raised' by some active and deliberate economic agent (Henderson and Hewings 1990). Of course, in the competitive market no individual agent has any power to influence price and this requires a way of talking that can match the insight that is being established. The original metaphor, in the context of the competitive market, has led to the generation of a style of talking in which, for example, demand as a noun is personified and the limited range of verbs associated with the elementary model (increase, shift, rise, demand, move) are either intransitive or used

356

in the passive mood. Two (authentic) examples are enough to make the point: 'With the amount of fish supplied unchanged, the stronger demand bids up the momentary price of fish'. 'Bids up' is an active verb but 'demand' is the actor. 'Gas and electric cookers are substitutes for each other and when gas cookers rise in price some households will buy electric rather than gas cookers, and the demand for electric cookers will thus rise'. Anyone new to the discipline is likely to find this sentence a puzzle. Apart from problems with substitutes in the opening part of the sentence, occasioned by the lack of reference to any consumers, 'rise' is an intransitive verb and without the adjunct 'in price', the clause, 'gas cookers rise in price' would not be awkward, but nonsense. Details of the language used carefully reflect the intention of removing human agents: abstract language to sustain abstract forces. Such language has to be formally learned and needs to be socialized through the use of textbooks.

The endless repetition of the underlying metaphor has helped it to decay (so it is 'dead' rather than 'living') (Ricoeur 1975). Firm traces are left in the language of the subject at an elementary level, for the metaphor, despite its long use, is to be found just below the surface.[5] Repetition, in the introductory textbooks, adds to the strength of equilibrium notions in economics, making it difficult for new ideas to take hold. Joan Robinson, criticizing the notion of equilibrium, added persuasive power to her writing by bringing the metaphor back to life:

> There is also a psychological element in the survival of equilibrium theory. There is an irresistible attraction about the concept of equilibrium – the almost silent hum of a perfectly running machine; the apparent stillness of the exact balance of counteracting pressures; the automatic smooth recovery from a chance disturbance .... We have to look for a psychological explanation to account for the powerful influence of an idea that is intellectually unsatisfactory.
>
> (Robinson 1964: 77–8)

Robinson chose her image with care: we are dealing here with metaphor as 'incisive communication' (Crider and Cirillo 1991: 174). Had she chosen something less soporific and more dangerous, such as a steam-engine, it would have been more difficult for her to make the point that she was making. There is a difference between the silent hum of her machine and the powerful noise of the engine of growth! Marshall, in reviewing the role played by analogies in the development of economic theory, illustrated his notion of 'relative rest' by reference to the experience of the 'man in the train', a train pulled by a disruptive steam-engine, and the action of stowing a parcel on the luggage rack. Experience taught such a person 'to look out for the disruptive dynamical element' (Pigou 1925: 312). The point to note here is not that metaphors mislead, all useful metaphors have that potential, but that a rhetorical awareness of what it is that is being suppressed by the metaphor can be as important as an understanding of what is being expressed.[6] Was Marshall using the metaphor and were later economists used by the metaphor? Joan Robinson might have turned to the way in which the mechanistic metaphor became embedded in the language of economics rather than to psychology as a means of understanding the institutionalization of equilibrium.

If we return to the notion of economic agents and decide to focus on their behaviour then entrepreneurship and theories of entrepreneurship come to the fore. Suppose we substitute the term 'actor' for 'agent' and take the term to point towards economy as drama. This very simple shift of noun allows for a new set of 'generating principles' with which to think about the construction of economic activity. This set consists of terms drawn from the work of Kenneth Burke in which he set out to analyse basic forms of thought and the attribution of motives: act, scene, agent, agency and purpose (Burke 1945). Each term is capable of further elaboration: agent, co-agent and counter-agent. It is not difficult to think of 'market scenarios' within which this type of dramatic, but nonetheless analytical, analysis could be usefully developed. We are here dealing with metaphor as 'revealing something new' (Crider and Cirillo 1991: 177). Although the economic actor in such an approach would be located, the point of view would be based on external interpretation. The overall narrative would not be conducted in mechanistic terms but the sequence, initial equilibrium, change causing event, followed by a new equilibrium may still apply since this is the sequence of events in classical drama. As far as I know there has been no such general application of Burke's ideas to the economic analysis of markets. Von Wright's concern with goals and purposes of human action certainly uses parts of the elements of this set (see Mäki 1990) though, of course, independent of Burke. It is not my intention to spell out the way or ways in which the dramatistic approach could develop into a theory of market action. Rather it is to illustrate that by a simple substitution of nouns, a new set of ideas becomes available. The development of such ideas would also involve the use of abstract language, but the details of such language would differ from a method which was initially concerned with the removal of human actors.

It is part of the generative aspect of metaphor to assist in the development of a routine vocabulary for handling economic ideas. This was recognized by nineteenth-century writers on economics, particularly Marx (who made an analysis of the language of property), Marshall (who stressed the pedagogic value of metaphor as well as its usefulness in the direct exploration of ideas about economic analysis) and Edgeworth (who used metaphors drawn from thermodynamics and other aspects of contemporary physics to extend his own understanding of economic processes). In this sense, metaphor 'increases what we can significantly say ... with the vocabulary we have' (Loewenberg 1973: 44).

There are other instances. Watery images, some derived directly, others indirectly, from hydraulics, abound: liquidity, floating exchange-rates, flotations, flows, circulation, leakages, injections, trickle-down effects. Walras and Edgeworth used images of lakes to picture equilibrium and disequilibrium. Irving Fisher used a hydraulic model as the basis for analogical argument in working out features of general equilibrium (Inrgrao and Israel 1990: 247). The physical model has long since gone, elements of the language remain.

It is pointless to ask in what medium floating exchange-rates float (they bob up and down on a graph) but not quite so pointless to wonder why, when money so clearly accumulates in company and some individual bank accounts, we insist upon the circulation of money. The circulation of money is derived by analogy from William Harvey's discovery of the circulation of the blood (Viner 1937: 37).[7] Money as 'blood' sits uncomfortably with 'money as a commodity like any other' for if 'money as blood' flows in one direction, commodities must flow in the other direction! It is also pertinent to ask what it is that circulates when money is said to circulate. The advent of coined money in the ancient world gave rise not only to economic and political symbols and to epigrams but to the notion of words and thoughts as coins. What physically moved from hand to hand was not hermeneutically simple. Much later, Nietzsche depicts truths as '... metaphors worn out and without sensuous powers, coins which have lost their impressions and now seen only as metal, no longer as coins' (Hinman 1982: 189).[8] The symbolic value of money is never far from sight in the political arena. 'The pound had a good day ...'; 'the pound must be able to look the dollar in the eye ...' are personifications of some significance. If then we are thinking seriously about 'money' then it is unlikely that the idea of money is likely to be fully understood within any *single* metaphor.

The use of metaphor in the generation of a new way of talking about ideas at a level beyond the level of the individual (simple) sentence challenges the notion that 'vocabulary is somehow out there in the world, waiting for us to discover it' (Rorty 1989: 6). The generative role of metaphor is in keeping with Quine's view that metaphor is to be found alive and well in the growing areas of a discipline (Quine 1979: 160). But in academic discourse it is the research community, rather than the reader, that traces out the implication of the metaphor beyond the level of the sentence.

Analogy and model: metaphor at the frontier

Argument by analogy, from thermodynamics, formed a very significant part of the way in which Edgeworth developed his ideas on contract and competition in *Mathematical Psychics*. Edgeworth seemed to see competition as atoms in motion and he hit upon the analogy 'kinetic energy: potential energy: expenditure: utility' (Mirowski, forthcoming). This is, again, metaphor as 'revealing something new' or 'transforming a perspective' (Crider and Cirillo 1991: 181). In *Mathematical Psychics* numerous analogies are drawn. The fact that Edgeworth works out some of the analogies and leaves others implicit, contributes to the difficult nature of his work (Henderson 1993: 213). However, Edgeworth clearly distinguished between two levels of figures, the 'elegant and convenient' metaphors and 'deep and real analogy' (Mirowski, forthcoming: 23). Marshall, writing in 1898, considered mechanics and biology to be significant sources for 'serviceable analogy' for the development of economic theory. The mechanical metaphor as we have seen, provides a basis for a study of equilibrium as can the biological metaphor, based on the organism and homeostatic adjustments to maintain equilibrium. The choice of metaphor will influence the way in which the analysis develops in language terms and the relationship between metaphor and narrative is continuously reinforced. Marshall's concern was, in the terms established earlier in the chapter, that the static mechanistic analogy suppresses the dynamic aspects of individual and system growth: trees of the forest and the cycle of youth, maturity and decay express aspects of economic life that become reduced to 'exit' and 'entry' conditions in the mechanistic model. In the life history of an actual economy or industry (for example, in the Japanese notion of the UK economy as a 'sun-set' economy where sunset is metaphorically linked to old age) such notions might be relevant. Mixing metaphors, often frowned upon in literary criticism, might be something to be valued in heuristic as well as in other terms. In the view being developed here, metaphor, model and narrative are not alternatives but interwoven parts of economics discourse. Analogies, like metaphor, are to be found in the growing parts of a discipline: the early stages of an expanding research programme.[9] Once the research programme has been articulated the force of the original metaphor is dulled as its useful elements become incorporated into the routine language of the discipline.

A single metaphor rarely gives rise to concept and vocabulary development. Repeated use is needed. Nineteenth-century economics writers resorted to mechanical analogies but the use of mechanical analogies has a longer history. The nature of the analogies used has been determined by the kind of machines available: clock mechanisms in the seventeenth and eighteenth centuries, heat engines in the nineteenth century and computer technologies in the late twentieth century (Hesse 1972: 173; Pepper 1942: 186). The implications of this view of the development of the analysis of economic life is that with each advance in technology, new vocabularies became available which in turn imply the reworking of previously held ideas. The 'invisible hand' metaphor is still used to shape and challenge notions of the market (Baumol and Blackman 1991: 1). References to 'clockwork' are now rare but can be found. Lachmann entitles an appendix to a work on market process as 'The market is not a clockwork' (Lachmann 1986: 156). The seductive power of the mechanistic metaphor is to be found in the success of Newton's celestial mechanics and in the practical progress of machines from clocks and automata to steam and other engines. The progression of the Newtonian ideal in the development of economic thought is set out in detail by Ingrao and Israel. There cannot be any presumption that changes in technology or in scientific understanding lead to a more direct understanding of human behaviour. It is, of course, analogical argument that some see as the basis for scientific models though with the extension of analogies from science to economics it is not always clear that strict Aristotelian analogy is being, or could be, followed. In both respects an understanding of argument by analogy will be useful in an exploration of what it is, if anything, an economic model is a model. 'Models' in the eighteenth and nineteenth centuries implied mechanisms that could be pictured as in the following example from the writings of Adam Smith:

> Systems in many respects resemble machines. A machine is a little system, created to perform, as well as to connect together, in reality, those different movements and effects which the artist has occasion for. A system is an imaginary machine, invented to connect together in the fancy those different movements and effects which are already in reality performed.
>
> (*Astronomy*, IV. 19)

The understanding of the imaginary machine, despite its contrast 'in reality' (i.e. the metaphor following nature rather than our understanding of nature following the metaphor), suggests that Smith held a very narrow view of metaphor and that argument by analogy was not strictly part of that view. Note the clever, double reversion of word order in the passage 'machine is a little system', 'a system is an imaginary machine' and the crossing over of 'in reality' and 'in the fancy'. These two perfectly balanced sentences can be taken as an early example of what Gide and Rist refer to as the 'literary charm' of Smith's writing (Gide and Rist 1948: 70).

Today's theoretical models imply the use of mathematics to structure a situation such that it can be mathematically processed. Israel and Ingrao argue that the change from mechanism to mathematical process occurred, in economics, from 1910 onwards. In this move, forced upon economics by strains within physics, the central position of 'mechanical analogy' gave way to 'mathematical analogy' in economic theorizing about 'equilibrium' (Ingrao and Israel 1990: 171).

Assessing metaphors in economics

The relationship between metaphor, models and contemporary economics language suggests that current linguistic practices are heavily influenced by past metaphors used to explore the frontiers of knowledge as they existed in the past. Historically, then, the fruitfulness of particular metaphors is partly revealed by the traces that they leave in the language of the discipline. The question of the wider assessment of metaphors, particularly of extended metaphors, remains. Literary metaphors contribute towards painting a beautiful picture or pictures, and this is not an inappropriate idea in economics where aesthetic judgements about the elegance of a theory or model can also apply. But, in rational discourse, the usefulness of metaphors and indeed even their truth-value are likely also to be of interest to some people. The vocabulary-generating role has been illustrated, but what about other aspects of assessing metaphor? Mirowski, for example, argues that neo-Classical economics is scientifically flawed because in making use of analogies from science, it failed to achieve a complete mapping of nineteenth-century physics on to the field of economics. For a rigorous argument complete mapping may be essential (though see below) but for starting to think about a topic or recasting a topic, something less will do. Metaphor is a complex idea and is related to argument, communication, language and thought in a number of different ways. Aristotelian analogy is properly about proportionality. The inferences made are inferences and are not deductively necessary. Further argument is required.

The question of the completeness of the mapping from physics to economics is an interesting one but care must be taken not to mis-state the significance of incomplete mapping. The power of the analogy to suggest lines of inquiry, implications, ways of proceeding, is also important. The sense in which mappings can and cannot be made is an essential part of the exploration process itself. Marshall must have intended something along these lines when he said that analogies were useful for 'getting into the saddle'. Once there, they were an 'encumbrance'. It is the suggestiveness of the ideas that is important and not necessarily the direct mapping of one idea onto another. Metaphor is not an identity. There are no sets of definitions and the relationship between terms in a metaphor is not the relationship that exists between synonyms. This is the case as much with a biological as with a mechanical metaphor. It is also the case with other overarching metaphors such as organicism and contextualism. The metaphor may supply a vocabulary but the fit is not likely to be perfect. The usefulness of imperfect similarities is recognized in science. Take, for example, the 'model of electron spin in which the electron is certainly not spinning in the normal sense of, say, the earth spinning on its axis' but the metaphor is the 'best we can do right now' (Eisenberg 1992: 95). Imperfect fit means that the words themselves take on new meanings. The ambiguity of metaphor is also widely understood and illustrated by the domains of discourse within which light is understood as a wave or as a particle. These examples from the scientific field show that usefulness does not imply total mapping. Fruitfulness, a suggestive way of thinking, is what is significant with respect to cognition. Argument by analogy is essentially about inference, about what could be the case. Only investigation over time will say how far the inference is justified. The idea that in metaphor or analogy that the transference is, or can ever be complete, is naive unless the one thing really *is* the other. If society really were available to (say) an analysis founded upon thermodynamics then economics would be physics and the metaphorical 'is' would have literal force. The 'best we can do right now' is, provided it is not complacent, the best that we can do right now.

CONCLUSIONS

Metaphor is slippery. In talking about ways of talking, clarity and precision are both needed. When working upon metaphor in economic thought, care has also to be taken in the specification of a theoretical perspective or perspectives through which it will be discussed. Are we stressing questions of style, of novel association, of framing and changing ideas, of synthesizing different viewpoints or of developing an argument? Are we concerned with the level of the sentence or metaphor's wider role in the development of the discourse? No single theory of metaphor is appropriate in all such differing circumstances. Literary theory is useful for considering style and some aspects of persuasion in economics whereas other aspects of metaphor, such as the suggestiveness of a vision or the generation of a vocabulary, might best be handled within the context of extended metaphor.

Also, we must go beyond the naive view that a metaphor fails because it is not a complete mapping of one domain of language upon another. A complete mapping eliminates metaphor. The terms in a metaphor are neither synonyms nor definitions. What is important is the 'fruitfulness' of a given approach. Sooner or later any metaphor will cease to be fruitful. Useful metaphors *extend* meanings. They work in social science by promoting comparisons and achieve their promotional success by suppressing aspects that are either less relevant or potentially even more relevant. At some stage the suppressed elements will come to our notice.

Marshall understood this. To avoid being used by the dominant metaphor, perhaps Marshall's version of stereoscopic vision is what is required of us all. We can no longer base good practice in a discourse community upon the work practices of Marshall, specialization alone works against it. A plurality of vision can, however, also imply a plurality of collective vision and hence colleagues exploring the areas of economic life suppressed by the prevailing metaphor and metaphors (such as contextualism) excluded by the predominant metaphor. Mechanistic metaphors are currently being exposed but similar exposure can be given to contextualism and to organicism. In the light of this re-examination, I have attempted to avoid using 'the' economist or 'the' economic way of thinking or even 'the' new conversation, preferring to use the indefinite article. Even such a minor change of linguistic practice required an effort far greater than the simple substitution of an 'an' for a 'the' suggests. Metaphors are habits of language and, hence, habits of mind, changing, or even assessing them, is likely to prove much more difficult.

ACKNOWLEDGEMENTS

I am grateful for comments from Roger Backhouse, Leone Burton, Tony Davies, Michael Goulder, Dan Hausman, Lynda Thomas and David Whitehead. I also appreciated two lengthy conversations with Vivienne Brown on metaphor and other topics. Any errors remain my own responsibility.

NOTES

1 The philosopher Tim Moore has pointed out that many cultures designate some uses of language as metaphorical and use metaphors to describe such uses. In Arabic, for example, words for metaphor imply 'bridge' or 'transfer'. The word metaphor in Greek was, according to Stanford, first used by Isocrates (Stanford 1973: 3).
2 Hobbes's attack on metaphor is riddled with it: '... the light of human minds is perspicuous words, but by exact definitions first snuffed, and purged from ambiguity; *reason* is the *pace*; increase of *science*, the way; and the benefit of mankind, the *end*. And on the contrary, metaphors, and senseless and ambiguous words, are like *ignes fatui*; and reasoning upon them is wandering amongst innumerable absurdities; and their end, contention and sedition, or contempt' (Hobbes 1651: 29–30).
3 In September 1800, Coleridge wrote to Godwin: 'I would endeavour to destroy the old antithesis of Words and Things: Elevating as it were Words into Things and living things too' (Stanford 1973: 17).
4 Such a stance carries with it the possibility of falling into the trap of the never-ending classification of tropes.
5 A more complex, though perhaps more useful, way of looking at 'living' and 'dead' metaphor is to recognize that for some new students some of the metaphorical language will be very much alive whereas for staff it will be considerably decayed (Henderson 1982).
6 Schumpeter concentrated on the dynamics of capitalism and moved freely between biological and mechanistic metaphors: 'an evolutionary process'; 'the capitalist engine in motion'; 'the same process of industrial mutation'. Both metaphors stress the ever-changing nature of capitalism as a whole. See Schumpeter (1976: 82–3).
7 For an exploration of 'wheel' metaphors, the origins of circular flow and the early uses of hydraulic diagrams, see Patinkin (1973).
8 For a very striking example of this from a piece of economics writing see F. Y. Edgeworth (1881). On page 3, the lengthy Edgeworthian sentence which begins:

'He that will not verify his conclusions as far as possible by mathematics, as it were bringing the ingots of common sense to be assayed and coined in the mint of the sovereign science . . .' is an example of thought as intellectual gold coin. For Edgeworth's use of metaphor see Henderson (1993).

9 Analogies have not only come from science to economics. Economics has been a source of ideas about text and about symbolization. Turgot draws analogies between symbolization in economics and in language. Marx also was aware of the connections between language and economics (Shell 1978).

BIBLIOGRAPHY

Aristotle (1965) 'On the art of poetry', *Classical Literary Criticism*, trans. T. S. Dorsch, Harmondsworth: Penguin Classics.

Aristotle (1987) *Topics*, in *A New Aristotle Reader*, J. L. Ackrill (ed.), Oxford: Clarendon Press, pp. 60–78.

Baumol, W. J. and Blackman, S. A. B. (1991) *Perfect Markets and Easy Virtue*, Cambridge, MA and Oxford: Basil Blackwell.

Black, M. (1979) 'More about metaphors', in A. Ortony (ed.), *Metaphor and Thought*, Cambridge: Cambridge University Press pp. 19–43.

Booth, W. C. (1978) 'Metaphor as rhetoric; the problem of evaluation', *Critical Inquiry* 5: 49–72.

Booth, W. C. (1979) 'Metaphor and rhetoric', in S. Sacks (ed.), *On Metaphor*. Chicago: University of Chicago Press.

Boyd, R. (1979) 'Metaphor and theory change: what is "Metaphor" a metaphor for', in A. Ortony (ed.), *Metaphor and Thought*, Cambridge: Cambridge University Press.

Brooks, C. (1965) 'Metaphor, paradox and stereotype', *Journal of the British Society of Aesthetics* 5: 315–28.

Burke, K. (1945) *A Grammar of Motives*, New York: Prentice Hall.

Burrell, D. (1973) *Analogy and Philosophical Language*, Yale: Yale University Press.

Cohen, T. (1976) 'Notes on metaphor', *Journal of Aesthetics and Art Criticism* xxxiv, no. 3, Spring: 249–59.

Cooper, D. E. (1986) *Metaphor*, Oxford: Basil Blackwell.

Crider, C. and Cirillo, L. (1991) 'Systems of interpretation and the function of metaphor', *Journal for the Theory of Social Behaviour* 22(2): 171–95.

Dammann, R. M. J. (1977–8) 'Metaphor and other things', *Proceedings of the Aristotelian Society*, new series, LXXVIII: 125–40.

De Quincey, T. (1824) *Dialogues of Three Templars on Political Economy*, republished in *De Quincey on Self-Education, Style, Rhetoric and Political Economy*, London: James Hogg & Sons (undated).

Edgeworth, F. Y. (1881) *Mathematical Psychics*, London: Kegan Paul.

Eisenberg, A. (1992) 'Metaphor in the language of science', *Scientific American* 266(5): 95.

Fowler, R. (1977) *Linguistics and the Novel*, London: Routledge & Kegan Paul.

Gide, C. and Rist, C. (1948) *A History of Economic Doctrines*, 2nd edn, trans. R. Richards, London: Harrap & Co.

Hawkes, T. (1972) *Metaphor*, London: Methuen.

Henderson, W. (1982) 'Metaphor in economics', *Economics*, Winter. Reprinted in M. Coulthard (ed.), *Talking about Text*, discourse analysis monograph no. 13, English Language Research, University of Birmingham, pp. 109–27.

Henderson, W. (1993) 'The problem of Edgeworth's style', in W. Henderson,

T. Dudley-Evans and R. Backhouse (eds), *Economics and Language*, London: Routledge, pp. 200–22.

Henderson, W. and Hewings, A. (1990) 'A language of model-building?', in A. Dudley-Evans and W. Henderson (eds), *The Language of Economics: The Analysis of Economics Discourse*, ELT Docs. no. 134, Oxford: Modern English Publications in Association with the British Council.

Hesse, M. (1972) 'Scientific models', reprinted in W. A. Shible (ed.), *Essays on Metaphor*, Whitewater, WI: The Language Press, pp. 169–80.

Hinman, L. W. (1982) 'Nietzsche, metaphor, and truth', *Philosophy and Phenomonological Research* xliii, no. 2, December: 179–99.

Hobbes, T. (1651) *Leviathan*, M. Oakeshott (ed.) (undated) Oxford: Basil Blackwell.

Hoover, K. D. (1991) 'Mirowski's screed: a review of Philip Mirowski's *More Heat than Light: Economics as Social Physics, Physics as Nature's Economics*', *Methodus* 3(1): 139–45.

Ingrao, B. and Israel, G. (1990) *The Invisible Hand: Economic Equilibrium in the History of Science*, Cambridge, MA and London: MIT Press.

Kuhn, T. S. (1979) 'Metaphor in science', in A. Ortony (ed.), *Metaphor and Thought*, Cambridge: Cambridge University Press.

Lachmann, L. M. (1986) *The Market as an Economic Process*, Oxford and New York: Basil Blackwell.

Lakoff, G. (1990) *Women, Fire, and Dangerous Things*, Chicago and London: University of Chicago Press.

Lakoff, G. and Johnson, M. (1980) *Metaphors We Live By*, Chicago: University of Chicago Press.

Leech, G. N. and Short, M. H. (1981) *Style in Fiction*, London: Longman.

Locke, J. (1706) *An Essay Concerning Human Understanding*, abridged and edited by J. W. Yolton (reissued 1991), London: J. M. Dent & Sons.

Lodge, D. (1977) *The Modes of Modern Writing, Metaphor, Metonymy, and the Typology of Modern Literature*, London: Edward Arnold.

Loewenberg, I. (1973) 'Truth and the consequences of metaphor', *Philosophy and Rhetoric* 6(1): 30–46.

'Longinus on the sublime', 'On the sublime' in Aristotle, *Classical Literary Criticism, op. cit.*

McCloskey, D. N. (1986) *The Rhetoric of Economics*, Brighton: Wheatsheaf.

Mäki, U. (1990) 'Practical syllogism, entrepreneurship and the invisible hand', in D. Lavoie, (ed.), *Economics and Hermeneutics*, London and New York: Routledge.

Mandeville, B. de (1714, 1957) *Fable of the Bees* (with a critical, historical and explanatory commentary by F. K. Kayel), Oxford: Clarendon Press.

Marshall, A. (1925) 'Mechanical and biological analogies in economics (1898)', in A. C. Pigou (ed.), *Memorials of Alfred Marshall*, London: Macmillan, pp. 312–18.

Medawar, P. (1984) *Pluto's Republic*, Oxford: Oxford University Press.

Mirowski, P. (1989) *More Heat than Light*, Cambridge: Cambridge University Press.

Mirowski, P. (forthcoming) 'Marshalling the unruly atoms: understanding Edgeworth's career'.

Ortony, A. (ed.) (1979) *Metaphor and Thought*, Cambridge: Cambridge University Press.

Patinkin, D. (1973) 'In search of the "wheel of wealth": on the origins of Frank Knight's circular flow diagram', *American Economic Review* 63: 1037–46.

Pepper, S. (1942) *World Hypothesis: A Study in Evidence*, Berkeley: University of California Press; London: Cambridge University Press.

Pigou, A. C. (ed.) (1925) *Memorials of Alfred Marshall*, London: Macmillan.

Quine, W. V. (1979) 'A postscript on metaphor', in S. Sacks (ed.), *On Metaphor*, Chicago: University of Chicago Press, pp. 159–60.

Ricoeur, P. (1974–5) 'Metaphor and the main problem of hermeneutics', *New Literary History* 6: 95–110.

Ricoeur, P. (1975) *The Rule of Metaphor*, Toronto: Toronto University Press.

Robinson, J. (1964) *Economic Philosophy*, Harmondsworth: Penguin Books.

Rorty, R. (1989) *Contingency, Irony and Solidarity*, Cambridge: Cambridge University Press.

Sacks, S. (ed.) (1979) *On Metaphor*, Chicago: University of Chicago Press.

Schumpeter, J. (1976) *Capitalism, Socialism and Democracy*, London: Allen & Unwin. First published 1943.

Shell, M. (1978) *The Economy of Literature*, Baltimore and London: Johns Hopkins University Press.

Smith, A. (1976a) *The Wealth of Nations*, Oxford: Clarendon Press.

Smith, A. (1976b) *The Theory of Moral Sentiments*, Oxford: Clarendon Press.

Smith, A. (1980) *Astronomy* [1758] vol. IV, p. 19, in W. P. D. Wightman and J. C. Boyce (eds), *Essays on Philosophical Subjects*, vol. 3 of the Glasgow edition of the Works and Correspondence of Adam Smith, Oxford: Clarendon Press, p. 66.

Smith, A. (1983) *Lectures on Rhetoric and Belles Lettres*, Oxford: Clarendon Press.

Stanford, W. B. (1973) *Greek Metaphor*, New York and London: Johnson Reprint Corporation.

Swales, J. (1993) 'The paradox of value: six treatments in search of the reader', in W. Henderson, T. Dudley-Evans and R. Backhouse (eds), *Economics and Language*, London: Routledge, pp. 223–39.

Viner, J. (1937) *Studies in the Theory of International Trade*, London and New York: Allen & Unwin.

Weimann, R. (1974–5) 'Shakespeare and the study of metaphor', *New Literary History* 6: 149–67.

West, J. F. (1965) *The Great Intellectual Revolution*, London: John Murray.

17

THE ECONOMY AS TEXT

Vivienne Brown

INTRODUCTION

Developments in philosophy and literary theory have begun to alert economists to the significance of language. In problematizing the role of language
as a means of communicating ideas, conducting arguments and describing
the empirical world, such developments have initiated a wide-ranging
debate across disparate academic disciplines. This has resulted in an
acknowledgement of the literariness of many forms of academic endeavour,
and the importance of rhetoric in the process of academic argument and
debate. Within economics, these developments have stimulated a new
interest in language, with different approaches emphasizing rhetoric, hermeneutics, literary theory, discourse analysis and constructivism.[1]

This chapter will examine some implications of the importance of language for economics, and in doing this it will approach economic discourse
by means of a specifically literary metaphor, that of seeing the economy
as text. If the economy is like a text, then economic discourse involves
reading that text. This implies that economic discourse is an interpretative
activity; the economy as text is composed of systems of signification, and
the signs have to be interpreted. Instead of seeing the economist as rhetor,
as one who seeks to persuade, the focus shifts to seeing economic discourse as a process of reading and interpreting the signs of the economy,
and so here the economist becomes a reader or interpreter. This leads on
to the issue of the kind of text that the economy may be thought to be,
and some of the ways in which this text may be read as a narrative. As
some readings have become more powerful or influential over time, this
connects with the notion of a 'canon' of readings which have become
authoritative as interpretations of the economy. Thus by drawing analogically on the terms of literary theory, this chapter offers an alternative
account of some features of economic discourse.

THE DEBATE ABOUT LANGUAGE

Construing the object of knowledge as a text to be read or deciphered does not represent a new metaphor for the pursuit of knowledge. In the Middle Ages, the physical world was seen as God's great book in which might be read the wonders of His creation. Here the great book of nature was a sign of the greatness of its Author, and those who read it might gain a glimpse of His design for the world. Thus the metaphor of the great book of nature functioned within a discursive space in which God's power was manifested in the signs of nature which He had made available for mortals to interpret, and in which God was the author of man's being.

The medieval conception of the physical world as God's great book thus presents one approach to seeing the substantive world as a text to be read. In this case, the meaning of the metaphor for the medieval conception of knowledge-creation depended on a broader discursive context which included theological dominance of intellectual endeavour and a world view based on the pre-eminence of the Roman Catholic church. One lesson to be learnt from this is that a metaphor may well be subject to different interpretations depending on the discursive context in which it is located and the current theoretical debates associated with it. To suggest in the late twentieth century that the economy is a text will therefore represent a particular way of conceiving the issue of textuality, one that is the product of an intense twentieth-century debate about the nature of language, texts and reading.

One view of language is that it should ideally function as a transparent means of communication such that the ideas which the author intends to convey are transmitted unproblematically to the mind of the listener/reader. If the author follows standard grammatical usage and adheres to the normal definitions of words, then the well-intentioned (and appropriately well-informed) reader will have no difficulties in understanding the author's meaning. As the purpose of language is to enable communication between the author and reader, the 'true' meaning of the text is determined by the author's intentions in writing. Cases of misreading, whether from mistakes, ignorance or ill-intent, thus result in interpretations that are at odds with what the author had in mind, and the extent of the misreading is measured by its distance from the author's meaning. Such a view of language may be taken as a 'literalist' or copy theory of language where the words literally represent what is in the author's mind. Here there is only one absolutely correct reading of a text, and this is given by the author's intended meaning. A corollary of this view is that language functions transparently as a means of communication; it can itself have no independent power to compel assent in argument which must be the result only of the objective strength of the argument. In the hands of unscrupulous users, however, language may be turned away from its proper role, and here the powers of a deceitful rhetoric may be deployed to subvert the cause of truth by playing on emotion and prejudice. In this case, language is something to be distrusted and castigated as a perversion of its proper role.

An opposing view of language, however, is that this 'literalness' is greatly overestimated. Whether or not language should ideally be capable of such an all-encompassing literalness, it is argued that language as it has actually developed is intensely figurative and open to alternative readings. Apart from the issue of the unscrupulous or deliberately deceitful use of language, this argument maintains that language use is necessarily a more open and contestable affair than the view of language as a transparent medium can accept. One reason for this is that there is a kind of 'plenitude' about language such that meanings can never quite be contained and confined but seem to overflow the boundaries of a text. In this sense, meanings seem to slide off the surface of the text in a regenerative and never-ending interpretative process. Partly this derives from the ways in which texts can take on different meanings according to the interpretative grid or discursive frame in which they are placed. Any process of reading requires that the interpretation of the text is constructed in terms of some kind of prior knowledge or context which then renders that text intelligible. When a text is read in terms of different discursive frames, then different readings of that text will inevitably be made and, given the wide range of potential frames of reference that are possible, the number of potential readings that are conceivable for a single text begins to multiply. Without any prior knowledge or discursive frame of reference, however, such a text would be meaningless or pointless for someone who attempted to read it.

Instruction in or induction into any academic discipline such as economics may thus be seen as an institutionalized means for equipping students with an 'appropriate' or discipline-based frame of reference. By requiring that the new learner is introduced to the 'literature' of the subject, the student learns the language, norms, presuppositions, current and historic disputes, arguments and issues of that field of learning. When the student is able to read this literature fluently, this process of induction is complete and the student has acquired the appropriate frame of reference and is equipped as an independent and competent reader. Within some academic disciplines this frame of reference is relatively homogeneous, and it can be expected that its practitioners will produce similar readings of any text. In other disciplines, however, this frame of reference is much more differentiated, perhaps heavily contested, and so there the reading process will produce much more diverse readings.

The possibility of alternative readings also results from the ways in which metaphorical and other analogical modes of expression may be interpreted. Consider the use of figurative means of expression. One aspect of the power of these expressions lies in the ways in which they appear to explain the unknown or unfamiliar in terms of the known, but this process is inevitably open-ended and subject to differently nuanced interpretations. Also given the extreme fecundity of many figurative expressions, it also frequently happens that their semantic resonances lie far beyond what any individual author might have deliberately or consciously intended in all its ramifications. For this reason, instead of simply providing an illustrative gloss or a persuasively compelling cognitive insight, or even an unexpected probe into the author's individual psychology, the presence of figurative language in a text provides the occasion for a more textured interpretative response which takes into account the different ways in which the figure may be pointing up important structural characteristics or internal tensions within the text itself. In this way too, the presence of figurative language may open the text to a deconstructive reading which highlights the tensions between different interpretative structures and between different systems of figuration within a text.

Partly, too, the range of alternative readings derives from inherent ambiguities and the polysemous nature of words themselves. Many expressions are susceptible to more than one interpretation. Dictionary definitions provide a first indication of the range of meanings attached to words, but even detailed etymological dictionaries cannot capture the range of nuances and subtle shifts of meaning that words undergo when embedded in complex texts. Sometimes too these alternative meanings are themselves metaphorically produced as when the extensions to the meaning of a word are the product of metaphorical accretions.

These arguments concerning the plenitude of meaning have resulted in a much more critical appraisal of the role of the author in establishing the meaning of a text. Once it is accepted that a text may proliferate a range of meanings, the view of the relation between the author and the text is subject to serious reappraisal, especially as the author's own intended meaning can never be known independently of the process of interpretation itself. If there is a plenitude of meaning in a text, then the author cannot have full control over every ramification of what is actually written down or uttered, but must to some degree relinquish control over the text when it is delivered into the public arena in either written or spoken form. This argument has sometimes been summarized in terms of the slogan 'death of the author'. This does not mean that authors have literally been done away with, nor that the named authorship of a piece of work is not significant in a number of ways (for example, in terms of its critical reception within academic or literary communities), but that interpretations of a text can no longer be bolstered by claiming a privileged access to the mind and intentions of the author of it. Such intentions are not available as a 'brute' presence independently of the process of interpretation itself, whether of the text in question, other parts of the author's 'oeuvre', or private notes, memoirs or correspondence.

The text is therefore no longer understood as the emanation of the author as origin whose unique life, historical circumstances or individual mind-set explain the work. According to one account of this, the author as custodian of the text's meaning is replaced by the 'scriptor' who simply occupies the subject position inscribed in the text itself:

> The Author, when believed in, is always conceived of as the past of his own book: book and author stand automatically on a single line divided into a *before* and an *after*. The Author is thought to *nourish* the book, which is to say that he exists before it, thinks, suffers, lives for it, is in the same relation of antecedence to his work as a father to his child. In complete contrast, the modern scriptor is born simultaneously with the text, is in no way equipped with a being preceding or exceeding the writing, is not the subject with the book as predicate . . . .
>
> (Barthes 1977: 145; original emphasis)

Demoting the author from the position of the origin and guarantor of a unique textual meaning, and emphasizing instead the notion of a scriptor, follows from the argument that the meaning which the reader ascribes to a text is the product of a process of reading within specific historical and discursive conditions, and this may not coincide with the intentions of the author. But demoting the author in this way also in turn underlines the crucial role that language itself plays in any text, not as the transparent medium through which the author shares intimate thoughts with the reader, but as the source of meaning itself.

Within the purview of literary criticism, this approach underlies the practice of critical readings of literary texts or 'literature'. The explosion of academic interest in language, however, has resulted from extending this view of the non-literalness of language from the relatively restricted sphere of 'literary' artefacts such as novels and poems, to a more inclusive category of 'non-literary' texts. Reappraising the nature of language in this broader way has also resulted in a growth of interest in the language of serious academic and scientific endeavour. For some, the recognition of the figurative power of language has resulted in a sort of celebration of this linguistic fecundity by deliberately trying to exploit the interpretative potential of language. Here, writers may try explicitly to work from within a multiplicity of meanings even as they write, exploring a complex polyphony of interpretation even as part of the writing process. For others, the complexity of the language-forms of academic debate has been seen as a means of exploring the rhetorical characteristics and unrecognized presuppositions of established academic disciplines. Others, too, have tried to call a halt to the extent to which alternative meanings may be attributed to a text, and have tried to redefine a legitimate area within which appropriate readings may properly take place.

Transposing this account of language to the textual analogy of the economy implies that just as no single interpretation of text can contain its linguistic plenitude and exhaust all the possible meanings that can be derived from it, so there is no single economic reading which can encompass the complexities and analytical plenitude of the text of the economy. There is thus inevitably a range of different theories with different emphases and nuances; sometimes these theories are in direct conflict with each other, sometimes they are tangential or complementary. The reason for this diverse range of theoretical approaches is not so much to be attributed to the deficiences of existing theories (which may or may not be found wanting), but to the analogical implication that the text of the economy is not susceptible to a unitheoretical interpretation. Thus the analytical plenitude of the economy as a text should alert its readers to the impossibility of containing it within a single theoretical schema. It is inevitable that a plurality of economic theories should characterize economic discourse, and that different theoretical approaches should be seen as alternative ways of reading the economy. For this reason, because plural readings of the economy necessarily proliferate from the economy as text, 'the economy' does not exist as an entity in the singular. In this sense, to use the expression 'the economy as text', is itself an acknowledgement of conventional linguistic usage as, from a textual point of view, the notion of 'the economy' itself dissolves in the presence of multiple readings.

As an example, consider how 'competition' is interpreted in different theoretical approaches. One account of competition is provided by the Walrasian model of competitive equilibrium. Here price is exogenous to the model and the competitive process is denoted by a series of comparative static competitive equilibrium positions. The characteristics of these competitive outcomes have been explored mathematically but the process by which one competitive outcome is superseded by another is left unaccounted for; a convenient fiction is that of the auctioneer who announces prices in a process of *tâtonnement*, but this itself lies outside the model. Another account is provided by Hayek's emphasis on the dynamics arising from the incentive structure of changing prices in a model not characterized by equilibrium. Here the emphasis is on the informational and incentive properties of disequilibrium situations, but the actual competitive process by which agents respond to and alter prices is obscure. Another version of competition is provided by Schumpeter's account of 'creative destruction'. Here firms are clearly able to alter prices as they face downward-sloping demand curves, but the point of this approach is not to emphasize monopoly as the opposite of competition, but rather to argue that a profits-driven incentive to innovate means that in the longer run firms are competing not just over price but for control of the expanding new markets of the day. These examples suggest that 'competition' denotes not a single process, but derives from alternative ways of reading a linguistically fertile text about markets.

Furthermore, this view of the nature of the reading process implies that there are no external guarantees to underwrite any particular reading. Each reading accounts for the text in its own way and embodies a distinct protocol for reading the text, but the text itself cannot definitively be used to discriminate between different readings. Some readings will appear to be better justified textually than others, but there is no way to assess one reading against another by using anything other than the text. If demoting the author as proprietor of meaning makes problematic the reference to authorial intentions in discussing the meaning of texts then, *a fortiori*, the absence of an author for the text of the economy implies that it is not possible to validate meanings by reference to something that stands outside it. The text of the economy is truly an authorless text whose meaning cannot be deciphered by reference to an external legitimating authority.

This analytical plenitude does not, however, mean that economists are unconstrained in their reading of the text of the economy, or that economic discourse is inevitably liable to the vagaries of totally indiscriminate readings. The act of reading a text takes place within certain established and often clearly-defined protocols of reading within specific discursive and institutional contexts. In this sense, readers do not just see anything at all when they come to read a text, and for this reason the reading process is not a subjective free-for-all in which readers may cavalierly disregard the signs of the text. Protocols of academic reading are derived from the community of scholars and scientists, and the conventions and practices that are embedded in these communities. Part of the process of academic and professional training thus serves to instill in its novitiates the skills and attitudes which are implicit in that particular discourse. Acquiring an academic training may therefore be seen as a process of coming to identify with the subject positions that are inscribed within an academic discourse at a certain period in history. Economists are trained in a range of conceptual, mathematical and econometric skills that give them particular perspectives and specific discursive frames of reference that facilitate particular kinds of reading processes, and which distinguish their readings from those of non-economists who read the text of the economy according to other discursive frames. Thus, alternative readings of the text of the economy are not arbitrary or subjectively determined in a wilful sense of disregard for established standards of analytical clarity and coherence, but derive from different discursive practices within economic discourse itself and the different subject positions that these subdiscourses occupy. Different and competing economic theories therefore derive not from individual aberrant behaviour, but from the discursive complexity of the text of the economy which facilitates and even requires a polyphonic reading process.

READING A FRAGMENTARY TEXT

In economic discourse it is taken for granted that the object of investigation is the 'economy', a clearly substantive entity. Theories are put forward to explain different aspects of the economy, but what is the evidence constituted by the substantive being of the economy itself? The most important component of this evidence is provided by empirical data of one sort or another, for example, time series on GNP, inflation, unemployment, profits, balance of payments, etc. Sometimes this data is produced by governments or other agencies of one sort or another, and sometimes it is produced by field research. The evidence may also take the form of reports or documentary evidence produced by the economic agents themselves, by their regulatory bodies, by their respective pressure group organizations, or by government departments. It is a commonplace that economic statistics have to be 'interpreted'; this means that the empirical evidence has to be interpreted or read in terms of the theories of economic reading that are current. Different statistical series are scrutinized in terms of the analytical frameworks that constitute these variables as significant and interesting. Before econometrics became well established, this process of interpretation might require only visual interpretation of the data presented graphically or in tabular form, perhaps combined with some elementary computation. With the increasingly sophisticated development of econometric techniques and computer software, the empirical data is subjected to a battery of interpretative techniques in order to construct their economic meaning. The kinds of reading that are possible depend on the current interests of theoretical debate as well as the econometric techniques available. These different econometric methods may also be compared with the different practices of reading that are employed in the case of literary texts, and the interpretations arising from them will also be as diverse.

In spite of the substantive nature of the economy as an independently existing entity, evidence of its functioning is not simply given to observation but has to be sought for, constructed and pieced together. This means that the text of the economy is not simply given, as the text of a book or a poem is given. It has to be compiled, sifted and sorted. Whereas the text of a book or poem may be regarded as a complete entity with no missing parts, this cannot be said of the text of the economy. Data have to be collected, produced or constructed. There are many data series that are not available to economists, or have to be interpolated or inferred from other data sources. Time lags in the production of data mean that current events cannot be interpreted until some time in the future, and even then such data series may have to be heavily revised later as new statistics are produced. Inevitably, too, most data series are approximate to some degree or another, and are clearly inconsistent with other data series. Thus economists may be regarded as the readers of a highly fragmentary text with missing pages, blanks and erasures. In this, economists may be compared with classical philologists, poring over fragments of ancient texts, trying to interpolate or deduce the meaning of the larger text from the extant parts that can be deciphered.

As with classical philologists, too, there may well be problems in deciphering the language or cracking the code of these fragments of a submerged language. Some data series refer to physical entities whereas others refer to monetary values. In order to make comparisons across sectors, across commodities, across time or across countries and currencies, various techniques for conversion have been developed which may be understood as a form of translation from one script to another, but in this case the translation has to proceed without the use of a definitive diction-ary; here the different scripts must be decoded from scratch according to basic linguistic principles. In some respects, monetary values function as a meta-language in so far as all physical entities may be translated into it. Thus different kinds of output, different kinds of labour and different kinds of capital goods may be rendered comparable by translating them into the common language of a monetary system of valuation. In this way, the monetary valuation of physical entities functions analogously with the role of Latin as the *lingua franca* of the medieval world of international scholarship. But here, too, translation proves intractably difficult. Problems of imputation, indexation, depreciation and obsolescence render such valu-ation procedures approximate, and the existence of different trading cur-rencies introduces further difficulties of establishing a common and internationally reliable monetary language.

The text of the economy is fragmentary in another way too. A text such as a book or poem normally has a clearly defined border or edge in a physical sense. The margins of the page enclose the text and frame it, separating it from its non-text, that which stands outside that particular text.[2] But in the case of the economy as text, there is no such border or frame; instead there is a ragged edge as the text becomes patchy, faint or illegible, or where the parchment has worn away. As the empirical evidence on the economy is not comprehensive but fragmentary, it cannot by itself define the boundaries of the economy. For this reason the bound-aries of the economy are inevitably subject to contestation and reinter-pretation even in the context of the kind of empirical evidence that counts as economic. Issues of moral evaluation, for example, are included within this contested liminal zone. Issues may concern distributional outcomes, the moral implications of a consumer society, the economic erosion of traditional communities or skills, the nature of business ethics, the extent of rights (and duties?) of property, intergenerational obligations and environmental degradation. Political issues regarding the proper role of government involvement, and the extent of national or regional economic areas have also been included along with feminist and ethnic issues relating to gender and racial differences. Such contestations are challenging the boundaries of the economy as an object of knowledge, and so may be understood as alternative ways of constituting and reading the text of the economy. As new evidence is adduced concerning these issues, say on the relation between entitlements and hunger, or on the relation between property rights and market efficiency, the working text of the economy is enlarged; new chapters are added, blank pages are filled in and additional footnotes are added to the existing text. Thus the economy is a text which is constantly subject to emendation. As classical philologists discover missing pages or succeed in deciphering a previously illegible piece of parchment, so the text of the economy is constantly being reconstructed.

TEXT AND NARRATIVE

It has been argued so far that the economy may be seen as a text, albeit a fragmentary one. This raises the question of what kind of text it is. Unlike an ancient text which is physically given at a point in time, the economy is a text that unfolds in the course of time, and so it has a temporal dimension in a way that a given text does not. This suggests that the economy may be seen as a narrative text in that narrative presupposes temporality: 'narrative is opposed to atemporal laws that depict what is, whether past or future. Any explanation that unfolds in time, with surprises during its progress and knowledge through hindsight, is just a story, no matter how factual' (Martin 1986: 187).[3] It has been argued by literary theorists that the narrative form seems to be well-nigh universal in that it appears in diverse cultures, languages and historical periods. Young children are particularly responsive to storytelling and love to hear the same stories again and again, and this attachment to stories is often sustained into adulthood with a desire for narratives as diverse as soap operas, novels, movies, biographies and national histories. Just as the implications deriving from seeing the economy as a text depend on what is meant by a text, so the implications deriving from seeing the text of the economy as a form of narrative depend on what is meant by narrative, and here different accounts have been put forward by literary theorists.[4]

One account of narrative emphasizes the importance of the sequence of plot structure and its invariance across very different stories. Drawing on this structuralist approach to narrative, it has been argued that much of economic analysis can be understood in terms of an invariant form of storytelling in three acts in which an initial and a final state are linked by an intermediate event which causes the final one (McCloskey 1990: chs 1–2). This is seen as indicative of the kinds of historical stories that economists tell, and it is also seen as a paradigm plot structure of comparative static analysis with its determinate transition from one equilibrium to another in response to a parameter change.[5] Such an approach to narrative, however, implies a kind of narrative unity to a story in the sense that the narrator exercises full control. It is the narrator's voice which fashions this systemic unity and produces a story which coheres as an integrated piece of work, where all the elements are articulated in producing the inevitable outcome. There is, therefore, a kind of analytical orderliness about the structuring of the elements of the narrative such that extraneous events are disallowed, and the incorporated elements are made to be functional with respect to producing the final conclusion to the narrative.

For this reason, a conception of narrative based on the centrality of this invariance of plot structure is not appropriate to the analogy of the economy as text which has been developed so far in this chapter and which has stressed the disparate and polyphonic readings of the text of economy. Instead of having a single narrator's voice in full control of the story, the text of the economy is characterized by the absence of an authoritative authorial or narrating presence. Instead of the univocity of the determinate story, there is instead a plenitude of language and a multivocal text. This means that the same text of the economy can generate different interpretations and different processes of reading. For example, statistical series on post-war inflation can be read as different narratives of inflation: they may be read in terms of a story about the weakness of political and economic will in democratically elected governments which are not tough-minded enough to exercise proper control over the money supply; they may be read in terms of a world of sophisticated financial institutions where the money supply is endogenous; or they may be read in terms of the institutional structures of government and the organizations of the workplace and the degrees and types of corporatist structures. In view of the multivocity of the text of the economy, therefore, the story of the economy does not have a determinate narrative point or conclusion but is discursively differentiated.

An account of narrative which is in greater accord with this argument concerning the economy as text is provided in the writings of Mikhail Bakhtin (1981, 1984, 1986) which challenge univocal conceptions of narrative by postulating a 'dialogic' or multi-voiced conception of narrative or 'novelistic discourse'.[6] In a series of analyses of the development of the European novel, Bakhtin argues that the novel is characterized by the confrontation of different 'voices' representing different axiological, political or cultural positions, and that a primary aspect of the radical nature of novelistic discourse lies in the way in which these different voices are organized within the text:

> The novel can be defined as a diversity of social speech types (sometimes even diversity of languages) and a diversity of individual voices, artistically organized. The internal stratification of any single national language ... at any given moment of its historical existence

is the indispensable prerequisite for the novel as a genre. The novel orchestrates all its themes, the totality of the world of objects and ideas depicted and expressed in it, by means of the social diversity of speech types and by the differing individual voices that flourish under such conditions.

(Bakhtin 1981: 262–3)

These different voices are the manifestations of the different speech types and different inflections which are the result of an internal differentiation of language which Bakhtin termed 'heteroglossia'. The dialogic interplay of these different voices derives not so much from a conception of dialogue as an orderly process of questioning and debate, but rather from a process of intersection and contestation of irreconcilable points of view, opposing value systems and contradictory conceptions of reality.

One effect of this contestation is to decentre the author's voice to some degree so that it becomes one voice structured among many within the novel, or engages in a more self-questioning or ironic relationship with other voices in the novel. Alternatively, the multi-voiced nature of novelistic discourse may provide the mechanism for the eclipse of the authorial voice altogether; in this case the story of the novel is delivered by the interplay between a range of alternative voices. Thus Bakhtin's work emphasizes the diologic nature of texts where meaning is the result of the interplay and contestation of different voices, and where there may be an absence of any final authoritative voice providing an ultimate meaning or determinate conclusion.

Stressing the dialogic nature of the text of the economy implies that the economy too is characterized by disparate voices. In engaging with a text of this sort, economic discourse inevitably proliferates a range of theoretical approaches. But as even the heterogeneous interpretative resources of the discipline cannot exhaust the dialogic potential of the text of the economy, this process of proliferation is never complete. Just as the text of the economy has no determinate conclusion, so the process of reading it is open-ended.

In trying to read the text of the economy, however, economists attempt to impose order on this polyphony of voices; they try to compose order out of this analytical plenitude, but inevitably this leads to different ways of conceiving order and disorder in economic relations. In this process the multivocity and dialogism of the text of the economy is rendered into a more univocal narrative which reflects the economist's attempt to impose order and coherence. Similarly, within economics as an academic discipline, there are pressures to compress this multivocity into a more unified discursive field. In Bakhtin's writings, the other or opposite of a dialogic discourse is a monologic discourse where a single authoritative voice denies the validity of dissenting or competing voices. For Bakhtin, paradigm

379

instances of monologic discourse are provided by the epic as a literary form, and by scientific and academic discourses. Here the text is characterized by a unified language and unified value system where heteroglossia is absent or much muted. This distinction seems to set up monologic and dialogic forms of discourse as antitheses of each other, and much of Bakhtin's writings do subscribe to this view. In view, however, of the wide range of academic and scientific discourses as well as the linguistic complexity of the epic form, it is probably better to take this distinction as one referring to differences of degree and type, rather than as a distinction that holds in an absolute sense.

Thus as an academic discipline, economics can be understood as an institutionalized form in which the multivocity of the text of the economy is continually being rendered into a more univocal or monologic form of discourse epitomizing a unified language and value system. Different readings are accorded a different status, but the different success rates of these readings may depend on institutional, sociological and political factors as well as theoretical and conceptual ones. This process may be compared with the production of the 'canon' in literary or religious contexts, where the canon functions authoritatively in fixing certain texts as embodying valued norms and characteristics. This process of canonization is, however, continually being challenged by means of the proliferation of new ways of reading the text of the economy, but in the course of time the diversity of the range of different readings of the economy slips from view. There is thus a constant tension between the multivocity of the text of the economy and the institutional tendencies towards a more univocal means of accounting for that text, or between the centrifugal forces of theoretical dispersion and the centripetal forces of theoretical conformity and agreement. In Bakhtin's writings, this centripetal process by which a heterogeneous polyphony of voices is reduced and constrained by the tightly structured requirements of an integrated discourse is presented as the process of canonization: 'Canonization is that process that blurs heteroglossia, that is, that facilitates a naive, single-voiced reading' (Bakhtin 1981: 425; editor's glossary entry).[7]

The 'canonic' readings of the text of the economy are the authorized readings that help to constitute and consolidate the economics discipline as an integrated form of discourse with an institutionalized presence in the community. These canonic readings of the economy provide economic discourse with its own sense of identity, its own language, its own conception of the nature of economic explanation, and its own construction of the text of the economy as an object of knowledge. Readings of the economy that fall outside the authorized version can be seen as a challenge to the canonic status of received readings, and are thus providing a centripetal counterpoint to the process by which the multivocity of the text of the economy is rendered into a more univocal form of economic discourse.

CONCLUSION

This chapter has examined some implications of seeing the substantive entity of the economy as a text which economists attempt to read, and by examining economic discourse analogically as the interpretation of a text. Seeing the economy in this way raises the issue of the kind of reading process that is involved in studying and analysing the economy, and how it is that there are different ways of reading it. The argument of the chapter has emphasized the problematic nature of textuality, and so it has proposed a conception of the economy as a multivocal but fragmentary text which has to be pieced together evidentially.

ACKNOWLEDGEMENTS

I would like to thank Roger Backhouse, D. Wade Hands, Daniel Hausman and Willie Henderson for their comments on an earlier draft of this chapter. The usual disclaimer applies.

NOTES

1 See for example Henderson (1982 and this volume), McCloskey (1986, 1990 and this volume), Klamer *et al.* (1988), Lavoie (1990), Samuels (1990), Henderson *et al.* (1993), Weintraub (1989, 1991), Brown (1993, 1994a, 1994b, 1994c).

2 A written text such as a novel or treatise has a border or margin in a physical sense which defines the limits of the text and this is absent from the economy as text. In terms of the process of reading, however, this notion of a given defining border is challenged in the stress on the importance of discursive frame and linguistic plenitude. Here what is significant is the context of interpretation, and this too becomes an arena in which the construction of the economy and the economic becomes a matter of continual redefinition and contestation.

3 Hamouda and Price (1991) present a methodological discussion of economics and history as related disciplines.

4 Introductions to recent debates can be found in Mitchell (1981), Martin (1986) and Miller (1990).

5 For competitive comparative static analysis, however, this is a story without a process of transition as it lacks a dynamic account of disequilibrium.

6 For introductions to Bakhtin's work see Clark and Holquist (1984), Todorov (1984), Holquist (1990) and Morson and Emerson (1990). Bakhtin's work is discussed in relation to the history of economic thought in Brown (1993), and in the context of Adam Smith's discourse in Brown (1994a).

7 The process of canonization is discussed in Brown (1993) with respect to reading practices in the history of economic thought.

BIBLIOGRAPHY

Bakhtin, M. M. (1981) *The Dialogic Imagination: Four Essays by M. M. Bakhtin*, Austin: University of Texas Press.

Bakhtin, M. M. (1984) *Problems of Dostoevsky's Poetics*, Manchester: Manchester University Press.

Bakhtin, M. M. (1986) *Speech Genres and Other Late Essays*, Austin: University of Texas Press.

Barthes, R. (1977) 'The death of the author', in S. Heath (ed. and trans.), *Image Music Text*, London: Fontana (Flamingo edn 1984), pp. 142–8.

Brown, V. (1993) 'Decanonizing discourses: textual analysis and the history of economic thought', in Henderson, Dudley-Evans and Backhouse (1993), pp. 64–84.

Brown, V. (1994a) *Adam Smith's Discourse: Canonicity, Commerce and Conscience*, London: Routledge, forthcoming.

Brown, V. (1994b) 'Higgling: the language of markets in economic discourse', in *History of Political Economy*, annual supplement, forthcoming.

Brown, V. (1994c) 'Metanarratives and economic discourse', *Scandinavian Journal of Economics* 96: forthcoming.

Hamouda, O. F. and Price, B. B. (1991) *Verification in Economics and History*, London and New York: Routledge.

Henderson, W. (1982) 'Metaphor in Economics', *Economics* xviii: 147–53.

Henderson, W., Dudley-Evans, T. and Backhouse, R. (1993) *Economics and Language*, London: Routledge.

Klamer, A., McCloskey, D. N. and Solow, R. M. (1988) *The Consequences of Economic Rhetoric*, Cambridge: Cambridge University Press.

Lavoie, D. (ed.) (1990) *Economics and Hermeneutics*, London: Routledge.

McCloskey, D. N. (1986) *The Rhetoric of Economics*, Brighton: Harvester.

McCloskey, D. N. (1990) *If You're So Smart: The Narrative of Economic Expertise*, Chicago and London: University of Chicago Press.

Martin, W. (1986) *Recent Theories of Narrative*, Ithaca and London: Cornell University Press.

Miller, J. H. (1990) 'Narrative', in F. Lentricchia and T. McLaughlin (eds), *Critical Terms for Literary Study*, Chicago and London: University of Chicago Press, pp. 66–79.

Mitchell, W. J. T. (ed.) (1981) *On Narrative*, Chicago: University of Chicago Press.

Morson, G. S. and Emerson, C. (1990) *Mikhail Bakhtin: Creation of a Prosaics*, Stanford, CA: Stanford University Press.

Samuels, W. J. (1990) *Economics as Discourse: An Analysis of the Language of Economists*, London: Kluwer.

Weintraub, E. R. (1989) 'Methodology doesn't matter, but the history of thought might', *Scandinavian Journal of Economics* 91: 477–93. (Reprinted in S. Honkapohja (ed.) (1990) *The State of Macroeconomics*, Oxford: Basil Blackwell, pp. 263–79.)

Weintraub, E. R. (1991) *Stabilizing Dynamics: Constructing Economic Knowledge*, Cambridge: Cambridge University Press.

INDEX